P9-CEZ-040

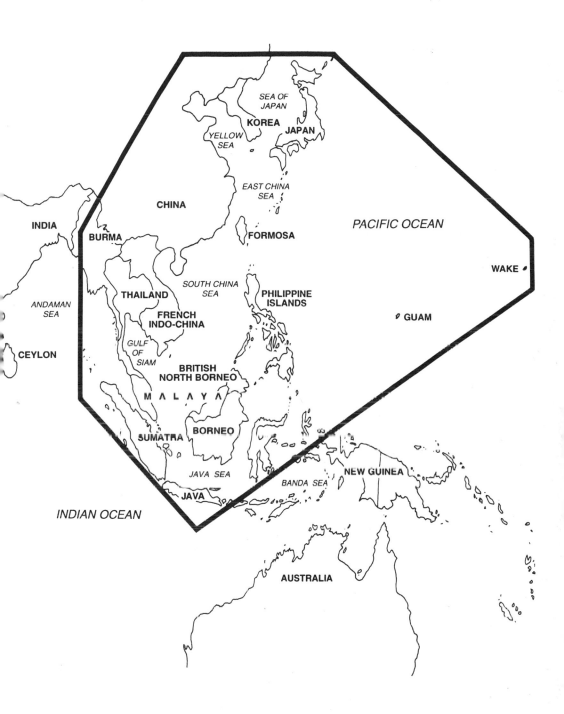

SEA OF
JAPAN

KOREA
YELLOW   JAPAN
SEA

EAST CHINA
SEA

CHINA

INDIA   FORMOSA   PACIFIC OCEAN

BURMA

WAKE

SOUTH CHINA   PHILIPPINE
SEA   ISLANDS

ANDAMAN   GUAM
SEA   THAILAND

FRENCH
INDO-CHINA

GULF
OF
SIAM

CEYLON   BRITISH
NORTH BORNEO

M A L A Y A

SUMATRA   BORNEO

JAVA SEA   NEW GUINEA

BANDA SEA

JAVA

INDIAN OCEAN

AUSTRALIA

WITH ONLY THE
WILL to LIVE

WITH ONLY THE
WILL to LIVE,

Accounts of Americans

in Japanese Prison Camps,

1941—1945

Edited by

Robert S. La Forte

Ronald E. Marcello

Richard L. Himmel

SR
BOOKS

A Scholarly Resources Inc. Imprint
Wilmington, Delaware

The paper used in this publication meets the minimum requirements of the American National Standard for permanence of paper for printed library materials, Z39.48, 1984.

Scholarly Resources Inc.
104 Greenhill Avenue
Wilmington, DE 19805-1897

Library of Congress Cataloging-in-Publication Data

With only the will to live : accounts of Americans in Japanese
    prison camps, 1941–1945 / edited by Robert S. La Forte,
    Ronald E. Marcello, and Richard L. Himmel.
        p.   cm.
    Topically arranged excerpts from interviews conducted from
1970 to 1989 by the University of North Texas Oral History
Program in Denton.
    Includes bibliographical references and index.
    ISBN 0-8420-2464-6 (cloth)
    1. World War, 1939–1945—Prisoners and prisons, Japanese.
2. World War, 1939–1945—Concentration camps—Asia, Southeastern. 3. World War, 1939–1945—Personal narratives, American.
4. Oral history. I. La Forte, Robert S. (Robert Sherman), 1933–   .
II. Marcello, Ronald E.   III. Himmel, Richard L., 1950–   .
D805.A785W57   1994
940.54'7252—dc20   93-42419
                                                            CIP

Contents

Prisoners of War Interviewed

Captain William G. Adair, Alabama, commander of the First Battalion, 21st Infantry Regiment, Philippine Division, was captured when Bataan fell on April 9, 1942. He followed the route of the infamous Death March but rode in an Army ambulance most of the way to Camp O'Donnell. During captivity, Adair was at O'Donnell, Cabanatuan, Osaka, and Zentsuji.

Corporal Billy W. Allen, Texas, was with the 4th Marines in Shanghai, China, and shifted with them to Manila and then into the Bataan Peninsula. He was captured on Corregidor when the fortress fell on May 6, 1942. Allen was held at Cabanatuan, Osaka, and Tsuruga.

Private First Class Roy Allen, Jr., Texas, was a member of the Seventh Materiel, 19th Heavy Bombardment Group, on detached duty at a new air base on Del Monte Plantation, Mindanao, Philippine Islands. He was captured there and spent most of his prison time at Camp Casisang and Davao Penal Colony on Mindanao. Allen was also at several locations in Japan, particularly at Yokkaichi.

Private Roy G. Armstrong, Texas, a member of F Battery, Second Battalion, 131st Field Artillery, 36th Division, was captured on Java and held at Tanjong Priok and Bicycle Camp in Batavia. He later worked on the Burma-Thailand Railway and finally was transferred to Da Lat in French Indochina.

Captain Leland D. Bartlett, Massachusetts, commissioned as a reserve officer in 1924, was called to active duty in April 1941 and was assigned to the Fourth Separate Chemical Company, Philippine Division, at Fort McKinley. He served on Bataan but was taken prisoner on Corregidor. Bartlett was held at Cabanatuan, Tanagawa, Zentsuji, and Roku Rushi.

Private Willie L. Benton, Texas, was part of the American Embassy Guard in Peking, China, a member of what is known as the North China Marines. After brief periods of imprisonment in Peking and Tientsin, he and his fellow Marines were interned at Woosung and Kiangwan, on the outskirts of Shanghai, and in 1945 at a mining camp near Hakodate.

Private Tom Blaylock, Texas, was a member of the 34th Pursuit Squadron in central Luzon. Shortly after the Japanese bombed the Philippines, he was sent to the Bataan Peninsula, where he was captured. Blaylock spent time at Camp O'Donnell, Cabanatuan, Bilibid Prison, and Omine.

Private First Class Hayes H. Bolitho, Montana, was a gunner on a B-17 at Clark Field. He was sent to one of the Del Monte air bases on Mindanao and was taken captive there. Bolitho was placed in Camp Casisang, near Malaybalay, and later in the Davao Penal Colony on Mindanao. While he was being transferred to Japan, his ship was sunk off Mindanao. He swam ashore and ultimately was liberated by Filipino guerrillas.

Corporal Loren H. Brantley, Texas, at the outbreak of war was a military policeman at Headquarters, First Battalion, Shanghai Marines. He was sent to Corregidor to help prepare beach defenses and was taken prisoner when the island fortress fell. Brantley was held at Bilibid Prison, Cabanatuan, Yodogawa Prison Camp, and at a coal-mining camp near Nagasaki.

Sergeant Philip Brodsky, New Jersey, was a medic attached to the field dispensary at Nichols Field near Manila. When American forces surrendered in early April, he was at an aid station near Mariveles on the southern part of the Bataan Peninsula. He spent most of his time as a captive at Camp O'Donnell and Palawan. Later, the ship carrying him to Japan was sunk, and Brodsky was interned on Formosa.

Private Karl A. Bugbee, Louisiana, was at Cavite Navy Yard as part of a Marine antiaircraft unit. Retreating with other base personnel into the Bataan Peninsula, he was captured on Corregidor and then imprisoned at Cabanatuan and Ashio.

Captain Harcourt G. Bull was born in London, England, but grew up in Pasadena, California. He graduated from The Citadel in 1929 with a reserve Army commission. Bull was recalled to active duty in October 1940 and was assigned to Manila one year later; prior to capture, he served as Post Exchange officer for Corregidor. He was incarcerated at Cabanatuan, Tanagawa, Zentsuji, and Roku Rushi.

Corporal William P. Bunch, Missouri, was a member of Battery F, 200th Coast Artillery, an antiaircraft unit of the New Mexico National Guard stationed at Clark Field. After that airfield was destroyed by Japanese bombers, he was transferred to the Bataan Peninsula, where he became a prisoner of war. Bunch spent time at Camp O'Donnell, Cabanatuan, Yodogawa, and Miyazu.

Sergeant Volnie S. Burk, Texas, was assigned to Battery G, 59th Coast Artillery, on Fort Hughes, where he was captured shortly after the fall of Corregidor. He spent his entire captivity in the Philippines at Bilibid Prison, Cabanatuan, the port area of Manila, and Nielson Field.

Corporal George Burlage, California, was with the Third Battalion, 4th Marine Regiment, at Cavite. He was shifted to Corregidor and surrendered with the garrison in early May 1942. Burlage spent most of his time in prison camps on Palawan and at Las Pinas but ended up working in a Mitsubishi lead mine in Japan at Hosakura.

Private Jonathan P. Burns, New Mexico, was in Battery F, 200th Coast Artillery, Antiaircraft, New Mexico National Guard, at Clark Field. After the Japanese bombers obliterated Clark, he moved into the Bataan Peninsula and was taken prisoner. Burns was held at Camp O'Donnell, Cabanatuan, and Moji.

Second Lieutenant Charles W. Burris, Oklahoma, was a pilot in the 17th Pursuit Squadron at Iba Field in the Philippines. After American airfields were virtually destroyed, he transferred to Battery B, 200th Coast Artillery, Antiaircraft, and surrendered with the unit at Bataan on April 9, 1942. Burris was interned at Camp O'Donnell, Cabanatuan, Fukuoka, and Inchon.

Captain Charles A. Cates, Texas, a member of D Battery, Second Battalion, 131st Field Artillery, 36th Division, was captured on Java and imprisoned at Bicycle Camp and Tanjong Priok in Batavia before being sent to Burma and the camps along the Burma-Thailand Railway. He was liberated in Bangkok in 1945.

Private Martin J. Chambers, Texas, served in D Battery, Second Battalion, 131st Field Artillery, 36th Division, and was captured on Java. He spent his remaining war years at Tanjong Priok and Bicycle Camp in Batavia and at camps along the Burma-Thailand Railway.

Corporal Onnie Clem, Texas, was a member of the Third Battalion, 4th Marine Regiment, at Cavite Navy Yard. He was captured on Corregidor and spent time at Camp O'Donnell, Cabanatuan, and the Davao Penal Colony. Clem was on board one of the infamous Death Ships when it was torpedoed a couple of miles outside Zamboanga, Mindanao. He swam ashore, was found by Filipino guerrillas, and ultimately was evacuated by an American submarine.

Corporal T. G. Crews, Texas, was an American Embassy Guard, North China Marines, Peking, and at the Consulate General in Tientsin, China. As a captive, he spent most of his time at camps in Woosung and Kiangwan, in the northern suburbs of Shanghai. Late in the war he was shifted to a mining camp near Hakodate.

Lieutenant M. L. Daman, Kansas, served in the Philippines but quit the Army to work for the largest Ford dealership in the islands, Manila Trading & Supply Co. He joined the Army reserves, received a commission, and volunteered in 1940 for one year of active duty in the 12th Quartermaster Regiment, Philippine Division. Daman was captured on Corregidor and kept at Bilibid Prison, Cabanatuan, and Davao Penal Colony.

Petty Officer Second Class George E. Detre, Ohio, swam ashore to Java when the USS *Houston* sank following the Battle of the Sunda Strait on February 29, 1942. He was captured by the Japanese, spent time at Bicycle Camp in Batavia, and then was sent to work on the Burma-Thailand Railway. Detre later was imprisoned in Sendryu, Japan.

Private First Class Pete Evans, Texas, a member of E Battery, Second Battalion, 131st Field Artillery, 36th Division, was captured at

Surabaja on Java. After a short stay in camps at Tanjong Priok and Changi, Evans was transported to Nagasaki. He was liberated from Orio in 1945.

Private First Class Marshall E. Fields, Arkansas, was assigned to a Marine antiaircraft battery but was part of the beach defense when the Japanese landed at Wake Island on December 28, 1941. After the surrender he spent two weeks at Wake and then was shipped via Japan to the Woosung camp near Shanghai. The remainder of his time as a prisoner was spent at Kiangwan, Fengtai, Pusan, and Hakodate.

Sergeant Frank ("Foo") Fujita, Texas, served in Battery E, Second Battalion, 131st Field Artillery Regiment, 36th Division. One of the few Japanese-American prisoners of war in the Far East, he was interned at various camps on Java and in Japan.

Private First Class John Breckenridge ("Brack") Garrison, Oklahoma and Texas, was a member of the 2d Marines on detached duty in Guam. As one of a handful of Marines on the island, his primary function was as policeman and guard. After the surrender, Garrison was sent to Japan and spent time in several camps there, including those at Zentsuji, Osaka, and Hirohata.

Captain Bryghte D. Godbold, Alabama, was commander of E Battery, 1st Defense Battalion, on Wake Island. Although an officer, he stayed with his men at Woosung and Kiangwan throughout their imprisonment in China. Godbold was separated from them in 1945 when he was sent to Sapporo, Japan.

Private J. L. ("Jake") Guiles, Oklahoma, was a member of Headquarters and Headquarters Squadron, Far Eastern Air Force, at Nichols Field. He was captured, however, on Bataan while attached to an infantry unit. Guiles was imprisoned at Camp O'Donnell, Cabanatuan, Hitachi, Ashio, and Niigata.

Corporal Alton C. Halbrook, Texas, served in the 4th Marines, Headquarters Company, at Shanghai, China, and then in Motor Transport at Cavite Navy Yard near Manila. He was captured on Corregidor, sent to Cabanatuan, and later served on work details at Camp

O'Donnell and Batangas. Halbrook was imprisoned for a time at Clark Field before he was shipped to Formosa and then to Japan.

First Sergeant M. T. Harrelson, Texas, a member of the Service Battery, Second Battalion, 131st Field Artillery, 36th Division, was captured on Java and held prisoner in a number of camps, including Tanjong Priok and Bicycle Camp in Batavia. His longest internment was at Camp No. 4 in Sumatra.

Fireman First Class Albert E. Kennedy, Texas, was picked up at sea after Japanese warships sank the USS *Houston* in Sunda Strait in March 1942. Kennedy was imprisoned in the Serang jail and Bicycle Camp before being sent to work on the Burma-Thailand Railway. He was liberated in Saigon, French Indochina, in 1945.

Private James L. Kent, Texas, was a Marine stationed at Cavite Navy Yard before moving to Bataan and Corregidor, where he was captured. He was held at Cabanatuan, Bilibid Prison, a copper mine north of Tokyo, and Mitsushima.

Corporal George Koury, Texas, was assigned to the 19th Bombardment Group at Clark Field near Manila. Following Japan's destruction of Clark, Koury was sent to Bataan, where he was captured. He was imprisoned at Camp O'Donnell, Cabanatuan, Nichols Field, Taiwan, and Honshu Camp No. 7.

Corporal Dean M. McCall, Kansas, was with the 19th Bombardment Group, Headquarters and Headquarters Squadron, at Clark Field. He moved with part of his unit to Corregidor and was captured when the fortress surrendered on May 6, 1942. McCall was at various camps, including Cabanatuan and Bilibid Prison, and on work details in the Philippines. His imprisonment ended at Hitachi Motoyama.

Corporal George W. McDaniel, Oklahoma and California, was a member of the First Defense Battalion, Fleet Marine Force, on Wake Island when he was captured. He was placed in the Woosung and Kiangwan camps near Shanghai. When the Americans were transferred to Japan, McDaniel was sent to a mine in the vicinity of Sapporo.

Corporal Cecil T. Minshew, Texas, who served in E Battery, Second Battalion, 131st Field Artillery, 36th Division, was captured on the Dutch East Indies island of Madura in early 1942. He spent one year in camps on Java and in Singapore before being transported to Japan. After a long period at Fukuoka, near Nagasaki, Minshew was transferred to the mining town of Orio, where he was liberated in 1945.

Private C. L. Permenter, Texas, was a member of the North China Marines taken prisoner in Peking. He spent time at Woosung, Kiangwan, and Hakodate.

Corporal Louis B. Read, Texas, was assigned to Headquarters Company, 31st Infantry, at Fort McKinley, and went with it into the Bataan Peninsula, where he surrendered. He was imprisoned at Camp O'Donnell, Cabanatuan, Las Pinas, Toroku on Formosa, and Moji.

Private First Class Marvin E. Robinson, Texas, was a member of the Marine detachment aboard the USS *Houston* when it sank in the Sunda Strait. Picked up by a Japanese boat, he was sent to Serang and then to Bicycle Camp in Batavia. Robinson later worked on the Burma-Thailand Railway and was liberated at Nakhon Nayok, near Bangkok.

Corporal J. L. Sherman, Texas, was a member of the 60th Coast Artillery, Antiaircraft, at Corregidor. After the fall of Corregidor, he escaped to Luzon with six other soldiers and fought as a guerilla for six months before surrendering. He was imprisoned at Cabanatuan, shipped to Formosa, and ended his captivity at Maibara.

Corporal Rufus W. Smith, Arkansas, was in the 4th Marine Regiment at Cavite Navy Yard. He was captured after moving to Corregidor and spent the majority of his time as a prisoner at Palawan, where he survived the Palawan Massacre.

Private First Class O. R. Sparkman, Texas, was part of the American guard stationed at the Consulate General in Tientsin. When the North China Marines surrendered, however, he was on guard duty at the American embassy in Peking. He was imprisoned at Woosung, Kiangwan, and Hakodate.

Technical Sergeant Jess H. Stanbrough, Texas, who served with Head-quarters Battery, Second Battalion, 131st Field Artillery, 36th Division, was captured on Java. In October 1942 he was shipped to Changi Prison in Singapore. Stanbrough was later sent to a camp near Ohasi.

Private Henry Stanley, Georgia, 454th Ordnance Squadron, 27th Bomb Group, went from Fort McKinley to Bataan soon after the war started and was there when the Americans surrendered. He took part in the Bataan Death March and was later held at Camp O'Donnell, Clark Field, and Hanawa.

Seaman First Class William J. Stewart, Kansas, was captured on Java after the USS *Houston* sank. In October 1942 he was transported first to Singapore and then to Ohasi.

Master Gunnery Sergeant Henry B. ("Hank") Stowers, Alabama, was part of the American Embassy and Legation Guard in Peking. He was imprisoned at Woosung, Kiangwan, and Hakodate.

First Lieutenant Robert Preston Taylor, Texas, was posted at the Cuartel de Espana, headquarters for the U.S. Philippine Division, as chaplain for the 31st Infantry Regiment. After the attack on Pearl Harbor, he moved to Nichols Field and then into the Bataan Peninsula. After his capture, Taylor was imprisoned at Bilibid Prison, Cabanatuan, Moji, Fukuoka, and the Hoten prison camp near Mukden, Manchuria.

Private First Class James C. Venable, Texas, was in E Battery, First Defense Battalion, on Wake Island. He was interned mostly at Woosung, Kiangwan, and Hakodate.

Private First Class William A. Visage, Texas, was a member of E Battery, Second Battalion, 131st Field Artillery, 36th Division. Captured on Madura, Dutch East Indies, he was sent to Changi before arriving at Arao, his final destination.

Captain Harvey D. Weidman, Wisconsin, was a member of the Corps of Engineers, Philippine Division, U.S. Army. After a period with Filipino guerrillas, he was captured on the island of Cebu in the fall of 1942. Weidman was held in Cebu Provincial Jail and at Bilibid Prison before being transported to Kobe.

Private John W. Wisecup, Louisiana, was on board the USS *Houston* when it sank in the Sunda Strait. After three days on a raft, he and fifty others reached a beach on Java. After capture by the Japanese, Wisecup was among the first Americans transferred to Bicycle Camp on Java, although he spent the remainder of the war as a prisoner in Changi and at various camps in Thailand working on the Death Railway. He was liberated at Changi in 1945.

Prison Camps, Work Sites, and Other Places Where POWs Were Held

Arao
> City in Kumamoto prefecture, west central Kyushu Island, south- ernmost of the four main islands of Japan.

Ashio
> City in Tochigi prefecture, central Honshu Island, Japan; copper- mining area.

Bangkok
> Capital city of Thailand near the coast of south central Thailand.

Ban Pong
> Southern terminus of the Burma-Thailand Railway in south cen- tral Thailand.

Bataan
> Province and peninsula, western Luzon, Philippine Islands.

Batangas
> City in Batangas province, southern Luzon, Philippine Islands.

Batavia (now Jakarta)
> City in northwestern Java, headquarters of the Dutch East India Company.

Bicycle Camp
> Prison compound in Batavia that had been a Dutch army installation.

Bilibid Prison
   Old Spanish prison built in 1865 in Manila, Philippine Islands.

Burma-Thailand Railway
   Railroad from Thanbyuzayat, Burma, to Ban Pong, Thailand, built
   by prisoners of war.

Cabanatuan
   City in Nueva Ecija province, central Luzon, Philippine Islands,
   where a number of POW camps were located near Cabu village.

Capas
   Town in Tarlac province, Luzon, Philippine Islands.

Casisang
   Camp located in central Mindanao, Philippine Islands.

Cebu Provincial Jail
   Located in Cebu, oldest Spanish town in the Philippine Islands,
   on Cebu Island.

Changi
   Former British garrison located in southern Singapore and the
   major internment camp for British and British Empire prisoners
   of war.

Clark Field
   Former U.S. airfield located northwest of Manila, near Tarlac,
   Luzon, Philippine Islands.

Corregidor
   Island group fortress at the entrance to Manila Bay, Philippine
   Islands.

Da Lat
   Town in southeastern French Indochina, now part of Vietnam.

Davao Penal Colony
   Located on the south coast of Mindanao, Philippine Islands.

Fengtai
   Railroad junction town near Peking in northern Hopeh province,
   northeastern China.

Formosa (now Taiwan, Republic of China)
  Island opposite Fukien province, southeastern China.

Fort Hughes
  Located on the south coast of Manila Bay, west central Luzon,
  Philippine Islands.

Fukuoka Camps
  Located in Fukuoka prefecture, north central Kyushu Island,
  Japan; manufacturing area.

Guam
  Largest and southernmost of the Mariana Islands in the western
  Pacific; U.S. naval station and civil aviation stop.

Hakodate
  Seaport in Hokkaido prefecture, southwestern Hokkaido Island,
  northernmost of the four main islands of Japan; coal-mining area.

Hanawa
  Located in Akita prefecture, northern Honshu Island, Japan.

Hintok
  City and camp on the Burma-Thailand Railway in west central
  Thailand.

Hirohata
  Located in Hyogo prefecture, western Honshu Island, Japan.

Hitachi
  City in northeastern Ibaraki prefecture, northeast of Tokyo,
  Honshu Island, Japan; industrial area.

Hitachi Motoyama
  Village in northeastern Ibaraki prefecture, near Hitachi, Japan.

Honshu Camp No. 7
  Located on the northern tip of Honshu Island, largest of the four
  main islands of Japan.

Hosakura
  Town in Miyagi prefecture, northern Honshu Island, Japan.

Hoten
    Village near Mukden, Manchuria, northeastern China.

Inchon
    Seaport in west central Korea, then called Jinsen.

Jaarmarkt
    Market on outskirts of Surabaja, northeastern Java.

Java
    Island in the Dutch East Indies in the Malaya archipelago, now
    part of Indonesia.

Kanchanaburi
    City and camp on the Burma-Thailand Railway in west central
    Thailand.

Kawasaki
    Southern suburb of Tokyo in Tokyo prefecture; area of heavy elec-
    trical equipment, chemical, and aircraft production.

Kiangwan
    Camp in suburb of Shanghai, China.

Kilo Camps
    POW camps on the Burma-Thailand Railway, so-called because
    of kilometer distances from the base camp at Thanbyuzayat,
    Thailand.

Kobe
    Seaport in Hyogo prefecture, southwest coast of Honshu Island,
    Japan; area of manufacturing, rubber, and aircraft production.

Las Pinas
    Located south of Nichols Field, near Manila, Philippine Islands;
    Japanese airfield.

Luzon
    Chief island of the Philippines in northern part of the group.

Madura
    Island off the northeast coast of Java.

Maibara
Located in Shiga prefecture, central Honshu Island, Japan.

Manila
Capital of the Philippine Islands in west central Luzon.

Mindanao
Southernmost major island of the Philippines.

Mitsushima
Located in Nagano prefecture, central Honshu Island, Japan.

Miyazu
Town in Kyoto prefecture, west central Honshu Island, Japan.

Moji
Seaport in Fukuoka prefecture, northern Kyushu Island, Japan.

Moulmein Prison
Located in Moulmein, southwestern Burma.

Nagasaki
Seaport in Nagasaki prefecture, west central Kyushu Island, Japan; shipbuilding, aircraft, general manufacturing, and coal.

Nakhon Nayok
Town in southeastern Thailand, near Bangkok.

Nanking (now Nanjing)
City in Kiangsu province, southeastern China, northwest of Shanghai; literally "southern capital."

Nichols Field
Located in Manila, Philippine Islands; U.S. airfield used by Japanese.

Nielson Field
Located in Manila, Philippine Islands; U.S. airfield used by Japanese.

Niigata
Seaport in Niigata prefecture, northwestern Honshu Island, Japan; petroleum and manufacturing.

O'Donnell
     U.S. Army camp near Tarlac, central Luzon, Philippine Islands;
     ultimate destination of the Death March.

Ohasi
     Town in Iwate prefecture, northern Honshu Island, Japan.

Omi
     Small island near southern tip of Honshu, opposite Omine.

Omine
     Located in Yamaguchi prefecture, near the southern tip of Honshu
     Island, Japan.

Orio
     Town in Fukuoka prefecture, northern Kyushu Island, Japan; coal-
     mining region.

Osaka
     Seaport in Osaka prefecture, southeastern Honshu Island, Japan;
     chemicals and manufacturing.

Palawan
     Island in southwestern region of the Philippine Islands.

Peking (now Beijing)
     City in Hopeh province, northeastern China; literally "northern
     capital."

Pusan
     Seaport in southeastern Korea.

Roku Rushi
     Located in central Honshu, twenty miles from Fukui in Fukui
     prefecture, west central Honshu Island, Japan.

Saigon
     Inland seaport in southeastern French Indochina, now Vietnam.

San Fernando
     City in central Luzon, Philippine Islands, on the route of the Death
     March.

Sapporo
> City in Hokkaido prefecture, west coast of Hokkaido Island, Japan; coal-mining and manufacturing.

Sendai
> City in Miyagi prefecture, northeastern Honshu Island, Japan; industrial and cultural center.

Sendryu
> Village in northern Nagasaki prefecture, northwestern Kyushu Island, Japan; coal-mining region.

Serang Jail
> Located in Serang, western Java, Dutch East Indies.

Serang Theater
> Located in Serang, western Java, Dutch East Indies.

Shanghai
> Seaport in Kiangsu province, southeastern China.

Shinogawa
> Located west of Tokyo, Tokyo prefecture, Honshu Island, Japan.

Singapore
> Island and city off southern end of the Malaya peninsula, then a British Crown colony and now an independent state; major military post.

Sumatra Camp No. 4
> Located in southern Sumatra, largest island in the Dutch East Indies, south of the Malaya peninsula and west of Java.

Surabaja
> Seaport on northeast coast of Java.

Taihoku (now Taipeh, Taiwan)
> City in northern Formosa.

Takao
> City on southwest coast of Formosa; agricultural region.

Tanagawa
  Town in Osaka prefecture, southeastern Honshu Island, Japan.

Tanjong Priok
  Port of Batavia, Java, Dutch East Indies.

Thanbyuzayat
  Town in southern Burma and northern base camp for the Burma-Thailand Railway.

Tientsin (now Tianjin)
  City in Hopeh province, northeastern China, southeast of Peking.

Tokyo
  Capital city of Japan, Tokyo prefecture, east central Honshu Island.

Toroku
  Located in south central Formosa.

Tsuruga
  Seaport in Fukui prefecture, west coast of Honshu Island, Japan.

Wake Island
  One of three islets—Wake, Peale, and Wilkes—around a lagoon, located in the northern Pacific; U.S. naval and air stations.

Woosung
  Camp and city in northern suburb of Shanghai, China.

Yodogawa Prison Camp
  Located in Osaka prefecture, west central Honshu Island, Japan.

Yokkaichi
  Seaport in Mie prefecture, southeastern Honshu Island, Japan.

Yokohama
  Seaport in Kanagawa prefecture, east central Honshu Island, and chief port of Japan; automobiles, shipbuilding, and heavy electrical equipment.

Zamboanga
  Seaport on west coast of Mindanao, Philippine Islands.

Zentsuji

Town in Kagawa prefecture, northeastern Shikoku Island, south-easternmost and smallest of the four main islands of Japan.

POW INTERNMENT SITES IN THE FAR EAST
(map refers only to those camps where interviewed POWs were held)

POW CAMPS IN JAPAN
(map refers only to those camps where interviewed POWs were held)

> In all American wars, inordinate public and
> official attention has been paid to the death and
> suffering of POWs, their heroism and coward-
> ice, their loyalty and disloyalty, their selfish-
> ness and altruism relative to the concern toward
> the fate and behavior of men in battle.[1]
>
> —Albert D. Biderman

Introduction: Prisoners of the Sun

During the first few months of World War II the Japanese military in
the Far East captured approximately 25,600 American servicemen.
For the next three and one-half years, they were kept at various POW
camps and work sites stretching from Burma north to Manchuria and
Hokkaido, south to Wake, Guam, and the Celebes (including the Philippines), west to Java and Sumatra, and north again to Burma. (See
the map reproduced on the endpapers.) The treatment that these men
and women received from December 1941 to September 1945 was a
major reason why war crimes trials were held in Singapore, Manila,
and elsewhere after the conflict. By then only about 15,000 American captives were still alive, over 10,000 having died or been killed
directly or indirectly by the Japanese.

From the testimonies and affidavits that former prisoners of war
gave afterward, a picture of privation, hardship, mistreatment, physical and psychological abuse, agony, and death emerges. For many,
atrocities began as soon as they were captured and lasted throughout
their imprisonment. For a few, their experiences never approximated
the horror and indignities revealed later at the war crimes trials. This
book, based on 174 oral history interviews conducted by the University of North Texas Oral History Program in Denton, gives insight
into these prisoners' experiences. It does not cover every camp in
which prisoners were kept; that task would be impossible. It does
include, however, descriptions of many of the major internment sites

---

[1]Biderman, *March to Calumny*, 17.

outside Japan and some of the important POW camps on the Japanese home islands. (See maps, "POW Internment Sites in the Far East" and "POW Camps in Japan.")

Like others writing about prisoners of war, we have been unable to ascertain the precise number of Americans taken by the Japanese and of the internment camps and work sites where they were held. We have relied on E. Bartlett Kerr, *Surrender and Survival: The Experience of American POWs in the Pacific, 1941–1945*, for the number of men and women captured, although his estimates may not be completely accurate. For the number and location of the over six hundred camp sites and work areas, we used a variety of sources but depended heavily on the map of Japanese prisoner-of-war camps found in volume two of Peter Calvocoressi et al., *Total War: The Causes and Courses of the Second World War*.

The U.S. government, which has spent considerable effort in writing excellent official histories of World War II, has failed to produce a study of prisoners of war or reliable statistics about them. Unlike Albert D. Biderman's opinion quoted above, Americans held prisoner by Japan during World War II have not received the same attention, statistical or otherwise, accorded the nation's fighting men and their military campaigns. And while statistics assist us in understanding the enormity of the plight of the American GIs held by Japan, to comprehend their lives as prisoners we must examine their reactions to and interactions with their captors. Nothing reaches the depth of experience with as much empathy as reminiscences, commentaries, memoirs, and oral histories—and oral history has the advantage of allowing those who otherwise cannot formulate and express their thoughts clearly to articulate them with the oral historian's help. Shortly before America entered World War II, Clarence R. Johnson wrote that "a significant point of view suggested by a former soldier is that the way to judge a prisoner-of-war camp is by looking out on the world through the barbed wire and not by looking through the barbed wire into the prison camp."[2]

In the following pages the prisoners tell their stories, not chronologically but topically. We have isolated major aspects of the men's experiences and used their quotes to illustrate the full range of what these aspects meant to America's "Prisoners of the Sun." To include the most frequent and most significant responses from the prisoners'

---

[2]Johnson, *Prisoners of War*, 10.

perspective, we interviewed men held primarily at the larger POW camps established by the Japanese. Although all 174 interviews were read, we chose to excerpt only 52 extensively. We also refer to others. Unfortunately, none of our interviews was with any of the sixty-seven "Angels of Bataan," the heroic nurses of Bataan and Corregidor held at Santo Tomas Camp in Manila. Also, none was with any American airmen shot down over territory controlled by the Japanese.

The topical, or mosaic, approach taken with these interviews allows the reader to sample what men say that they felt when captured, beaten, terrorized, bored, or released. Their experiences run the gamut of human emotion, with the darker side of life prevailing. Dr. Henri Hekking, medical officer of the former Royal Dutch East Indian Army, Medical Corps, who was attached to Americans working on the Burma-Thailand Railway, commented in 1978 on the number of requests he received from former prisoners making claims for disability to the Veterans Bureau:

> In the past I made several statements about American ex-POWs who returned to their country from prison camps along the Burma Railroad. They came back home alive, yes, but damaged in body and soul. My statements were necessary in their struggle—that started some years later—for a war-connected pension. For most doctors of the pension boards, it was extremely difficult to insert the not always directly visible traces of the tremendous impact of the POW time on body and soul, into the general state of ill health that caused the disability for which the pension was claimed. The 1st few years I received a growing number of requests. . , . As the drawing up of the requested reports—especially for an old and busy man, in [what is for me] a foreign language—is rather time-consuming, I decided to make this general statement. In my opinion this is quite justified, because all the men along the Burma Railroad sustained the same hardships and suffered from practically all diseases mentioned later on in this statement. The only difference is the variability in resistance of the different victims.

Dr. Hekking, then cataloging starvation, diseases, and maltreatment, concluded that of the extent of "damage . . . done to the intricate system of the many enzymes, necessary to maintain life, one can only guess. There probably won't be a single tissue or vital organ not badly affected for life by all the influences mentioned above."[3] Most of the medical personnel quoted in *The Japanese Story*, where Dr. Hekking's statement appeared, express similar sentiments regarding the

---

[3] American Ex-Prisoners of War Inc., *The Japanese Story*, 71.

experiences of the prisoners, whose suffering brought the label "Death Railway" to the project.

The problems of long-term disability also are addressed in a study by Bernard M. Cohen and Maurice Z. Cooper, whose purpose was to compare POWs of Japan (PWJs) with Americans captured in Europe (PWEs) in regard to the lingering effects of prisoner-of-war status. They conclude that "considerably greater disability level, . . . appreciably more frequent complaints of sickness, and the indications of less satisfactory work adjustment . . . of the PWJs as compared with those of the PWEs represent specific suggestive evidence of a continued excess of unhospitalized morbidity in the Pacific group."[4] A. J. Barker believes that "the Japanese treatment of prisoners in the Far East is comparable to that of the Russians."[5] He is referring to the Russian treatment of German prisoners during World War II, but he may as well have spoken of the German treatment of Russian prisoners.

In this volume the reader must remember that the prisoners of war are giving their own recollections and opinions. What one man says may not agree in all particulars with another's statement, and at times an interviewee may contradict himself. Memory is at best a fragile tool, especially when recalling experiences as horrifying as these. Moreover, individuals do not always perceive events in the same way—a chaplain, Lt. Robert Preston Taylor, no doubt sees the world differently from an agnostic. At times the interviewees may make statements contrary to the logical circumstances of a situation. In such instances the reader must decide which is the more probable, keeping in mind that truth is often stranger than fiction and that the whims of the Japanese determined the Americans' fate. As a result, a prisoner's life varied from camp to camp and from day to day throughout the long months of his captivity, and the perception of each situation he experienced also varied, captive by captive.

While disparity of treatment and individual discernment make it difficult to generalize about what it meant to be a Prisoner of the Sun, in general what Americans suffered was dreadful. Many writers have provided explanations for the savageries visited upon their prisoners by the Japanese; the best explanations combine the evil side of

---

[4]Cohen and Cooper, *A Follow-up Study of World War II Prisoners of War*, 65.
[5]Barker, *Prisoners of War*, 106.

human nature, racism, and the Code of Bushido, or the Way of the Warrior. During basic training, Japanese soldiers were taught that the greatest honor was to die for the emperor and that the ultimate shame was to surrender to the enemy. Barker points out that "soldiers of the Imperial Japanese Army were brought up to believe that military honor dictated no surrender, and training manuals of the Japanese fighting forces contained the warning that 'Those becoming prisoners of war will suffer the death penalty.' "[6] Moreover, capture not only disgraced the soldier but it also dishonored his family.

Harold K. Johnson, who was assigned to a Philippine Scout regiment when captured, writes that the Japanese repeatedly asked, "Why did you not commit suicide?"[7] Had those same Japanese been taken captive early in the war, they undoubtedly would have committed hara-kiri. Thus, they could not readily comprehend why American troops surrendered, and they despised the GIs for doing so. Their disgust and disdain led them to believe that the prisoners, by surrendering, had forfeited all right to self-respect or even to life itself. According to Barker, "The attitude of Japanese troops towards the prisoners of war of their enemies tended to be one of contempt, and this was reflected in the attitudes of the guards. Since POWs were little better than dead men, their living conditions were of no importance."[8] Stewart Wolf and Herbert S. Ripley agree that because "Japanese culture recognized suicide as the honorable recourse in defeat they held those who surrendered in special contempt. It was their policy to humiliate and degrade by physical violence."[9]

The Code of Bushido determined discipline in the Japanese Army, justifying harsh treatment within its ranks. Officers violently attacked noncoms; noncoms brutalized privates, who in turn visited their fury on prisoners of war, which according to many prisoners was the Oriental way of saving face. In some areas, Koreans and Formosans, whom the Japanese treated almost as badly as they did the American captives, were pressed into service as guards. Generally, the conscripts' fury, when passed on to American prisoners, was worse than the treatment by any Japanese guard. Years later, Cpl. Edward Fung,

---

[6]Ibid., 121–22.

[7]James, ed., *South to Bataan, North to Mukden*, xiii.

[8]Barker, *Prisoners of War*, 122.

[9]Wolf and Ripley, "Reactions among Allied Prisoners of War Subjected to Three Years of Imprisonment and Torture by the Japanese," 183.

a Chinese-American in the Second Battalion, 131st Field Artillery
Regiment, who had worked on the Death Railway, said: "I will dis-
like Koreans to the day I die"; and Sgt. Luther Prunty, a member of
the same unit, summed up widespread disgust in a three-word de-
scription of his Korean guards: "ignorant, sadistic, cruel."[10] Thus,
the prisoners found themselves at the bottom of a social system that
was harsh, punitive, fanatical, and often deadly. Of the Japanese—
officers as well as enlisted men—guilty of atrocities against prisoners, Richard Garrett has written: "Nobody who was not a prisoner
of Nippon during World War II can say whether there should be
forgiveness."[11]

Another view of why Allied prisoners were mistreated is offered
by Barker: "As British and American POWs were members of enemy
nations which in the past had been patronizing and superior, their
loss of face should be made apparent to themselves and to the people
of the East which Japan was supposed to be liberating."[12] This attitude may explain why Americans were paraded at times before native populations by the Japanese, who were making the point that a
white skin did not necessarily mean superiority.

Pat Reid and Maurice Michael offer similar opinions as well as a
different angle: "A great determinant in the treatment of the POW
has always been numbers. Small numbers are easy to deal with in a
humane and civilized manner, while logistical difficulties make it
impossible to deal with large numbers in anything approaching a humane manner."[13] Indeed, the Japanese captured more Allied troops
than they expected to, but it is difficult to see how numbers alone can
explain the beatings, mass punishments, tortures, beheadings, and
murders of these prisoners. Nor does it account for medical experi-
mentation and cannibalism, as described by Waller F. Jones: "At
Kyushu Imperial University . . . Professor Fukujiro Ishiyama conducted the dismemberment of captives, removing lungs, stomachs,
and even drilled holes in their skulls. This was all done without anesthesia!" He adds that "irrefutable proof that field commanders and

[10]La Forte and Marcello, *Building the Death Railway*, 280.
[11]Garrett, *P.O.W: The Uncivil Face of War*, 203. For an interpretation
that modifies what is said here, in the hope of rationalizing Japanese action
by explaining away American reporting as due to racial attitudes and prac-
tices, see John W. Dower, *War without Mercy*, 48–52 and passim.
[12]Barker, *Prisoners of War*, 122.
[13]Reid and Michael, *Prisoners of War*, 13.

their troops indulged in [cannibalism] . . . exists because a captured field order announced that *it was 'permissible to eat the flesh of the enemy only,'* " and that "in 1946 an Allied military tribunal tried Major Suso Matoba on charges of cannibalism."[14]

These and other Japanese brutalities happened despite Tokyo's ratification of The Hague Conference Agreement of 1907, part of which applied to war prisoners. Japan's delegates also signed the 1929 Geneva Accords that specified principles and rules for the treatment of prisoners of war, although their government never ratified it. However, Tokyo did approve the Geneva Red Cross Convention on the treatment of wounded, sick, and dead in wartime. In fact, the Japanese promised to observe the Red Cross and Geneva conventions if they did not conflict with existing home government regulations, laws, and policies. Additionally, Japan established the Prisoner of War Administrative Division in its War Ministry and placed Gen. Seitaro Uemura in charge. He and his staff also acted as the POW Information Bureau, the source of official pronouncements about prisoners.

Paper protections, however, were misleading. In fact, the Japanese had no standard way of behaving toward prisoners of war. Treatment varied according to the attitude or whim of the highest or lowest Japanese officer, enlisted man, or Korean or Formosan conscript guard. To quote again Harold K. Johnson, who retired from the Army with the rank of general: "Conditions in each prison camp differed in both minor and major degrees. Moreover, conditions in each camp varied over a period of time."[15]

In addition, the course of the war played a role. In some ways continuous American victories during 1944 and 1945 resulted in better treatment as some Japanese began to expect an ultimate victory by the Allies—but during and after air raids near POW camps, prisoners were beaten and kicked viciously. Also, as invading forces neared the camps, the Japanese drafted a plan to execute American prisoners. According to Ronald H. Bailey, as the war concluded the "Japanese attitudes toward defeat and capture—their own and their enemies'—made the future look grim for Allied prisoners. It appeared likely that they would be massacred by their Japanese guards, who

---

[14]Jones, "Japanese Attitudes toward Prisoners of War," 18–20 (author's emphasis).

[15]James, ed., *South to Bataan, North to Mukden*, xii–xiii.

would then commit suicide."[16] As related in *Building the Death Railway*, Field Marshal Count Juichi Terauchi, commander of the Southern Army in Saigon, concocted a grisly plan to massacre all prisoners in Thailand if and when an Allied invasion took place. Only intervention by the emperor's brother, Prince Chichibu, and the dropping of atomic bombs on Hiroshima and Nagasaki kept Terauchi from carrying out his ghastly project.[17] (An equally gruesome plan was implemented, on a smaller scale, at Palawan in the Philippines. As U.S. forces approached the island, 141 Americans were massacred.)

During the interviews some prisoners state that they were held at Cabanatuan, Fukuoka, Hakodate, Honshu, or Sapporo; in fact, there were several prison camps around a particular town or city or on an island. Sometimes the interviewee refers to Cabanatuan No. 1, Fukuoka No. 4, or Honshu Camp No. 7; more often than not, he fails to distinguish which numbered camp he means, or he uses the name of another town or village closer to the numbered camp—for example, Sendryu or Arao on Kyushu Island, Japan. Either the Japanese used both village names and numbers for camps or the prisoners, on their own, designated the camps this way. In any case, we have been forced to use Cabanatuan, Hakodate, or others without their numbers. Thus, the reader should remember that Hakodate, as it appears in the interviews, refers to several different sites near that port city on Hokkaido Island. The same is true for other citations as well.

The interviews presented here were conducted from 1970 to 1989 in accordance with the guidelines prescribed by the Oral History Association, with each former prisoner of war interviewed individually and in private. A core of similar questions was asked each person, followed by more precise inquiries to clarify and expand on certain responses. After being transcribed and copyread, the interviews were placed along with one copy of the transcription in the Archives Department of Willis Library at the University of North Texas.

A number of individuals helped us in preparing this volume. Otto Schwarz, who survived the sinking of the USS *Houston* and the building of the Death Railway, supplied us with POW documents and counsel; his support was invaluable. Glenn E. Helm, reference librarian, Naval Historical Center, Washington, DC, provided data about U.S. Navy prisoners of war. Professor Edward J. Coomes, former sailor

---

[16]Bailey, *Prisoners of War: World War II*, 181.
[17]La Forte and Marcello, *Building the Death Railway*, 233–34.

and Korean War veteran, read the entire manuscript for errors. Georgia Mann, teaching fellow and graduate student in history at the University of North Texas, also reviewed parts of the manuscript. Betty Burch, the History Department's superb administrative assistant, shared with us her expertise in the use of personal computers. Toshla Kimball and Sandy Weldin, graduate students and departmental secretaries, copyread the manuscript, and Sandy proofread the galleys. The Interlibrary Loan Office of Willis Library helped secure journal articles and books not otherwise available. The maps were prepared by Chad Maloney, media specialist, Center for Instructional Services, University of North Texas. Finally, Donald Knox's masterful oral history, *Death March: The Survivors of Bataan* (1981), served as the inspiration and something of a model for this book.

Robert S. La Forte

Chapter I

Capture

The American officers and soldiers who surrendered to the Japanese made one of the most agonizing and difficult choices of World War II. Whether by Maj. Gen. Jonathan M. Wainwright amid the ruins of Corregidor, or by PFC John Breckenridge Garrison after hiding for eleven days in the rugged hills of Guam following its capitulation, the decision to give up seared itself forever into the prisoners' minds.

Amazingly, the Japanese generally treated Americans captured without a fight better than those taken after battle. The soldiers of Nippon, devotees of the Code of Bushido, respected other warriors but hated with a greater passion the U.S. servicemen who, minutes before surrender, had been trying to kill them. This elemental reality made the difference in treatment. The residue of battlefield anger caused some Americans to receive rough handling by Japan's frontline troops. Other reasons for brutality, soon after capture, ranged from disgust and contempt to indifference toward the enemy, but individual acts of sadism by Japanese soldiers should not be discounted. It is difficult to determine whether the relationship between Americans and Japanese frontline troops was substantially different from the relationships surrounding surrender in other wars. Richard Holmes, who describes a variety of treatments that conquerors visited upon the conquered in *Acts of War: The Behavior of Men in Battle*, makes it seem similar.[1]

For many of America's prisoners of war in the Orient, the enduring remembrance of surrender was the shame and humiliation of defeat. Representatives of a nation that had taught them that their country had never lost a war, they believed that as the unvanquished they were a superior people. They were unprepared for defeat and believed that they were betraying their nation's trust and their families back

---

[1]Holmes, *Acts of War*, 319–20, 323–25, 382–88.

home. Some worried about their immediate fate. They had heard of Japanese viciousness in China, and for those captured at Bataan and involved in the Death March, or for survivors of the USS *Houston* taken captive on Java, their fear of Japanese barbarity seemed realized.

In these interviews, however, the Japanese frontline troops who captured most Americans are remembered as significantly better and more humane than the men who guarded them for the duration of their imprisonment. Still, many accounts given during or immediately after the war do not square with the prisoners' nostalgic appreciation of the better qualities of their battle-tested captors. There seems to be no explanation for the disparity, other than that time has healed many of the worst wounds—the psychological ones.

Most of the men who surrendered in the first several months of the war did so after battle, either in the Philippines on Bataan, Corregidor, or Mindanao; at Wake Island, on Java, or Guam; or from sinking ships, most notably the heavy cruiser *Houston* and the destroyer *Pope*. The men who jumped from these ships into the sea were either picked up by Japanese vessels or else made it to land and were captured on shore. A number of other American warships, including the destroyers *Edsall* and *Pillsbury* and the gunboat *Asheville*, were reported missing in the southwest Pacific during the early months of 1942. All were lost in the Java Sea. The submarine *Perch* also was reported missing in the Pacific in April 1942. (We have been unable to learn whether any of these ships' crews were captured and survived.)

Other American fighting men were taken prisoner without a struggle, in their barracks in Peking or Tientsin, on the streets in Japan proper, or at scattered places throughout the Far East and southwest Pacific. They include the crew of the gunboat *Wake*, the only American ship to surrender to the Japanese during World War II, taken at Shanghai on December 8, 1941. In the following pages the reader will discover how some of the Americans reacted to capture and their captors.

American Attitudes toward Surrender

Cpl. Sherman (Luzon) "We knew we were going to die, one way or the other, but then there was a possibility that they might keep us alive. So we decided we'd surrender. But first we sat down and ate all the fruit we had. We had taken our guns and torn them up, piece by piece, and threw them four ways to the wind. All we had on us was a change of clothes and a couple of blankets. We shook hands with each other, and we took off. We walked down to the Cabanatuan Camp."

Capt. Adair (Bataan) "Frankly, surrender didn't enter my mind, and I didn't hear any talk about it. Of course, things happened so fast that it's hard to describe your feelings. You don't want to even think about surrender. An American doesn't think about it. You might think about what would happen and that sort of thing, but you try to push it out of your mind. I know the other guys felt the same way, too. That's the way we were thinking. We didn't even talk about it, knowing in the back of your mind that it could happen at any time. We wouldn't face reality, I guess you could say. We were hoping against hope that aid would come. But once it happened, it came so fast that you didn't have time to think about what you would do. No one I knew had made any plans to surrender or to make any escape plans because they just couldn't believe it."

Cpl. Bunch (Bataan) "Finally, word came back that the American command was trying to set up a meeting with the Japanese to surrender the Bataan Peninsula and that we were to pull back. I and some other fellows considered going to the hills, and a lot of them did this for a while, but in most cases I don't think it paid off. I think most of them changed their minds and went ahead and surrendered

"I felt like the thing to do was to stay with a mass of people than go off with a small group and no supplies and really not knowing whether the Filipinos would turn you in or protect you or help you or what. So I felt that the thing to do was to stay with a large group, and that's what I did. I really didn't have a great desire to run off to the mountains without any supplies or anything because I felt like I'd just be hunted down and shot or turned in. So my reaction was, of course, one of great disappointment when I got the word that we had surrendered, but I never had the feeling that we'd be a prisoner of war for three and a half years. I thought, 'Well, okay, they got us now, but just wait.' I thought that eventually we'd be rescued and that there would be a million troops to come in and take this place back. And I more or less resolved to myself that I was going to be a prisoner and hoped that they wouldn't shoot us all like I thought they might."

Cpl. Koury (Bataan) "I think a bunch of us went back to Mount Mariveles, and we started planning what we were going to do, that we were not going to surrender. We'd seen evidence of some of the things the Japs did to prisoners. We'd seen some Filipino Scouts who had been overrun, and they had been very badly mutilated and one thing and another. Really, in our minds we kept thinking that somebody was going to come and get us. [Gen. Douglas] MacArthur had sent out the message before he left that he had more troops than the enemy and this, that, and the other, and all kinds of stuff, and what he could do, and that we had to hold. We believed that—we really did—until the surrender.

"Like I said, a bunch of us—forty or fifty—had already decided that we weren't going to surrender. We were going to split up, and, in fact, we were getting medical kits together, and money, because money was most important, and food and handguns, stuff like that. We were going to take off and stay around Mount Mariveles because it was a good place to hide. The next day when the colonel told us to stack our weapons and turn them in, well, we just took off for the hills. We broke into smaller groups, not forty or fifty of us. We had no plans, really. We were just trying to hide. We still felt that in maybe six months from then, or a year, but not more than that, that they'd be back. We just hid. There weren't many people around, really. There was plenty of food and water, and so we just slept and stood watch. Like I say, we had no firm plan for what we were going to do, except try to hide, stay out of the way.

"It was about seven or eight days after we were supposed to have surrendered that they caught us. We woke up one morning, and there a Japanese stood. He had one of these little guns pointed at me, and other Japs had guns on the other guys who were laying there. They were most unhappy to find us up there. They wanted to know why we hadn't honored our word to surrender like we should. The sickening part is that they were all little bitty guys. I've seen a lot of Japs that weren't small, but this bunch that caught us were short."

Pvt. Guiles (Bataan) "We were ordered by General Wainwright via radio that for us the war had ended, and we were to surrender. At that time I thought that surrendering was one of the most disgraceful things that a person could do, but I was ordered to stack my arms, and that's what I did along with the rest of the Americans."

Lt. Burris (Bataan) "The fact is, I think, that it would have been better if we had gotten as many fliers out of there as possible—me included. Let us fight someplace else rather than let us wither on the ground there and do nothing. I had the thought the entire time, I guess, that I would be evacuated. I just couldn't see why they would let somebody that they had spent a full year training just hang there, sit there and be inefficient and do nothing. I figured they'd pull us back someplace where they had airplanes so that we could fight. This seemed like the sensible thing to me. The British evacuated Dunkirk, didn't they, and brought their men back so they could fight again with a better situation for themselves? That makes sense to me. We were doing nothing except losing there on Bataan. At least that's what I thought. I knew there was a lot of trouble up there on the front, but it still didn't dawn on me that we were stuck there. I couldn't see anything wrong with leaving because as soon as we got back in American hands we'd be put right into the conflict where we could do some good. We really wouldn't have been deserting. It would just be doing the sensible thing, as far as I was concerned. I figured that that was what they were going to do, but, by golly, they didn't do it. They just let us stay there."

Cpl. Read (Bataan) "My first thought was to try to get to the beach and swim to Corregidor, and I think a lot of people had the same idea. It was about three miles across the strait, and I was a fair swimmer. I then just went through the jungle trails, and one trail came out on a road somewhere around Limay, and the place was swarming with Japs already. I realized that they were on the beaches already, so there was no way to get to the beach.

"I eventually wound up down in the vicinity of Mariveles and ran into what was left of my divisional command post. It was kind of disorganized, but I decided to stay around and see what happened. They had radio communications, and before long we found out that the surrender was taking place. We had a lot of division records; we had the colors of all the regiments there; we had the service records of everybody. So they put us to work digging a bunch of big holes, and we buried all that stuff. Everybody figured that we'd come back later on and get everything.

"About this time I fell in with a guy by the name of [Benjamin] Dunn from McKinney, Texas. He and I decided that we didn't like the sound of things because there were a lot of scare stories going around that the Japs were shooting all the prisoners and such stuff. So he and I got hold of some canned salmon there, fixed us some packs, loaded ourselves with bandoliers of ammunition and a couple of rifles, and we were heading for the hills. We were in a good place to do it, too, because we were in the foothills of Mount Mariveles there, which was all heavy jungle. Then a lieutenant stopped us, and he says, 'Where are you guys going?' We told him, and he says, 'Oh, you're foolish to do that! The war will be over in four or five weeks! The Japs are treating prisoners according to the Geneva Convention, and we've got absolute confirmation on that.' He says, 'You're crazy to go out there and fight in the jungle with all that malaria and all that kind of thing!' So we didn't go, and I've always wondered how things would have turned out. But we stayed there just waiting for some kind of word."

Pvt. Stanley (Bataan) "I'll never forget the surrender, but I don't know how to describe it. You just felt like you were on a boat, and the boat just went out from under you, and you were out in the middle of the ocean. You just felt that the world had come to an end almost, and yet—this sounds funny—we had it so rough, starved for so long— we thought we had it rough, I'll put it that way—that in a lot of ways it was kind of a relief to get to surrender. We had been starved for so long and had been under these air raids, and I was too stupid to real- ize that I was really going to be in for something. I thought the Japs would just take us and pen us up and treat us like we were human beings. Does that make sense? Anyway, it was kind of a relief to surrender, but yet I felt like a whipped dog."

Lt. Taylor (Bataan) "It wasn't so much hearing about the surren- der as it was seeing the white flags go up, which is a symbol of sur- render. I guess around 8:00 or 9:00 in the morning the surrender flags went up, and we got the word that General [Edward P.] King had been ordered to surrender and that he had sent his contact people forward to confer with the Japanese and effect the surrender. This was a rather sad moment in the lives of most of us, and you just can't imagine what the feeling is unless you've been there to see the white flag being hoisted and the American flag being lowered in defeat. This is something we had never witnessed and had never expected and never experienced. We were not prepared for it at all, no. So this was somewhat of a shock. To see all those white flags flying was degrading and rather suffocating to all of us in spirit and in feeling."

Cpl. McCall (Corregidor) "I can't recall exactly what my feel- ings were, but I felt sort of sorry about surrendering. I felt ashamed that we lost, I know that."

Cpl. Brantley (Corregidor) "They sent in orders for us to surrender, and our colonel said, 'Marines never surrender, and I'm not going to be the first!' Then he calmed down and called us all together and told us the news. Well, it stunned us. We didn't know what to expect because we had heard rumors that the Japanese didn't take prisoners and that they killed them. So we didn't know if surrendering was going to change the situation. Really, I had hidden some pistols, kept them close by, after we ran up the white flag, so I sort of had a gun in my possession."

Capt. Bartlett (Corregidor) "I guess I was numb when I first heard about the surrender. I don't know. I knew it was coming. It was just like you see a baseball heading for a window. It hits it, but you have no reaction. You know it is coming. When we first headed to Bataan, I didn't ever think I would come out of there, but it didn't worry me very much. I still have that attitude toward death. It wouldn't worry me in the least to know that when I step out that door that I would drop dead. Not that I'm looking for death, but I'm a fatalist, so I can't think back on any point where fear entered my system. I don't know. Maybe I'm a nut, but I can't fear anything. Fear is a normal reaction, so maybe I'm not a normal human being. I had no worry about it."

Pvt. Bugbee (Corregidor) "We had an awful lot of apprehension about surrendering because we knew we had been told that the Japs used POWs for bayonet practice, and it was a proven fact that they had used the Chinese this way. So we just didn't know how long we would be alive; I mean, we just felt that when the Japs did come in, we wouldn't know what to expect. Then there was our own disbelief that it really could have happened to us. There's just no way to express an individual's feelings when he sees his country's flag come down and the enemy flag go up. We were ordered to congregate in a certain area and watch this ceremony take place, and I don't guess there was an American eye that didn't have tears in it when we saw the Stars and Stripes go down and the Rising Sun go up."

Capt. Bull (Corregidor) "Surrender was a great surprise to me. I thought we would fight to the last man, so I wasn't prepared for the surrender, and neither were the officers in my immediate vicinity. I remember having a copy of War Plan Orange [the contingency plan for war with Japan] in my safe as the Post Exchange officer and probably as battery commander, too, so surrender or even evacuation wasn't thinkable at all until it actually occurred. When we received the rumors of a surrender, the regimental supply officer and myself took steps to destroy things that might be of value to the enemy should we be taken. I recall our dropping hand grenades in searchlights and destroying them and saying to ourselves, 'If there isn't a surrender, we'll certainly owe the government a lot of money for destroying government property.' We put our small arms in a shell crater and put gasoline in on top of them and tried to destroy them as best we could. We also destroyed the two 155-millimeter guns by bottling up their ends and firing a round so that it would destroy the barrel. So at that time it did look like we were going to surrender and not fight to the last man, which was to me a great surprise."

Sgt. Burk (Fort Hughes) "When our lieutenant told us that we were surrendering, we all made light of it, really. You'd see a guy light a cigarette with a twenty-dollar bill. Nobody thought about money. What good was it? The Japs would take it if they found it. After the constant pounding we had taken from artillery and bombs, we felt both relief that it was over and apprehension of not knowing what was going to happen next."

PFC R. Allen (Mindanao) "For about nine hours they bombarded us, and at daylight they made this second landing, and they pushed us back. We retreated and after three days our commanders said we were giving up, surrendering. We were to stack our arms and surrender the next morning. Well, the boys didn't like that too much, but that was orders. There were orders that if you went to the hills, you'd be court-martialed. I for one said that I'd never become a Japanese prisoner. I'd blow my brains out first, but that's the talk of an eighteen-year-old boy. I tried. I was going to blow my brains out. I put the gun to my head, put my finger on the trigger, and for some reason that thumb paralyzed. I couldn't do it. There were a lot of the men that tried this. Surrendering makes you feel inadequate. It makes you feel that you weren't much of a man to be taken. But after that, a little later in the day, I was called to headquarters and was told to go into the hills to form guerrilla warfare groups. Four of us had taken six months of combat training and Spanish, and they picked us and two other boys to go. There were six of us.

"We spent most of our time trying to form guerrilla warfare units. We did this for approximately six months. I don't think we'd have ever been captured if we hadn't been turned in. A Filipino had turned us in."

PFC Bolitho (Mindanao) "We were the last to be captured as a unit in the Philippines, but it was either give up or be annihilated. We were surrounded by the Japanese. So we took sheets and put them over the top of the ambulances and trucks and drove into this area where we were told to get off the trucks and raise our hands. We were searched; our pens and pencils, wristwatches, and rings were taken."

Capt. Godbold (Wake Island) "We were engaged in light, not heavy, activity against the enemy. They didn't overwhelm our position. I guess in time they would have, but we held them off and the island surrendered while we were still engaged in fighting the Japanese. As far as I could tell from my position, things were going along very well. We were holding the Japanese off with relatively little difficulty. When [Maj. James P. S.] Devereux, our commanding officer, went through my position toward the Japanese line carrying a white flag, it was obvious we were going to surrender. My reaction, from my limited viewpoint, was that I saw no reason for surrendering because we were doing very well there. Obviously, I didn't know the situation at other points on the island, and to some extent neither did Devereux, but he knew a lot more than I did. So from my standpoint, I thought at the time it was a mistake to surrender. There were rumors, as you'd expect, that the Japanese would shoot all the prisoners. This didn't seem reasonable, and I didn't expect it. So Devereux came back with Japanese soldiers, and we were told by him to cease firing and lay down our arms. Gradually, Japanese soldiers came up and disarmed anyone who still hadn't given up their guns."

PFC Venable (Wake Island) "It seems to me that it was like 10:00 or 11:00 in the morning when we were given the word that we were surrendering, and I must admit that this was probably the lowest point of our lives because we had been trained to fight, not to surrender, and to be commanded that we must surrender was a very tremendous blow to our pride, to the esprit de corps that we had. I know that the guys cried to think of it. Lieutenant Lewis pulled out his pistol, and I know he emptied it into the height finder in order to destroy the mechanism. We destroyed the guns as best we could by placing grenades in them. We packed blankets in the barrels and then rolled up grenades in them and pulled the pin. We threw away our firing pins to all the rifles. We completely destroyed our equipment as well as we could. But, frankly, it was a very, very low point at this time."

PFC Garrison (Guam) "Word came down from the governor, who was a captain in the Navy and governor of the island [Capt. G. J.

McMillin], that the island had surrendered. We had been led to believe that the Japanese took no prisoners. So nine of us decided that if we were going to get killed we might as well be shooting back. So we didn't surrender. Nine of us got all the ammunition and rifles and weapons that we could accumulate and what stores we could get and went out in the hills. We stayed out there for about eleven days, I guess. We foraged for food, tried to live, because if we ran into a Japanese patrol, well, that's when I did my fighting. We killed pigs, deer, iguanas, and there's all the fruit and vegetables, if you know what to look for.

"Had there not been that large of a group, I might not have turned myself in. I think I could have gotten by with just myself and another man. There were nine of us altogether. The word finally came down to us, through some natives that we'd run into and were friendly to us, that the Japs weren't going to kill everybody, and that everybody was going to Japan, but that anybody left on the island would be shot on sight. Of course, we knew that anyway. The Japs wanted all of us to turn in. So we decided that that would be the best thing to do. Guam is so small that at one time or another the Japs were going to trap you. There just wasn't enough area for hiding.

"We took all of our weapons, took the bolts out of them, and threw the bolts in the ocean so that the rifles would be rendered useless to anybody, and we marched in with a white flag. We marched within one hundred yards of the main Japanese headquarters before anybody saw us. There were Japanese soldiers all over the place, and they didn't even notice us. We were waving this white flag, you know. They finally saw us, and, of course, they started jabbering. There was one sailor on Guam, a radioman, who took off for the hills. He made it all through the war. I can't remember his name, but he was never captured. He wrote a book later."[2]

Fireman 1/C Kennedy (Sunda Strait) "I was on the raft at daybreak. We floated through a fleet of Japanese merchant ships for an hour or two. Finally, a landing boat came out and circled us with its machine guns on us. I started to swim away, but I didn't go very far when I decided,' This is stupid.' So I swam back to the raft, and then

---

[2]Garrison is referring to Radioman First Class George Ray Tweed. His book, *Robinson Crusoe, USN: The Adventures of George Tweed as Told to Blake Clark* (New York: Whittlesey House, 1945), was made into the movie *No Man Is an Island* (1962), starring Jeffrey Hunter as Tweed.

they put us aboard the landing barge. I had been on two other rafts that night and those men were never heard from. I'm sure they were machine-gunned. I think I am alive today because the officer who captured us was a graduate of UCLA."

Sgt. Fujita (Java) "When we were first captured, there wasn't a one of us that thought that it would not be two months later until we would be out of there. It was fairly early when we had to change our original estimate. Now it dawned on us that we might possibly be there two years or so. Later, when we got to Japan it finally dawned on us, 'Hell, we may be here for twenty years.' "

Cpl. Crews (Peking) "Word came down that we were going to have to go to the parade ground, bring our rifles and all of our ammunition, stack arms, and turn it over to the Japs. We didn't like it. We didn't like it at all, but what could we do? It's hard to relay the impression it had on us. It wasn't just me; it was the whole outfit. We were out on the parade ground when the flag came down. I don't think there was a dry eye in the crowd. I think there were eighty or ninety of us there. I may be wrong. We started out with four or five hundred in Tientsin and four or five hundred in Peking and forty or fifty in Chinwangtao. I think when we surrendered there were only about two hundred left in the area, because for at least a year we had no replacements when somebody was sent back home."

Pvt. Benton (Peking) "Our captain, Captain Hester, assembled us. Each company was handled the same way. He told us, 'We don't know what's going to happen. They might come in here, take us all out there on the parade ground, and mow us down.' He said, 'We do have what is known as the protocol, which was signed in 1900 during the Boxer Rebellion.' Then he went on to explain that we were part of the embassy and that we had a good chance at being repatriated with the diplomats. Well, of course, that made us feel good. But as we later learned, I learned this from Captain White, that he researched and never has found that document that was supposed to have been signed. I don't know, but we didn't get out."

Frontline Troops of Japan

Cpl. Clem (Bataan) "All these fellows were combat troops, and they did not rough us up. They had a lot of respect for us, and we had a lot of respect for them. They were good soldiers, and they treated us real well. We got to ride in a truck up to the first stop, which was O'Donnell. We didn't have to do the actual walking ourselves. They were kind of in awe of us. I think they were amazed that we were prisoners, and that we weren't killed. Death for the emperor was drilled into the rank and file so much. I think they were surprised that anybody would go through a war and be captured."

Capt. Adair (Bataan) "Immediately, they started taking personal property that you had, like rings, watches, anything like that. I threw away a ring and my watch to keep them from getting it. I couldn't see giving them personal belongings. Of course, they searched you thoroughly and took anything they wanted. They weren't roughing us up at all while we were sitting on the side of that hill. They weren't the least bit friendly, but they didn't really bother us at that time. We were put on trucks and were just sitting there while waiting to be taken out of Bataan. We had no helmets, just the gear we were allowed to take with us. As we were sitting there, just a constant stream of Japanese troops of all types—infantry, some on trucks, some in tanks—passed us. They were just constant, just solid all the way. Well, they threw rocks at us and tried to jab us with bayonets, and you had to be on your toes all the time, particularly if you were sitting closer to the edge of the truck, because they could reach up and hit you or throw rocks at you. You had to sit there and try to protect yourself. We put up with quite a bit of that at first, but, actually, as far as abuse down in Bataan after we surrendered, that was the only time I saw real serious abuse. That, of course, could have been serious, but the worst that could have happened was somebody getting hit on the head with a rock or something, or they got hit with a gun butt just because some Japanese soldier was mad at us or something."

Cpl. Koury (Bataan) "This bunch that caught us were regulars, and they were good soldiers. They roughed us up, but they didn't beat us or anything. They took our watches, our rings, our billfolds. If you were a little hesitant in moving, they hit you with a gun butt or something, or kicked you. Then they tied us up, which I learned later was unusual. Most of the troops, when they surrendered, weren't tied up or anything. They tied us up and started us down the mountain, and we got there in time to join the last exodus out."

Lt. Burris (Bataan) "I had a pretty good set of clothes. I think I had two extra pairs of shorts and two undershirts, maybe some socks, a couple of towels, a razor and other shaving equipment. If I could have kept those things, I would have been in good shape. On the first day of the march, though, I ran into this great big Japanese soldier. He must have been six feet tall and as broad as a man can get—just a big, burly type of soldier. He was lots bigger than any Japanese soldier I thought I was ever going to see, and this one was tremendous. He took my musette bag with all the clothes in it, and he made me empty my pockets. He took my money and everything I had in the musette bag—my fountain pen, my watch, my mess kit. I guess you'd say I meekly gave everything to him, but when he pointed to my shoes, I told him no. He put his bayonet against my stomach and pressed it a little bit and looked at me real mean and then pointed to my shoes again. I knew I was going to have to do some fast talking then, so I showed him—using my hands—that his shoe was almost twice as long. I thought he was going to kill me, but the reason I took this tack was because I was afraid to be without shoes. I had seen these Filipinos going barefooted, and they all had sores with running pus all over their feet. They were deep sores that were as big around as fifty-cent pieces. So I guess I was more afraid of going without shoes than I was of the man with the bayonet. It was not bravery because I almost panicked, and my heart almost took a flip-flop. When I told him no a second time, I just turned and started walking down the road, and he let me go. Anyway, I walked away from there with my canteen and the clothes I was wearing."

Cpl. Read (Bataan) "Quite a few guys had souvenirs that they had picked up along the way—and I was one of them—off dead Japs in battle, things such as Japanese paper money, and in more extreme cases mess kits and even guns. I think the guys with guns threw them away, knowing full well they couldn't get by with those items. Some of the guys did hang on to mess kits and money and such souvenirs as that, and the Japs didn't make any bones about that. When they caught a guy with one of those things, they took him out and summarily executed him. They just took them over to the side and shot them without any ceremony. These Japs were the most ill-tempered people you ever saw when it came to things like that. There wasn't a lot of shoving, kicking, and things like that, but they just couldn't tolerate anybody having Jap souvenirs. I didn't have too much for them to take. I recall that I had a gold pocket watch, and it was probably the only thing I had on me that was worth anything, and they took that. A lot of people, officers especially, had West Point rings, and the Japs took that stuff. The Japs loved Parker fountain pens, and they were particularly on the lookout for those. If you ever want to sell fountain pens in Japan, just get Parker pens! In my case, I was allowed to keep a mess kit, canteen, and the set of khaki clothes I was wearing."

Pvt. Stanley (Bataan) "Once or twice I got hit with a flat hand, but as far as being hit with a gun, no. The first time I really got roughed up was when I started to go after a drink of water. It was getting pretty hot over there, and several hours after I got captured I got roughed up, slapped, when I went after that water. But I was a little fellow, and the Japanese picked on the big Americans because it meant that they had control, and it made them look a lot stronger if they got the big man rather than the little man. So I was lucky there. I maneuvered around and tried to stay out of the way as much as possible."

Lt. Taylor (Bataan) "At first they did not seem to want to recognize chaplains as noncombatants. Then later on they did, and they recognized us. They didn't give Captain Oliver any static about assigning a couple or three of us to this hospital group that was going to remain here. In the hospital area they never bothered us, and they never questioned us. They just looked on all of us as prisoners of war. They kind of ignored us, except they used us. They placed their guns all around the hospital—the artillery to shell Corregidor and Fort Drum—but they didn't harass us."

Cpl. B. Allen (Corregidor) "The day after the surrender they came for work details to clean up the island and pick up the dead bodies. I remember that that afternoon I developed a very severe headache, and I thought my head was about to split. I was afraid to tell the Jap guard that I had this headache because I thought that he would think I didn't want to work and he might shoot me. Finally, it got so bad that I said, 'Well, okay, they'll shoot me, but my head is hurting too bad.' I went over to this Jap sergeant, and I made gestures that my head was hurting bad. Well, he gave me something, a pill, and had me lie down. I took the pill, and he gave me something to drink. It must have been a strong pill because within fifteen minutes my headache was gone. I got up and went back to work, not scared any longer. These were still frontline troops because they didn't have time yet to pull them out and bring in others.

"Now these frontline troops did loot us. I lost my watch. I also had a little basketball that I treasured more than anything I ever had. I was a basketball player and had played with our company team in Shanghai, and we won the International Settlement championship. Each of us had a little gold basketball with our name on it and inscribed: 'International Champions, Shanghai, China, 1940.' That was just something special to me because that's the only thing I ever won. Well, they got that. I also had photographs of the aftermath of a rape that I had seen committed by Japanese troops in Shanghai. I had pictures of that and many other brutalities similar to that. They didn't get those pictures because I burned them."

Capt. Bartlett (Corregidor) "When they separated the enlisted men from the officers, I somehow got mixed in with the enlisted men in the general confusion. I was going back to where the officers were when this Jap guard, probably through ignorance, thought I was going the wrong way, so he slammed me. He hit me twice with his gun butt. One pop injured my tailbone, and the other one went higher and hit me in the sacrum. He then shoved me back toward the enlisted men, and I stayed with them the first night. At that time I didn't know how seriously I was hurt, and I didn't feel it so much as I felt it later. That's what I'm now retired on. I knew it hurt back there during that whole prison setup, but I didn't know how bad it was until later. At the time it was more of a numbness. See, there was so much bumping around and jostling around that you couldn't lay anything like that to any particular setup. I just knew I was hurt."

Pvt. Bugbee (Corregidor) "When the Japanese did come, they were actually the fighting troops. Here again, there's a certain amount of love between thieves, so to speak. The actual Japanese fighting man had more compassion for our military men than did some of the home guard after we were actually taken off Corregidor. The front line troops did make it known in no uncertain terms that they had been victorious, but they did not treat us all that badly. For example, we soon learned that they were dying for sweets. Apparently they had been rationed on any kind of sugar and stuff, and when they saw the canned pineapple that we'd gotten hold of, they'd point with their bayonet and yell, 'Pineapple! Pineapple!' They wouldn't say it that distinctly, but that's what they wanted, and they would go hog-wild over anything that was sweet. Like I said, they had apparently been starved for sweets, and, of course, the Japs loved sweets anyhow."

Capt. Bull (Corregidor) "These Japanese could speak in broken English. We were approached by three or four of them with bayonets affixed to their rifles, and we were put in one area. We were searched. My gold-rimmed glasses were taken, and I was threatened with my finger being cut off if I didn't remove my tight-fitting class ring. They also took our money and fountain pens. In essence, they looted us thoroughly. I can't recall if I lost my wristwatch at this time, but I do know that it was gone within a month's time. We were not roughed up at this time. The ones with the bayonets were kind of shaking, too, because I guess they feared that there might be somebody who might shoot them. A couple of days after the surrender, I can remember a lot of irritating things happening, such as a Japanese soldier coming up and opening a billfold and taking some American's girlfriend's picture, tearing it up, and then stomping on it. Some individuals were also spat upon. Maybe this kind of thing happens among all frontline troops, but it was, to say the least, unexpected. On the whole, I recall very little hitting or slapping or anything of this nature. We were so disorganized that half our troubles were of our own making."

Sgt. Burk (Fort Hughes) "They had us sitting around our mess tables, and this one big, ugly Jap came up to us. Well, I'm goosey and he came up and punched me in the ribs, and I like to have torn up that table because I wasn't expecting him to do that. He was wanting a watch, and I didn't have one. But a friend of mine did have an ol' pocket watch that he'd bought in Manila for four or five pesos. It had an imitation gold case on it, and it was one of those that closed. You'd mash the stem in, and the front of it would pop open to where you could see the face. I asked him if he still had it, and when he said that he did, I said, 'Give it to me. This ugly bastard wants a watch.' I gave it to him, and I made quite a hit with him. He gave me a little jar of hard candy. I took a couple of pieces and passed it around, and that seemed to please him. Then he went off and came back with a can of hash, cold and mostly grease. He took his bayonet and opened it, and a couple of buddies and I ate it. Then he went off again and brought back a bunch of this hash. Well, then he brought his buddy over, and this guy also wanted a watch. Well, I still didn't have a watch, so I asked another ol' boy if he had one, and he said that he had a Mickey Mouse pocket watch. But I made a better hit with the ugly one because I had gotten him a better watch. All this time I hadn't seen anybody get hit."

PFC Bolitho (Camp Casisang) "These were frontline troops. They were entirely different. They would come down and try to learn English with their Japanese-English dictionaries. They had no fear of laying their rifle down, coming in the barracks, and sitting down and talking to you."

PFC Venable (Wake Island) "We were brought into a group and lined up in a solid body, several ranks deep. Suddenly, machine-gun crews came running out, and they set up their machine guns. They lined up a number of machine guns in front of the group, and they loaded them with ammunition, they jumped down behind them, they cocked them. Then there was a deadly silence. And I recall one guy said, 'Well, this looks like it's it. So let me tell you, when they start pulling the trigger let's just jump up and get a gut full. Let's not just get caught here in a pile and have them come through and shoot us.' He said it would be a lot easier to jump up and get a gut full. At the time it sounded like a very logical thing to do, and I was mentally prepared to do it. I think that I felt that I was closer to death at that point than at any time in my life. So, consequently, had they pulled the trigger, I would not have been really disappointed. That's not the word. I would not have been surprised, would be a better word. But it didn't happen, and it didn't happen, and it didn't happen. And, then, here comes a Japanese officer followed by his staff. I don't know what his rank was. He was accompanied by an interpreter, and they made a rather lengthy speech in which the gist of it was that the emperor had decreed that our lives were to be spared and that we were going to be treated as prisoners of war, and we were expected to work for them and to help establish the Greater East Asia Co-Prosperity Sphere. Then, the machine gunners backed off their machine guns. We were given instructions that we were to react to orders that we received and if anyone didn't, why, he'd be shot. You know, the usual instructions. Well, they had made their point. The message got across."

Cpl. McDaniel (Wake Island) "The Japs lined us up. They roughed us up a little bit, shoved, yelled, cursed you, and then they put us in an underground ammunition bunker. It had had ammunition and bombs in it, but we had used them all up. They put part of us in there. They may have put some others in other ones of them. We had two or three of them. They slammed the door to the ammunition bunker and then opened the door and shot in there two or three times. They killed one or two of the fellows, I think, after we were in there. After we'd been in there a little while, they took us out and took all our clothes away from us. They stripped us naked. Some had underwear and some didn't. They took everything we had, but I didn't have anything. Well, we weren't given clothes for two or three days.

"When they took us out of this ammunition depot, which was underground, they took us outside and lined us up along the road. That's when we thought they were going to shoot us. They had .50-caliber machine guns in front of us and lined us all up. I still think to this day that that's what their intentions were. I think there was a Japanese officer who came up and stopped the ordeal. I think they had five or six .50-caliber machine guns, and they had three or four men to each one. We were all lined up in front of them. Then we were sent out on the airport without clothes, without clothing."

PO2 Detre (Java) "The Japanese had six horses in this unit to carry their machine guns. These horses came in on a barge. They weren't even tied, they were so well trained. They let the gate down, and those horses walked out of there. The soldiers didn't even get their feet wet. I always have to admire that. These guys were real soldiers. There was nothing second-rate about these guys. They knew their job, and they did it.

"These Japanese were all combat troops, and they had a good billet and knew it. They were just taking all the advantage of it that they could. They were relaxing and doing the least amount of work they could and getting a few drinks in. They weren't about to go over and raise hell with the prisoners. There wasn't any guarding to it. They just shut the door and that was that."

Cpl. Minshew (Madura Island) "Midgets! To me personally, I couldn't understand how a bunch of little sawed-off people like that could take over the whole Asiatic world. As we went along in our association with the Japanese, we found out that they were so dedicated to their emperor and their war effort. They were just so indoctrinated that they didn't mind walking right into the guns. We always thought they were doped up when they did that, but I don't think they were. They were fanatics. Their tropic uniforms looked like a poor grade of our khaki, and their shirts were lighter material than khaki. They wore a little cloth cap with a neck cloth hanging down, sewed to the back of it, to keep the neck from blistering. They had on tennis shoes, and the big toe was separated from the rest of the shoe. I didn't know that from the time they were little bitty things they wore those clompers that separated their big toe from the rest."

M/Sgt. Stowers (Woosung) "Occasionally, we would get a group of old regulars who had been in New Guinea, Guadalcanal, and so forth, that would be pulled in for a rest after many months of hard battle to guard us. They were old pros. We would get them, and they would say, 'Ah, the hell with it. Take it easy!' They'd give us cigarettes, and they were really good to us—the old pro soldiers. The 4-Fs they brought in there were pure hell. They were people who weren't trusted to ever get into battle, and they were the terrors. They were dangerous. They'd kill you; they'd bayonet you. They thought by treating the prisoners rough that they were winning the war."

Chapter II

Adjustment to POW Status

When America's ill-prepared armies were overrun in Southeast Asia in 1942, its fighting men had to make their hardest decision: whether to surrender. Once captured, however, they confronted an even more important choice: adjustment to being prisoners of war. Adjustment to POW status meant being servile, which young men have always found difficult. Moreover, these Americans were predominantly white and had been reared in a society that generally considered racial groups other than white to be inferior. Being submissive to Japanese and Korean guards was an especially bitter experience for them. They soon found that to be defiant could, and no doubt would, result in death. Lester Rasbury, who worked on the Burma-Thailand Railway, said it best: "You have to go along with things and learn to live a different life. You've got to make up your mind: . . . if you want to survive, you've got to adjust because if you try to get rough with them, well, they can just get rougher."[1]

The Japanese had not expected to capture as many prisoners as they did. This fact exacerbated the harshness of the GIs' physical conditions, as did the unwillingness or inability of Japanese officers to force their troops to treat prisoners humanely. The capriciousness of the guards—who were sometimes Japanese but more often conscripts taken from within the empire, especially from Korea—was totally unexpected in a well-disciplined army that represented a nation of regimented people.

In their recent study, Meirion and Susie Harries point out that "the Japanese army, like any other, had its share of sadists and psychopaths. It is likely, too, that a high proportion of these may have found their way to guarding prisoners of war, since this duty was considered almost as dishonorable as being a captive, and many misfits were assigned to it—drunks, troublemakers, even the insane."

---

[1]La Forte and Marcello, *Building the Death Railway*, 43.

They add that "former peasants who became NCOs and regular army men were able to vent all their pent-up anger and frustration, the rage accumulated from the social and economic deprivation they had suffered in the countryside. A large proportion of the ordinary soldiers themselves came from extremely harsh backgrounds." They conclude that on the "ladder of oppression, beneath the Japanese rank and file came prisoners of war and the natives of occupied countries, and by the time transferred fury and brutality touched them, it had been magnified to a terrible intensity."[2]

Generalizations do not apply validly to Japanese punishments for rule violations or to the sadistic treatment given prisoners for reasons that seem irrational or remain unknown. Among the punishments mentioned most often are beatings with rifles and sticks, sometimes until a prisoner was rendered senseless. Slapping with hands, punching with fists, and kicking were also frequently used ways of forcing Americans to obey. Prisoners stood at attention for hours on end, or were made to look into the sun until they were blinded, or were forced to squat with bamboo poles placed in the fold of their legs behind the knee joints. They were hanged by their arms or fingers, or placed in a "sweatbox" in the summer and an "icebox" in the winter.

The Japanese in the Philippines used the water treatment, filling a prisoner's empty stomach with water and then beating, kicking, or jumping on his abdomen. And punishment was unpredictable. For the same offense one man might be whipped, another might be shot or beheaded. The prisoners often had to watch their comrades being punished or killed. "I guess they wanted to impress on us what would happen," Cpl. Paul Bunch said. "We got the message."

After the war a number of Japanese guards were brought to trials less publicized than those held by the International Military Tribunal for the Far East in Tokyo. Two of the guards mentioned in this volume were found guilty of war crimes: Isamu Ishihara ("Beast of the East") and Tatsuo Tsuchiya ("Little Glass Eye"). By researching the *New York Times*, we also know that many other guards or camp administrators were tried and sentenced, including those held to be guilty of some of the atrocities mentioned in this chapter. For example, Japanese involved in the Palawan Massacre were tried in Yokohama in 1948.

---

[2]Harries and Harries, *Soldiers of the Sun*, 478.

During their internment most Americans believed that their successful adjustment depended upon maintaining the discipline that had existed while they were part of fighting units. However, some sources indicate that discipline in a POW camp was not as easy to perpetuate as our interviewees suggest. Charles J. Katz acknowledges that a "chaotic, anarchistic state of affairs" existed in some camps, and that "enlisted men and some of the junior-grade officers often refused to obey orders or to carry out instructions."[3] The great majority of those interviewed here claim that discipline was maintained in their compounds, but at times their recollections contradict this contention.

Resistance, sabotage, and collaboration in POW camps were not as commonplace as popular representations make them seem. In movies and television programs, prisoners often spend much of their free time engaged in one of these three activities. In fact, each was infrequent. (Our interviews were with men captured at the onset of war, many of whom were enlisted personnel and therefore had little to reveal to interrogators.) Resistance, sabotage, and collaboration jeopardized the safety and wellbeing of individuals who engaged in any of them, and this kept such activity at a minimum. Still, there were cases of all three, from concealing a ring to seeking better treatment to causing real damage to the Japanese war machine. They are discussed in this chapter as one of the many adjustments that were made to captivity. The reader should remember that this adjustment continued throughout the duration of a prisoner's incarceration. Because we have included punishment, resistance, and sabotage here, we have selected quotations that go beyond the first weeks of adjustment to captivity. Some describe activities that lasted almost until the end.

Japanese Rules

Cpl. Clem (Camp O'Donnell) "I think everybody suddenly realized that they were in pretty dire straits and kind of sobered up to the fact that they were prisoners. It was hard to realize that here you are,

---

[3]Katz, "Experiences in a Prison Camp as a Background for Therapy," 93.

you've never been caged up in your life before, and all of a sudden you're caged up and somebody has the power of life and death over you. It was a very sobering thought, and it was hard to get that through everybody's mind that that was the predicament we were in."

Cpl. Bunch (Cabanatuan) "When you get that many guys together, some of them are going to figure out a way to get some food, and you have some Filipinos on the outside who are ready to make a buck. In addition, there was a lot of money in this camp because people had money that had not been taken away from them, and, of course, the American dollar was still in demand over in the Philippines. So we had guys who had the guts to climb the fences at night and go into Cabanatuan and deal with the Filipinos and come back before daylight. There was no problem to get over the fence. It was a barbed-wire fence, and they had guards patrolling; but you could jump that fence in the darkness and be gone and then get back in. I never had the desire to do this, really. Some people were more daring to do that, and if they could make it back with some canned salmon or something, they could not only eat it themselves but they could sell it for a lot of money and go out and buy more. Cigarettes were a dollar apiece for all you could sell and all you could get."

Cpl. Koury (Cabanatuan) "They had two fences, an inner fence and an outer fence—the inner fence for Americans to walk guard and an outer fence for the Japs to walk guard. The rule was that you were in squads of ten, and if one guy left, the other nine got shot! So we walked guard in self-defense which, I think, is fairly easily understood. Like in a family, they had rules, and you'd better obey them. If you didn't, you got into trouble."

Lt. Burris (Cabanatuan) "There were some people who traded with the Japs, but I didn't have anything to trade with them. Even if I had've, I don't know whether or not I would have traded with them because it was dangerous. Some guys would go outside the fence to trade with a guard. If a Japanese officer came up there and found them in that situation, that guard wouldn't admit that they were trading. He'd say, 'No! No! This man got out here!' And the prisoner would be taken away and killed, so it didn't pay to be too friendly with the Japs because they'd turn on you. They wouldn't take no blame. I think they were told to stay away from us—socially or trading or anything. They'd get beat up pretty good if they didn't. A Jap officer—I guess right on down the line—would make the next lower rank stand at attention while he beat him up, just hit him in the face over and over and over. The guards obviously didn't like that, so if they could blame somebody else, they'd go ahead and do it."

Capt. Bartlett (Cabanatuan) "Ten men on a sheet of paper, ten names. If one of these men escaped, the other nine would be executed. One of the enlisted men did escape but not of his own volition. He was on a working party with the guards. The guerrillas attacked the guards and released him. They shot up the Jap guards, and they rescued him. I don't think he had a damn thing to say about it! Anyway, the other nine men were executed."

Capt. Bull (Cabanatuan) "We were formed into groups of ten and were told that if one man escaped, the other nine would be shot. I felt that they were not bluffing, that they meant every word they said. In fact, they did execute four Americans for trying to escape while I was there. I did not personally witness them being shot, but I was only about two hundred yards away when I heard the shots. But I did see them tied up all day. So there was that fear and mental strain on us to be put in those ten-man squads, to say the least, because it was so inhumane to do a thing like that. It wasn't fair punishment; it wasn't fair treatment. Another surprising thing is that they told us that we were hostages, not prisoners of war. We were just hostages, which in international law may have had a different connotation."

Pvt. Stanley (Clark Field) "It was amazing how much authority a sergeant had in the Jap Army. I believe that a lieutenant was in charge of the whole works here, and usually someone like a buck sergeant would be in charge of each work shift. Most of the time—I'll give the Japanese credit—they didn't mess with you inside the camp when you wasn't working. Every once in a while a smart Jap would come through, and he would be a troublemaker; he just wanted to show off. But so many times we would go for days, and a Jap wouldn't come through the camp except to walk through and inspect it, looking around to see if somebody was making something he wasn't supposed to. Of course, we worked every day here, but as far as bothering you in the camp, they let you alone."

Cpl. Clem (Davao Penal Colony) "The only clothing that we had was a loincloth. We'd go on these work parties and secretly obtain bananas, pineapples, potatoes, and lemons, and we'd put them in these loincloths. We weren't supposed to have a thing. We'd come marching up to the gate, and the guards would go down the line searching everybody's hands. Of course, they found nothing. So one day they got wise to it, and they'd have everybody take their loincloth off there at the gate. Naturally, all the food would fall out, and there'd be little piles of food sitting around. They wouldn't discipline you about that. They'd just confiscate the food themselves because they wanted it."

Pvt. Armstrong (Tanjong Priok) "You just have to adjust. You know you're going to have to do it because if you don't do it, they were going to be rough on you. I just made up my mind that if they told me to do something, I was going to try to do it. If I can keep one of them off me, I'll go ahead and do what I'm supposed to do. Because if they tell you they're going to whip you, they're going to whip you. They don't bluff you at all. They just come up there and go to kicking and scratching. If you don't understand, why, you try to make them know that you don't understand."

PFC Evans (Jaarmarkt, Surabaja) "If you had a cap on, you saluted to the Japanese. If you didn't have a cap on, you bowed, which we took as an insult to us. Of course, now I realize that they bowed to each other as a form of respect. It wasn't a form of subordination as such. Of course, the Japanese gave us no respect, so as a result we felt we didn't owe them any, either. The best way to get along with the Japanese soldiers is not only to do what they want you to do, or what you know they want you to do, but also what you anticipate that they might want. I'll tell you, when you're faced with either living or dying, you're going to pretty well do whatever is necessary to live."

T/Sgt. Stanbrough (Bicycle Camp) "Captain Zeigler called his senior sergeants up and told them that the Japanese had insisted that we sign an oath of absolute obedience to the Imperial Japanese Army. He said that they resisted this, but we would have to sign. At the first signing of the oath, we modified it to except conditions where it was contrary to our oath of allegiance to our own country. The Japanese commandant was very pleased because he probably got our group to sign quicker than anyone. He found out later that he'd been taken, and the sergeants were called together and told there was to be no more of this modifying. Our officer took complete responsibility for our signing under duress. We signed the little things, but some of the other people didn't sign and all hell broke loose. We lost our privileges for the camp; the food situation got a lot worse because we didn't have the canteen supplies coming in. They all eventually signed, even the hard-core Australians."

Fireman 1/C Kennedy (Bicycle Camp) "I always resented bowing. That little son of a bitch! I didn't want to bow to him, but I had to. It's a way of life, and you soon learn. They looked down on us because we became prisoners, and evidently in their army it's something that's disgraceful to do."

Pvt. Permenter (Tientsin) "We had a real good deal there in Tientsin going out and buying our own food and stuff. The Japanese were all on our side, that is, the privates. When the Japanese lieutenant would leave, the guards would all go out and line up. I asked a fellow with me, 'What are these idiots doing?' He said, 'If you want to go anyplace, just walk out toward the gate and just motion for one of them to follow you. If you want to go to the grocery store, if you want a bottle of beer, or anyplace you want to go, go on. When you get back, give him a couple of dollars.' I said, 'You're crazy!' He said, 'No, they don't make but two or three dollars a month, and they'll make more in one night taking us out in town than they will in a whole month's pay.' But I still didn't believe him and wouldn't try it. A couple of days later—I don't remember who—a couple of us guys got together, and we went to a grocery store down the street, just walked out and motioned, and here one of the guards came. He followed us down there and followed us back, and we gave him a couple of dollars. He was happy, and he went to the end of the line. Of course, the lieutenant had to leave before they could do that."

Capt. Godbold (Woosung) "Saluting the Japanese was sort of a cyclical type of thing. At times with the changes of administration in the camp, a turnover of personnel, this would rise and fall, and sometimes they would go to an unreasonable extent to require military courtesies and so on. Then, at other times they were very lax and didn't care. Occasionally, there would be this upsurge in 'Well, we've got to have more respect from these Americans,' and so they would come around and harangue us about the need for respecting the emperor's soldiers. But this was really just a minor irritation."

Pvt. Permenter (Woosung) "We would have to count off in Japanese when they'd have roll call in the morning. Boy, that was something else. *Ichi, ni, san, shi, go, roku* [one, two, three, four, five, six]. And if anybody fouled up you'd have to start all over again. It was something else learning how to count in Japanese. But the longer you'd stay around them you'd pick up enough that you could tell what they were talking about."

Pvt. Benton (Woosung or Kiangwan) "We found that the Japanese soldier had a one-track mind. He's not like you and me. If you were searching somebody for dope and you found a gun, you'd take it; if you found something he'd stole, you'd take it. But the way they ran searches, they'd be looking for one thing. If they didn't find it, but you had a machine gun, you could carry that gun through there. That's the way we had them pegged. Now I could be wrong. I might be a little extreme by saying you could keep a machine gun. But the reason I say that is that we'd bring things in and get it past them on a particular day, and the next day they'd take it away from you because they would be looking for it that day. So we'd figured out, 'Well, if they were looking for this yesterday, we can get by with it today.' So the next day we'd try, and nine times out of ten we'd make it. That's the reason I say they had a one-track mind as I see it."

Capt. Bull (Zentsuji) "The Japanese definition of contraband varied from place to place. In one camp it would be knives, in another it would be pencils, in another it would be razor blades, so it was hard to predict. On occasions they would pull sneak inspections of our barracks, but the word would be passed along, so we would be able to hide the things that we were not allowed to have.

"From time to time they would encourage the officers to work on agricultural projects by telling us we would get more food if we worked. Being so unpredictable, as usual, they'd sometimes tell us that officers had to work, so we weren't given any choice of working or not. Whichever, we'd be taken out a month at a time to clear an area under pine trees. We'd march through town and on the way pass a shrine. They'd have us all stop at that point, face the shrine, and bow down. Then they'd use some Japanese words to pray, but under our breaths we would always mumble, 'We hope that they bring in ten thousand more white boxes today' because at the shrine the Japanese would always bring their dead, whom they had cremated, in a white box. So that was our morale builder—to do that as we passed the shrine."

Cpl. B. Allen (Osaka) "The Japanese warned us that we would be severely punished if we were caught stealing, but we did it anyway. For example, we invented devices to smuggle food into the camp. We'd take a handkerchief or a square of cloth and sew it together on two sides and make a sack out of it—leave it open with a drawstring in the top and then put straps at each corner and wear it like a jockey strap. They didn't fool around in this area of your body when they searched you, so that device became an old standby. We'd make bags ten or twelve inches long sometimes with four inches in width, and maybe with raw rice that might hold three pounds of rice strapped underneath you."

Japanese Punishment

Capt. Adair (Camp O'Donnell) "I might sound prejudiced, having been an officer, but I believe that they treated us worse because it was the Japanese enlisted men that we came in contact with, and they took advantage of their position and pushed the officers around a little more. Later on I know we very definitely got worse treatment because we wouldn't work. Enlisted men were forced to work, but officers were only supposed to volunteer to work. But we wouldn't work, and they hated us for this. As a result, they gave us worse treatment and constantly harassed us."

Pvt. Burns (Camp O'Donnell) "A lot of the punishment would depend on what you did. I know that they would take you and tie you up against a post with your hands stretched out in the hot sun, and they wouldn't give you any water for hours and hours. Some of them would take you and make you lie down underneath a spigot and tie your hands down, and your forehead would be positioned under the spigot, and they would turn the water on, and just a little drop of water would drop on your forehead. You couldn't move or anything. You would be surprised how heavy a little drop of water can get after so long a period of time."

Cpl. Read (Camp O'Donnell) "This interpreter got up and said, 'The captain, he say if you try to escape you will be shot!' That's just the way he went on. Now, bear in mind that all Japanese officers and enlisted men, no matter what their rank, their title is captain if they're in charge of anything. So this guy was the camp commandant, and he was a captain. He would say something in Japanese, and then the interpreter would shout, 'The captain, he say. . . .' That was his greeting, and that was it. And we believed him! You bet we did! He looked the part, too. He was a fierce-looking man. He had a bristly, big mustache and glasses, and he wore the Jap Army uniform with their funny-looking helmet on and all that stuff, big ol' sword and all that. We had had a little experience along the way with those swords. We believed every word he said, and he didn't say many."

Pvt. Blaylock (Cabanatuan) "Three American officers tried to escape and got caught. I witnessed the Japanese beating them to death little by little, and they tied them to the barbed-wire fence and let them stay all day in the sun with no hat or anything. They'd beat them several times a day, through the night, and then the next day, before they finally pronounced them dead. They had used the butts of their rifles to beat them.

"I witnessed a Mexican kid being executed. He had been crawling through the fence and trading with a Jap guard. A Jap officer came by one night and caught him. Of course, the officer started shouting that the Mexican had been trying to escape, and in a day or two, as well as I can remember, they marched him off from camp and stood him up against a tree with his hands tied behind him and shot him. I actually witnessed that.

"There was a fellow I knew from Oklahoma, and I don't know why in the hell he tried to escape. He didn't have the use of his right arm, and he didn't know where to go. But he did escape, and then he came back. We had a farm at that time around the prison camp there, and he didn't know where to go, so he'd hide out and at night he'd eat these vegetables, and he got so weak that they found him. The Japs had to carry him on a litter to execute him. I didn't see them execute him, but I heard the rifles, and then the Jap officer gave him the coup de grace. Then they brought him back into camp and buried him."

Cpl. Bunch (Cabanatuan) "The only abuse, what I consider a real abuse, was the incident where the fellows were caught coming back into camp and were eventually executed. The Japanese had a punishment that we called the seventy-two-hour sun cure. They would tie you up to a post, as they did these guys, in front of the guard shack for seventy-two hours without food or drink. In some way or other, these guys got their hands loose, and, of course, the only thing they could do was come back into camp. It wouldn't have done them any good to run off someplace else, particularly in broad daylight. Anyway, they came back into camp, ran into a barracks, and proceeded to drink all the water they could hold. Of course, the guards found them, beat them severely with gun butts, picked them up by their heels, and dragged them a quarter mile back down to the guard shack. The next morning they got those three out, made them dig their own graves, and executed them with a firing squad. And they forced us to get out there and watch the whole thing because I guess they wanted to impress on us what would happen. We got the message."

Cpl. Brantley (Cabanatuan) "Prisoners would take things, and the Japanese would catch them and carry them out there and stand them in the sun. Sometimes they'd get caught buying something from the Filipinos, and the Japs would stand them up, take a bamboo pole, and beat them. They caught one guy buying from a Filipino, and they stood him up and beat him. He finally broke down and ran and got some water to drink because they wouldn't give him any water. Of course, after he did that, they shot him and killed him."

Pvt. Guiles (Cabanatuan) "There was one time when I couldn't hold myself back from hitting one of the guards. Of course, I regretted it afterward, but at the time you can only take so much, and then you say to hell with it. This incident occurred one time when I was working outside on the prison farm. I had just worked and worked and worked until I didn't think I could go on any longer. In the meantime, this one particular guard had been on my case, and then he really zeroed in on me. He could speak some English, and he started cursing me, and that did it. I said to myself, 'I don't care,' and I lowered the boom on him—I hit him with my fist. Immediately, he and two of his buddies pounced on me with their vitamin sticks [clubs], and the first couple of blows knocked me unconscious. The other prisoners had to carry me back into camp. That whole episode was a pretty valuable lesson to me.

"You've heard of the water treatment, I'm sure. Well, that happened to me one time. They caught me talking to one of the Japanese guards on perimeter duty, and this is something that you were not supposed to do at all. They took a water hose and stuck it down my throat and turned it on. Believe it or not, your stomach can swell to where you look like you're pregnant. Then they put their boot on my stomach, and it was just like a geyser—here it comes. And I wonder sometimes to this day why I have stomach cramps now and then! I was lucky to survive that because in most cases it resulted in death."

Lt. Burris (Cabanatuan) "The guards got mean here at Cabanatuan. They would harass you all the time. You'd be working on the farm, and they'd come up behind you and whack you with a stick. They didn't always need a reason to do it, either. Some of them would come screaming at you with their club, which was usually a hoe handle. Now we used those ol' British-type hoes that had a handle about the size of a pick handle, and that's what those guards used for a club. They'd come waving it at you and screaming bloody murder, like they were going to tear you to pieces. Most people would just get scared to death."

Cpl. Read (Cabanatuan) "They caught a guy who had tried to escape, and they had him on display over at the hospital camp for a while. He'd been beaten up a little and put on display after a couple of weeks. Then I just happened to be out by the fence, and we watched the whole thing as it took place. Here come the guards with this guy, and they had a leash on him, just like you'd have a leash on a dog, and he had to go in front of the guard. The guard has got a rifle with a bayonet, and then another guard had a shovel, and they went down the road. I could see them, and they walked over to the low ground, and this guy was digging his own grave. He dug his grave and stood in it, and they shot him and covered him up—just like that. You always wonder what you'd do in a case like that. I think that I'd be inclined to make a break for it under those circumstances. What have you got to lose by trying that?"

Cpl. B. Allen (Cabanatuan) "We were a little scared of getting too close to the fence. Four guys were at the fence one day, and the Japs claimed they were trying to escape. They took those four men and put them in a torturous position and tied them up for about forty-eight hours out in the hot sun. They were down on their knees with boards behind their legs and their hands tied behind them. Those men were begging the Japs to shoot them, which they did after forty-eight hours. I watched the shooting. The four men dug their own grave— one long trench. They then stood in front of it. They were each given a cigarette. Then the Japs blindfolded them, and the firing squad was ordered to fire. They did. The four prisoners just kind of tumbled back into the hole, and that was it. Not one of them asked for any mercy. They stood like men, smoked their cigarette, put on their blindfold, and uttered not one sound. They were fired upon and struck several times in the head.

"The Japs liked to put you in those uncomfortable positions for long periods of time. I know of one that I was in, and I thought I couldn't make it. They thought I had stolen something, and they pulled two tables far enough apart that I could just put my hands on one and my feet on the other. I had to support myself face down in this position. They kept a rifle pointed at me, so I didn't dare turn loose. Finally, they let me down, and I was very, very weak. I couldn't stand at first when I got down off it. But they had one worse than that where they would tie you with something like a two-by-four behind your knees and then tie your legs behind you and tie your hands, and you kneeled there. Sometimes they'd keep you in that position for forty-eight hours, and you couldn't walk when they turned you loose from that, either."

Pvt. Bugbee (Cabanatuan) "The only time that I was actually really physically manhandled was when one of the Jap sergeants saw a guard give me a cigarette. He worked over the guard, and he worked me over, and then he worked over the guard once again. They all had sticks that they carried around with them out there in the field as we were working, and this sergeant just worked me over pretty good with his stick. It didn't really do too much physical harm, but I do remember that the guard got it twice to my once because he had given me a cigarette. Even today, when people ask me about my animosity toward Japs, I can't really have a whole lot of animosity because the Japs treated their own people almost as bad as they treated us."

Cpl. Halbrook (Corregidor) "Jack Kirkland, a Marine, refused to do what the Japanese asked him to do. They'd tell him to bow, and he'd say, 'Bullshit!' So they made an example of him in front of all of us at the Malinta Tunnel. First, they tied him up by the thumbs with his hands behind his back on an A-frame where his feet are touching the ground. They worked him over real good, but they couldn't make him give up. After they got his arms out of shape where he couldn't do anything, they untied him. He was absolutely helpless, but he would run at them like a bull, and they would just beat him up. They finally got him where he couldn't move and broke both of his arms between the elbow and the wrist. He was the meanest mother going, and they took him, and they broke him. They showed everybody what would happen if they did the same thing.

"I was driving a sixteen-cylinder Lincoln on a Japanese detail, taking General [Tomoyuki] Yamashita around Corregidor. The Japanese officer of the day told me to move the car forward. I told him I couldn't move because this goddamned high-powered engine would throw gravel on General Yamashita and that he had to move the damned general. The officer got out a cheese knife [samurai sword] to give me a little incentive, so I reached down and threw it down into second gear. Those damned wheels caught in that gravel and threw it on that damned general. Just as the officer got ready to put the knife to me, Yamashita said something to him. I don't know what he said, but it stopped him. After I dropped them off from their tour, five guards bodily dragged me out of the car and hauled me over to the guard shack. They tied me up on the A-frame in front of everybody, where my feet just barely touched the ground and my hands were behind my back. They left me standing there the rest of the afternoon. After dark, they cut me down and took me inside and put me in a dungeon. It was a fifty-five-gallon drum deal down in a hole in the ground. They left me there that night. I don't remember how many days they kept me, but they took me off the island after dark and put me on a little old barge and hauled me over to Bilibid Prison in Manila. In three days, I'm in Cabanatuan."

Cpl. Smith (Palawan) "Brutality was common, what I call common, everyday occurrences. It was beatings, clubbings. Maybe one Jap would treat you decent if you was on his work detail; and then maybe another Jap would come along that didn't like your looks, and he'd knock the hell out of you for no reason at all but other than the fact that you were an American."

PFC R. Allen (Davao Penal Colony) "I've seen boys hung by their thumbs for two and three days at a time. In fact, I've seen their thumbs just pulled off, cut off where the wire was they were strung up with. I've seen a boy have a beard, and they'd just happen to pull his beard out just a few hairs at a time. Fingernails and toenails a lot, hands, arms, feet, legs crushed. I think one of the worst punishments was when they hung me one time by my thumbs. Before they hung me, they tied my feet together and put a two-by-four under my knees and made me squat down on that two-by-four. They tied my legs this way and then hung me by my thumbs. I still have trouble with my knees. I'd hit a Jap. So they gave me a little treatment, and I didn't hit no more. Later on they broke both of my feet.

"I worked in a tailor shop, of sorts. We had an Indian boy, Chief, who was in charge of the Americans in the shop. We were making shirts out of sugar and flour sacks, and then they brought in an American flag, and they wanted us to cut up this flag and make it part of their insignia. They gave it to me, and I handed it to Chief and told him I wouldn't do it. He wouldn't cut it up, either. He was an American Indian boy from Tulsa, Oklahoma. He's no longer with us. They killed him before we left. He hit a Jap major, and they killed him. But we wouldn't cut up the American flag, so they broke both of our feet with rifle butts. That was one of their favorite tricks, to hit you on the feet with rifle butts. They could break your feet with just one lick.

"If they'd catch a cook getting a little rice to eat, he'd had it. He'd take a whipping that wouldn't quit. I've seen men whipped with barbed wire. I've seen them whipped with big leather straps. I've seen them hit with sticks up to the size of a two-inch piece of wood. I've seen boys' heads broken open with a stick like that. The Japs are some of the cruelest people I've ever seen.

"They'd put you in the little hot house that they had. It was just some sheet metal that would absorb the heat. They'd stick you in it.

It felt like it'd get about 170, 180 degrees in there. It was four foot high and three foot square. You'd get put in today for one thing and tomorrow for something else. You may do the same thing next time, and they'd punish you some other way. It seemed to me that whatever hit their mind as right at the time, that's what they'd give you."

Pvt. Armstrong (Tanjong Priok) "We were rolling and stacking barrels, empty barrels, at the docks. You'd have to stack them up on one another, and you'd have to put a scotch [chock] under it or they'd all roll off. I went up there and threw a barrel on this stack of 150 barrels, and the scotch didn't hold. All those barrels fell and rolled all over the docks in every direction. Two of the Jap guards got me, one of them was hitting me and the other kicking me. They worked me over real good. They kicked me for something like ten minutes."

PFC Robinson (Bicycle Camp) "Physical punishment took many different forms. It consisted of open palm, fists, rifle, rifle butt. Down the line bamboo, especially male bamboo, entered in. Bamboo was about as deadly a punishment as there was because they cause sores that were hard to get rid of. To me the most extreme form of punishment was when you had to kneel in the hot sun, bareheaded, on your ankles with a pole behind your knees. This gets to be a pretty severe punishment over a period of several hours. The guards could kneel you in front of the guardhouse and have their eyes on you continuously, so there was no opportunity to do any cheating."

Pvt. Wisecup (Bicycle Camp) "I got more than my share of clouts because I was a big guy. They had an inferiority complex about a tall guy. They singled out tall guys not only at Bicycle Camp but at any place."

Fireman 1/C Kennedy (Burma-Thailand Railway) "An engineer said something to me, and I called him a son of a bitch. He could understand English, he had a club, and he beat the hell out of me. Another punishment was a case of my missing my number when counting off. I was number eight in line, and the guy that was number six said he was seven in the wrong way. I just had a blank and got the hell beat out of me. The worst part of it is the frustration of not being able to strike back."

Pvt. Permenter (Woosung) "The worst punishment I ever got in my life was while I was in camp in March of the first year—1942. Somebody threw a piece of wire on the electric fence to see what would happen. Well, it shorted out and set the alarm. Here come the guards. Well, we got away with it. I don't know how it happened the second time. I think they may have made it up because the first time made them mad. It turned out that we stood at attention for seven hours in the cold March rain that day. A lot of guys passed out. I didn't, but couldn't any [of them] walk when they got through with us. In fact, a fellow by the name of Bennett said he did it. They said they were going to keep us there until the one who had done it admitted it. He told them he did it, but he didn't. They locked him up with three or four guys and let the rest of us go. It was my understanding that they beat up on him when they got him in the guardhouse."

Pvt. Benton (Woosung or Kiangwan) "I can tell you of one incident when I got beat up. We had what we called night watch. I don't remember whether it was Woosung or Kiangwan, but I had watch. Fire watch is what the Japs called it then. You weren't to smoke, and I was smoking, and I got caught. Well, I got worked over for it. I brought it on myself. If I hadn't been smoking, I wouldn't have gotten caught and worked over. We all smoked, but the guard just happened to come by and caught me. I heard him coming, but he had seen me through the window. He came in and worked me over. He hit me with his fist and then with a rifle butt. That was about it. My pride hurt more than he did. I couldn't fight back, that's what hurt. I mean, I knew I could have torn him apart with my bare hands, but I knew if I did he'd stick that bayonet in me."

PFC Venable (Kiangwan) "We were punished as a group on a number of occasions. On one occasion they took us out, and they made us lay out in this muddy field all night because they said that the American bombers were going to come, and they were going to destroy the camp. We stood out there while they harangued us for hours. A number of times someone would do something, and in trying to catch the culprit they would instigate mass punishment. They would make everyone stand at attention for hours and hours. But as far as atrocities, no, our camp was relatively free of that."

PFC Garrison (Osaka) "An insane person is pampered in Japan, I'll put it that way. They could walk in anybody's house and get food because they're insane. That's something I don't understand. Well, one day this prisoner, Hammel, was lined up and ready to go to camp, and the 'White Bull' walked past Hammel, and Hammel knocked him in the moat around the camp. We thought, 'Well, Hammel's dead. He's gone. That's it for him.' Well, the Bull came out, and they started beating on Hammel. They beat him down, and finally they quit. And he started jabbering and went just completely out of his head. This went on for two or three days. And finally, the Japanese were convinced that he was insane. They moved him out of the barracks, put him in the brig—what was supposedly the brig—gave him a brazier of charcoal so he could stay warm, fed him real good food the rest of the time. Now he'd go outside naked in the snow with a big ol' hat on with strings tied to it with a piece of wood tied here, a rock there, and a piece of glass over here—just nutty as a fruitcake. The day peace was signed, he came around shaking hands with everybody. And he said, 'Fellows, I just didn't think I was going to make it.' There was nothing wrong with him. He was the greatest actor that's ever been."

Cpl. Brantley (Yodogawa Steel Mill) "One time I had accidentally frozen up the furnace. In other words, I was to charge this furnace by adding so much metal and so much scrap and so much coke and so much ore. Anyhow, they couldn't afford to shoot me or turn me in because they had previously let all the Japanese who should have been there to supervise me leave, so these guys would have been involved, too. So they just hung me up to where my toes barely touched the ground, and then they beat me around. They took their time about it. I finally passed out. In fact, you can still see the scars where they hung me up.

"Another time I bought some food off a civilian. They'd give us so many yen [Japanese money] for doing this work, so I bought some potato bread. Well, they caught me with it, and they wanted to know where I had gotten it. I wouldn't tell them who sold it to me because I didn't want to get him in trouble. So then they put me in a little dungeon or wooden cage and kept me in that for three days without anything to eat. That was in the wintertime, and I had no clothes or anything, and it was cold, rainy, and snowy."

PFC Evans (Nagasaki) "One evening I was a little delinquent when I sat down on my bunk, which we were not allowed to do when the guards were in close proximity of counting us. It just so happened that I had some chewing gum in my mouth. The guard held out his hand, and I spit the gum out. He took the chewing gum on the end of his thumb and plastered one of my eyes shut, and then he proceeded to try to knock my other eye out. After he got tired of whupping around my head, he called our first sergeant and told him to hit me a few times. The first sergeant hit me a few times with the soft part of his hand. After everybody had gone to bed, the guard came back with a few others and took me to the guardhouse. The guard grabbed up an ax and hit me with the flat part, the head, and he knocked me down, over some of the other guards. A Japanese sergeant came in and put a stop to it. That was as close as I ever came to being permanently injured.

"We had a guy that I was raised with called Corky, who was born tongue-tied. They never clipped his tongue when he was a child. When he got into the Army, they clipped his tongue. They didn't give him any voice therapy, and, of course, he talked just like he always did. When we got to Japan, they put a *baka* [fool or idiot] tag on him. He could go anywhere and do anything he wanted. A Sergeant Yastagi found out that Corky was from Texas and asked him if he was a cowboy. He said he was a cowboy. They got him a rope, made a loop in it, and asked him who he was going to rope. The guards let a Dutchman, who was in a cell in solitary confinement, out for Corky to rope. Yastagi got the Dutchman running, but, instead of roping the Dutchman, Corky caught the Japanese sergeant with the rope and threw him down in the damn dirt and dusted him off real good. Yastagi took Corky to a cell and kept him there an hour. Then they took him to the guardhouse where they fed him. They turned him loose and didn't do a thing to him. The Japanese treated people they thought were deranged differently than they did the other prisoners."

PFC Visage (Nagasaki) "This particular night I went into the *mizu* room [storeroom] and had my fill. As I opened the door to leave, a Japanese guard saw me. I ran, thinking that I could outrun him, but he tackled me. He took me to the guard shack, and they started working me over. Then they took me to this air-raid shelter and worked me over, trying to find out who had keys to the *mizu* room. They started beating me across the face with their fists, and they had gloves on. They beat me and beat me. They broke both my jaws, and I was just out on my feet. I got to where I had no feelings. They called my first sergeant in and told him to start beating me. He told me, 'All I'm going to do is hit you one time and knock you out. If I don't knock you out, fall down and fake it.' Sure enough, he knocked me out.

"They threw me into a cell and the next morning took me to a Japanese doctor who examined my jaws. The Japanese guard told the doctor what had happened, and the doctor had a temper fit, and he hit me. They took me out and tied me to a post in front of the guard shack. They had four soldiers put bayonets on their rifles and lunge at me. The first time they came, they veered off and hit the post. The second time they also veered off and hit the post. They'd stick the bayonet against my throat, and then they'd back off. They did this for about fifteen minutes. After they had left me tied to the post for a while, they released me and let me to go back to my room. My jaw remained broken, and I could hardly eat for three or four weeks."

Escape

Cpl. Clem (Cabanatuan) "About that time some of the fellows started trying to escape, and that's the first time I saw them put into effect the business that if one man escaped they'd shoot ten others. When a man escaped, they'd just walk into camp and pull out ten men at random. I witnessed two such executions here. I remember one tall red-headed boy. They took the ten men they were going to shoot and tied them up to consecutive posts on a fence, and they left them there all day long in the hot sun. They wouldn't give them any water, and they were out there a couple of days. And this red-headed boy managed to get himself untied, and he ran down to one of the barracks. All he wanted was a drink of water; he wasn't trying to run off. The guards came down and got him, and they beat the devil out of him and took him back up there and tied him up again. After two days the Japanese took them up on a hill and made them dig their own graves and then executed them by firing squad. In the volley everybody went down except this red-headed boy. We were about one hundred or two hundred yards away, and we saw him stagger. They shot him again, and he still didn't go down. Before they could shoot him a third time, his knees finally buckled. Then the officer went up, and he fired only one shot in his head. The execution scared the hell out of us, we knew they'd kill us for trying to escape."

Cpl. McCall (Cabanatuan) "There was an escape attempt on the march to Cabanatuan because the Japanese brought these boys in and tied them up. There were five of them. I guess they were mistreated pretty badly, beaten. The Japs sent all of us to the barracks, and just a little ways from the barracks I lay there and watched them execute these boys. They shot five of them. They stood in the trench, and it was about knee high, and they offered them a cigarette. I don't know if they blindfolded them or not. It seems like a couple were. Seems like they fell, and then the Jap went up and gave them a mercy shot with a pistol. Those five had tried to escape, and they were turned in by a Filipino sheriff, and that's how they got caught. I'm sure there were a few others who did escape because we were getting into a mountainous region."

Sgt. Burk (Cabanatuan) "I never thought about escape because I didn't see where I could gain anything. I had opportunities to escape, but where was I going to go—a redhead amongst dark people? You know, I'd kind of stand out. As I say, I never even gave it a thought. I just thought I'd make the best of a bad situation."

Cpl. McCall (Clark Field) "We had an escape at Clark Field. A fellow left there and went over the fence one night. And they took us out and made us sit in a group and brought out machine guns, lined them up. And, of course, we stood out there a couple of hours. And we weren't sure whether they were going to kill us or what. And it turned out that nothing happened, but it was quite a tense couple of hours there for a while. The joke used to be that if you're going to tell me you're escaping, I won't stop you. I'll go with you. That was the truth. If the man would tell me that he was going, I'd have gone with him. Of course, we were up there at the base of the mountains, and I don't think they were watching us too closely. But where could you go? In a strange country that you didn't know and no food, no rations, no contact. You didn't know where to go. But that's about the size of it at Clark Field."

Cpl. Burlage (Palawan) "After the first escape, the Japs seemed very hurt. The commandant seemed very hurt that these people would do this to him. He lined us up. Of course, they had a big parade ground, constabulary parade ground, and they lined us up there. But first they kept us in our barracks for two days. No food. We weren't allowed to come out of the barracks. Then this commandant called us out, and we went out and lined up, and he came out, and he was so mad he was incoherent. He was screaming and taking off. He said that we were honorable warriors, and we could not treat honorable captors that way. He went on and on about this. He said, 'There are three things I can do to you. I can put you in chains and take you back to the field, and you can work in chains. I could order my men to shoot you right here and now, or I could forget about it.' He said, 'I'm going to give you one more chance.' And that was it. The next day we were all put in ten-man squads—your death squads of ten men. He never did carry out the death threat when the other people escaped, but he did starve us for a couple of days at a time or something along that line. And I must say, this is the same Palawan camp where they had the massacre at the very end. The 150 or about, what they had left."

Lt. Daman (Davao Penal Colony) "While the guard had gone to get his chow, twelve men on this work detail took off into the jungle. This is when the Japs came in with this buddy system and counted ten men who slept next to any man who had escaped. We were told that these ten would be executed if this man escaped. They said they wanted to know if there were any other plans afoot for more escapes of this sort. It was also at this time, because these fellows had escaped, that the Japs took our shoes away from us. They also took our trousers, our hats, and our shirts so that we had nothing but absolute bare skin. You couldn't live very long in these tropical jungles with all these thorns and thickets without any kind of protective clothing. So all we had to wear was an improvised G-string."

Cpl. Clem (Zamboanga) "The Japanese put 250 of us in this forward hold, and in the after hold they put another 500 men. The ship would travel a little ways and stop; it might stop several hours and then start up again. We were aboard this ship altogether about nineteen days and eighteen nights. You had room to sit and lay down; the food was a little better. Well, late one afternoon we heard the Japanese bugler blowing general quarters, and in the process of blowing it he trailed off. He just pooped out, hit some sour notes. Suddenly the Japanese pulled the hatch covers off and dropped hand grenades down in there and then turned machine guns down in the hold. Well, just about the time they started that, there was this explosion. What had happened was that a torpedo had hit this ship. Personally, the only thing that I remember was that I saw a flash, and everything turned an orangish-colored red. No feeling, no nothing. Everything just turned a solid color. I don't know if the grenades went off first or the torpedo because it all meshed together. But then they started shooting; you could see the fire coming out of the machine guns. As I said, everything turned red on me, and I assume that that's when the torpedo hit. The next thing I knew, I was kind of flying, just twisting and turning, and there were clouds of smoke all around me. I couldn't see anything but these billowy forms like pillows. I thought I was dead.

"Then I opened my eyes, and reality came back. I was underwater in the hold of this ship, and these pillows were the bodies of other guys in there. Some of them were dead; some of them were trying to get out. The ship was filling up with water, and I thought it had already sunk; and I thought I was trapped down in it, and I thought I was going to die, sure enough. So I figured the quickest way to get it over with was to go ahead and drown myself. So I opened my mouth and thought I'd drink in some water.

"I found that my head was above water, and I was just gulping air. I looked up, and I could see light coming through this open hatch. Then I thought, 'Well, I can get out of here.' In the meantime, all this water was rushing up toward this hatch, and the ship was filling up and sinking. I had actually been forced into a corner and was away from the hatch, and this was one place where it was everybody for themselves—survival of the fittest. Everybody was clawing at each other trying to get to the hatch. You'd pull one person out of the way to get a little closer to the hatch. I finally reached the hatch, and two other guys and I pulled ourselves out at the same time.

"Up on the bridge there was a machine gun spraying the hatch. A burst of machine-gun fire caught all three of us and knocked us back down in the hold. We'd all been hit. I got plowed in the skull, and it got split half in two. Another bullet chipped out my chin. Nevertheless, I was able to work myself back up on deck, and I was eyeing that bridge when I came out that time. The gun was still there, but the gunner was laying out on deck. Somebody had apparently got up there and killed him. At this time I found out that we were out in the ocean about two or three miles from shore. All I had on was a loincloth.

"All I could think of was getting to that land and getting some water or coconut milk. I couldn't see out of one eye on account of the blood. I'd reach up there, and I knew I was shot. I figured I was in pretty bad shape, but I still wanted to get to shore and get something to drink. You could barely see the land.

"So the first thing I thought of was that I had a long swim. I pulled off my loincloth so that I had nothing to encumber me in swimming. Also, I had been down in that hold for nineteen days and eighteen nights, so I didn't have a lot of strength. Anyway, I dove over the side, and when I hit the water I happened to look up, and I saw that we were part of a convoy because there were many ships around. The other ships had put out lifeboats to pick up Japanese, but they were shooting all the Americans. They were shooting them, or some of the officers were taking swipes at their heads with sabers. There were Japs all around me. Hell, there were a lot of Jap troops on this ship.

"Then there was a seaplane patrolling for this convoy, and we had to contend with him. He'd make a pass and strafe us. In the meantime, I couldn't hear a thing because, I later found out, both my eardrums had been perforated in the concussion of this explosion. I was as deaf as I could be, so in the swimming all I could sense was little shocks in the water, and I didn't know what it was. I'd look around and the water would be spraying up, and it was where somebody was shooting.

"We swam and we swam, and my right arm just finally got to where I couldn't swim, couldn't move it, couldn't pull it over my head. It was completely paralyzed, useless. I found out later that while I had been swimming I'd been shot twice—once in the arm and once in the shoulder. We got to the beach a little before sundown. Two of us got into some trees off the beach, and a Filipino walked up. He had on a pair of cut-off sailor dungarees, and he took them off and gave them to me, and then he climbed up this coconut tree and got a bunch of coconuts and cut them down for us.

"We walked about a mile inland and came upon this hut with several Filipinos standing around. They gave us some water—I never could get enough water—and then they took us to a village probably five or six miles away. Then they started bringing other Americans into this village. We stayed there that night, and there were eighty-three of us that showed up. There were 750 of us on that ship, and only eighty-three of us got ashore.

"They moved us into a main guerrilla camp about ten miles back in the hills. They took the slugs out of my arm, but they never did take the one out of my back. This guerrilla encampment had radio contact with Australia, and they promised us that the next time they brought in supplies by submarine they would take out the wounded. We were supposed to be down at the beach at a certain time. One night after we'd been with the guerrillas about a month we went down to the beach and this submarine surfaced, and the Filipinos took us out to the sub in dugout canoes."

PFC Bolitho (sunk in transit, Davao Penal Colony to Japan, 1944)
"We left and got around the tip of Zamboanga and came up the western coast of Mindanao. It was afternoon, and we were hit by a wolf pack of American submarines. We probably weren't more than three or four miles from the coast. There were eight ships and a tanker in the convoy, and they sank six, and the tanker was beached. When the torpedo hit our ship it killed all the men in the forward part, almost

all the men on the right side, and all the men in the middle. Out of 850 people on the ship, there were only eighty-two of us that survived. All I remember is that water was coming in, and I thought I was pushing sponges away, but they were dead bodies. The Japs were firing and throwing hand grenades down at us. So the only way we could get out—at least I did—was through the hole that the torpedo made.

"I went out through the hole, and somehow the rushing water slammed me against the side of the ship and threw me up on deck. When it did, I broke five ribs, had my right arm broken, and a broken jaw. I can remember looking around, and machine-gun bullets whizzing by. They had this machine gun, and they were sweeping the deck. I was so dazed that I just walked right across and never got hit. I went over the side as the ship listed. When I got in the water there was another American close to me—E. L. Browning from Centralia, Washington. We were surrounded by Jap guards who were in the water. One had a bayonet and one had a small bat about two feet long. Browning said, 'Are you hurt?' And I said, 'Yes, I think I have a broken arm. I don't think I can make it.' He said, 'Well, I'm not hurt. The next time this Jap makes a lunge at me I'm going to get that bat. Can you grab the bayonet?' I said, 'Sure.' He grabbed the bat and hit this guy with it and then swung around to hit the other Jap that had the bayonet. I grabbed the bayonet, and we fought our way out of there. We found a hatch cover, and I hung on to it. Oh, I had got hit with the bayonet on the right side, and I was bleeding profusely.

"Fortunately, the tide was going in. It was probably 4:00 in the afternoon. So we swam as much as we could until the Japs catapulted a plane from, I believe, a light cruiser. The plane came back and forth strafing the water. When it did, we'd have to dive under the water, and we got separated. Then they lowered a motor launch, and they were strafing everybody. I kept swimming as best I could, trying to paddle in, and, fortunately, the tide carried me in on that hatch. I'd never have made it without the hatch because I couldn't swim with my right arm.

"It was getting dark as I got close in. The beach was all coral. And I saw another American sitting there. He was Lieutenant Tresnewski of the 31st Infantry. He had a gash between his eyes that was about four inches long and half an inch wide and probably three quarters of an inch deep. He wasn't bleeding—just oozing this gray stuff. He was blind, completely blind. I told him my name, and he said, 'Yes, Hayes, I know you.' He said, 'I can't go into the jungle because I'm blind.' I said, 'I can't go. I've got a broken right arm, and my jaw's broken.' So he said, 'Let's give ourselves up.' I said, 'There's a Jap tanker beached up here.' So we stood up in the water and waved, and they waved back at us. Then down on the right, an American crossed the beach, and when he did, they opened up on him. When this happened, I said to Tresnewski, 'They're firing at us, we've no choice.' His sight came back, and he went one way, and I went the other.

"I could see tracer bullets coming, and I dived behind this mound of coral, and they cut the top right off of it. Then they went on after Tresnewski. I ran through a clearing and headed for a big tree. As I did, I could see the tracers coming again. I hit the ground and rolled behind the tree. When I did, a shell exploded. I got hit through the bottom of my right foot and across the right finger. Then they almost cut that tree down firing back and forth. I had no idea where Tresnewski was. My foot was bleeding, my side was bleeding, my hand was bleeding, and I was drooling blood from my jaw, but I didn't hurt anyplace, really. I took off my G-string and wound it around my foot. Why my foot? I don't know. Instead of tying up my arm, I wrapped it around my foot.

"So I walked into the jungle and down this path. I had no idea where I was going, and I came to a clearing and here was another American—Snowden. Finally, we came into another clearing, and here was a little Filipino boy and an old man. All the old man could say was, 'Americano, Americano.' The little kid could speak English, and he took us by the hand down this path and pointed to another path and said, 'Go that way.' It was dark as we walked down this path for, say, about twenty minutes to half an hour, and all of a sudden we heard a lot of noise. We stopped, fell in the path and rolled into the jungle, and laid real quiet. We couldn't make out if they were Filipinos or Japs. Then all of a sudden a torch was thrown into the clearing on this path. So Snowden said, 'Well, I think we're caught.' I said, 'I think you're right.' So instead of having them fire blindly, which we thought they would do, we stood up and raised our hands, and into the clearing came these Filipino guerrillas. I never saw such a good-looking sight in my life. They just looked great.

"This one guy pointed to me and asked if I were hurt and I said, 'Yes.' He saw my foot. He turned around and said, 'Climb on.' I climbed on his back. They picked Snowden up, and they dogtrotted with us through that jungle for about four hours. Never stopped, right straight through, and brought us up into the hills where there was a schoolhouse. This is the area where they were gathering all of the Americans that got off of this ship—Liloy Point, Sindangan, Zamboanga, Misamas Oriental, Mindanao.

"So they took us to the hospital they had prepared—a bamboo shack. There were two doctors, one of whom was a dentist. He got hold of some piano wire, and he tied my jaw together with this piano wire. It was absolutely terrible pain. I was there thirty days, and when I got on the submarine that took us out I weighed ninety-eight pounds. I had been living and eating like a king in the jungle. So I must have put on twenty pounds in those thirty days. I imagine at one point I was probably down to seventy pounds."

PFC Evans (Surabaja) "We had two guys try to escape in Java, and they were put into a cage, like a chicken cage, and tied up. The Japanese would go out there once in a while and put cigarettes out on them and that sort of thing. They'd be in that cage in the hot sun tied up with their hands behind their backs and kneeling on the ground with a bamboo pole under the backsides of their knees, which virtually crippled them. They were not allowed to relieve themselves. I think they gave them a little water once in a while and a little food—enough to keep them alive. They were using them as an example for us. We were told that if we tried to escape, we'd be killed. We absolutely had no possible way of escaping because the facts are that a man would show up like a lump of coal in a bale of cotton."

PO2 Detre (Java) "We talked endlessly about escape. But it was cheap talk because we were a bunch of sailors, and we didn't know where we were. We had no idea of direction. A soldier might tell you, 'We'll get a boat and go.' But he doesn't know how big that sea is. The sailors never seriously entertained escaping."

PFC Robinson (Thanbyuzayat) "Two Australians who had escaped were recaptured and brought to Thanbyuzayat. The Nips supposedly tried them. I doubt that they ever got a trial. We were well aware of the fact that they were to be executed. When the day came, they marched them right through the camp and out the back of the camp and into the woods. I'm assuming that they shot them. We did hear shots, and we never saw either of them again."

Pvt. Benton (Tientsin) "We were planning a break all the time we were in Tientsin, about three weeks. We were trying to figure out how to do it, how to get out. We were serious, no big talk. Of course, the rumor got around, and our commanding officer put out the word that there would be no escape attempts. Well, being Marines, even though we didn't like it, we didn't question him. The reason he said he gave the order was that we had quite a few old men in our midst. The colonel himself was in his fifties. He said that if we left, the Japs would catch the old men, and they'd execute all of them. But anyway, we dropped it."

Cpl. Crews (Tientsin) "We stayed in Tientsin maybe six weeks, two months. A patrol guarded us and the only thing that happened of consequence was that George Stone and his partner decided to try to make a break for it, holed up in the attic on the day that we left. These were real old ancient-type barracks that had acres of area upstairs. What happened is the Japs let us know when we were leaving. So George and this other guy just got up in the attic some way and got some water and some corned beef and stuff to survive for a little while. When we pulled out, well, we were missing two men. Stone had been a pilot in civilian life. The Japanese searched but never found them.

"After we got to Shanghai—I guess it might have been two or three weeks—the Japs brought them into camp one day, and they told the story of how they stayed up in the attic as long as they could. They got cold, and Peking is like New York, not like Texas, in the wintertime. It is zero weather practically all the time. So George and these guys—it may have been three guys, but I believe it was two—well, they had to come down. Their water had froze up, their food was frozen, and they had frostbite. They came down to get water and food, and the Japs had left somebody in the area and they caught them. They had bruises on them, and they didn't seem like they were in too good shape when they got back."

PFC Venable (Woosung) "There were four people. There was Captain Willy and Captain Smith and Teters, that's Dan Teters. He was in charge of the Morrison-Knudsen construction work on Wake. There was these two and Teters plus one other who made arrangements to escape some way. They got out of the prison camp by going under the wire prior to a place being fixed in the fence. And they escaped. They had money, and they made contact with Chinese people. But the Chinese turned them in to the Japanese, and the Japs brought them back into camp, marched them around, tied them up, and then sentenced them all to be killed. But then they commuted this to life imprisonment at hard labor. And then they interned them in jail in

Shanghai for most of the war. They finally brought them back to us, but they were really broken people."

Capt. Godbold (Woosung or Kiangwan) "We were always planning to escape but were discouraged by the senior American colonel named Ashurst. He said if you escaped, the Chinese would kill you for your shoes. None of us believed this. I expect he knew pretty well that if we got well away from camp, the chances of escape were extremely good. He just felt, I believe, that the good that would accrue to our country's cause by two or three people escaping and coming back to America would be detrimental to the prisoners who were still there. It was not really worth the effort, and I just think that he felt that for all things concerned the best thing to do was to stay there and wait the war out, but, of course, none of the young officers agreed with that."

Cpl. Crews (Kiangwan) "I was racked up quite a bit and put in solitary without blankets for two or three weeks one time when Corporal Story and PFC Battles dug under the electric fence and escaped. I was bunking right next to them. The Japs took the whole bunch of us—probably twenty-five—and said, 'Now, you didn't tell us those boys were going to escape. You're going to suffer for it.' So they threw us in this old dark room, and they didn't feed us. They kept us there for about three weeks, and they'd give us a bowl of rice every two or three days. They took all of our clothes away from us except our skivvy shorts, and this was in cold weather. I forget whether it was the first year or the second year, but it was extremely cold. We would run and jump every night. And in the daytime we had one little area where we would get a little light, and we'd take turns trying to sleep in the area where the sun was coming in. They caught Story and Battles, but they never brought them back to our camp. I understand they kept them in a dungeon in Shanghai, but Corporal Story made it out some way because he is out in the West someplace."

Cpl. Crews (in transit, near Nanking, 1945) "We were in this area ten or fifteen miles past Nanking, after we had been loaded on the freight cars in Nanking en route to Peking. Lieutenant [Lewis S.] Bishop, this ex-Flying Tiger, Lieutenant [James D.] McBrayer, and this other lieutenant whose name I can't remember had a can rigged up in the back to use as a rest room. They got the Japanese to thinking that they wanted a little privacy back there, so they put a blanket up shielding the can off from the guards, who were in the middle of the boxcars. The Japs didn't think about it, but there was a window opening in that area. So behind the blanket they either sawed the bars loose or unscrewed them or whatever they had to do. The Japs couldn't see them, and they had plenty of time to work. Somehow they got it open, and one by one they dropped out of the train—five of them [Bishop, McBrayer, Richard M. Huizenga, John F. Kinney, and John G. McAlister].

"Of course, the Japs didn't know they were missing until they took a count. Every so often they'd line you up and count you off. When they found that they were missing, well, they stopped the train, and they got some clothes that they left behind. Evidently, Bishop was familiar with the area since he'd been a pilot, a professional fighter pilot over there for years, and he figured he could contact the guerrillas near the railroad. So they didn't take their clothing. Well, the Japs brought some bloodhounds in and let them smell the clothing, and they took off down the track presumably to find where they'd left the railroad. That's the last time we saw or heard of them until after the war when we found that they really and truly made their escape. They got in contact with the guerrillas."

M/Sgt. Stowers (in transit, near Nanking, 1945) "Jim McBrayer told me what happened to them. He asked me, 'Hank, do you want to go with us?' I told him, thanks, but no thanks. I didn't believe that they could make it. It was a dark, stormy night, and we were going along about thirty or forty miles an hour in this train. They were going to have to go out of the window headfirst, and Jim said, 'I don't know what we are going to hit. It may be a concrete bridge. I don't know. It's pitch dark out there.' We talked it over for an hour, and that's when I said that I was going to pass. I noticed that two of the bars were out of the window, but the Japs didn't notice it. I guess we had gone ten or fifteen miles out of Nanking when they decided to go out headfirst. They had more guts than I had. Well, they all went out maybe at a mile or half-mile intervals. McBrayer hit and rolled down an embankment, and then he went walking through China, and he came to a river. He swam the river and was so tired that he crawled up under some rocks, and he just passed out. When he woke up, it was the middle of the day and the sun was shining, and a lot of Chinese were around him. One guy walked up and said, 'Come on with me.' He went with him, and he fed him, and he put him in a little hut, and about a week later some guerrillas came and took him to an airfield, a disguised airfield, and they picked him up and took him to Chungking. McBrayer was a close friend of mine, and I remember that particular deal. They were the only prisoners that successfully escaped during our time. Many tried it, and most of them were killed."

Guards and Camp Administrators

Lt. Taylor (Philippines) "My personal feelings—and I think this was pretty universal—toward the Japanese leaders, especially the commanding general in the Philippines who knew what was being done by the commissioned and noncommissioned officers under his command, were that he was absolutely no good. We could not feel kindly toward a guy who would permit men to suffer and die when in the early days they could have brought in adequate food and medicine, because there was plenty of American stores right there in Manila and other places, these bases that they had captured. There were plenty of library books and everything else they could have brought into prison camp to establish a comfortable prison camp, if you can call a prison camp comfortable. But they could have at least made it livable. They could have permitted the men to go out and build latrines, and they could have brought in disinfectant-type things for sanitation. They could have helped us make the camps sanitary, which they did not. As one Japanese commander told the Americans at O'Donnell, 'We are not concerned about how many die. The only thing we want to know in the morning is how many died the night before—just so we know how many are left in the camp.' This tells us something. They were not concerned with human lives. It was just a matter of getting rid of as many as possible, and I think they did."

Cpl. Burlage (Philippines) "We had names for all the guards. They weren't too complimentary. But this one guy had a nice name. We called him Donald Duck because that's what he sounded like. He had ears that were of a pretty good size because he could hear us talking about him, and he wasn't anywhere in sight, you know. He would come over and slap you two or three times and accuse you of defaming his character. This one particular time he came over, and he said, 'You call me Donald Duck. Bad name.' And he started in on us. 'No, that's not a bad name. It's a movie star.' And we convinced him that it was a movie star. He felt pretty good there for a long, long time. A supply boat would come in about every three months, and sometimes they would bring some films. It just so happened they did bring some film sometime later, and there was a Donald Duck film in there. Well, we were told about it the next day in a rough way.

"There was one little goofy guy, who wasn't too bright, either. We called him Blinky because he was always blinking his eyes. He would come up, and he would want to play this game where you guess how many fingers that you're going to slap across a man's wrist. He would always lose, and his wrist was always red from someone slapping him.

"Then there was this guy, I can't remember the exact name, maybe something like Timex or something of that sort, I guess. Anyway, he was always trying to get some of the prisoners to send him a wrist-watch when they got back home. He wanted an American wristwatch. I guess he didn't know that the Japs would rule the world some day with watches and other goods.

"At another camp we had Porky Pig. We used Disney characters. Porky Pig looked and grunted like a pig. And, boy, you stayed out of his way, there was no question about it. He was the equivalent of our Navy chief. He was a reservist. The meanest bunch were mostly re-servists. You could tell when something went wrong because these people were even a little bit meaner. It was nothing to get hit over the shoulder or the head with a pick handle. They carried pick handles, and, boy, I mean to tell you, I was beat up more than once by those people, for nothing at all. They were sadistic."

Lt. Daman (Cabanatuan) "There was one particular guard that we disliked, called Laughing Boy. He was one of the meanest indi-viduals I have ever met on the face of the earth. I was on a detail one time, and I saw him break the arm of one of the other prisoners. The boy was told to get down off a stack of straw that we were on. He started to get down, but I guess he didn't move as fast as Laughing Boy wanted him to. Well, this guard carried a hardwood replica of a samurai sword, and he hit this boy across the arm and broke his arm. This guard got his nickname because every time he beat up some-body he would practically go into hysterics from laughing.

"Another guard named Air Raid shot a very good friend of mine. This friend, Major Harrison, had hollowed out an area in the heel of his shoe and hid some seeds there. When Harrison went through the gate, Air Raid happened to be on guard duty and evidently saw some of the seeds fall out. He made Harrison take off his shoe. Well, Harrison knew he was going to be beaten pretty badly, so instead of stopping to take that beating, which he obviously would have received, he decided to run. He ran down the street and out toward the back of the camp, and Air Raid just up and shot him right there in the camp.

"We had another guard here whose name was Wada, and we called him Running Wada. He was an interpreter. When we first arrived here, they put us out in this field and took our hats away from us and made us sit there for two and a half hours in the hot tropical sun. He said, 'We're leaving you out here to meditate because we don't want disturbances of any kind. If you meditate on this, we're sure that you won't want to commit any crimes against Japan.' Boy, two and a half hours in that sun and sitting down with no hat on, you become a Christian in a hurry."

Cpl. Halbrook (Cabanatuan) "They called him Air Raid because on one end of the work detail, when he would start to work on somebody, you would holler, Air Raid. And it meant to get the hell out or move around and get away from him because this was a mother that's coming out looking for trouble, and he carried a stick with him."

Cpl. Sherman (Cabanatuan) " 'Clark Gable' was like a cocky little rooster. He had a little mustache, and he thought he was *it*. It didn't make any difference to him. He'd just as soon cut your throat as anything."

Cpl. Halbrook (Clark Field) " 'Big Ass' Adams escaped out of camp, and then he slipped back in camp. The Japs had already missed him. They had us lined up, and they already had us sectioned out. A guy named the White Angel had decided he was going to execute ten of us. We called him the White Angel because he was a naval officer with a white uniform who spoke perfect English, a graduate of UCLA. The White Angel told Adams that if he would lay his head down across a stump that was there, he would cut his head off. Adams asked only one thing—untie his hands. They untied his hands and stuck his head across there. The White Angel took his damn sword—we called it a cheese knife or a samurai sword—and pulled it up above his head. Adams's eyes were still open when his head hit the ground."

Cpl. Halbrook (Batangas) "Koreans hated us. For some reason the Koreans were always trying to impress the Japanese. They worked our butt over every time they got a chance. If you had a Korean or a northern Japanese or a Japanese Marine, and you were an American Marine, you were in deep, deep trouble."

Cpl. Clem (Davao Penal Colony) "The Japanese took out the regular troops and brought in a bunch of youngsters from Formosa. They weren't combat troops. They had the power of life and death over us, and they dealt us misery. On the slightest provocation they just beat the devil out of somebody just to be doing it. They would stand somebody up and take a pistol and point it at him and pull the trigger. It wasn't loaded, but you never knew for sure. They had the power to kill you if they wanted to, and they kept your nerves on edge with all this harassing they'd do."

Lt. Daman (Davao Penal Colony) "These guards that we had were Taiwanese yardbirds. They were poor caliber troops and were not combat troops in any sense of the word. They were quite brutal out on work details. The Japs had occupied Taiwan for many years, and they just took some of these people and made them guards. Of course, they were scared to death that the Japs were going to kill them if they didn't do the job right, so they were a rough, tough lot."

PFC Bolitho (Davao Penal Colony) "One of the benefits of working in the kitchen was when you went for supplies. We had a good Japanese soldier who was a two-star private. His name was Okomoto. Okomoto-san was a pretty good guy. When we went to the grocery store, we'd pick up these sacks of dried fish, and he'd always turn his head, and we'd make a raid on the canned milk which was there and throw so much canned milk in fish bags. We also managed to hide a sack of brown sugar—and when I mean sack, it was like fifty-five pounds—and bring it back to camp. There was one Jap officer who understood English and was a pretty good Jap officer. But we had a little sadistic character. I can't remember his name either, but he was a little syphilitic Jap second lieutenant. He was forever practicing judo on some big, tall American. He was about five foot, but he was a great one for trying to inflict as much punishment as possible."

Sgt. Brodsky (Palawan) "The Japanese commander at Palawan seemed like a really fair guy. He made a speech to us and told us that we would have Sundays off and that we would have athletic contests as long as we worked. He gave us the usual speech that a commander would give."

Pvt. Armstrong (Bicycle Camp) "We had one guard called the Brown Bomber. He was short, heavyset, but small. He'd come through the barracks at night just banging on you, beating on you. If he caught you going to the latrine, he'd stand you up and beat the hell out of you for no reason at all. I don't know whether he was drunk, but he'd scream and holler and get everybody out in the night, line them up, and count."

Fireman 1/C Kennedy (Bicycle Camp) "In the beginning you tried to get close to the guards. You soon learned that that was an error, especially if they spoke English. We would talk to those who spoke English and, before we knew it, we'd say something we shouldn't say and find out that that's what they were trying to get us to do. You didn't try to be friends with them. You learned to keep a low profile and not call attention to yourself under any condition."

Sgt. Fujita (in transit, Java to Japan) "From Java to Singapore to Formosa to Japan, we were under this one sergeant all the way. He looked like an ape and was great big. We called him The Bull, and he was just a bull of a fellow. He was mean as hell, but he was fair. What I mean is, if you goofed up you knew you had it coming, because you knew you goofed up. He didn't let anything pass. But if his own soldiers goofed up, I saw him line them up out there in front of all the prisoners of war, and he beat every one of them unmercifully just because one of them goofed up. He wasn't having any of that in his outfit. His word was law—period!"

Pvt. Chambers (Burma-Thailand Railway) "We had a guard called Makan who got a lot of thrills out of beating on the guys. He was always talking about eating with us—that's why we called him Makan, Malayan for eat or food. When we first started knowing him, he was a pretty good guard to have around. He was a Korean. Boy, he soured. He went to another camp and got away from us. When he returned, we were talking about how glad we were to see him. But he had changed and become one of the worst of the lot."

Cpl. Crews (Peking) "The first couple of weeks, we had a guard that we nicknamed Hollywood, who was always around with a bunch of photographers. They wanted some pictures. They wanted to throw everything in a good light for them, of course. I think they tried to make us a showcase prisoner-of-war camp there for about three weeks to be used later on for propaganda."

Pvt. Benton (Woosung) "I found out very quick to leave the Japs alone. In other words, the less you had to do with them, the better off you were, because I've seen quite a few guys that would get chummy with a guard, and he'd go and cut up with him today, and the next day the guard would come around and the guy would say something to him, and the guard would just knock the hell out of him. I could see right quick that they were moody, and you never knew what mood they would be in. So when I found out, I made my mind up that the least I could have to do with them, that's what I was going to do. I

learned before the war was over that it paid off as far as I was concerned because I was only beaten twice in forty-four months, which I
consider very lucky. They were not torture beatings. The guard would
just get mad at you and work you over with a rifle butt or something.
Other guys went through torture and things that I never had to en-
dure. And a lot of that was brought on by being friendly with the
guards. Different things would happen, and the Japs would try to find
out who was doing that, and they'd torture the friendly guys, give
them the water treatment and stuff to make them talk.

"Anyway, when we arrived in Shanghai, this Colonel Yuse made
a speech. He just rambled on, telling us, 'If you try to escape, you
will be shot.' He died in the fall of 1942, and Colonel Otera replaced
him. We called him Handlebar Hank. He didn't spend much time in
camp. I heard he was a drunk, but I don't know. He would generally
go to Shanghai. He left most details up to the Beast of the East,
Ishihara."

Capt. Godbold (Woosung) "I remember that there was a guard
called Tiny Tim. I remember that he was highly regarded among the
prisoners. He gave them information about the war. Whether he ever
dealt in selling things for the prisoners, I don't know. As I recall,
maybe he was a Taiwanese, I'm not sure. He had a good reputation
among the prisoners. Evidently he was humane in his treatment and
very favorably regarded.

"I [also] remember Otera. He had a handlebar mustache. He was
an old-line professional soldier who was probably too old for active
combat or else had not distinguished himself in combat and had been
shunted off to be commanding officer of a little prisoner-of-war camp.
I expect he had a drinking problem, although I don't recall this spe-
cifically, but I do remember there was talk about him being quite a
drinker. He liked softball. We played a great deal of softball, and he
always came to the games. I think he sort of liked me because he
liked softball, and I was, I expect, the most proficient softball player
among the Marines."

PFC Fields (Woosung) "We had a sentry, a guard, we always called
Crash Dive, because he was so tough and mean, rugged. He was a
rugged individual. He was one of those tough guys, I think a frontline soldier. We didn't know he could speak English. We started making fun of him, and he said, 'You don't think I know what you mean!'
And he started working a few of us over. We had another called
Mortimer Snerd [dummy on ventriloquist Edgar Bergen's popular

1940s radio program]. He got to asking us who Mortimer Snerd was, and we told him, 'a big Hollywood movie star.' I don't know how, but he found out who Mortimer Snerd was, and then after that, if you'd call him Mortimer Snerd, it was a sad moment."

Cpl. Crews (Woosung) "We also had Formosan guards. I understand that there was some other Marines that gave bad reports on the Formosan type. I didn't find them to be that bad, really. But the Formosans were looked down on by the Japanese, and it looked like the Japanese were kicking them around a little bit. My relations and the relations of the Marines around me with the Formosan guards was better than with the Jap guards."

Pvt. Permenter (Woosung or Kiangwan) "The Japanese guards were just like I was. You'd get him off to himself, and, as a rule, the majority of them would be pretty nice to you. But now when you'd get him in a group, it was a different thing altogether. That's when you had to watch them, especially around their officers or some other guards."

Cpl. McDaniel (Woosung or Kiangwan) "There was a black market everywhere we went. You'd contact guards or Chinese when you were on work parties. With the guards you get back to saving face again. If you'd get them one on one, you could deal with them. But if there was a third party, it was an insult to try to deal with them. One day you could deal with a fellow and go back the next day, and if you had someone else with you, you didn't deal. It was an insult. I mean, you stood a chance of getting beat up or what have you, harassed. I mean, it's something that he took as an insult."

Capt. Godbold (Kiangwan) "The guards were sometimes brutal, sometimes stupid, sometimes kindly, sometimes thoughtful. Mostly they were indifferent in that they did their job, and I thought they handled themselves reasonably well."

PFC Fields (Kiangwan) "There was one foreman in Shanghai, a Japanese soldier, that I'd like to see today. I think he was a wonderful person. He would take care of us. He'd give us a few cigarettes, and he would divide some of his food with us. He was just a good guy. He was well educated. I understand that when the war broke out he was an engineer on a train from, I believe, Osaka to someplace. I don't remember, but he was a fine fellow."

Pvt. Benton (Kiangwan) "This guard was raised—born and raised—in San Francisco. He spoke the old slang just like I do. You could sit there and talk to him, and he talked just like I do. He was a real fine fellow, really, but he was in a situation where he could only do so much. He had a little guard with him, a lance corporal. He was just meaner than hell when he first came out there. He'd slap you around for this and that. The longer he stayed around us, the more mellow he got. Finally, after about a month, he got to be one of the best guys you ever saw. I guess we won him over.

"Then we had another little guard who stands out in my mind. He was from Formosa. You know, the Japs occupied Formosa, and they had taken kids in, and they had some of them guarding us. He could speak real good English. I don't know where he learned it. He used to tell us that he'd swap places with any of us. He'd come over and be a prisoner, and a prisoner could have his guard duty. As far as I know, he never bothered anybody. I guess those three are the ones I remember more than any others.

"We had an interpreter named Ishihara. We called him the Beast of the East. He was mean; he was mean. He was raised in Honolulu, so I understand. He seemed to get a kick out of trying to put you down, make you feel inferior to him, which he was never able to do. That's what irritated him, because he could never bring you to his level. He punished quite a few guys pretty severely. He put quite a few of them through the water treatment. It's an Oriental torture that they put you through. They'd tie you down on a board and just keep pouring water down you. Finally, you get so much water that you throw up and pass out. I've heard say they would even jump on you when you're full of water."

M/Sgt Stowers (Kiangwan) "Ishihara was the interpreter and couldn't speak English very well. He carried a short riding crop, and he'd been turned down by the Army, was 4-F, and he was trying to win the war by using that riding crop and whipping everybody and screaming. He was a bundle of energy, I'll tell you that much! I don't know why the Army couldn't use him, whether he was mentally or physically defective, probably mentally. But he was a terror."

PFC Venable (Kiangwan) "Ishihara—in gutter terminology he was a dirty, rotten son of a bitch. The guy worked at being mean. He was personally vindictive toward us. He made life miserable. I understand that he received twenty years in trials following World War II."

PFC Sparkman (Kiangwan) "They had one guy called G-2 [Ishihara]. I guess he was a little tougher. He was mean for a Jap and a little larger than the rest of them. We called him G-2, or maybe they did—I don't remember—because he checked on the guards. He was the main guy running the guard detail. He'd have us standing up there, and he jabbered to us. He'd come down the line, and he'd slap us on one side, and then he'd go back up the other side, and he'd slap us alongside of the face. I kind of rolled with mine, so it didn't bother me much. But some of the guys he knocked out. You can hit a man very light behind his jawbone or right on it, and it don't take much to knock him out.

"This one guy I called Cat Eyes. His eyes were slanted quite a bit. He was always after me. If we lined up for inspection, and if I didn't have my shoes fixed right, he'd point it out. One day he wanted me to jump over the electric fence. He told me to jump over it. And I told him, 'No, I don't want to do it.' The guards thought it would be funny to pull the juice on when I jumped up on the fence. I told him I wasn't going to do it, but he kept insisting, and I said, 'Okay.' So I put my foot on one of the insulators, and I vaulted over, and that made him mad. So he slapped me around a little.

"We had another little Jap, but he was just as friendly as he could be. He was nice. He gave the guys cigarettes. He'd talk to them. He was going to an English school in Shanghai to learn to speak English, and he liked to talk to us all the time. He'd treat you like a human being."

Pvt. Burns (Moji) "We had one guard there who we called Peg Leg because he had lost a leg in some battle. We knew that he was out to get you; he was going to try to catch you doing something on detail, and he was going to nail you one way or the other. I guess maybe this was so he would have the privilege of beating the heck out of you.

"We had another one that we called Old Sailor. He had been in the Japanese Navy, and he was now too old for combat. When he was in charge of a detail by himself, if you wanted to wander about the warehouse and put some sugar in your pocket, he would look the other way. He didn't care. But if he was with three or four other guards and they would catch somebody who had stolen something, he would have to join in with the punishment. For instance, they might line us up, and each one would come down the line and hit you in the small of the back with an iron pipe. Well, the Old Sailor would come by, and he had to save face, but he would just go through the motions of swinging. You could do almost anything you wanted to do in front of him if he was alone."

PFC Garrison (Hirohata) "We had this one officer that we called the White Bull. There's no way to describe the man. There's no way. He was inhuman. It was an absolute pleasure to him to whip somebody. It was his greatest love. He was the most vicious person I've ever seen. He did things that he was not ordered to do, and he did them for his own pure pleasure. About a year after the war, the FBI like to have scared me to death. I walked home and there sat an FBI agent in the living room. I thought, 'What have I done?' He came for information on the White Bull. He was to be punished as a war criminal.

"Another fellow that stands out was this Japanese man, we called him Sikidushi-san. He and the White Bull were the two who got the greatest pleasure out of punishing us. They beat you with clubs, 're-form bats,' until you were unconscious. Whatever they decided to do, they did it. Well, when peace was signed, we took over, and naturally we started looking for specific people. We were going by the railroad station one day, and I just happened to glance in there, three of us, and there he was—Sikidushi-san. Well, he saw us about this time and ran. He ran out of one side of the building to a Japanese house. So we got up there, and the fellow that owned the house came out and wanted to know what we wanted. We said, 'We want that man who came into your house.' He said, 'Well, he isn't here.' We said, 'Well, we saw him come in.' And he said, 'No, no, no, he's not here.' We said, 'We'll tell you what. If he isn't here, it won't hurt him if we burn your house down, would it?' So we lit matches, and we were going to burn that house, but the man turned around and went back into the house and called upstairs, and Sikidushi-san came out So then we commandeered a truck and took him out in the hills. We tied him to a tree, and we reciprocated and left him there. I don't know whether he lived or not. We had the same reform bat that they used, and we used it."

Pvt. Kent (Mitsushima) "Two Japanese soldiers who had fought in China, Big Glass Eye and Little Glass Eye, knocked my back out of place. They were rough. They worked together. They'd come by and tell you just what they were going to do to your country, and that they were coming to get American girls—just to agitate you. They both had their right eyes knocked out during the China war, and that was the reason they were so rough on the Chinese prisoners."

PFC Evans (Orio) "We had one guy in the mines we called Three-Ringer. He had this big spotlight that would just knock your eyes out.

He had three red rings on the inside of his light. He carried an inspector's pick that was like a mountaineer's pick. It was a walking stick with a sharp point on the end which you could use to test roofs. On the other side was a hammer to test the braces. This guy was a big, tall Manchurian. We called him a Mongolian. He was better than six feet tall and was pretty mean. If he thought you were goofing off or not doing what he wanted you to do, he'd take that mine inspector's pick and knock your light off. Then he'd try to beat you to death with the other end of it."

PFC Visage (Nagasaki) "Tank Happy got his name because he was a big, overgrown Japanese; and he was always walking around grinning all the time. He was well liked by the prisoners for the simple reason that he did a lot of things for people. Once I was in solitary confinement for six days in a cubicle that you couldn't stand up, sit down, or lie down in. He was on guard shift at nighttime. I was on a no-food basis, but when he was on guard shift, he would untie my hands and give me a handful of rice. He did this at his own risk."

PFC Fields (Hakodate) "One of the supervisors in the mine was a Jap we called Mousey. He was the one that came down one day and flailed us all with his little ol' hammer. He beat us up with one of the little hammers. It's sharp on one end and flat on the other. I don't know what you call that thing, where you check for shale. They'd give us a lunch period, and we didn't have watches. But it seemed like we had worked long enough that it should've been what we called chow time, so we sat down and started eating. When he came in, he just started slamming that hammer and hitting us and beating us up with that hammer and said that it wasn't time to eat."

American Discipline

Lt. Burris (Bataan) "On the march, there was an incident that just gave me the idea of what was coming. I didn't realize it at the time, but it was selfishness. It was *me*, take care of *me*. It was, 'To hell with everybody else! I'm going to take care of me.' This one soldier was eating some weeds he'd picked up off the road some- where. It was some kind of weed, I think it was pigweed; we called it pigweed in Arkansas. So he was eating it and kind of hiding it from me. I asked him to let me see what he was eating so that I could get some. He wouldn't tell me and wouldn't tell me where he got it. Even though he was going to have to walk away from that spot the same as me, he still didn't want me to have something that might deprive him of something. We were beginning to show evidence of selfishness and disbelief in what the other person said."

Cpl. Clem (Cabanatuan) "The Japanese always had a lot of respect for the Marines, and they kept all the Marines segregated from the Army personnel. We were in a barracks all to our own. The Marine Corps had a lot of discipline. We followed orders and instructions from our officers, and we got to know them real well while we were prisoners. Of course, back at that time there was a lot of distinction between an officer and enlisted personnel, and we were very surprised to find out that some of these officers who we thought had been sons of bitches could actually be human beings. There wasn't anybody who fussed with what the officers told them to do."

Capt. Adair (Cabanatuan) "By the time we got to Cabanatuan we were able to organize. The Japanese segregated the enlisted men from the officers, and the officers were separated by rank. As I recall, the captains were in one group of houses. We set up mess halls for each group, and we had our leaders then appointed according to seniority. The Japanese left that up to us, so we had a lot better discipline at Cabanatuan than at O'Donnell."

Pvt. Burns (Cabanatuan) "The Japanese had their camp commander, and then the Americans had one of their own officers who functioned almost like one of the commanding officers on a post in the States. He had his own staff, his sergeant major, and right on down from there. Then you had so many men in a barracks, so many barracks to a company. I think there were four or five or six barracks to a company. A higher-ranking officer was in charge of each company, and each barracks had a leader and an assistant leader who could be anything from a second lieutenant to a captain or major. This was the way the camp was set up—more or less on the basis of your regular Army post. Orders went from the Japanese commandant down through the chain of command to the barracks leader."

Cpl. Koury (Cabanatuan) "At this stage in time the old American system of 'he who has, gets' began to take hold. Guys would get a little clique going, and a captain might say that you are in charge of distributing chow, and these guys get two thirds and you get one third. This is why many people died—things weren't equally divided. I think that if a man has a choice to make under these circumstances, I don't know of many who wouldn't take care of themselves. There were a few who didn't, but by and large I'd say that 99 percent of them, when it came down to a point of life or death, was going to make it for themselves.

"We received our first Red Cross packages here, and this is when all the bandits showed up. People started stealing from one another. Of course, you handled this yourself. I saw some guys beaten rather severely for stealing."

Lt. Burris (Cabanatuan) "There was very little cooperation among the prisoners—very little. It was mostly fighting each other. Everybody was selfish. It was dog-eat-dog. The fact is, they caught a dog. A group caught a dog in camp, and they killed him and ate him. I didn't see it, but another guy saw these guys and said, 'What are you guys eating there?' They said, 'Dog.' He said, 'You know, I never had any dog. I sure would like to have a taste of dog so I could tell my folks back home what it tastes like.' These guys said, 'You go get your own dog!'

"That was one place where I learned that a human being is a marauder. I believe he would steal from his own mother if he was starving hard enough. You couldn't keep food around because they'd steal it. You ate it right away. I had a little plot of land maybe a couple of feet square on each side, and I planted five or six okra plants there, and I ate them real quick. When they'd get just a little bit big, I ate them. I'd have liked to let them stay on longer, but I couldn't stay around that garden when I was working, so I had to eat them before somebody else would take them. There was quite a bit of stealing. People would take things that they could use to their advantage, like cigarettes. They didn't mind seeing a guy die. They just wanted his food. Everybody was concerned about themselves."

Lt. Taylor (Cabanatuan) "We didn't go every man his own way. We tried to help each other even though we were all in great need. I recall we had a TB [tuberculosis] ward. When the Red Cross food parcels came in December, the first year we were in there, the doctors sent out word to all of us: 'Even though we know you need your tin of powdered milk, these TB patients need it worse than any of us. All of you who will, please donate yours.' Man, they donated that stuff like they had a storehouse full of it, out of their graciousness, you know, their consideration for the TB patients. Now, if every man had been dog-eat-dog, you could never have done a thing like that.

"The enlisted men obeyed and respected their officers even though it was a prisoner-of-war situation. This was the secret to the whole thing. We had an organization, and the men did respect their leaders. Even enlisted men respected their sergeants just like they had done in the military. There may have been a few infractions, but very few. We had a guardhouse right there in camp, but we never did have very many in it."

Pvt. Bugbee (Cabanatuan) "There were stories that filtered back that if you went over to the hospital with a ring or gold tooth or a watch or something like that, you'd very seldom come back. Here again, this was some of our people, not the Japs. It was our people over there that were doing some of these things. All of us had reverted back to the beast in man, I'll say. It was survival of the fittest.

"I will never forget that one time I asked a chaplain if he would take some bananas over to a buddy of mine in the hospital. He said, 'The only way I'll take them over there is if I can have half of them.' There was another time when I saw a man of the cloth get a little extra food, and he ran into one of the huts and gobbled it down so nobody would see him have it. But these are things that you cannot criticize people for. We all reverted back."

Sgt. Burk (Cabanatuan) "There weren't really any orders given here. Some took advantage of being put in charge, and others didn't. Our barracks had Navy people, Marines, and civilians as well as Army personnel, and we more or less elected a Navy chief as barracks leader. He was louder than the rest of us, I guess, so we put him in charge. He would tell you what the Japs wanted done, and if you did it, no trouble came. If you didn't do it, then there'd be trouble for everybody."

Lt. Daman (Cabanatuan) "The veneer of civilization is extremely thin. When you had full colonels fighting over the division of a few grains of rice, why, there was a lot of griping about the servings."

Capt. Bull (Cabanatuan) "I volunteered to take charge of a company of five hundred men, and I supervised it. I had one lieutenant under me for each separate barracks. We had probably 100 or 150 in each barracks. I didn't go out on work parties because my assignment was to supervise the men as well as we could and to call them for mess and see that they stayed out of trouble. All orders came through some colonel above me, but once in a while the whole camp was called to listen to a Japanese officer talk. He would speak in Japanese, and then an interpreter would translate his message to us.

"I did feel that there was some animosity between the officers and the enlisted men, possibly because we didn't work. I tried my best not to create anything like that. For example, at mealtime I would always be the last one to eat. But I personally didn't experience any firsthand animosity. On the other hand, there was a lot of breakdown in discipline, and cussing by enlisted men to officers and blaming them for the predicament we were in. Our hands were tied, and there was no effective way to punish men, so it was an impossible situation. I think we did have some form of minor punishment, but I've forgotten what it was."

Sgt. Burk (Bilibid Prison) "While I was here, a Navy doctor operated on my eye to remove the corneal ulcer. Well, they bandaged my eyes, both of them, and this fellow would come around at mealtime and feed me because I was down and couldn't raise my head up. So he'd feed me my rice. Well, I went along for a week or so, maybe ten days, and then he took a pencil and made this hole in this cover over my one good eye so I could see out. A couple of days later, he took it off. The first day after that, I just remarked to the guy next door to me that they had served more rice that day at mealtime. He said, 'No, the same amount.' I said, 'Yours may be the same amount, but mine is not.' He said, 'No, the guy who has been feeding you has been eating more of yours than he's been giving you.' I saw this guy later, and I remarked to him that he seemed to have gained a little weight. He just walked off. He was hungry, I guess. So was I. But prisoners would do anything to stay alive, to get a little bit more to eat, even to the point of taking it from their buddies. It comes back to that old business of self-survival."

PFC Bolitho (Davao Penal Colony) "The discipline was excellent. We had our own commanding officer of the camp. In our camp, he was a Navy commander. We had our own officers in each barracks. We had details assigned to us in each barracks. The officers generally had the good details. Also, it was almost an unwritten law that you didn't steal your friend's food ration. Now, if somebody came in from another barracks, he was watched closely. But in our own barracks, nothing was touched."

Cpl. Burlage (Palawan) "We kept rank. The Japs were fairly savvy, I would say, on this subject. They would take a group of two hundred enlisted men, and they usually tried to get about four officers with them. The senior officer would be responsible for everything within the walls, within the fence. Then he would take his other officers and give them responsibility. Then he would take his first sergeants or sergeants major and so on. We were always formed into companies; I guess you might call them that. There were fifty, maybe a hundred, people in each group, and they would get the senior NCO and put him in charge of the rest. We had the regular line of authority right down the line—just like the military. That's how you survived. Everybody couldn't go his own separate way."

Pvt. Armstrong (Bicycle Camp) "The officers initiated the policy of stopping formalities such as saluting. We still called them 'Lieutenant' or 'Captain' and we'd say 'Sir,' but the saluting had already stopped. We had all we could salute in the Jap deal of it."

PFC Visage (Surabaja) "Nobody respected our officers. Not a man respected them because they didn't tell us what was going on before we were captured. The officers were running around, dating and partying, and we had no supervision. The military discipline that came about in the prison camp was from our first sergeant, Farris Gilliam. He treated guys equally and did lots of favors for them. He would also stand up to the Dutch and argue with them about policy and about turning guys in."

PO2 Detre (Java) "Chief A. R. DeMoen was a real leader. He maintained order. A couple of arguments came up, but he had no problems whatsoever. Respect for the chief petty officer was there. We were professional sailors. If a second class petty officer told me I had to do something, I would do it. As far as we were concerned, we were still in the Navy and the chief was in charge."

PFC Robinson (Burma-Thailand Railway) "Lieutenant Roy Stensland was very helpful. He could cheat a Nip on a work detail with the Nip standing there watching him. He was the bull type. He was all man. He had a knack for getting along with the Nips, although he received many beatings when he stepped in to take the place of someone not as willing to accept them. On occasions he drank with the Nips and got away with it. That's something I don't recall any of the rest of us being able to do. I honestly never felt that there was any reason to have an officer guiding a work detail. Overall respect for officers decreased 80 percent. They were not participating physically in the building of the railroad and were not participating, when they should have been, in decisions being made."

Capt. Godbold (Woosung) "There was a chain of command in the prison camp with the Japanese dealing through the senior American officers, although this sometimes broke down, and there were direct relationships between some of the subordinate Japanese with some of the lower-ranking Americans in regard to issuing orders and so on.

But essentially the Japanese respected the chain of command. Of course, with the civilians you had a different situation; however, they did respect the position of the head man from Wake Island, Mr. [Dan] Teters, in regard to the civilians. So I think all in all the Japanese from this standpoint generally honored the military and civilian hierarchy, and I think wisely so. It made their system of control of prisoners a lot easier rather than dealing with each prisoner as an individual.

"Discipline was maintained essentially as you would maintain it if you had not been in prison. We worked through the noncommissioned officers, and if there were grave infringements of discipline, while we had no power to inflict punishment as such, there was a hearing held and records made with the understanding that this would be considered after the war insofar as the individual was concerned. And this generally worked pretty well. There were some minor problems. Some individuals felt that they were subject to Japanese discipline alone and took advantage of this or tried to, but generally this was taken care of by the views of their own contemporaries, and such individuals would soon come into line and say, 'Well, I will respect the decisions of my own people rather than the Japanese.' There were problems, but, essentially, this was handled in a generally satisfactory way."

M/Sgt. Stowers (Woosung) "Discipline was sort of second nature in the old Marine Corps. They looked to the old-timers—the sergeants and corporals—and they looked to them with respect for advice, and it was, I'd say, pretty good. If, for instance, I was senior noncom and you were a private and you didn't bathe, I'd say, 'You didn't take a bath tonight. If you don't get a bath, I'm going to put two men on you and scrub you down.' And he'd say, 'Yes, sir!' He'd go out there and bathe. Actually, I couldn't have enforced it, no way in the world. I had no backing, not even from the Japanese. I'd bluff them. I guess I could say I'd bring charges after the war, but they knew better than that. They weren't that dumb."

Cpl. Crews (Woosung) "We had our own system to deal with somebody that would steal. To give you an example, we had a young sailor off of Wake Island who got hungry and stole some food from one of his buddies. I can't remember this boy's name and wouldn't say it if I could because he was a good boy. But they stripped him and publicly whipped him, and there was no more stealing. That's the way we handled it. That's the only case of stealing I can remember."

PFC Venable (Woosung or Kiangwan) "There was never any question about it. Discipline was maintained by our own NCOs. Discipline was not nearly as rigid in civilian barracks, but the Marines maintained discipline throughout."

Pvt. Permenter (Woosung or Kiangwan) "I think for about the first year, as best I can recollect, they required us to salute our officers. Then it was knocked off, but we did continue to salute our colonel. We didn't salute the rest of the officers, but we did the colonel because we had respect for him."

PFC Garrison (Osaka) "We had our own discipline. When eighty of us got together, we'd stay clean. Nobody got out of line, because if somebody did, we'd straighten them up ourselves. We had certain rules. You didn't steal from anybody else, and you didn't take advantage of anybody else. It was just unwritten. This was a team. Things weren't very bad; we were all living pretty good."

Interrogation and Collaboration

Pvt. Guiles (San Fernando) "This is where the Japs started compiling rosters of the prisoners. I recall one instance when each morning they were calling in a certain group for interrogation. The morning they called me in, of course, the first thing they wanted was your name. Actually, my legal name is J. L., initials only, and the Japs couldn't understand that. They didn't accept initials as a name, and they beat the living daylights out of me, trying to get me to tell them my name. Well, that was my name. They sent me back to my quarters after working me over good with their fists. The second morning they called me in, and they used what I call their vitamin sticks [clubs] on me. The third morning they called me in, and by this time I had decided the night before that I'd had enough of that. So they called me in the third morning and were interrogating me and asked me my name, and I told them my name was John L."

Capt. Adair (Camp O'Donnell) "I never saw any collaboration—very definitely not. Not only there, but I never saw it anyplace that I was located. You never heard of anything like that."

Cpl. Koury (Cabanatuan) "To the best of my knowledge, there was no collaboration whatsoever. Of course, give the devil his due. I don't believe the Japs made any effort to encourage it. At least I didn't see any attempts. They definitely made no attempts to convert us to the Japanese cause."

Cpl. Read (Cabanatuan) "I always felt that we didn't have anything the Japanese wanted, really. They had the whole thing. I don't know of any way that our people could have helped them if they'd been inclined to, really. I don't think the Japs ever asked for help. They left us pretty well alone inside the camp, as long as the work details produced."

Pvt. Bugbee (Cabanatuan) "At that point collaboration would have meant nothing. They had everything in the Philippines, and we didn't know what was going on back in the States. We had no information on that, so we had nothing we could collaborate with them about. I don't know of anything that anybody would have had any information about, unless it would have been somebody who would go up and inform them about somebody who was going to try to escape or something like that."

Cpl. Halbrook (Corregidor) "We had our first contact with John David Provoo when we went down into Malinta Tunnel with wounded Japanese. Provoo was an American that was a traitor to the Americans. He was an American, but he was Japanese-hearted. At this time he was a cook for the Japanese, but he had been in our Intelligence Corps because he was a man who spoke Japanese fluently, had taught Japanese in Japan before the war. The minute the war was over, when the Americans surrendered, he shaved his head and got into a Japanese uniform and joined the Japanese Army. We hollered at him—who he was—and he would say something back such as, 'You bastards, you deserve what you got.' Anything the Japanese wanted, Provoo was getting.

"Provoo requested that an American Army captain, who had food for wounded soldiers in Malinta Tunnel, give him some sliced peaches for the Japanese one night for dessert. The captain told him to go blow it, that he wasn't giving him nothing. The captain was put on trial. All the conversation at the trial was between Provoo and the Japanese. The captain didn't say anything because he didn't know what they were talking about. A Japanese corporal drove the captain out to Monkey Point and shot him five times and killed him. Two Japanese soldiers helped me bury him the next day. After the war they spent a ton of money on a trial for Provoo. I was never called for the trial because my testimony conflicted with three other people. I couldn't identify any of the Japanese. Provoo was finally convicted in New York, but then he got out because of a mistrial."

PFC Bolitho (Davao Penal Colony) "You've heard of collaborators that they had in Vietnam. We had them over there, too. But we took care of them in camp. I mean, we didn't kill them, but they were beat up, they were harassed. These were individuals who were pretty selfish and only thought of themselves, regardless of what happened to their comrades. To benefit themselves, they did almost anything. When I say it was every man for himself, it was. But you were not going to rat on your friends or anybody—any American, let me put it that way."

Cpl. Burlage (Palawan) "There was only one time, one time only, when we had a collaborator. This man was an Army man, and he was not American-born. Can I mention his ethnic background? He was Jewish. He was born in Germany. He just didn't like to work, I guess. And he had written a note. I don't know where he got the pencil and paper, from an interpreter, I guess. He wrote a note to the commandant of the camp, saying that he was a German, and he believed in the Axis cause, and he would like to join the Jap Army. The American officer in charge of the camp was an American Marine, a captain who I had known for a long time, and we more or less chatted quite a bit. I remember I was talking to him this evening when we came in from work. In fact, my bunk space was right around the corner from where he had a little kind of office. But, anyway, we were out on the veranda talking, and this commandant and the interpreter walked up. The commandant gave this Marine captain the note, and through the interpreter he said, 'I got this from one of your men.' He said, 'I don't want it.' I remember what the interpreter said very well. He said, 'There you are. I don't want it. If that man is no good to you people, he would be no good for us, either.' That is the only case I've ever known. Well, this commandant asked the captain, 'What would you do with him?' And, of course, the captain hesitated, and he looked at me, and he said, 'What would you do?' And I said, 'I would hang him.' Then the captain said, 'We don't want him. To avoid trouble I think you should take him.' They took him away. As I understand it, they sent him back to Manila, where they had a prison for people like that."

Cpl. Crews (Woosung) "My answer to whether we had collaborators is that this was the old Marine Corps. It was a different breed. I think that breed of collaborators came on later. We were all volunteers. We were in the Marine Corps because we wanted to be. We knew what we had to face up to when we went in the Marines. Nobody told us we had to be a Marine, and we were proud of that. I don't think there was one Marine in the entire detachment that ever looked for a favor from the Japs."

Pvt. Permenter (Woosung) "We had people in there that were traitors. In fact, Mark Streeter had gotten a bad-conduct discharge from the Marine Corps before the war began, and he became one of the twenty most-wanted men in Japan. I wonder what happened to him. I wonder if they ever caught him or if they ever tried him. I never did hear. I know on the ship that picked us up after we got out, they put out a little ship's paper, and on the list of the most-wanted men he was the seventh one listed.

"Streeter didn't stay too long in Shanghai after he got there. See, Streeter was a civilian on Wake Island in defense work. Herman Wolfe, a sergeant in our outfit, the North China bunch, recognized Streeter after he'd been in camp there several months. Herman was a Jew from New York and a sergeant in the Marines. When Streeter got kicked out of the Corps, Wolfe was a prisoner chaser. When a person got kicked out, they gave him a suit of clothes and fifty dollars and carried them to the camp limits and kicked them out. That's how they treated them way back then. Herman was a prisoner chaser who guarded Streeter, carrying him to the camp limits. And at first he kept his mouth shut about it until Streeter started writing articles and stuff, especially against President Roosevelt. Then Wolfe told us that he was on to Streeter. But the articles kept getting worse, and so the Japanese took him and shipped him to Japan, and I understand that he went on the radio over there. He started making a lot of speeches against the United States. There were other collaborators, but I didn't know any of them, if they were in our bunch. We didn't have any, so far as I know."

Cpl. McDaniel (Woosung or Kiangwan) "I've seen civilian construction workers from Wake Island collaborate with the Japs, but not Marine personnel. They'd do anything to get favors. But anybody that had any authority or any knowledge, anything beneficial to offer the Japs, I don't think that type of person would collaborate with them."

PFC Venable (Woosung or Kiangwan) "Time has dimmed that, but we had some rat finks. I will always suspect one Marine that I prefer not to name, but I suspect that we had several in our camp who collaborated with the Japanese. A major from North China, he received far better treatment from the Japanese than he should have. Let me clarify that and say that he received far better treatment than our own major received. Therefore, the only thing that I would question is why. And I really don't know, but frankly he stood an enlisted Marine up at attention and hit him and broke his jaw. So this type of guy we could have done without!"

M/Sgt. Stowers (Kiangwan) "Ishihara was the interrogator and a very poor one. He says, 'Confess!' And we'd say, 'Confess to what?' 'You know what we want!' And we'd get another slapping and working over with the bullwhip he had. Then the sentries would work us over and kick us. We didn't know what to confess to. And we didn't. We didn't know anything except that swapping of letters with the Chinese government agent. Of course, that's sort of why Ishihara had started this thing. This sentry told him that he saw this agent giving us balls of rice. We didn't know this at first; we thought it was in connection with the letters.

"It lasted for hours. Each one of us was given the water treatment and tied down with wet towels over your nose and mouth, and they would pour water over the towel, and when you tried to breathe, you'd suck water. You'd choke and almost drown and were almost unconscious. Sometimes you would be unconscious, and they would revive you and say, 'Confess!' And we'd say, 'Confess to what?' And they never would say exactly what they wanted. Then they'd give you what we called the double lockup. They'd put you in the little room, and you sat naked and cross-legged on nothing but just concrete, like in a dog pen. Some of the guards would come in, you know, and they'd throw a bucket of cold water over you. Of course, this was freezing weather, and the water would form ice over you. It was pretty rough."

Sgt. Brodsky (Formosa) "They unloaded us in Formosa, and when we got over to the *Kempei-tai* [thought police], I told the guy in charge that we were American prisoners of the Japanese on a ship that was sunk by Americans, and I was picked up by the ship that delivered us here. They didn't want to believe that. They thought that we were American sailors off of a submarine that they had sunk and then were picked up. While we were being interrogated—we couldn't understand this guy very well—they blindfolded us when they brought us up there. Before blindfolding us, the guy pulled out his sword, and he put it on my neck. I honestly didn't think that he would do anything. I mean, I was telling him the truth. I didn't know anything else; I had been a prisoner all this time. There wasn't a damn thing I could tell him, except what I had already told him."

Capt. Bartlett (Tanagawa) "There was one American who was squealing on the boys—a stool pigeon. The Japs were always looking for contraband and things of that nature, and he'd tell them where to find it and who had it, and the boys would get in trouble. He didn't know that they suspected him, so they framed him. To prove it out, they let him see one of the boys hide some contraband, and then they went out to work. He squealed to this guard while on the way to work at the shipyards. The two boys who went with him were the only others who knew about this, and the three of them stayed together all the time out there. The first thing, that Jap guard went right up there and grabbed that contraband when they came back from work. The next day this guy went to work, and when work was over they found him where he had fallen off a scaffold and was dead."

Sgt. Fujita (Nagasaki) "I got thinking, hell, if I change my name to Joe Martinez or something, well, when they kill me they might have me listed as Joe Martinez, and then my folks would never know what happened to me. So I figured, hell, I was born with this name, and I might as well die with it. Well, this little guard was showing off how he could read English, so he was reading the roster. He'd go in and call attention and make everyone listen to him, and he'd go down the roster. . . . He came to my name and said, 'Oh, my God, what's this? This is Japanese!' He was excited. He told the officers of the camp, so they kept me off of work the next day. And the camp commander interviewed me and decided, well, he'd just make me his private servant. He assigned an English-speaking corporal to teach me Japanese during the day. And so I figured only one thing— nothing but trouble if I learned to speak Japanese. I figured my best bet was to not learn anything. I realized the corporal was in a hard position. They'd take him out, work him over because I wasn't learning Japanese. I guess he figured one day that if he's going to go down the drain on account of me, he's going to take me with him. So he got his cheese knife out, his samurai sword, and backed me up against the wall, and he started swinging this thing just as hard as he could and, boy, he was furiously mad. And, of course, I was as flat against that wall as I could get, and, boy, he'd come so close I even felt it once, you know, but I just felt the breeze of it every time. Just a little miscalculation and he'd split my throat open or cut my head off. And he was so mad. And this just went on like that, his threatening to kill me."

Sgt. Fujita (Japan) "There were twenty-five of us. They called us fellows out and told us that they were going to start some sort of radio program, and that we would all cooperate or our lives would not be guaranteed. Well, this was after two years in prison camp, and we already knew that they didn't usually talk too lightly. They weren't usually joking when they said they meant to kill you. Anyhow, they decided they'd have this radio program, just strictly a radio program. So I figured, 'Well, I could see where everyone else could fit into a radio program, but how in the hell are they going to use an artist on a radio program?' So they started everybody out, and they'd assign a topic, and everybody had to write on this topic. They said, 'If you will not cooperate, your life will not be guaranteed.' So everybody was writing sloppy, something like a first grader. Well, they knew that all of us were not that stupid. So by the time they worked us over two or three times, well, then they made their point, and people started writing. But I never could bring myself to do it because I'm not a writer to start with. And I didn't know what to write about, and what they wanted you to write on was politics. And politics hadn't entered my head at the tender age of twenty. It was the farthest thing from my mind.

"So I'd try to write something; I'd deliberately make it as bad as I could. I guess my ignorance had preceded me, too. 'Well, this stupid guy, this freak, can't even learn Japanese.' So that went over. They decided well, hell, they couldn't use me on the program so they made me the janitor, and I had to clean up the toilets. So I spent the rest of the war cleaning up the toilets.

"One of the guys who slept next to me and who was tried for treason later was John D. Provoo. It was found out right off the bat that he and one other guy [Mark Streeter] were very definitely traitors, and quite a stink was made of it. So when it looked like the war was about over, the Americans gained the command from the Australians, and then we placed this Provoo under guard. And this Streeter, a guy from Idaho, he was avidly for the program, and he was very vitriolic about America and called the American flag a dirty piece of rag, and he couldn't say too many bad things about President Roosevelt, you know. He was strictly a Japanese boy. Come to find out, that guy was a Communist. I didn't know anything about communism in

those days, but now after all these years, I can look back and see, but
in those days a Communist didn't mean anything to me."

Resistance and Sabotage

Cpl. Clem (Camp O'Donnell) "I had a Marine Corps ring that I
had had made out in China that I wore all the time except when the
Japanese were around. Then I kept it up my rectum the whole time
the Japanese were around. I eventually lost it, but I was able to keep
it for about two and a half years."

Cpl. Halbrook (Clark Field) "The Japs didn't know anything about
driving, and they didn't know anything about mechanic's work. As
long as you acted natural, you could just tear the hell out of anything.
If you started looking over your shoulder, acting like something you
were doing was wrong, that's when you got in trouble. We'd take
sugar and fill up the gas tanks, but it wouldn't do a damn thing to the
engine. We pulled wiring loose underneath the dash. If a cylinder
was missing, we just pulled all the sparkplug wires off it and turned
them around and screwed it up a bit.

"In the Japanese hangars at Clark Field, they had welding shops.
They had so many explosions out there they'd have the Americans
go over to show the Japanese how to hook up the oxygen tanks. They
wore these greasy, old leather gloves. We'd tell them to always wipe
the threads off of that damn oxygen bottle with their greasy gloves
before screwing her down. And just as soon as he wiped her down
and screwed her up real tight and he'd turn her on, why, you'd just
lose your Jap because it would blow him up! The Japs thought it was
just bad equipment, and we'd go along with them—stupid American
equipment that's not any good."

PFC R. Allen (Davao Penal Colony) "There wasn't much sabotage in the penal colony. There wasn't anything that we could destroy. But we had electricians that the Japs would have do different
things. One day this truck pulled up and stopped, and this electrician
was up on a pole. The lines weren't over ten foot off the ground, and
he's working right in the middle of the poles, more or less, with the
trucks underneath. There was a truck full of soldiers. They had metal
beds and metal seats and everything. So this boy on the pole thought,
well, it'd be funny if the electric line were to drop across that truck.

And that idiot cut the wire and let it go. Now you talk about a bunch of Japs that were doing some dancing—they were doing some dancing. It wasn't strong enough to kill them, but it was strong enough that they couldn't get loose from it, and they sat there squalling and hollering.

"That's just one incident that happened. If the boys got a chance in any way, shape, form, or fashion, they did others. I knew some boy putting out poison in the garden. We knew he was, because he sprinkled some on his own food and liked to died. It tasted sort of like peanut butter. So he thought it'd be real funny to put this in the Japs' food. He carried a little ol' bottle of that stuff for almost eight months. They'd take boys to work around the Jap kitchen—wood detail, cutting wood, and what have you. Well, he carried some of that stuff over, and he poured it on their food. He should've known better, because they knew that stuff wasn't just going to jump into their food. The boys that were on that detail that day—you talk about getting a whipping. They really got whipped, and if they're alive today they're carrying marks of that whipping. It's a wonder they hadn't shot all of us."

Cpl. Burlage (Palawan) "A boat would come in down there at three- or four- month intervals, and they got us down there and worked us from early in the morning until way into the night getting this boat unloaded. The Japs wouldn't get on the ship because the ship was too darn hot. They wouldn't get down in the holds. So we got down in this hold, and we found several cases of beer, San Miguel beer, made in Manila. Well, we changed shifts about every thirty minutes, and we arranged it so everybody could get a beer. We would take the beer and drink it, put the cap back on it, and put it back in the cases. The darn Jap in charge was out in the shade of a palm tree, and we finally loaded the beer on the truck, but by now they were all empty. We loaded the truck, and the old Jap was happy and said, 'Ah, Japanese, we have party!' He could speak a little English, and he was telling us about what he was going to do. You know, 'Americans nothing.' Well, some of us were feeling pretty good by that time. There was a school building where the Japs had their barracks, where they lived. So that night they got over there, and they decorated the place, and they had a little extra food, and they got in there and started a little singing and dancing with each other and everything else—waiting for the beer to come. Finally, the beer came, and there wasn't a drop left. That's one time we actually got the upper hand on them. They never

did think we took it. They thought someone had made a mistake somewhere else."

PO2 Detre (Burma-Thailand Railway) "Many times we'd pull
things that we thought would sabotage the bridges. The bridges were
held together with long staples made out of reinforcing rods. Sometimes we wouldn't drive them in, or we'd leave one out. This was
about all you could do because the Japs worked right with you doing
the mortising."

PFC Sparkman (Woosung) "We had a detail over at a garage not
far from the camp where they worked on trucks for the Shanghai
area. I guess it was their motor pool. And the guys there would put
shavings or anything else that they could in their motors and leave
batteries out and everything like that."

Pvt. Benton (Kiangwan) "Before we worked on the 'Mount
Fujiyama' project [a rifle-range abutment] we had a detail that worked
in a garage. This is where we did a lot of sabotage. We'd take the
wrenches and put cheaters on them and break them. A wrench handle
will take so much pressure, and we'd put a piece of pipe on the end
of it, and, well, you could get a whole lot more pressure on the wrench
than it would stand. When you put the cheaters on there, you'd just
pop the handle, break it. They finally got wise to us and quit letting
us use the wrenches. Or, the guys would take a truck and overhaul it.
It would be in A-1 condition, but they'd take valve-grinding compound and put it on top of a cylinder and put the head on. Man, it'd
run like a top. But in about three days the Japs dragged it back in
there with the motor burned out. We did little things like that.

"After Mount Fuji I went to work in the foundry. We'd have to
get up on top of that old furnace and throw scrap iron in there. Man,
that was hot work working on the old blast furnace. It gets to be 100
to 150 degrees up there. Well, we'd get the scrap all melted down,
and then we'd have molds. We were pouring mostly pistons. We'd
get our molds all set up, and just before we'd start pouring, we'd
throw a little rock or something in it. Then we'd pour the pistons and
take them out, and you'd always have a bubble. Well, then they'd
have to scrap them. We did hundreds of them that way—little sabotage—and they never did really get wise to us. We always wondered,
but they never did get wise to us.

"Later, the Japs were getting desperate for gasoline, and they
started burning a lot of alcohol in their trucks. We were on this detail
at this racetrack to dig holes and take fifty-five-gallon drums of alco-

hol and bury them there, and cover them over with grass. Now in the burying detail, we would get a little nail or a piece of metal and before we'd turn a barrel up, we'd stick a hole in it. We'd fill our own bottle with alcohol. Then we'd turn the barrels upside down. Then the alcohol would gradually run out—leak out. There's no telling how many thousands of gallons of that alcohol ran out on the ground because we buried thousands of barrels of that stuff in these fifty-five-gallon drums. We were big saboteurs. Also, we'd bring that alcohol in and swap it for rice and cigarettes. We got to be the biggest bootleggers in Shanghai, the Al Capones of Shanghai."

Cpl. Minshew (Nagasaki) "There was very little opportunity to sabotage in the dry dock, but once the ship was out on the water, I shot ten thousand caulking tools over the side. The boys who were riveting out over the water were shooting those riveting hammers, the hammerhead itself, into the water, too. They'd always go to work with several and turn in their gun that night. The Japanese didn't clamp down on this for a long time. Then they started issuing each POW three caulking tools, and when you checked in, you had to check in three tools."

PFC Visage (Nagasaki) "We managed to get to their dynamos that served all their electricity in the shipyard, and we put drill shavings in it. It would flash out the whole electricity. We caused a fire in the boiler shop by running the boiler up way past the danger point and backing off, unbeknown to the Japanese, and letting the thing explode. It exploded all this creosote and caught the hoses on fire there."

PFC Garrison (Osaka) "We started unloading this bauxite, and we had to go through this warehouse, and there was some great big crates with monstrous beakers like a chemistry lab would use. Right on the bottom of these things there was a mercury-filled bulb. Most of us didn't have any idea what it was, but we had a radioman who told us that they were used in radios. He said the best thing for us to do was when we went by with a load of bauxite to reach out and knock the tit off one of those things, and all the mercury would run out.

"Of course, mercury was priceless at that time, I guess. We hadn't been working there two hours, and this mercury was under the dirt. You couldn't see it was there, but the first thing you know, it was splashing. You're just walking along, and mercury was splashing everywhere! The Japanese begin to get inquisitive: 'What's going on here?' Of course, none of us knew anything. But we ruined a lot of beakers for them that day.

"Another time we were transferring some Standard Oil aviation oil in barrels from a warehouse, and they started stacks of it on the ground. Then when they got it so far, they put runners up, and you would roll the barrels up and put on a second layer. Well, every once in a while we would see one of these bungs that had a ring of wet oil in it. It would be a little loose. You could unscrew it with your hand. Well, we unscrewed it to where just one thread was holding it, and we would roll the barrel upon this second layer and bump it against the next barrel pretty hard, and every time the bung would come out. But we would do it so the bung was on the inside where they couldn't see the oil running out. The area of barrels was monstrous. It must have been a block or two long and half a block wide on the bottom row. Well, it took a long time for this oil to run out. The next day there was oil everywhere. Of course, they couldn't figure out who did it, who was on the detail. This is how lax they were at the beginning."

Chapter III

Atrocities

The horrors recounted here are distinguished by their enormity from other dreadful conditions described by the interviewees. Certainly, the starvation diets and other specifics of mistreatment and punishment were abominable and could be included as atrocities. This inclusion, however, would detract from the premeditated, vicious, and inhuman acts that took place on the Death Ships and during the Death Marches, to name only two examples of mass hypercruelty. The depth of depravity that Japanese officers and men plumbed in their treatment not only of the prisoners of Bataan or on the Death Ships but also of those at Palawan (where 141 Americans were massacred), in the jungles of Burma (where 19 percent of the Lost Battalion died), or elsewhere in the Orient was without limits.

Joan and Clay Blair in *Return from the River Kwai* describe the sinking of the *Kachidoki Maru* and *Rokyu Maru*, two Japanese transports carrying Allied prisoners to Japan in late 1944 that were attacked by U.S. Navy submarines. All of the men who traveled in the overcrowded Death Ships suffered from hunger, thirst, and lack of sanitation. Death was a companion for them, but even more so when submarines torpedoed their vessels. As the men tried to escape the sinking ships, Japanese sailors fired on them or threw hand grenades at them. If the survivors were lucky enough to make it into the sea, Japanese boats raked them with machine-gun fire.

In explaining the causes of the Bataan Death March, Donald Knox cites three faulty assumptions that the Japanese made in their plan for evacuating the peninsula: 1) they thought that the captives would be in good physical condition; 2) they allowed insufficient time to work out details of the evacuation; and 3) they underestimated by one half the number of American troops that finally were moved.[1]

---

[1]Knox, *Death March*, 118–19.

Nevertheless, the raw brutality exhibited by Japanese soldiers is incomprehensible and can only be explained by the existence of evil.

Secretary of State Cordell Hull, in responding to news of the Death March, said that it would "be necessary to summon, to assemble together, all the demons available from anywhere and combine the fiendishness which all of them embody to describe the conduct of those who inflicted these unthinkable tortures on Americans and Filipinos."[2] According to Stanley L. Falk, between 600 to 650 Americans and 5,000 to 10,000 Filipinos died or were killed.[3]

In a halting manner some of these Americans, who endured the unendurable, relate their experiences years later. Many admit that they could not have told their stories during the first decades after the war. These men, who smelled, tasted, and saw death, survived. Perhaps their survival, mixed with a sense of guilt that assuredly was not theirs, makes their voices falter. Whatever the case, their memories remain vivid.

Death Marches

Pvt. Stanley (Bataan Death March, 1942) "I can remember some of the details of the march, but I can't pinpoint those towns. This first day on the march we got pretty thirsty, and the only thing that kept me going for a while was that I had a little bottle of iodine in the Air Corps coveralls I had on. The Japs had missed that iodine. They didn't want us to have any water, but after it got so hot we would come across all these ditches that were bloody with dead carabao and Americans. The water was not fit to drink, but I would get a little water with my canteen cup and put a little iodine in there. That's what kept me from losing my head and getting a drink of water and getting myself killed. I do not know how I was smart enough to do that, but I just happened to have that little bottle of iodine about the size of your thumb, and I would put a drop of iodine in that water, and I guess it purified it. Of course, I had several attacks of malaria on that trip, and that was what I was afraid of—going out of my head while I was having an attack of malaria.

---

[2]Falk, *Bataan*, 197–98.
[3]Ibid., 209.

"What I saw that was worse than anything was after we got so thirsty. All along this road where we marched was good artesian wells setting on the right. After you got so thirsty, your tongue was so dry, and you would almost give your life for a sip of water. The Japanese were standing around there, and the Americans—some of them— would lose control of themselves and run up there and get a drink of water, and the Japs would stab them. We had men laying around those wells. At almost every well you'd see a few dead Americans laying around them.

"I never was hit seriously during the Death March. I did, however, get slapped across the head. One time I was marching along there, and I met one of these Jap trucks going in the opposite direction, and one of these guys hit me so hard that it knocked me down. Every once in a while two or three Japs would come along and just start swinging and hitting everything. I got hit several times that way, but none ever threw a bayonet at me or shot at me. Like I say, I was little and I maneuvered around and tried to stay behind somebody. I don't know whether I was a coward or not, but, anyway, I was trying to stay out of the line of fire."

Cpl. Read (Bataan Death March, 1942) "If I had to guess, I'd say we started out with two thousand men in a column. Then they formed us up in columns of fours, and we marched down the left side of an asphalt highway; and on the right side there were Jap troops pouring down the highway on the right of us as we went. There was Jap cavalry, horses, tanks, and artillery, and they were all going down to the beach and setting up for Corregidor. It was very common for these Japs to take swipes at you or try to hit you as they went past. It didn't take me long to wise up on that score. Whenever we would stop for a break, I always jumped up and saw to it that I was on the inside column when they reformed the four columns. The guys on the outside got clobbered. As these cavalry people rode by, they would sometimes whop you over the head with a rifle butt or anything like that.

"There was another reason why I tried to get on the inside ranks everywhere I could. That's because I had a better chance of getting water. Water throughout the Death March was a problem. It was dry and it was hot, and I was always thirsty. Officially, they never at any time while you were marching allowed you to leave ranks to refill your canteen or get any water. Some who tried it were shot; some were bayoneted. I broke ranks myself occasionally and made a dive for a stream of water trickling over a bluff in the road and tried to fill my canteen. The Japanese guards, if they saw you, would kneel down in the road and shoot at you. They weren't the best shots in the world. I got shot at several times and never got hit, but it was a risk you had to take because you were starving for water.

"We had other problems, too. Keep in mind that some people had dysentery and malaria, and the hot sun wasn't so kind to people who had malaria, especially, and these guys were constantly dropping out. Other people would try to hold them up and keep them going, but when they did drop out, the Japs would bayonet them or shoot them or just not bother with them. Now, I am aware that some rode in trucks, but I never personally saw over a half-dozen trucks the whole time I was on the march, and I was on the march a long time.

"I would like to clarify a point because many people think that the Death March was a great distance made in a short time. But it was not. I don't know how far it was, but I have always figured it was about seventy miles at the most. I was on the march for the better part of a week, and the actual rigors of actually walking on this march were absolutely nothing—absolutely nothing. The fact is I was on this march for ten or eleven days, but some of this time was spent in holding camps for two or three days at a time. Most of the walking was for short distances. The Japs themselves didn't want to walk in the heat of the day, so it wasn't so much that they didn't want us to walk in the heat of the day as it was that they didn't want to walk in the heat of the day! They changed guard shifts every few miles, but even so they would march us into a rice paddy or an open field, and they would make us sit down in ranks and stay there through the heat of the day. Then, in the evening, we would move out and march a few miles. And that's why it took so long.

"But the really tough part of it, aside from not having anything to eat, was having to sit in ranks all through the heat of the day, right in the sun, and having no water. They had guards all around you, and periodically, every three or four hours, they might let you line up and get some water from a hydrant and fill your canteen. Sometimes they did, and sometimes they didn't. Sometimes there was none.

"Off to the side of the road we often saw beheaded Filipinos. You know, the Japs were great about chopping off people's heads, and all the noncoms carried these two-handed swords, and they were allowed to use them. Everywhere you looked almost, you would see some-body who had their head cut off. We were pretty much used to it after a while. It was the same way with the filth. You don't think too much about it after a while, and, for that matter, I could say the same thing about food. After a while you just get used to it; you don't have pain or hunger or anything.

"In the early stages of the march, it was still pretty much everybody looking out for everybody else as best you could. If a guy was stumbling and acting like he was going to fall out, you would grab him and try to hold him up and march him until the column stopped. This was very common, but you couldn't always do it. Then what happened was that as some of these guys fell back in the ranks, they were just passed along back through until they came to the end. Nobody could hold them any longer, and they fell out. I am quite sure that some guys were sustained that way until they were able to come to a stopping point and rest and sit. I have no doubt about that.

"There were civilians along the way looking at us, you know, observing us, but they pretty much stayed out of sight because I think they were afraid of what might happen to them at that point. Later on down the march, beyond Balanga, there were a lot of civilians along the way, but I found none of them to be helpful. They were trying to sell stuff to the prisoners, but unfortunately most of us had had our money taken away. I never had any Filipino offer me food or anything along the march; they were trying to sell it. Now, later on there were occasions when the Filipinos gave us food, but that was after the march was over, when the cattle-car part of the thing to O'Donnell had started.

"I don't know why they wouldn't allow the prisoners to get water. I think it was just a matter of organization. They were afraid they would lose control if they let us all dive out into these streams and wallows that we passed. If they had done it in an organized manner, it would have taken all day for a couple of thousand people to go and fill their canteens. I am sure they felt like they would lose control with the number of guards they had and so forth.

"I remember one stop at Lubao that was the worst. There were more Japs there that were picking people out and taking them across the road and bayoneting them. I had a little brush with this kind of thing there, and I guess that's why I thought it was so bad there. I was standing in the water hydrant line—they had a single water hydrant in this whole thing—and the line was so long that you couldn't see where the end was. Maybe you'd stay in line six to eight hours to work your way up to it. I must have been about a dozen people away from the hydrant when a Jap officer—he looked like the cartoon prototype—came up and put his hand on the fellow right in front of me and pulled him out of line. Well, this Jap officer called some guards over, and they took him across the road where they proceeded to bayonet him. Just like that! Then they picked up his body and carried it over to a clump of bamboo and slung it in there. Just as I got to the hydrant, a Jap soldier jostled me out of the way and washed the blood off their bayonets under the hydrant. So that's how close I was to that specific incident, and that was a kind of horrifying thing to me, and maybe that's why I think Lubao is so bad.

"I would like to interject something here. I take some exception to [Stanley] Falk's book about the Bataan Death March and the Japanese being unprepared. He held, I think, that they simply didn't have the food to feed these people. At least three times on this march, at various places, right by the road, we passed dumps of U.S. Army canned goods that were maybe a city block square and like a hundred feet high—nothing but case after case of miscellaneous canned goods. At least three times we saw dumps like that right beside the road, and they had Jap guards standing on top of them. The Japs themselves didn't have any interest in that particular type of food, actually, at that point. There was an enormous amount of food, and when we passed by that stuff we were really slobbering when we saw that stuff. It always occurred to me that if they were really interested in feeding us, they could have cut some of this stuff loose."

Pvt. Blaylock (Bataan Death March, 1942) "We sat around at Mariveles for three days, and then we started marching. This is where the Bataan Death March started. Well, it was a living nightmare. You had no water, no food. If you dropped to the ground, and you weren't on your feet by the time the Japs got there, they shot you or stuck a bayonet in you. I called them the Clean-up Squad because every so many yards behind the Americans there were two, three, or four Japanese guards, and anybody on the ground by the time they got there was a dead man. I helped one or two men on the march in five or six days, however long we marched at one time or another, and I was helped some. But if an American was down, and you were trying to pick him up, help him up, you might get shot, too.

"Their trucks were coming in the opposite direction going toward Corregidor, and if there was a dead body on the road and in their way, the truck just ran over it. And the Japs would reach out and try to bash our heads in. I don't remember how many killings I did witness. I didn't actually witness a Jap chopping off a head, but I did see the results once.

"One of the things that the Japanese did on this march was to show off the Americans in front of the local Filipino population. I guess they did it to show that they were the superior race. There was nothing that delighted a short Jap more than to reach up and slap a tall, skinny American who was about a foot or two taller than him in front of a Filipino. It was humiliating.

"I was just craving food. We had been cut down to one meal before the Bataan Peninsula fell. No matter where you stopped on the march and in prison camp, you always ended up talking about food in any conversation.

"Each day we'd march, and when we stopped, we just fell out by the side of the road, usually in a predesignated area. And, boy, we just piled down! You used the latrine wherever and whenever you could. When we got up, there would always be a few still there who had died. I guess most of them died from sheer exhaustion or from dysentery or malaria."

Pvt. Burns (Bataan Death March, 1942) "I would say there were about one thousand or fifteen hundred or something like that when we started the Death March. After so long guys were carrying only what they could. I had a few extra things like a bedroll and a blanket and a pillow, but it didn't take long until I abandoned it. The only things I ended up carrying was my mess kit and my two canteens. That is what I wound up with. As far as I can remember, I had my two canteens full when I started.

"It was fairly hot, but, really, I didn't pay a whole lot of attention to that. This being April, it was the hot part of the season in the Philippines. It was more or less a dirt road that we were marching on.

"There weren't any organized guards with us at this particular time, and that's how I wound up with some medics that were in our outfit. I guess there were about eight of us, and they gave me an armband that the medics wore. So I stayed with them, and we were more or less just following the marching. There really weren't any guards with us at this particular time.

"As we were laying down at night at these various places, you had to sleep with your shoes under your head, if you had any shoes, because at night the Japanese would sneak through there and steal your shoes or anything they thought was of value. A lot of guys lost their shoes that way, or they'd take mess kits or watches or anything like that.

"The next day we started out, and we started marching. I would say it was around 10:00 in the morning. They divided us into groups of a hundred men, and you had a column of four across and twenty-five deep. There was one guard assigned to each group. You might have four or five columns, and you'd have the first Jap at the head of the first group and another at the head of the second group, and so forth. They were supposed to march us twenty-five miles, so that night we stopped and were herded into another area.

"The next day we started out again, and we had a new guard. It just so happened that we got a good guard that day, and he was one of the biggest Japs I have ever seen. So my group was pretty fortunate because this guard told us we could break ranks whenever we came to one of these artesian wells that might be off the road a little ways and get some water. So the word was passed back. He said that we could not fill our canteens because the holes were too small and it would take too long to fill them, but we could take our canteen cup and get water. The other guards didn't bother our guard, and whatever he wanted to do was his business. I do remember that I was in the fourth column from the front, and I do remember this Jap guard pulling a couple of guys out by the shirt because they didn't go and get water. He made them get water. So what we'd do, before we came to a well we'd run out of the column, and by the time the column got abreast of the well, why, we were back in line.

"On the third day I saw my first atrocity. Again, we had a new set of guards. This particular day one of the fellows had to go to the bathroom—let's put it that way—because he had dysentery. The guy tried to do what was right, so he fell out and went over to the guard and asked for permission to go off the side of the road. I guess the guard didn't understand him or thought he was trying to escape. Anyway, the guy didn't make himself clear, and he was so weak he could hardly stand up. They scuffled a bit, and the guy almost got up to his knees, and the Jap scuffled with him again, and this went on about three times. He was trying to explain to the guard what he wanted to do, and the guard didn't know or didn't want to know. About the third time, he got halfway up to his knees, and the Jap shot him right through the heart. Like I said, each guard had a different disposition."

Cpl. Koury (Bataan Death March, 1942) "At Mariveles they had these big open areas where the troops were, and we just went there and sat down. Then they took you out in numbers, and you started up the road. Our group had several hundred people in it, and I think we were all fairly healthy. We went from Mariveles to Cabcaben to Limay to Balanga, and we made that portion in one day without too much strain. This is where they started trying to get our attention—that we were prisoners of war and that they were God's children. You kept going, and you didn't stop, and you didn't go to the bathroom, and you didn't do anything, or they would knock you on the head or stick you with a saber or shoot you or whatever. There was no hanky-panky at all. We didn't have any water because they had taken our canteens and made us drop everything before we ever started. It was awfully hot and humid. I only had an overseas cap to protect me from the sun, but that was absolutely useless. As I say, most of our group made it without any problem, but we were all hot and tired and thirsty.

"I'd say there was one guard for every hundred guys, maybe, and every one of them was mean and unhappy. There were several people who were shot, guys who would break the rules or do something they weren't supposed to do. They would see a stream or a pump or an artesian well, which were plentiful in that country; and if a guy had been walking for four or five hours, he gets thirsty and sees an artesian well, and he thinks, 'My God, I'll get a drink of water!' Well, they would shoot him because they told him not to do this. Who is to say they were wrong? I can't criticize the Japs too severely for it. I think they should have let us have that water, but, on the other hand, they told me not to drink that water, so I wasn't going to drink it. I never saw anybody shot, beaten, or stabbed unless they did something that was against what we had already been told not to do. I did see a friend of mine get bayoneted after first being shot that first day. He took some food from a native alongside the road and sat down; and the Jap guard walked up to him and hit him beside the head with his rifle and then shot him and then stabbed him.

"When we got to Balanga, they herded us into this pen. They wouldn't let us sit down, and then they said they were going to turn on the water for so many minutes. I think there was one spigot, and I know I didn't get any water. This was one of the most serious parts of the march—not getting water. At this time everybody starts to thinking, 'Well, the next day we've got to do something. We can't go on like this, for God knows how far we've got to walk.' It could've gone on for weeks, so a bunch of us started talking that night: 'Well, there aren't that many guards, and there are quite a few of us, and let's just take this thing over.' The next day the guards were probably doubled or tripled over what it had been the first day. I don't think they heard us talking or anything, so I think it was just one of those things that happened.

"On the second day, I did see some acts of compassion because some of the guys who fell down were picked up by the Japs and taken to prison camp in trucks. I also saw an interpreter pull an American into the shade and kind of prop him up and wipe his brow off and everything. Then there were some who for no rhyme or reason were killed. It all depended on who the guard was, I guess. I don't know."

Pvt. Guiles (Bataan Death March, 1942) "I believe there were about a hundred of us when we started the march from Mariveles to Balanga. This part of the march wasn't too bad, except that the Americans on Corregidor were firing over our heads. This artillery fire was quite frightening because you could hear them as well as see them, and not knowing where the shells were going to hit was scary. I guess the Japs didn't figure that the Americans would fire at them as long as they were marching us.

"As I said, this part of the march was not too bad because we were still being guarded by combat troops. Of course, we had no water, no food, nothing. In terms of gear, I had a blanket, and I believe I still had my mess kit, and that was it. I had no hat to protect myself from the extremely intense sun. They would march us for a distance, and then they would gather us all into a compact group for a rest period, as they called it. I think that the group I was in had eight guards.

"There wasn't too much suffering on this part of the trip. I'm speaking for me personally and the ones around me because we still had the strength to go on. I do remember that there were some wells along in here, but you still didn't dare get a drink of water. But once in a while you passed one of these cane fields, and you'd jump off to the side of the road and grab a stalk of cane. After so long you'd take those kind of chances. Nevertheless, after a few hours in that broiling sun and marching with no food or water, then it began to work on us pretty fast.

"We left Balanga the next morning, and that's when the brutality began to increase—that's where it really started. They really began to put it on us from here to Orani. I think what really made it tougher on us was the fact that we were out of water, we'd had no food to speak of, and our strength was gone. You'd walk along or stagger along while trying to carry one of your buddies, or helping to carry him and so on, so we just began to deteriorate. I mean, our strength was waning, and the Japs took every advantage of it. If you staggered or fell, that was it. If you weren't able to go on or your buddies weren't able to, there was no survival. They would shoot you or bayonet you, and I witnessed this more than once.

"One time I even saw a beheading at one of the wells that we passed. We had been advised to stay in formation and keep moving, and this fellow left formation. He'd just gone as far as he could without water, he thought, and he left formation. Of course, the guards were marching with fixed bayonets at all times, and then the officers had these two-handed sabers. So when this guy went over to get a drink at the well, he lost his head. I mean, those sabers were sharp enough to chop down a fence post, so with one swish that was it for this ol' boy.

"There were many guys who couldn't go on and on, and, like I say, at that time we were losing our strength so fast. We'd carry them as far as we could, and then it was a matter of self-survival. Once you hesitated or went down, that was it if you couldn't get back on your feet. I did not see one act of compassion on the part of the guards at any point along the way. Like I say, I only witnessed that one decapitation, but I saw the results of many more along the way.

"On the third day, we marched from Orani to Lubao, and things got worse by the hour. By this time it was a matter of every man on his own. Like I say, we started trying to help the men who couldn't make it on their own, but by the third day our energy was so depleted that we were lucky to stay on our feet and keep going. The larger individuals seemed to suffer the most because they had so much weight to carry. And it seemed like the Japs just relished picking on the big boys. For instance, if a big man and a small man were both caught doing the same thing at the same time, the small man could get away with it, but the big man couldn't. Most of the time, neither got away with it, but they just seemed to get more enjoyment out of whipping a big man. Also, although they were changing guards periodically by this time, I think they were getting tired, too, and the more tired they got the more they took it out on the prisoners. During this phase of the march, I had three fingers on one hand broken with what we called a vitamin stick [club] because I attempted to get a drink of water. In one way I was fortunate that the guard stopped me before I had an opportunity to go any further, but I was rapped on the back of the hand, and it broke three fingers.

"Now, I cannot remember the march on the fourth day from Lubao to San Fernando, where we picked up the train. I think that by this time I was kind of numb. All this brutality going on around me was pretty hard to comprehend. Meanwhile, when somebody fell, you just kept your eyes straight ahead and kept on marching. You went right on; you went straight ahead."

Lt. Burris (Bataan Death March, 1942) "We were in a column about three or four men wide. There were a few guards on each side of us and ahead of us and behind us, and we changed guards every so often. We just kept going. Some nights we walked all night with a few stops for a guard change. It was a stony road, real rough, dusty. The guards were not as bad as later on, but they were bad enough. They wouldn't let us get any water; they wouldn't let us have anything to eat. They'd set us out in the sun when it was hot in the daytime, and they'd keep us going into the night. I remember that the road had a lot of flat stones on it, and at night it would get cold, and when we'd fall out I'd lay down on these rocks because the heat that was coming up made them warm and comfortable. I just fit right into these rocks and went to sleep, even though maybe I'd be there no more than twenty or thirty minutes and then they'd get us up and get us going again.

"I ran through a gauntlet. They had a row of Japanese soldiers one night, and they were hitting us with the butts of their guns and long clubs. We had to go through that. Everybody who had to go through it would run, and I did, too. I ran. I tried to lean forward or bend over to avoid the clubs as I was running. I had some hits on the back of my head, but the full force was glancing on the top of my head and went down and hit me on the shoulders or upper back. I remember getting water once, but we never had anything to eat from the day we surrendered until the fifth or sixth day, whenever we reached San Fernando. And I was tired. Boy, was I tired! As soon as they said it was the end of the march, I just lay down and went to sleep. It didn't take me but two seconds to lay down, and once I lay down, in two or three seconds I was sound asleep. I was wore out."

Pvt. Wisecup (in transit, Ban Pong to Hintok, 1943) "We walked, I think, for ten days. We didn't lose as many men as they did in the

Bataan Death March, but what we lost on the railroad made that death march look like a picnic. I'll tell you what was bad about our march— not with the Americans but with all the others. Most of the Limeys and other guys were culls; they were sick people. We lost quite a few going up, and the Japs just left them in the jungle. We walked ninety-six miles. What made it hard was that you had to carry a lot of gear. We carried tents, which we shouldn't have brought, because the bastards leaked like sieves. We were carrying them and all the cooking gear and all kinds of shit. Plus, some of the guys carried a whole gang of gear that they discarded on the way.

"What we did was march at night because it was so hot. We'd march all night until daybreak. We'd take breaks about every hour, I think, for maybe five minutes. The guards kept you going. The guys in the rear were kicked and punched and beat. If someone couldn't make it, if he had to fall out, that was that. You just left them there. I don't know how many we left. I couldn't give you an accurate figure, but we must have lost quite a few. But we didn't lose any Americans, although some of them got sick en route. The hell of it was that when we got to the goddamned place, Hintok, we didn't even get a day's rest to put up a camp. We went right to work, and it started raining the day we got there!"

Death Ships

Capt. Bartlett (in transit, Manila to Japan, 1942) "I was in Cabanatuan for about four months, so I was in the first group they started shipping to Japan. I was philosophical when I heard the news because to my own mind I was already dead. I had no sadness about leaving, since there were still around thirty a day who were dying, but there wasn't any enjoyment in leaving, either. After you go through this stuff for a while, you just don't give a damn anymore.

"We were packed in boxcars like sardines and taken to the Manila docks. There we were loaded aboard a ship which we named the *Maggota Maru*. We were put in the bottom of the hold. There was planking there, and as you were laying down you could hear the bilge water sloshing just below you. We were packed in there so tight that there were two men in a space about eight inches wide and seven feet long. I know you could just lay down straight, and there would be room for a man to sit down at your feet. We slept in relays.

"There were two washtubs for the men with dysentery. I understand that there were eight hundred men in that hold, and there was always a waiting line to get to these tubs. When the tub would get full, the next two men in line would pack it up the ladders and dump it over the side and bring it back down.

"The rice came down in a big bucket. It wasn't full by any means, about a third full, and that would be for about twenty men on a platform. One of the boys divided it out. You had to go up on the open deck to get water. There were so many who were allowed to go up at one time; I think it was four or five at a time.

"It took us six weeks to get to Japan. We went slowly, and this ship was a junk pile to start with. I would say we lost 25 percent of the men on this trip, mainly due to starvation and disease."

Pvt. Guiles (in transit, Manila to Japan, 1943) "They put us on an old ship that had been used to haul cattle—flat-bottomed. It was hard for me to realize that the war had gone on this long, and then for me to be moving to Japan, just that much farther away from the American return, I just couldn't hardly comprehend it.

"It was a sixty-two-day trip, and it was holy hell! They herded us into the hold, which was an area approximately sixty by one hundred feet, and there again we were packed in just like sardines. We were made to kneel, and your knees were in somebody else's back, and somebody else's knees were in your back. Of course, the conditions since the day we were captured were awful, but they were heaven on earth compared to what we were to experience during the next few days. There were no sanitary facilities whatsoever. You cannot imagine or comprehend what it's like for approximately 250 men to be crowded into an area this small. You get seasick; the dysentery is rampant; there's no food, no water, no fresh air whatsoever. It's just about as bad as it can get. In fact, for the first day or two, they didn't even open the hatch. The only air that got to us came through the cracks and so on. We were never allowed to go topside.

"There was complete chaos down in the hold. If somebody had some water, he was fair game for someone else who was desperate enough to take it from him. I remember two prisoners who were twins, and one of them was actually killed by one of our own men for that very thing, a canteen of water. At night you could hear men stalking around in this hold and shaking canteens of other prisoners to see if there was any water in them. On one occasion the Japs lowered a bucket of salt water and said that it was for bathing, knowing full well that everybody was going to drink that water.

"Every morning we had to get rid of the men who had died during the night. We'd pick them up and just over our heads would pass them down below the hatch opening. Then they'd slip a rope under their armpits and pull them out of the hold. Boy, that was a sight, to see that corpse going up out of there with ropes under his arms pulling him out of there. It was a daily process.

"I can understand many things that happened, but this portion of my tenure over there was the hardest to understand, as far as I'm concerned—that boat trip. I'm sure the other fellows will bear me out on this. As far as my own personal physical being was concerned, I thought my chances were less than a couple of days into this trip. If somebody would sit down and try to tell me what happened in these conditions and circumstances and so on, I'd tend to disbelieve him. You can't comprehend these things happening. You just can't imagine the stench with that many men in the hold and probably 85 percent of us with dysentery and no sanitary facilities at all and no way to bathe or clean up.

"From time to time you could hear the pings from the sonar of American submarines bouncing off the hull of the ship. Those subs were shadowing our convoy, and daily you could hear torpedoes hitting those ships. Of course, we were below water level, and the sound would carry, and it would seem like the torpedo had hit right next to us. I guess we were fortunate that this old scow was so sorry looking that it wasn't a decent war prize. It wasn't a real target, or I guess they would have come after us."

Pvt. Stanley (in transit, Manila to Japan, 1943) "I do not remember the name of this ship, but it was part of a pretty good-sized convoy. We hadn't got out no far piece when one of the ships had trouble and we had to sit there in the harbor two or three days. That ship was the worst part of the whole deal; that ship made the Death March look like a picnic. They died like flies! You stayed in one position the whole time you were there unless you were lucky. We were so thick down in that hold that you couldn't move.

"I think we had one ration of food a day, and I think it was a short ration. A couple of Japanese, the best I remember, would bring it to you. Then we had an American officer more or less in charge, and he'd send a couple of men over to the hatch to get it. You would be real lucky if they got it rationed all the way. They tried to pass it around, and most of the time it got through because if one man took another man's ration . . . well, you had to be honest. You were out for number one, but, boy, you had better not fool with anybody else's stuff, or you would have the whole gang on you. So the best I remember, everybody got their ration.

"The water was the worst part of it. For a few days we could make it without too much food, but you cannot live without water. It was so hot down in that hold, and the only air we got was from one little open hatch up above us. Many of them actually suffocated away from the hatch, and for a drink I heard that a lot of the guys drank their own urine.

"I was in better shape than most of them, so I was put on the burial detail. They were dying just like flies down in this hold from suffocation and heat. I can't remember whether the Americans down there lifted them or if the Japs gave them a rope to pull them out, but it was my job to help throw them over the side. We just took them to the side and tossed them overboard. I got water on the burial detail. It rained almost every day on that trip, so I could get at least a pinch of water, enough to keep you from thirsting to death.

"This trip to Japan took seventeen days because they were zig-zagging all over that ocean on account of American submarines. These subs got most of the convoy before we got to Japan. See, we were on freighters, and the Japs didn't mark them. We heard some of the firing, but we didn't know what it was. When I was on these burial details, however, none of this was happening."

Lt. Burris (in transit, Manila to Japan, 1943) "It was packed like sardines in there. Pretty soon the group was moving and twisting and pulling, and I had to go with them. I ended up on the deck, the floor. Then people started walking on me, stepping on me. I struggled and was almost exhausted there. I wasn't going to last no time at all. All I was going to do, and all they were going to do, was wear ourselves out, just expending energy for nothing. So I crawled between their legs, and I went aft. I don't know why I did this. It was deep and pitch black in there, and you couldn't see back in there very far, but I was just trying to find a way out. We were so packed in there that I think some people died from suffocation before we even ate a meal. We were packed in so tight that some who were in the back didn't get enough air. Then when they covered the hatch over, there was no source of air to speak of.

"The first night it was bad. People were screaming for air and fighting and struggling. They were hot and thirsty, and they wanted water. They had evidently drunk their canteen of water real quick as well as whatever water they got from the Japs. One guy defecated in his mess kit and ate the defecation. Of course, I don't think he held it down very long. Another one urinated in his canteen, and he drank his urine. Now, there might have been more than one who did that. You know, common sense would tell them urine would just make things worse, and defecation would be as bad as brackish, slimy water, so you can't hold that down. But people were thirsty, and it was hot. Oh, the temperature was hot! It must have been at least 120 degrees. In that hold we were packed in there, and the body heat was there, and there were stinking and sweaty people struggling with no air to speak of. Almost everybody took off their clothes. Everybody around me took off their clothes, and I did, too.

"The second day, as we were slowly moving away from the dock, the ship was caught in an American air raid, and everybody was afraid. This lasted all day long, both bombing and strafing. We had some near misses on the front hold, and the back hold received a direct hit. Everybody was tense. I know that when every airplane came down, I waited for something to hit me, and I think everybody else felt the same way, too. Men went crazy because of the raid and a lack of water. They moved around or tried to, and it was just one big struggling mass of writhing men, like a bag of worms in there. Anyway, it was a madhouse during the bombing and strafing, and our ship went dead in the water that afternoon. They bombed it so bad that it couldn't go. Then they bombed several times when the ship was just stationary.

"I probably can't describe that second night. I was afraid of all these people. People were just like a bag of worms, struggling and fighting for space and screaming for water and fighting each other. Boy, it was just like a madhouse. During the daytime I had a full canteen of water, and I was hot and thirsty, too. It was dark, and nobody would have seen me, so I thought about taking a drink. But they might have felt me or heard me, so I decided not to take a swig. If they would have known about it, they would have taken it away from me, and they probably would have killed me in the process. Anyway, I wanted a drink, but I talked myself out of it. Several prisoners were cutting other prisoners' wrists and necks and drinking their blood. They got razor blades, and they were drinking their blood.

I didn't see it or anything, but I could hear them hollering. A guy would say, 'What are you doing? Hey, he cut me with a razor!' He's drinking my blood!' That happened different times at different places on the ship that night. Colonel Beecher had set up his command post at the bottom rung of the ladder, but he couldn't see these guys or get to them. He'd holler, 'Do you know who they are?' He'd say, 'Kill 'em! They're not gonna stop! Just kill 'em!' So he ordered them to be murdered, and they were murdered. He said, 'Beat 'em with a shoe! Choke 'em! Do anything! But kill 'em! Make sure they're dead!' You could hear them getting a beating, and they'd scream and holler. I don't remember their words, but some of them might have been begging for mercy. They went ahead and killed them. It got so bad at one point that even the Japs yelled down and threatened to shoot down in there. Finally, they did shoot down in there and killed a few people, but it didn't help any. These guys were completely out of their heads— most of them. One ol' boy yelled, 'How do you like it, Beecher? You ain't gettin' no water, either! You're gonna die like the rest of us!' He couldn't control them. Nobody could control them. The threat of death didn't even control them.

"We were in Formosa, Takao harbor, I guess it was, when we were again attacked by American planes. We were tied up there when four planes swooped in, and a bomb hit the forward hold, just like it had been in the Philippines. Thank goodness, I was in the back hold because it killed almost everybody in that front hold. After the planes had dropped their bombs, they started strafing with machine guns. The .50-caliber bullets came right through the deck and the bulkhead, and that's where I was. I know that around me people were dead, and others were wounded and crying and screaming.

"After it was over, the Japs stood around and looked down at us, and they'd laugh. They thought it was great that we were in such misery. We had no bandages or medicine, so most of the wounded died from infection, if nothing else. In addition, we were all in misery because we had not eaten at all that day. In fact, since we had left the Philippines, we only got to eat once a day, and that was just rice and one or two spoonfuls of mixed salt water and fresh water. So it was real bad, and we were miserable, and the Japs thought it was great. They'd just stand around and point to us and just die laughing. Of course, they knew they were losing the war, and their hatred must have been running pretty high.

"I think we stayed on there three days before they started to take the bodies out. They asked for volunteers to help put the bodies on a net. A big crane would drop down, and you'd put them in its net. I remember that I had lost my shoes during that raid in Manila Bay, and I wanted a pair of shoes. I was deathly afraid of being without shoes, and I'd go hysterical if I thought I didn't have shoes. Anyway, I went over to the dead bodies to scrounge for a pair, and when I got there, them guys had been stripped clean, and there was nothing to get.

"Anyway, I got put on this detail when I went over there. We would pick up a guy by his arms and legs, and when you did, well, his arms or legs would come loose and his body would just fall off because everything was rotten. The stench was terrible, and they had decomposed to the point that the body wouldn't hold together when it was lifted. Since the limbs would fall off, you had to grab them under the hips and shoulders to get them in the net."

Cpl. Read (in transit, Manila to Japan, 1944) "This ship represented perhaps the low point of my entire POW career. There were approximately a thousand of us that they put on this ship. I have to describe it. I do not know the name of this ship, but we came to refer to it as the *Benjo Maru. Benjo* is the Japanese word for toilet, and this was our opinion of it. It was an old steel vessel. It was so old that it had been a coal burner and had been converted to some other kind of fuel. It was not a large ship, but it had two large spaces to put things in. It had been used as a horse boat, apparently for Japanese cavalry. One end of the ship had stables for horses, and the other end had a huge coal bin for a hold. We were divided into two groups, and half went into the horse stables, and the other half went into the coal bin. I was in the half that went into the coal bin, and it was so crowded in there that you could not move or hardly breathe. There was no room to sit down, and there was such a crowd in there that you had to stand. It was dark in there, and the floor was littered with coal. It was quite hot in there at that time, too, so not only were we stifled from lack of space but also from the heat in this coal bin. In fact, all I could think of was the historical reference to the Black Hole of Calcutta because this place was truly a black, dark hole. Some of these people went stark raving mad in the next two or three days.

"To begin with, we stayed at the pier for two or three days before we actually left. We were all afraid. We had looked out over the bay before we got on board, and we had seen all the sunken ships from recent air attacks by the American forces. They had sunk every ship out in Manila Bay, and there were a lot of them sticking out of the water. We felt that the longer we stayed there the better the chance of us getting hit, so we began to get very nervous because we felt that they would come back and sink whatever they had missed the first time. As the thing dragged on and people got more despondent, some guys started raving and hollering real loud and saying unintelligible things; and then they started climbing on top of people and walking over their shoulders and heads and just tearing around in a generally maniacal manner. After doing this for a while, some of these people just dropped dead. There were others who in the darkness were dispatched by someone—just put out of their misery. These people later on were hoisted up to the top and thrown over the side. What probably made matters even worse was that among the five hundred prisoners in the coal bin were about two hundred Dutch and British prisoners who had survived a recent sinking of their ship off the Philippines. These people were particularly nervous and jittery. Their ship had come up from the Dutch East Indies, and they told me that they had been part of an increment of one thousand to twelve hundred men. They were either bombed or torpedoed and sunk, and this couple of hundred had survived by swimming ashore or had been picked up.

"Then we finally left as part of a convoy. We learned from the fellows up on deck who cooked our rice that we were with a convoy and we were the smallest ship in the group. We also found out from our rice cooks that the Japs had said we were on our way to Formosa. We went out of Manila Bay and turned north and stayed close to the shore in sight of land; but before we were out of sight of land, every ship in the convoy had been sunk except ours. Evidently, the convoy was hit by both planes and submarines. I guess they just missed us, is all I can say. It was a small scow, but there was no indication that it was a POW ship whatsoever. We had some Navy people on board, and they told us that down below the waterline they could hear the pings from a submarine's sonar bouncing off the hull of the ship. And we heard these things constantly, and this caused some more people to go off their rocker. I heard some of them in there, for example, praying for a torpedo to hit us and that kind of thing. I remember one loud voice calling out, 'Lord, send us a fish!' That meant to send us a torpedo, you know, and they were praying for that thing to sink us.

"Incidentally, while we were under these attacks, we never got fed. People had begun to die off in the hold and were hoisted up to the top and thrown over the side. In fact, there were so many in our crowd who had died that by the time the attacks were over, just about everybody had room to sit down. Also, I should mention that when the attacks began, the Japs had battened down the hatches, and there would have been no way to escape.

"At the same time, simultaneously, a typhoon blew up, and apparently the Japs decided to try to outrun it, so we headed right across the South China Sea. We didn't know where we were going at the time, but we wound up in Hong Kong. While we were on the open sea, the typhoon was in full force, and that ship was bouncing like a cork on the waves. It was just up and down, up and down. Although I personally didn't get seasick, the deck was a mess from other people vomiting and everything else. Fortunately, you couldn't see all of this stuff because the whole bottom of the thing was covered with coal, and that may have been a good thing. I don't know how deep the coal was, but a lot of that stuff was sifting down below where we were.

"Believe it or not, we always managed to have a little bit of internal organization under these circumstances. We had group leaders down there, and we were able to organize after so many had died and we were able to sit down. These leaders determined how the rice was rationed out, and everybody went along with it because it was the only way to do things. And these leaders served it. The bucket of rice came down to this guy, and he sat there, and somebody dished it out in your mess kit which you had passed on down there. I never knew of anybody to steal your rice as it was being passed back. Everybody was scrupulously honest because there was such a small amount. There really was a great deal of consideration on the part of one another. Everybody was in the same boat, and I don't care whether you were a major or a buck private, because by this time everybody considered themselves on a par."

Lt. Daman (in transit, Davao to Manila, 1944) "They put us in the hold of an old tramp freighter. The holds were small, and they put a large number in each hold. We had a lot of men die during this voyage. First, off of Cebu we got caught in an American air raid and had to put into Cebu, where we stayed for about two weeks. Second, the conditions aboard that ship were the worst you could possibly think about—filth of all kinds. They didn't build latrines of any kind, and they wouldn't let us up on deck at any time because earlier two men had escaped and made it safely to shore and they didn't want that to happen again. Our ration of rice was lowered down in buckets and was issued out. We had no way to sterilize our mess kits or anything. On this trip we had one man who went berserk; he went stark raving mad. They finally had to chain him to a post there to keep him from hurting any of the other prisoners. Altogether, we lost fifty-six men, and they were simply lifted up to the main deck by ropes and then thrown over the side."

Cpl. Burlage (in transit, Philippines to Japan, 1944) "They took us out to the waterfront and put us aboard ship, and they stacked us in there. They put us in the hold. They lined us up shoulder to shoulder and back to back. We started talking and saying, 'We can't get to Japan like this.' The word was passed that they were going to take us out and get us on a big ship, but this was it, we were going on this little ship. Before we ever got under way, people were dying from the heat and people were going crazy. When they died, you'd stand on them. You didn't remain a human very long in that place. Every morning the Japs would lower a rope down, and somebody would tie the rope around the dead people, and they'd hoist them up and throw them over the side. With the same rope they'd lower our food, a couple of buckets of rice. Once or twice a week they'd lower a bucket for a toilet. It was an old coal-carrying ship, and it still had coal in the hold. It was a good thing we had the coal there because we started going in it. About the third or fourth day out we had room because so many people had died. We were able to sit down. I would say twenty to fifty died each day.

"We wound up in Hong Kong. It's the one time in thirty-nine days that we were out of that hold. We were there about a week. They made us move out because a bunch of four-motor bombers and dive bombers came by and bombed the dock area. We were laying in the hold looking up through the cracks in the ship and seeing bombs come right over our ship. We were at sea about ten more days and wound up in Takao, a southern port in Formosa. I was down to where I couldn't walk. I couldn't stand up because we hadn't eaten in some time; we hadn't eaten for days at a time, and no water either. We were just living on reserve, I guess. Well, from Takao, they took us up to the northern part of the island, and we stayed there for about two and a half months, and I got my strength back. Anyway, we next went to Japan. It took two weeks, and it was cold. We crowded on a

ship with a bunch of Japanese soldiers. So, we came to Moji. Some
Jap came in and gave us a big speech and said, 'You're in luck now.
We're humane. You're in the homeland. We'll treat you kindly.
The Red Cross will take you to a hospital in Tokyo. You will enjoy
your stay there the rest of the war.' I didn't believe them, and nobody
else did.

"The worst conditions by all means was on the ship, because we
lost so many people there. We had people that would just go crazy.
Maybe you don't believe this, but people just tried to bite your throat
to get blood. You know, they were thirsty, just going out of their minds.
There was a young doctor by me one day, a fellow I got to know. He
had a medical bag, and we ended up talking. He said, 'I'm not going
to put up with this.' I said, 'Well, what's the trouble?' He said, 'Well,
I'm not going to put up with it. We aren't getting through. I have
some morphine.' He reached in his bag, and he gave me some morphine. It was broken in small pieces, and he said, 'If you get to hurting or something, take one of these.' And I did. He took some of his,
too. He took all of his. He killed himself. People were doing that.
They would go crazy, and somebody would hit them and they would
fall, and that would be the end of them. It wouldn't kill them, but
they would die. They were crazy—people in the tropics like that with
no water, and they go crazy. Somebody is trying to bite your throat, I
mean, it's unbelievable."

Cpl. Halbrook (in transit, Manila to Hong Kong, 1944) "We were
marched into a coal burner that had held horses before we went in.
They had two holds in the ship, a hold forward and a hold in the rear,
and we were in the forward hold. We marched up the gangplank in
single file, dropped our G-strings, and bent down and caught both
ankles and spread the cheeks of our butts. They rammed a glass rod
up our butts to make sure we were not carrying any valuables aboard.
They would take that same glass rod, open your mouth, and they'd
pull down your tongue to check under it, looking for valuables. Then
they handed you a new G-string and you went aboard and down into
the hold. The hold was about a fourth of the size of a football field,
big enough that twelve hundred men were put in there. Nobody could
sit down. They loaded everybody in there, and we were standing up
and cussing and raising hell down there just like cannibals. The Japanese brought two air-cooled machine guns and put them on either
side of the hold. The Japanese interpreter said, 'I don't need to take
you to Japan. I've got the numbers. Either sit down, or I'm going to

make a bunch of numbers.' So we sat down. They told us on the megaphone to get comfortable because we'd be aboard ship for twelve days. There wasn't any question about where we were going to be in case we got hit, and there wasn't no way to get out of there. With twelve hundred men, there ain't no way you are going to come up through a three-foot hole and get out.

"Twelve days to get from Manila to Hong Kong! The first evening we were out, the American submarines began to peck away at the damn convoy. The second day, the other prison ship got hit. We didn't know it at the time, but we were around Olongapo, down on the end of the Philippines. We had no sanitary facilities. On the third day they put salt water down in the hold and sent down rice in buckets. It was after dark, and as the canteen cups of rice would be passed back to their original owners, some guys would eat the rice and crap in the canteen cups. By the time the cups got back to the original owners, there already had been two or three guys who took a sample of it before they figured out what it was! There'd be a little bit of cussing going on there.

"Water was the main thing. My tongue swelled out where I could see it. They pulled the dead out of the hold every three days. They began to let little groups go up topside in the evening. The Korean guards made the guys with dysentery stand over the other guys, over the little hole, and crap down on top of everybody. The Korean guards would stand up, and they would tantalize you. They would make you say, 'Oh, please, Mr. Guard, can I come upstairs?' in Japanese. And 'Could I go to the *benjo*?', which was the crapper. And they would ask you how bad you wanted to go and whether you wanted to go real bad or not.

"But the dead details were the thing I remember most about the service, and I like to never get it out of my mind. When I came back to the States, I was afraid to get drunk because I'd see Taylor when I'd get drunk. I could always see Taylor that day they pulled him out of the hold. He was swelled up, and we were sitting on him. We were taking turns sitting on him. I know we ended up beating him, I mean, you were not your own self in your mind. You'd hit him in the face to try to make him quit grinning at you. Every place you looked, it seemed, he was looking at you. They finally pulled him out of that hold and took him out of there. When they hollered for the dead detail, we volunteered. They'd tie a rope under their arms, and they'd pull them up just like a sack of wheat. Ol' Taylor, when they pulled him out, they took him to the top and seemed to stop him. He just spun like a top. It seemed like he stopped and looked just straight down at ol' Black and I, grinning the same grin that he had on his face the three or four days we had been looking at him. And that was the grin that I saw everytime that I would get drunk. I had nightmares. Taylor would always wind up spinning around in front of me.

"On the first night, you could feel guys reaching around over your neck looking for a canteen. The guy right close to me had a canteen and some water in it, and you could hear the canteen going 'carumph' as they were hitting him on the head, killing him. Late in the evening, on the second or third day out, the Japanese announced they were going to send us down water, plenty for everybody. And the Navy guys let us know real quick not to drink it because it was salt water. Some guys started drinking it, and they started going crazy and wild. Salt water is like drinking kerosene that eats your guts out. Guys would get up and run just like a turpentined cat and then fall down and start kicking other people. We lost more people the first three days. I imagine we got to Japan with half the bunch that started."

Sgt. Brodsky (sunk in transit, Philippines to Japan, 1944) "We were loaded onto another ship called the *Arisan Maru*. Everybody went into the same hold, and it was jam-packed, like sardines. We headed south instead of toward Japan and docked at a place called Mindoro. We barely had enough room to move around. Food was lowered in a bucket by a rope through the hatch. All the bodily wastes were emptied into a wood bucket. Some men had dysentery bad, and it splashed all over the place. It was hauled up, and as it was hauled up, the overflow would just drop down all over everybody. This was as unsanitary as you can imagine. After two or three days we came back to Manila, but they docked outside of the breakwater. I don't know but I think it was October 20 when we left from Manila to head toward Japan.

"We were four days out, heading for Japan, when the ship was torpedoed. You could hear this sound, and the Navy personnel told us it was a submarine aiming at us. We had a chaplain give everybody Absolution, and he told us what might happen. Shortly thereafter, the ship was hit. Nobody was injured from the torpedo, but there was a Jap guard on top with a machine gun pointed down at the hold. But after about twenty minutes, all the Japs abandoned the ship. Somebody looked up and removed some hatch covers and made a ramp up to the deck. I had broken my hand and had put a splint on it, so I waited until the hold emptied out, and then somebody helped me up, and we got to the top.

"Everybody in our hold got out on deck, and stacked on deck were a bunch of life preservers, and most everybody got a life preserver. In the meantime a lot of people were jumping over the side because they saw these other ships in the convoy, and I guess they thought they would pick them up. A lot of guys ran up a ladder to the galley, and they came down with bottles of ketchup and handfuls of sugar and cigarettes. They were eating sugar and ketchup and smoking two cigarettes at a time. It was comical even if it was so urgent. I mean, it was just comical to watch some of the guys drinking bottles of ketchup and eating all this sugar. Then they would jump over. This was in October, and the water was cold.

"I stayed on board the thing, and I tried to talk to the other guys: 'Why don't you wait and see what happens—if anybody's being picked up—before you jump over? That water is cold.' I remember a couple just jumped over and said, 'We're following what the officers are doing. They jumped over.' Around dusk—it was just getting dark—when the water seemed to be coming up to the deck, instead of the ship sinking like I had always thought, and instead of any whirlpool pulling you down, it just floated right under so peacefully. Well, when the water came up to meet us, I just floated off the ship and swam away.

"The thing that I remember most about this time afloat was that in the daytime it was so blasted hot that I wished for nighttime; and when nighttime came, it was so cold that my mind just wished for daytime. We were afloat four days and four nights. Finally, we did see ships coming. They came right up beside us, pretty close to us. I swam over to a ship. There were a lot of barnacles on the side, and this guy threw me a rope over. I had this broken hand, but I grabbed hold of the rope, and they started pulling me up onto this destroyer.

"As they pulled me up, I was like one big burn from the sun. There were big scabs all over me. When they pulled me up along these barnacles, they pulled all the scabs off. I was bleeding and pussy. It was awful! They got me up on deck. The deck was metal, and I was barefooted. When I walked on that deck with my bare feet, I got blisters on the bottom of my feet from the heat. It was like stepping on fire. Right away I asked for water: 'Give us water! Water! Water!' I asked for *mizu,* which is their word for water. They brought out some water, and it was boiling. I went to drink it, and it burned my whole mouth. Finally, they brought out some of this *lugao*—this watery, watery rice. That was hot, but that was good. We had some of that, and we kept asking for more water all the time. We couldn't get enough water. They teased us a little bit with water, but we finally got enough water. I think it was about eighteen hours from the time they picked us up until they landed at Formosa. And I think I was in the water four or five days. I don't know where I floated during those four or five days."

Other Atrocities

Capt. Adair (in transit, San Fernando to Capas, 1942) "This was the most brutal thing the Japanese could have done outside of the march itself. As I recall, they loaded 120 men to a boxcar. These were not the real large boxcars like we have in the United States. Then they closed the doors. This was in hot summer, in the worst part of the summer, you might say. The heat must have been 120 or 130 degrees at least. We had no water at all. If you had any water, you'd already drunk it by that time. I had none. But air was more important than water in those boxcars at that time. You couldn't breathe; there wasn't enough air to breathe in this boxcar.

"After a short while, I went forward and worked my way to the door where the guard was and convinced him that we had to open that door. I guess he was hot himself, so he decided to crack the door a little bit. Naturally, everyone surged forward trying to get that air. As I recall, I was the senior man on that car, so I took over because it was getting out of hand. People were fighting to get to the door, so I got two stout enlisted men up there at the door. I would have them shuffle people forward two or three at a time and rotate them to get air.

"That was the point where morale was at its lowest because you're going to fight to get air; you'll kill to get air before you die. And it nearly got that bad. Of course, men were passing out from heat prostration. Well, this went on until finally they opened the door a little wider. Maybe the train stopped a couple of times, and maybe the noncoms gave orders to open the doors a little wider. Finally, we did get a little more air, but it was a brutal thing, a brutal experience that I hate to even think about."

Pvt. Stanley (in transit, San Fernando to Capas, 1942) "Those boxcars got dirty real fast because we were just like a bunch of pigs living in a pen or something. A lot of the guys by this time had dysentery, and their bowel movements were in their pants because they had nowhere else to go. If you had dysentery, your clothes got to where they stuck to you, and you were just like an animal—just like an animal."

Cpl. Clem (in transit, Camp O'Donnell to Cabanatuan, 1942) "We marched to the railroad, and then they loaded us on boxcars. They would pack as many as they could in a car, and then they would close the doors. It was way over 100 degrees. It had to be! It must have been around 130, 140 degrees. It was like being in an automobile on a summer day when you get in with all the windows up—about the same thing."

Lt. Taylor (Cabanatuan) "We had three men at Cabanatuan who were just thinking about, I guess, trying to escape. They hadn't even gotten out through the fence. The Japanese saw them as they were making some approach toward the fence. They tied them up, and after the third day they beheaded all three of them. They were taken just a short ways from the camp when this was done."

Pvt. Kent (Cabanatuan) "Two of the guards were going to push me into a fifty-gallon drum, what they called soup pots. Those pots were boiling all the time. My leg burned, third degree, all the way down to my ankle. I almost lost it as gangrene was setting up in it. A Navy corpsman took care of my leg, scraping it two or three times a day to keep the pus out of it."

Lt. Daman (in transit, Bilibid Prison to Davao Penal Colony, 1944) "There were two thousand of us who were too sick to work, so they selected us and decided to send us to Davao. They put us on these steel boxcars again, and it was the same kind of trip going out as it was coming in. It was pretty rough, and it took us the better part of a day to get to Bilibid Prison in Manila. We were only at Bilibid for a matter of days, and then they put six hundred of us in the hold of a ship. We were packed in there like sardines, too. The trip in the boxcar was bad, but this trip was twice as bad down there in the hold because of the motion of the ship and so on. They closed the hatches and would let us out just one time a day to relieve ourselves. It took us two weeks, I think, to reach Davao because this was an old scow and they were constantly afraid of American air raids. They were running for shelter at night and putting in at safe harbors, and then they'd take off the next morning.

"They provided us with a very meager quantity of rice, and it was horrible, horrible food. I think they did provide about a quart of water per day per person. They would take us up on deck to eat because that's where they did the cooking. So this gave us another chance to get up on deck for some air.

"Davao was about fifty-two kilometers from the Davao Penal Colony, which was a prison that had been built for Filipinos who had been convicted of serious crimes. It was a 22,000-hectare compound. Getting there was like another Bataan Death March. We had a number of people who never made it, that fell out along the road and were stabbed or bayoneted. Of course, we were all in a very weakened condition, and, finally, when they saw that we were not going to make it, they brought along some trucks. They put as many as fifty of us in each truck and hauled us the rest of the way in."

PFC Bolitho (Davao Penal Colony) "We had a fellow outside the compound, right underneath a guard tower, digging camotes, which is like a sweet potato. He hollered to one of his friends inside to throw him a canteen of water, and this guard misunderstood what he did. His friend threw the canteen, and this guard was right above him with his rifle and aiming down at him. He began begging the guard not to shoot him. The guard pumped two bullets into him, and then he fired at this other fellow running across the compound."

Cpl. Smith (Palawan) "The morning of December 14, 1944, started out about normal for that time. Everybody went out on the detail and went about their daily routine until probably 10:30 or 11:00 Then the Japs broke up all the work details and brought everybody back to camp under the pretense that a large number of American airplanes were on the way in. We had dug some little trenches and shelters for falling shrapnel—light stuff—down in back of the compound, so the Japs made us all get down in them. When they got everybody inside the trenches, then they started dumping gasoline in and followed with a torch. As I got down the steps—I had barely got down inside—all hell broke loose, the hollering and screaming taking place. The first thing that I thought of was that the danged guerrillas had landed.

"I stuck my head up to see what was going on, and even just at a glimpse I saw men running around coming out of the B Company trench. Men were burning, and the killing and shooting and bayoneting was going on. I ducked back down and told one of the other men what was happening. Well, Glen W. McDole, my real close buddy, stuck his head out. I told him, 'You better keep your head down! You'll get it shot off! There's a machine gun sitting up at the head of the stairs!' He did anyway, and they opened up on him. Then he hollered to me to pull the sandbag out of the wall. In digging our trench, we'd got a hunk of coral, knocked it away, and shoved it aside, then dug a hole and put dirt in a sandbag, and covered it all over with brush and everything. I thought it would make a good escape hatch, and it worked out that way. We were to get that sandbag out and get through the hole and get down to the beach! But the others wouldn't do it; they didn't believe us. About this time, one of the medics, Bancroft, jumped in with us. He was afire, burning, and he started screaming and telling us what was going on. About that time the Japs threw a torch in on us, but they forgot to throw gasoline in. There were nine of us in this little hole, just jammed into the hole, but McDole and I helped them go through it one at a time. McDole said he was the last one out, but I know I was the last one out. Anyway, we left the trench through the hole. Nine of us got down to the beach. McDole and I made it back, but the others were killed on the beach.

"The cliff over the beach was about 150 feet from the hole, then it was another forty feet or so straight down to the beach. The Japs had two patrol boats roaming the beach—keeping watch on the beach—with machine guns mounted on them, and they were shooting anybody and anything that moved. Then they had men stationed down on the beach with automatic rifles and bayonets. They were killing people. When I hit the beach, they fired at me. I ran down to the right—the west—a fairly short distance, and I got behind a bunch of coral for protection. There were three or four guys already there, and I told them, 'You'd better split up! You ain't going to be able to hide four and five at a time!' They wanted me to stay with them, but I wouldn't do it. I left. I went back up on top of the cliff and crawled to a wash or crevice and under a bunch of overlapping grass and weeds. I lay there until it got dark—laid there all afternoon.

"The Japs were still very active. I was a short distance from the west edge of our compound. I could see through the breaks in the grass and weeds what was going on. There were men running around on fire and being shot and bayoneted, and I could hear them hollering, off and on. Some of it was out of my sight, but I could hear it. This went on all afternoon. Now, I imagine it all started right at noontime, I'd say about 12:00, and by this time—the time I got down in the crevice—it was probably just before 1:00.

"Once I thought they had discovered me. A little ol' Jap came by and killed those four guys on the beach below me. I was hiding right over them. He killed all four, and then he came on up the same way I had come up, and he raised the grass and stuff and looked under there right at me. He wasn't over six or seven feet from me; but it was bright sunshine out where he was, and he looked under there and couldn't see a thing. I thought I had had it when he came up there, though, but he dropped the grass and went on down. When it came toward evening, the Japs came down through there with bayonets— they lined up solid and came through there with fixed bayonets— jabbing them in the ground every few feet and few inches. One of them stepped on me, but the bayonet missed me, so, again, I got by okay. After that, there were two Jap guards within ten or twelve feet of me. They sat down and stayed there the rest of the evening.

"In the evening, everything quieted down, real quiet. As soon as it got good and dark, I eased down this cliff the same way I came up and got to the edge of the water. I looked up and it turned out that the guard was standing on a tall hump of coral. When he turned his back to the bay, looking back toward the cliff, well, I eased in the water and went underneath and swam under water as far as I could. He never did discover me, so I straightened out and started swimming. I didn't think I was a good swimmer, but I guess I was. I figured I swam somewhere between five and seven miles. The Filipinos said five miles, and the combat engineers measured the shortest way across at seven miles.

"When I first got across, I couldn't even sit up; my back wouldn't support me. When I first started out walking, I was hoping to hit the southern boundary of the Iwahig Penal Colony. I stumbled and fell a lot, tore a lot of skin off of me. Then I spotted this little shack. It was quite a way up the side of the mountain, but I worked hard and got up there. There wasn't anyone there, but down on the other side of the mountain were five or six men working. The dogs found me and started barking. Finally, one of the men left the group and came up there. I told him what happened and he said, 'We'll take you in; we're your friends.' "

Cpl. Burlage (Palawan) "There was a massacre after I left Palawan. I was told by some of my buddies that afterwards the Japs took the American bodies and piled them up in such a way and then took dynamite and bounced the bodies around with dynamite to make it look like bomb explosions killed them, but it didn't fool the Americans. When they got there, they recognized that it was a massacre."

Pvt. Chambers (Burma-Thailand Railway) "A sailor off of the *Houston* had a big ulcer almost from his knee to his ankle, with just a piece of cloth hanging over it. He didn't have enough bandages to cover it and no medication to put on it. I guess that Jap thought he was kind of putting on. The sailor had a chill and was shaking. The Jap made him pull the cloth up on the ulcer to see if it was too bad to keep him from going to work. The sailor raised it up, and the Jap hauled off and kicked that ulcer with his hobnailed shoes. The blood just flew and the sailor died in a short time."

M/Sgt. Stowers (Woosung) "A good friend of mine, named Cash, and I were out working all day and came in. He was a staff sergeant, and we were at the faucets washing ourselves down. There was a sentry outside, and he sighted his rifle on me and then on Cash. Cash says, 'Hank, what is that bastard doing?' I said, 'Don't pay no attention to him, ignore him.' And suddenly, bang! He shot Cash through his throat. I tried to hold his jugular vein, but blood was just spurting, and he died in a second or two. Well, the officer came out and chewed the guard out a little bit—you shouldn't do that, that kind of stuff. It was real rough."

PFC Sparkman (Woosung) "One of the civilians from Wake Island was an electrician, so he was putting light bulbs and stuff in camp. There was a light on the back of the outhouse for his barracks, and this Jap who was standing guard on the road outside the fence told him to put a new light in it. I was brushing my teeth and listening to them. The Jap pointed the gun at him like he was going to shoot him if he didn't. The guy pointed right here at his throat: 'Shoot me there if that's what you're going to do.' The next thing that happened was the Jap shot him right in the throat, and he was dead before he hit the ground. I finished brushing my teeth and went in. The story they put out was that the civilian was trying to escape."

Cpl. Halbrook (Omi) "Omi was a little ol' island where there was this prison where they practiced doing spinal blocks, and on mine it was practicing driving you into shock or seeing whether they could put you into shock. They would tie a rubber band around my damn testicles, and they would beat on the damn things until it would drive me into shock, and then they would bring me back. They killed a lot of people, and they hurt a lot of people, and they killed some of my friends. It was a deal that causes me to stay awake at night. I don't want to talk about it."

Pvt. Kent (near Tokyo) "At this copper mine they had a hospital, and they operated on five of us. They took our appendix out. We didn't have appendicitis, but they took them out anyway. They were young doctors experimenting. It was a rough operation because they didn't have any anesthetics, and there was a whole bunch of little ol' Japanese nurses around to hold you. They cut so deep that I went out like a light. When I woke up, well, there was a whole bunch of little ol' Jap nurses standing around playing with my thing, trying to get it hard. And so, heck, there I was about dead, and I guess that's the lowest point that I ever was."

Chapter IV

General Treatment—The Physical

In one of the earliest studies of prisoners of war undertaken by an American scholar, Herbert C. Fooks pointed out that the Japanese, by establishing rules for the humane treatment of prisoners, had "manifested a desire to precede other nations on the road to civilization."[1] A great deal changed between Fooks's comments in 1924 and World War II, and civilization was not the beneficiary.

Early in the war, physical treatment of American prisoners varied from moderately good to absolutely dreadful. Conditions depended on where and when the men were captured. Logistically, the Japanese were not prepared for the surrender of a large number of Allied soldiers. That fact plus the hostile attitude of Japanese toward other peoples and their military's disdain for those who surrendered created brutal conditions, such as on the Bataan Death March. As the war progressed, men interned in areas where they later would suffer greatly received acceptable treatment at first. Special situations also played a role, as evidenced by the treatment afforded Americans captured in Java and sent to work on the Burma-Thailand Railway. Toward the war's end, in 1945, the status of almost all prisoners declined. By then, the Japanese had an excuse for their brutality: they were losing the conflict and could not supply prisoner-of-war camps adequately.

In the following pages, American servicemen interned for an average of three and one-half years recall their physical treatment, both in general and in specific terms. Their descriptions reveal not only Japanese attitudes but also their own. Some captives complain about conditions that others would have relished. For example, the reader should compare descriptions of captivity by the North China Marines with those of the men in Cabanatuan, Camp O'Donnell, or on the Death Railway.

---

[1]Fooks, *Prisoners of War*, 18–19.

While it is difficult to stress one physical problem over another, the prisoners were unanimous on the subject of food—it was always insufficient, both in quality and quantity. The lack of food manifested itself in constant hunger; and the poor quality, in disease, weakness, ill health, and death. When Pvt. Willie Benton, an embassy guard in Peking, came back home, "people [wanted] to hear horror tales," but the only story he had to tell was "one of starvation and hard work." This situation was repeated countless times. Men who had weighed 180 to 190 pounds when captured only weighed 80 or 90 pounds when freed. (Many prisoners believed that men who were thin when captured survived better than those who were muscular or heavyset.)

Because their rations were meager, the prisoners stole food from the Japanese, planted gardens, and bartered their few possessions or used money they had earned to buy food from local people. (The Americans were paid for the work they did: enlisted men, four to five dollars; officers, about twenty dollars, although they rarely, if ever, received this much.) Prisoners in the Burma jungle supplemented their rice diet by eating lizards, pythons, elephants, dogs, cats, monkeys, birds, and certain beetles. Most of the interviewees deny that they ate rats, but PFC O. R. Sparkman, a North China Marine, admits that at Woosung, near Shanghai, he once ate part of a rat that had fallen into the rice gruel he was served. "When you get hungry," he says, "your stomach don't care what you eat."[2]

Housing for the prisoners was usually primitive. The necessities of daily living, such as soap, toothbrushes, and razors, were nonexistent or were used over and over until they wore out or were used up. Many men ended the war in tattered clothing, although those sent to Japan generally were given winter clothing, which failed to keep them as warm as they wished. In the jungles they sometimes were given black G-strings, or they made crude ones out of their deteriorating uniforms.

All nationalities—underfed, poorly clad, and badly housed—were required to work, according to a Japanese directive issued early in the war. At Kiangwan, inmates built an abutment for a rifle range; in Thailand, French Indochina, and the Philippines they worked on air-

---

[2]In the 1965 movie *King Rat*, which chronicles the years that James Clavell spent at the Changi POW camp in Singapore, an American corporal named King survives by raising and selling rats to the British prisoners.

fields; in Japan they were employed in coal mines, at steel mills, on the docks, in railroad yards, and at a Chevrolet plant. They also worked at a machine-tool plant in Manchuria and at sites elsewhere doing various jobs, many of which were in conflict with the rules established by the Geneva Convention.

Not only did the Japanese violate accepted international law, but they also set tasks, such as the Burma-Thailand Railway, that were almost impossible to fulfill. In discussing charges before the International Military Tribunal for the Far East in Tokyo, which tried Japanese presumed to be guilty of war crimes, Philip R. Piccigallo writes that the prisoners daily gave testimony "to the horrible, often unbearable, conditions under which they had toiled and lived for so long." Indeed, Japanese treatment of the men is compared "to slave labor in [the] time of the pyramids or galley slaves."[3]

Even sick prisoners had to work. The list of maladies that they suffered is unending, but it includes fever, chills, malaise, pain, anorexia, tropical ulcers, abdominal cramps from recurrent malaria, and dysentery, which plagued nearly everyone and killed thousands. Beriberi caused painful feet, cardiac failure, and loss of vision. Xerophthalmia meant sore eyes, corneal ulcers, and impaired vision. Outbreaks of diphtheria, flu, typhoid fever, along with tuberculosis and pneumonia, were frequent. Operations by inadequately supplied "surgeons" often resulted in complications.

Although in this volume we have separated physical from psychological conditions, they were interrelated. J. E. Nardini, a U.S. Navy medical officer imprisoned in the Philippines, points out that even in relatively good times "emotional shock and reactive depression played a great part in individual inability to cope with physical symptoms and disease, and undoubtedly contributed much to massive death rate[s]."[4] Witnessing the daily burial details that carried bodies to makeshift cemeteries caused depression, and often heavy silence weighed on the men for hours after a funeral procession passed. However, a certain graveyard humor developed, at least as some of the prisoners relate their experiences, no doubt in testimony to the resilience of the human spirit.

---

[3]Piccigallo, *The Japanese on Trial*, 113.
[4]Nardini, "Survival Factors in American Prisoners of War of the Japanese," 240.

Transportation

Cpl. Bunch (in transit, Pilar to Camp O'Donnell) "I did not make the Death March. We were just more or less stretched out along the road near this village, which I think was Pilar. As we were waiting, three flatbed trucks pulled up and just happened to stop close to where I happened to be standing, myself and five or six close friends in my outfit. The Japanese troops got out, and they motioned for us to get on the truck. Well, when thirty-five men got on the truck, they stopped any more from getting on. I was on the first of the three trucks."

Capt. Bull (en route, Manila, 1942) "After about ten days or two weeks, they put us aboard a transport, a cattle ship, and we were herded down in the bottom and spent the night there in the hold next to the stalls that had been occupied by cattle. It smelled of cattle, and we were not allowed to clean it out. Then the next day we were taken into Manila. We were dumped into the water about a hundred yards from shore, and we had to wade ashore in water that was chest deep. It's hard to figure why they didn't take us farther in, but I guess it was to demean us. They took us up to one end of Dewey Boulevard and paraded us from one part of town to the other so as to demean us before the native Filipinos. We were in bad shape, and I think many of us had diarrhea, dysentery, and I remember having to humiliate ourselves, to relieve ourselves on the main street of town."

Cpl. B. Allen (en route, Manila, 1942) "They put us on a ship, and we went toward Manila. We could see Manila from Corregidor; it was twenty-five miles or so, I think. Then they forced us off the ship and into waist-deep water, and we had to wade ashore. The ship could have gone to a dock, but it didn't. Anyhow, they put us out in shallow water, made us wade ashore, and then marched us up Dewey Boulevard. All this was done to humiliate us in front of the Filipinos. This was pretty obvious. As we marched up Dewey Boulevard, they rode along on horses—their high-ranking officers—and used quirts and whipped us and hit us. The enlisted men sometimes walked along and hit men with rifle butts. Oh, yes, they were putting on a great show. The Filipinos seemed emotionless when a Japanese was nearby. But when one wasn't around, they'd say, 'Hang on, Joe! Hang on, Joe!' Nearly every American was 'Joe.' They were certainly sympathetic and were for us, and when they had an opportunity they tried to give us words of encouragement as we marched along."

Capt. Bull (in transit, Bilibid Prison to Cabanatuan, 1942) "We were put in small boxcars, smaller than American boxcars, and we were crammed in there. It must have easily been over 100 degrees inside. There were 100 to 150 in each car. When we got to the town of Cabanatuan, we then started on our march to the camp.[5] I was in charge of a hundred men, and our guard was quite civilized. He would allow us to stop at roadside stands, and when we told him we didn't have any money to buy bananas or something, why, he told the Filipinos to give them to us without charge, so we received some refreshments along the way."

Cpl. McDaniel (in transit, Wake Island to Woosung, 1942) "They took our watches and rings when we got aboard ship. They sprayed us with a kind of smelly insecticide before they put us aboard. We didn't have any belongings. We thought they'd take us to Japan, which they did first. I think we were on the ship about fifteen days. We were packed in the hold. We weren't allowed to stand up, and there was just barely room enough to lay down doubling over. They had five-gallon cans for toilets. Once, they said we were in Yokohama. I think we were there maybe a day or maybe a night. I wasn't allowed on deck, but I think some officers and some men were, for propaganda purposes. I imagine they took pictures of them. We had on our regular tropic uniforms, and it was freezing cold. Then they took us to Woosung. It was also very cold. They marched us through several Chinese villages. They were humiliating us for the Chinese. They pushed and shoved, and some of the Chinese laughed—a few of them, but I don't think it was very many."

Capt. Godbold (in transit, Wake Island to Woosung, 1942) "When we boarded the ship, we were placed in what I gather was the mail room, where the ship handled its mail for the passengers. The room was reasonably good-sized. We didn't have any extra room, but we were not too crowded. There were a few bunks and some of the older officers occupied those, and the rest of us had mats on the floor. We traveled on this ship to Japan. We were fed a couple of times a day, not very well, maybe three times a day. We had rice, soup, pickles,

---

[5]Three prison camps existed near Cabanatuan, but only Camp No. 1 continued until 1945. Camp No. 2 operated for only a few days, and Camp No. 3 was closed in late 1942. The prisoners held at these three sites do not always distinguish among them in the interviews.

and maybe some tea. The food was adequate even though not very palatable. I don't recall any particular hardship. It was not pleasant, but there was no brutality shown. The accommodations were about what you'd expect for prisoners of war. It was a monotonous trip."

PFC Garrison (in transit, Guam to Japan, 1942) "They sent us to Japan on the *Argentina Maru*. It was a luxury liner. Of course, we stayed down right above the engines. They let us up on deck once a day to get some exercise, to get a little sunshine, and then back down in the hold. There were approximately three hundred service personnel and four hundred civilians, primarily contractors who worked for the government, all Americans. We slept on steel, side by side. I weighed 140 pounds when I surrendered, and I weighed 110 by the time we got to Japan. The food was very meager. Of course, we were unaccustomed to rice, but that's what they gave us, with a side dish that we didn't know what it was. They called it *daikons*. It turns out that they were pickled radishes, big ol' white radishes that they cut up and pickled, and they were pretty hard to eat, even as hungry as we were."

PO2 Detre (en route, Penang to Moulmein, 1943) "When we got to Penang, we boarded a transport ship. It was exceptionally clean. It had all new bamboo mats laid on the decks. There was plenty of space. We were in the forward hold. The Aussies were in the rear of the ship. The captain spoke English and had apparently lived in Missouri. He asked if anybody was from Missouri, and H. T. Kelley said he was. They practically lived together on that trip. We had the run of the ship. From the forward part of the ship we could go back as far as the bridge. We had lots of water, and we could take saltwater baths.

"We were cruising in line astern, three ships total, with one small escort vessel. At 10:00 one morning, they passed the word that there was an air raid and all men had to go down below deck. This bomber came over and got three perfect hits on the other two ships. They were loaded with railroad equipment, and one of them had an engine on it. They just rolled over and sank. Some prisoners were lost, but mostly Japanese troops. The Japanese had moved into the good quarters below decks and made the Dutch deck cargo. So when the ship was sunk, the Dutch were on the surface. The bomber tried for us and got one hit off the starboard quarter, one hit right beside the beam, and one hit off the port beam. It was a perfect straddle and blew all the lifeboats off. It set the ammunition on fire on the gun platform aft and killed about thirty-four Aussies. It also killed several Japs, including a Japanese officer who was throwing the ammunition off when he died. The Aussies put the fire out. The little carpenter went up to the gun on the bow and aimed that little popgun at the bomber and shot at it. He shot the stay in two on the mast. He was happy—he'd done his duty.

"This bombing was as scared as I've ever been. It wasn't just a momentary thing—I was scared for about three days. Even after we got ashore I was scared. Kelley was told by the Japanese captain while we were circling to pick up survivors to take the ship over. He said, 'It's not far to India, you know.' We tried to get the Army officers to authorize us to take the ship over, and if they had known what we were getting into, they probably would have. But somebody missed out. We had enough people on board to man five ships. Somebody missed out on being a big hero. We had to stay prisoners."

PFC Visage (in transit, Singapore to Nagasaki, 1942) "The *Kamakura Maru* was a merchant ship loaded with contraband goods they were taking out of the Indies. That was probably one of the reasons we didn't get stuck in the hold. We got stuck on the deck. It was December, and before we ever got to Formosa we ran into an ice and sleet storm. We had been down in the tropics and were not dressed for cold weather. The waves were coming over the side of the ship and getting us wet. We had very few blankets, and the Japanese issued no gear at all on the ship. We were given rice once a day, about three scoops. It took five days to get from Singapore to Formosa. After six to eight hours we took off again for Nagasaki. It was getting colder, and the principal thing was to keep warm. Many of the guys pulled off practically all of their clothes but their shorts because they were wet and bundled up with each other to keep warm. We didn't lose any Americans, but we lost a few Dutch that contracted pneumonia."

M/Sgt. Stowers (en route, Tientsin to Shanghai, 1942) "It was ten below zero and very cold in these slatted railroad cars. Any train that had any priority at all, they would sidetrack us and pass us, and we might sit two or three days. The food was either nonexistent or very poor, just cold rice. They'd dish it out maybe once a day, a bowl of it. We suddenly began to realize that we were prisoners of war, and things were going to be tough. It took us three weeks to go five hundred miles."

Cpl. Crews (in transit, Kiangwan to Hakodate, 1945) "Just before we left Pusan, Korea, they made us do something that would probably be interesting. The Japs had sterilization plants. They called them sterilization plants. And we were told that since their soil in Japan was sacred and beautiful and clean and everything, they didn't want us dirty Americans going over and messing up their soil and land. So they took us out to this sterilization plant and made us all strip off our clothes. And they ran us through something, I don't know what—steam bath or something—and they kept us out there nearly all day sterilizing all our clothes and equipment. They didn't let us go back to the horrible barn we had been in. They immediately placed us aboard ship."

Pvt. Benton (in transit, Pusan to Kobe, 1945) "When I got back from loading baggage or something on the boat, I gave my water bottle to a guy named K. R. Clark, who had been my bunky in Peking for two years. After we got on the boat and got down in the hold, it was hot and the humidity was awful, and it wasn't long till your ol' tongue was beginning to swell—no water. Well, when I finally found Clark, he had drunk all my water. But I was lucky. It started raining and the Japs let some of us, who had bottles, up on top. They had a tarpaulin catching rainwater. I got my bottle filled up. I got all the water I wanted and refilled my bottle and carried it back down and shared it with the boys. It was a big ol' bottle—two quarts. We wouldn't let a guy have but about two or three swallows. They were suffering; they were desperate for water. Actually, our throats and tongues had swelled up and you couldn't eat."

PFC Sparkman (en route, Tokyo, 1945) "We were going to change trains in Tokyo, and I remember one of the boys raised the curtain, and all you could see were ships sunk, laying on their sides and burning. They just had a raid on the outskirts of Tokyo. Of course, this guy got caught, and the Jap hit him with a rifle butt. Then they got us off the train and walked us down under a subway or tunnel. When we went up to cross a street, the Japs were trying to get us to run, but I wouldn't run. I guess they all got ahead of me. I went a long way—I don't know how far—and I got up to the train as they were boarding. And there was a guy standing with a bloody head and cuts all over him. They said the women back there had been throwing rocks at them because of the air raids, and they got cut. I know after we were running in the tunnel we crossed the intersection up above, and you could see bodies still laying in the streets. They hadn't cleaned up. There were fires everywhere. It was burning; the whole town was burning. It didn't take them long to put us on a train and then another boat because we were going to Hakodate."

Pvt. Benton (en route, Tokyo, 1945) "We got aboard an electric train in Yokohama. Man, that thing traveled even back then. We got divided in Tokyo. I was in the first group, and lucky, because the civilians worked the second group over pretty well. Of course, the civilians would walk up to the train window and spit at us. The windows were closed, but they'd spit on the window like they were trying to spit in your face. It was quite a feeling to sit there knowing people were trying to spit in your face. I was uncomfortable. We didn't have enough guards on the train to protect us—not from a mob—unless they'd start shooting. We didn't know what would happen."

Housing and Camp Layout

Pvt. Blaylock (Camp O'Donnell) "I stayed at O'Donnell for four and a half months, and it was a hellhole. The barracks were made of bamboo, and you slept on bamboo slats. It rained a few times while I was there, and you just sloshed around in the mud. And there were maggots everywhere; I mean, the latrines were just crawling with them."

Cpl. Koury (Camp O'Donnell) "O'Donnell had been built for the Philippine Army. It was kind of a training camp, and it had bamboo barracks with thatched roofs. There was a barbed-wire fence around it, but the fence wasn't very high. They had constructed guard shacks up on stilts. We were all crowded into a small area, and then we were put into barracks by groups. These barracks had no beds or anything; they were just double-deck shelves. There were no doors, but just an opening down the middle."

Pvt. Burns (Cabanatuan) "They had a main gate to go in, and the road ran up through the camp. Then the barbed wire started there and went around the camp. The barracks were bamboo. Up so far, you have your bamboo, and from there you have your opening for about four feet, and then from there you had screening up to the roof. The sleeping area inside the barracks was nothing but a long platform about three feet off the floor, and it was nothing but bamboo slats. You had a lower berth and an upper berth, double deck. Some of the guys had a blanket or a little mattress with some padding that they slept on, but usually you had just bamboo slats, and that was about it. Your sleeping area on this platform was about three feet wide, and it was long enough to lay down."

Lt. Taylor (Bilibid Prison) "We were imprisoned there for several weeks. This was an old Spanish prison that had been there for centuries, and there were these dismal, gloomy walls. This was quite an experience because it was our first imprisonment even though we had surrendered a month before. For those who stayed behind in Bataan, this was our first imprisonment. It was a horrible setup. You can just imagine being thrown into a prison where the walls are high and there are Japanese guards all around."

Cpl. Burlage (Bilibid Prison) "Bilibid Prison was a walled prison. It had rows of buildings, an old auditorium-type building, administration building—the end of it had been partially destroyed—and a few towers, guard towers. Bilibid Prison had been more or less abandoned, and the new prison was built. It had just been completed by the Filipino government. Bilibid had been there forever. The Japs took it over in the state it was in, and they used it. Later on, they used it as a hospital, an American hospital. It was staffed by Navy corpsmen and native doctors. They didn't put you anywhere. You just found yourself a place to stretch out. That was all—outside, inside, anywhere you could find. It was more or less a receiving or casual facility for us. They moved us out the next morning to Cabanatuan, the main prison camp."

Cpl. Halbrook (Clark Field) "The camp had double rows of barbed wire, and the barbed wire was one row about six strands high around it, and was probably a hundred yards down one side and fifty yards wide. On the outer perimeter was another row of barbed wire. At night they said it could be charged, but I don't know if it was. At the end of the compound, the Japanese guard shack set out in front of the main gate. They had their barracks behind the guard shack. The infirmary was nothing more than a hut with three or four bays in it. There was a galley, and the kitchen there was a choice detail. From there we had the restrooms and the washrooms in the middle of the compound. Barracks were running down either side of it, and the barracks had two tiers or two decks. The bottom deck of the bay and the upper bay had five or six guys each. The choice spot to be was to stay on the top until rainy season started and then get on the bottom."

PFC R. Allen (Camp Casisang) "The Americans were in their camp, and the Filipinos were in theirs. The camp had two strings of barbed wire around it. That's all it was. It wasn't a real concentration camp. It had two or three guards posted outside. In fact, you could sneak out at night and slip over to the little barrio over there and see some of the girls."

PFC Bolitho (Camp Casisang) "They were the old Filipino Army cadre barracks which were probably, oh, maybe twenty, twenty-five feet wide and perhaps three quarters of a city block long and raised up from the path going through the middle, where you could put your bunk roll and just lay right on the boards."

Lt. Daman (Davao Penal Colony) "There were a bunch of buildings in a row. The roofs were galvanized metal, corrugated iron. Down through the center there would be an aisleway, and on each side built up about two feet would be a platform which would extend all the way back to the wall of the building. These were the sleeping platforms, and each man was assigned two and a half feet for his sleeping area. We had no blankets, no covering of any kind. If you had any spare clothes, you used them for a pillow. After a while, with all your fat gone from your body, it doesn't take long before the bones start jutting out. When you're lying on a hard surface, you got a lot of bedsores that were caused by that kind of thing."

PFC Bolitho (Davao Penal Colony) "Davao was quite a shock when I first saw it. It was probably two and a half or three city blocks long and perhaps one and a half to two city blocks wide and probably had ten or twelve barracks with corrugated roofs, corrugated tin-roof tops. In the Philippines, that's almost unbearable. The whole area was pretty dingy. They had three series of barbed wire and a guard tower on each corner. We had to go across a bridge, a small bridge over a little stream [moat], to get into the compound. See, this was a prison for political and incorrigible Filipinos."

PFC R. Allen (Davao Penal Colony) "The penal colony was a Filipino prison, and it was sort of the hellhole of the island. It was all swampy. They had some old barracks there that we stayed in. They had dirt floors in them, just long shotgun-looking buildings, and they came in and put in a board floor. It was about fourteen inches off the ground. They put straw mats down on it, and that's where we slept at night. There were lots of bedbugs, ticks, lice, and the water around was full of leeches. They were anywhere from a quarter of an inch to an inch to two inches long. If you never walked out in water with seventy-five to one hundred leeches on you, you wouldn't know what it was. They stick their head in and start sucking blood. It itches, and you reach down to scratch. If you break the head off, you'll get an infection, so you have to be careful how you get them off."

Cpl. Burlage (Palawan) "We were in a constabulary barracks built many, many years ago. You've probably seen replicas of them on television. They are built around a center. The whole building is built like a square. There are four wings, what you'd say were two sides and two ends. They had maybe an acre of ground in the center. The buildings had a veranda that faced inside, which was full of coconut trees and lawns. It was a very pretty place when it was built. They even had a brig there. The barracks was on a slope. We called it a slope, like a split-level. On one end, on the first floor, was a store-room. You had the galley and the storeroom. We could put three hundred people in there. We were allotted a space of about six feet long, three feet wide—a burial plot!"

Capt. Weidman (Cebu Provincial Jail) "There were seventeen Americans and about sixty Filipino officers and enlisted men who were captured. They took us all down and put us in the provincial jail in Cebu. It was an old Spanish prison with a twenty-foot wall around it. It was about a block square. It had watchtowers and a gate. It was a good prison."

First Sgt. Harrelson (Tanjong Priok) "In our mind Tanjong Priok was less than nothing. It had been a Dutch native army training camp, and the barracks as such, although they had a roof, were open. They had one center wall down that long barracks, and then every cubicle was open. We slept on the floor. There was a barbed-wire fence originally on the outside of the camp only. Later on, they put it around every hut. Those huts would hold 100 to 150 men. The camp was just downright dirty. The barracks were infested with body lice, chinch bugs, and cockroaches by the million."

First Sgt. Harrelson (Bicycle Camp) "Before you go into the gate you see barbed-wire fences, eight feet tall, with barbed-wire entanglements on the top. All of the fences are lined with atap mats so you couldn't see through in either direction. There was one main road that went straight through the camp from side to side. The barracks were at each side of the road, lengthwise running away from the road. Each barracks would hold from 100 to 150 men easily. There was a large corridor running straight through the center of the barracks with cubicles on either side. The front of the cubicle was open to the corridor, and there was a wall between you and the next cubicle on both sides. They also had cubicles that were open to the outside. The barracks had clay tile roofs and ceramic tile floors."

Pvt. Armstrong (Changi) "Changi had two-story barracks. There were verandas or porches on them, very close to the bay. The quarters weren't real bad. You had bamboo bunks to sleep on, but there wasn't any screen on the windows to keep the mosquitoes out. We had troubles with bedbugs and lice. The bamboo slats on the cots were just alive with lice and bedbugs. We'd use gasoline, and we'd sun our blankets and shake them out, but we never got rid of all of them."

Pvt. Armstrong (Moulmein Prison) "It had a high fence around it and a big iron gate. We went in there at night. We found a place to roll our bedrolls out and laid down. When daylight came the next morning, we found we were laying within twenty feet of a guillotine, and it had been used. Buster Ross looked at me and said, 'Oh, Lord, Armstrong, we've drawn the black bean!' We were put in cells the next day."

Pvt. Chambers (Burma-Thailand Railway) "When we came to 18 Kilo Camp, it was dry and deserted-looking. The buildings were made out of bamboo with palm leaves. They would take a bamboo stick and double the palm leaf over it and weave through it with another string. Then they would hang the panel of leaves up. It was approximately three feet long, and they would make a cover about ten inches to a foot wide, and they would hang those over the sides to make your wall. They had an aisle down the center of these huts that was dirt. Then on each side of the aisle they had a floor made of bamboo. The floor was of different heights. They didn't level the ground off to build the floor. The platform on either side of the dirt aisle was made to sleep on, not walk on. Some huts were 150 feet long. They gave us about two feet of space to sleep on. They had some fences around 18 Kilo, but it would have been no problem to get through it."

PO2 Detre (Burma-Thailand Railway) "80 Kilo [Camp] was a jungle clearing on high ground. When we got there, the buildings were all new and in good condition. There was a little fence at the gate on the road. The guardhouse was located there. There was no fence around the camp—the jungle was a thousand-mile fence. The barracks were very long and contained several hundred men. They were open in the middle with a shelf-like structure on the sides where you slept and kept your goods off the ground. The shelves were about two feet in height and usually had a slight slope to them. During the rainy season, when they frequently leaked water, a large pile of leaves was kept for repair material."

Capt. Godbold (Wake Island) "We were interned in one of the civilian contractors' barracks—one of the barracks where the civilians who were working on the island lived—and there was a barbed-wire fence placed around it, and we lived in this barracks really very comfortably. We just lived in this barracks for a period of two or three weeks."

PFC Venable (Woosung) "There must have been about seven barracks total in the camp. These barracks were surrounded by an electric fence, and then outside of this electric fence was the mess hall and the other things that they had to have around the camp—supporting buildings. And then around that was another outer perimeter fence—electric fence, also. I recall that we were spoken to by this interpreter, and he said, 'You know, you touch the fence, you die.' And after seeing a man go into the fence and die with a little more than just a groan and a grunt, you know, it demonstrated pretty clearly that they meant what they said. They did. You were killed instantly."

Pvt. Benton (Woosung) "We had one light bulb in the barracks right in the middle, and that was it. We had a wood stove, but we didn't have wood. It seems like if we did, we could burn the stove an hour in the morning and an hour in the afternoon. The barracks had windows and no insulation. You could feel the wind coming through the cracks. We left our mattresses in Tientsin, and now we had mattresses filled with straw. We had our wool blankets. The Japs' blankets were cotton. We left there in December of 1942."

Capt. Godbold (Woosung) "In at least one or two of the barracks, there were a good many individual rooms which had obviously been rooms for the Japanese officers. They placed the American officers in the officers' rooms."

Cpl. Crews (Woosung) "Rats were a problem. When we speak of rats, I can remember one time that we changed camps at Woosung, and the bulk of the prisoners went to the other camp. For some reason or other they kept a half dozen of us back with a couple of guards in the old camp to come on the next day. That night we had to stand guard against these rats that were as big as cats. They would actually attack you if you laid down and went to sleep, so we had to stand guard against rats. Funny thing about rats, it seemed if there were a lot of you, they didn't bother you. But if you got down to a few of you, and there were a lot of rats—that was a different story."

Pvt. Benton (Kiangwan) "The living quarters at Kiangwan were the same as in Woosung—the same kind of barracks, except the barracks were a bit better. They were better built against the weather, and they were newer. Our camp, the Shanghai International Airport, and the Chinese military airport were in sort of a triangle with our camp at the top. It wasn't marked to show it was a POW camp, so we got quite a few bombings and attacks from fighters."

Pvt. Permenter (Kiangwan) "We had what we called an inner electric fence which was cut off pretty early in the morning, and we had an outer fence that was an electric fence that stayed on all the time. We had several guys in the camp that got killed on that fence."

Pvt. Permenter (Fengtai) "The camp at Fengtai was the worst. I mean, boy! There were no toilet facilities, no water, no nothing! It was just a big warehouse they had us in. We didn't stay there too long. We didn't stay there but about three weeks or a month, to the best of my recollection."

PFC Garrison (Zentsuji) "Zentsuji was the first prison camp formed in Japan. There were about twenty-five or thirty Australians and Americans. The Americans had been captured on Wake, and I don't know where the Australians were from. It was mainly a three-story barracks that the wind blew through, and you could see through the eaves. There was no weather stripping at all. It gets cold in Japan. Heck, it snows there, and we didn't have much heat. They had a big fence, twelve or thirteen feet high, with barbed wire slanting in. You couldn't climb over it."

Pvt. Burns (Moji) "They had one building that we stayed in there at Moji. I don't know if you'd call it a barracks or not, but, anyway, it was just one big building where we stayed. They had a ground floor and an upstairs floor, and it wasn't in too big of an area where you had a lot of room because there were houses on each side of it and also across the street. It wasn't anything like the camps at O'Donnell or Cabanatuan. It was just one big building. There were no individual beds or anything. You had a little platform that you stepped up on, and you had a space there to spread your blanket. You had just so much space, and then there was the next man. I guess that it wasn't over two and a half or three feet wide. Above you was a shelf for your mess kit or maybe your shaving gear and stuff like that, and that was about it."

Cpl. Minshew (Nagasaki) "We landed on an island in a harbor at Nagasaki. We marched about three quarters of a mile to a prison camp that was more or less prepared for us. This prison camp was like an H with two crosses instead of one, and the halls were on the inside of the H, and the rooms were on the outside. Each room was about twenty by thirty feet and held approximately thirty POWs on two wooden shelves. The shelves were about twenty inches wide and six feet long. They had a roof over the building, walls dividing the rooms, but no ceiling. They had no doors on the north end—and the hall was big enough to drive a truck through—and no doors on the south. In December the wind would come in that north door, down that hall, right over those walls into our beds. I was in there with the one pair of socks that I'd gotten from the Salvation Army in Java and the English battle dress that had been given to me before I left Singapore and the one blanket."

PFC Evans (Orio) "Fukuoka No. 9 must have been some sort of a civilian quarters for mine workers. They were two-story buildings, and we were put in cubicles. There were four men to a cubicle. They had cubicles downstairs and porches along the bottom side. They were long units like a barracks, but they were also like apartments. The cubicles were covered with rice mats and, of course, were infested with the usual bedbugs. In the cold wintertime you had to bunk together. If you didn't, you would freeze to death."

Pvt. Blaylock (Omine) "There were four men to a room in the barracks. We had a straw mat, a comforter, one blanket, and no pillow. Luckily, the other three men in my room were on the opposite shift—there were only two shifts, one all day and the other all night—so while they were gone, I had plenty of cover. And the one night we were all together we'd double up to keep warm, sleep back to back and use each others' covers, so there was no problem for me to keep warm at night. On the other hand, the barracks were not well insulated because they had cracks and things. I don't know how cold it got in Japan, but some guys read the thermometer and said it was below zero. I know everything was frozen up. When you got ready to put on your rubber work shoes, they were frozen. If you washed your clothes, there was no way to dry them, so you put on these old clothes with the coal dust on them day after day."

Pvt. Guiles (Hitachi) "The barracks were smaller than those in the Philippines, and they were divided into smaller rooms. I believe they were eight-man rooms. In the center they had a charcoal pit.

Why, I don't know, because they never had any charcoal to burn in them. But that's what it was for, to supply heat for the room. Oh, it was miserably cold! It'd get down to twenty below pretty regularly. In fact, we slept two men together in order to stay warm."

Cpl. Read (Shinogawa) "The principal thing I remember about that camp was the sleeping conditions. This camp was right out on the water, out in the ocean on the bay. By this time we had a real heavy crop of lice, and lice live in the seams of your clothing, and they come out at night when you're still. So we'd lay on these bamboo slats and try to sleep, and about the time you'd get still and get a little bit sleepy, you'd feel these little, tiny feet come out and start walking around on you. Then about the time you'd get used to that, two or three big ol' wharf rats would start fighting at your feet. These were huge things, and they'd snarl and growl and spit and run over you. That happened every night."

Cpl. McCall (Hitachi Motoyama) "We were assigned to wooden barracks. There were three hundred of us. We were on a mountaintop; I was told Motoyama meant 'mountain village' in Japanese. They had papered over the cracks in the wood. The barracks were very thin, and they had sliding wooden doors, and then they had a hallway. There was five rooms to a barracks, and I believe twenty men to a room. You slept on straw mats on a platform as high up as a table. In the center they had a little charcoal pit made out of bricks, and we had electricity there, and we had a few lights for a change, which we didn't have in our camps in the Philippines."

Cpl. Burlage (Hosakura) "So finally we got to Hosakura. Mitsubishi had taken us in. We were going to work in a lead mine for them, and they built these barracks for us. The town was strictly owned by Mitsubishi. It was in the northern part of Honshu in the mountains. It was cold. They put us in these barracks, and there were a hundred to a barracks. Again, we had double bays, upstairs and downstairs. The bays were about four feet apart. There was snow on the ground, and it was cold. The wind whistled through the barracks. They gave us five blankets apiece. Well, three of us buddied up—Joe Romanelli, who is a pharmacist in Des Moines now, and George Fox, an appraiser of some sort in Little Rock. So we said, 'Well, it's too cold to try to sleep under one person's blankets, so let's all three get together.' So we put one blanket on the floor and fourteen over us, and we just about froze to death at night. The blankets were made out of wood pulp or something."

Seaman 1/C Stewart (Ohasi) "The barracks were made out of flimsy material, but they were sealed pretty well. The outside boards were paper thin, but inside they had bamboo covered with plaster, kind of like the stucco buildings. It wasn't really plaster but dried-up mud. In Ohasi the temperature was cold about ten months out of the year. These big, long barracks had three stoves to burn wood. You could build a fire in them when the temperature got down to twenty-five degrees. I think we got more heat from the two hundred men in the barracks than we did from all the stoves put together."

Capt. Weidman (Kobe) "We got up to Kobe, Japan, where they unloaded us. It was about a half mile up to the prison. The Japs had taken this old warehouse across from an old English soccer field. This warehouse was three stories, a brick warehouse where they used to store goods. On the ground floor were the toilets, the trenches, the cooking facilities. We were put on the second and third floors. The guards were just outside."

Cpl. McDaniel (Sapporo) "We got there in June or July. They took us to a coal mine, put us in a compound. It had a moat around it. I guess the fence was eight to ten foot tall. The barracks were just like they were in China, only they were two-story. It had an upper and a lower level. They weren't as good as the ones in China. They didn't have stoves in them, for one thing. As I say, they were two-story, and they were shoddy built, rough lumber."

Cpl. Crews (Hakodate) "We marched into the wilderness—hills and mountains—and after a long, long march we came to this area where you could see slag heaps of coal everywhere, and you could see a mine here and a mine there, and in between there was a stockade. It was like an old western stockade that you might see the Indians attacking, and they marched us into this thing. It had about twelve-foot-high split-rail logs for a fence and sentry towers on each corner. And they assigned us quarters, and the only difference here from the old barns we lived in since we had been in Japan was that they had racks. You had to pull your shoes off when you went in there and put your shoes in these racks. And there was no mats or anything, but it had double bunks. Anyway, they quartered us in these places."

Work

Cpl. Brantley (Cabanatuan) "They took me off the burial detail because the Japanese sergeant in charge had malaria real bad. I knew what he had because he was shaking real bad. So I took some quinine—I had my pockets full of quinine and iodine, and I was using the iodine to purify my drinking water—and I gave him some quinine and got his fever down. Thereafter, he took a liking to me and put me in charge of his barracks. There were four of them, and all I had to do was go over to the galley where they cooked the Japanese food and bring food over to them. I was kind of like their messboy. I'd set up the table, and for a day or two I'd wait outside while they ate. One day they came out and got me, sat me down, and I ate with them from then on. I was in good shape, and I weighed 195 pounds."

Cpl. Koury (Cabanatuan) "They got you up bright and early—I don't remember what time, but it was around 6:00. As I remember it, we worked thirteen straight days and were off one. They would work you from sunup to sundown pretty generally, and there wasn't much loafing going on. They didn't approve of that. I worked on the farm for a while, and it was nasty work because of the tools we had to use. They lined up people side by side and gave you a pickax, and that's the way we plowed the ground. You'd get out there and swing that pickax for two straight hours without stopping, and they didn't want you to straighten up and wipe your brow or anything. Then they had guys coming on behind us with rakes and hoes. It does a beautiful job if you have enough people to do it. The sad part is that as people got sicker their work got slower, even in spite of the beatings and the harassment and everything. A man with a fever of 105 degrees can only be beaten so much, and then he'll lay down and die. He doesn't care."

Cpl. Read (Cabanatuan) "The cook detail was a desirable one, even KP and things like that. I never observed a lot of resentment directed at guys who had these jobs. What would you expect? If a guy worked in the kitchen, he was going to get fat. I always thought to myself, 'Boy, if I was in there I'd do the same thing. I would get what was left over, scrape the pot or something.' Yes, that was a choice job."

Lt. Taylor (Cabanatuan) "The officers worked at Cabanatuan. They didn't make any preferences here at all. Usually, the officers went right along with the enlisted men and worked side by side with them. It was a violation of the Geneva Convention to require officers to work. However, at Cabanatuan I think for the most part officers felt that it was almost necessary, and, really, it was a great blessing for those men to get out and work with their fellow prisoners of war on the farm. I believe that for the most part the senior man of the group served as the supervisor. But the officers did work. I was the hospital chaplain for about two years there, and I worked right along with the doctors and with the patients in the hospital."

Lt. Daman (Cabanatuan) "We worked as slave labor all the time. We had to go out and dig cassava roots and haul them in big baskets to the kitchen. The officers also had to cut corn, cut stubble. The officers protested about having to work, that it was contrary to the Geneva Convention, but it didn't do any good. The Japs simply said, 'Look, you're our prisoners. If you want to live, you're going to work and feed yourselves. We're not going to feed you.'"

Cpl. Koury (Nichols Field) "We went there to build an airstrip parallel to the one the Japanese Navy was already using there. We worked thirteen out of fourteen days, and we were building this airstrip, believe it or not, with picks, shovels, and wheelbarrows. We would excavate this dirt, and we had these little cars on wheels that you pushed, and you had to do so many cars a day of dirt, or you got the hell beat out of you. It was a good day's work, but if you were healthy you could do it. They didn't play games with you, and it got to the point where it was all you could do to meet this quota. If you were sick, you went out on the work detail anyhow. They didn't leave anybody in the barracks."

Cpl. Read (Las Pinas) "We did work pretty hard here. We did pick-and-shovel work, rock picking. We were knocking down hills and filling valleys to flatten out a space for an airfield. It was a question of picking rock about twelve hours a day. We had a two-man crew, and we had cars on little tracks. We were working on embankments, and Filipino surveyors had laid out this thing. Engineers and surveyors laid these stakes indicating it was level. We had to move this track against the hill and pick away at the rock, fill the cars, roll them down the track, and dump them in the low places in the valley until we worked the hill off the common level. This we did every day, approximately twelve hours a day, on a diet of about twelve hundred calories a day. We didn't have a numerical quota at that time, but they stood over you, literally, with pick handles, beating on guys to make them hurry up. When the lead car was full, all the cars had to go, and if you went by and your car wasn't full, then they'd whop you as you went by. These cars held about a cubic meter. I learned to swing a fourteen-pound railroad pick during that year very well, and I can really do tricks with that fourteen-pound railroad pick to this day."

Cpl. Halbrook (Clark Field) "You had to be in good shape and look good for the Japanese to see you. Here was a big, strong Marine that was now a prisoner of the Japanese and a slave to them. And that's really what they wanted us for. Hell, we were slaves. If that's what they wanted, that's what we were."

Pvt. Stanley (Clark Field) "The Japanese had hit this base pretty hard and tore it up, so at first we went in there and cut grass around the runways and filled up holes. Then the last year we were there we were building revetments. In these little hills around Clark Field, we worked sometimes as much as thirty days straight. They'd give us each a pick and shovel to dig into this hard rock on the edge of these hills there, and they would push airplanes back in there and hide them. I guess we put in more hours on that than on any other thing. It was all just flunky work, but the average work detail wouldn't have been hard if a man had been in good shape. The average Jap there would leave you alone as long as you kept moving. They just didn't want you to stop. Sometimes we would cut grass. I was real short, and fortunately I could just squat for hours and hours with a sickle and cut grass around these runways. But when you would raise up, you had to be on your guard because they'd get on you. But some of those poor fellows—tall, ol' six-foot boys—just couldn't get down there. I was real fortunate. We did that for days and days."

Lt. Daman (Davao Penal Colony) "Both officers and enlisted men worked side by side in the rice paddies here. First, they'd plow it with carabaos, and then they'd flood the paddies. Then you would walk out there, and they would give you a basket of seedlings. You'd go along and plant these seedlings in rows. Of course, when it was harvested we used small knives, and we clipped the tops of the rice and put them in a sack and carried them out to the train and dumped them in a big car. Then they hauled the rice to the mill. This was back-breaking work because it was all stoop labor. If we didn't do what we were supposed to do, we were beat right on the spot. You couldn't goldbrick and get away with it. Given that this was a tropical climate, the growing season was constant, so we did this work 365 days a year. Moreover, we got up at 4:00 in the morning, and they would have us out there by 6:00. We were generally in the fields by 7:00 or 7:30, and we would stay out there until 5:30 or just before dark. This was a seven-day-a-week proposition.

"At first they were rough on us all the time, but after a while we were able to convince them that if they would give us a certain quota to do and leave us alone, we would fill that quota and maybe even more. They tried this and found that this was successful, so after that it began to be a little bit better out in the fields. They'd still harass us from time to time, though. They'd push us so that we'd fall down in the water and mud. Then, of course, you had no way to clean yourself. This dried mud would cake on you out there. They'd never let you go swimming to where you could clean yourself.

"Later, I worked on building roads out of coral. This was much harder work than being in the rice paddies. We'd dig the roadbed down to the level that the Japs wanted it, and then they'd bring in coral, and we'd take hammers and crush it until it was pulverized. The calluses on the bottom of my feet became at least three quarters of an inch to an inch thick from walking on this coral, and you know how it can cut you. We built coral roads all around Davao City out toward the penal colony."

PFC R. Allen (Davao Penal Colony) "We did a little bit of everything. Mostly we went to the rice fields. In the rice fields the men cultivated the rice. They planted rice; they pulled the plows. They didn't have carabaos there. If you didn't pull the plow fast enough, you were liable to get whopped across the back with a piece of barbed wire, a barbed-wire whip. We had wood details. You had so much wood to cut, and you'd get back at a certain time. We did all the work for our camps and for the Japs' camp."

Cpl. Burlage (Palawan) "I ended up going from Cabanatuan to Palawan. That's the southernmost island in the Philippines, right off Borneo. We went down by interisland boat. We got down there, and our job was to go into the jungle and, using picks, hoes, and shovels, clear the jungle of coconut trees, mango trees, and anything else that was in the way of building an airstrip. I tell you, it is a job to cut down a coconut tree with a grubbing hoe, or you were shoveling and pushing dirt in a wheelbarrow to level off the field. We went out into the fields at sunup and came in at sundown, day in and day out, rain or shine. About halfway through the morning usually they would holler that it was time to break because the tea wagon was coming. They'd come out with a big truck with a couple of drums of what was actually hot tea. So we had a fifteen- or twenty-minute break and then went back to work. At noon we took off for thirty minutes, and they came out with several buckets of rice and fed us our rations, and we went back to work. In the afternoon there was another break. I was down there fifteen months, and I got so much dingy [dengue] fever and malaria that they brought me back. When I left there, they were getting ready to start a runway, a concrete runway, which was eventually built after I left."

Sgt. Brodsky (Palawan) "The first airfield we built was a few kilometers from the compound. They would take us out in trucks every morning. We worked from sunup to sundown; then they would bring us back in trucks. We built the airfield using very crude tools— the tools consisted of an ax, a hoe, a scythe, and a spike and sledgehammer to break up the coral to level out the jungle in order to pour cement for an airfield. First, you cut down trees and shrubbery and whatnot in the jungles and haul the logs out, and then you chop the coral to level the field out. Chipping this coral caused a lot of injuries from the coral digging into the flesh of the people and flying all over. People were injured by trees falling on them. We had some very severe injuries and a few deaths in building these airfields. I was a medical man, and I worked in the field with the men to take care of them and also at the prison camp itself in the dispensary holding sick call."

First Sgt. Harrelson (Bicycle Camp) "For every fifty men detailed for work, there would be one Japanese or Korean guard. We dismantled automobiles. They took all the automobiles from the civilians, which we dismantled and loaded aboard ships going to Japan. Steel girders on bridges and steel lightposts also came down and were loaded on ships. We also built dirt emplacements for machine guns and bomb trenches. One of the hardest things to do was mowing the lawn at the governor's mansion. You had to line up a hundred men or so, drop down on your haunches, and crop the grass with your fingers. It was hard at first for us to squat down on our heels and to stay bent over like that."

First Sgt. Harrelson (Sumatra Camp No. 4) "We had to work on details for the railroad. There were details for clearing the right-of-way, for building up the right-of-way with dirt, for cutting and placing crossties, for setting rails, for spiking rails, and for ballasting and trueing up the lines. We had quotas on all the different kinds of work. Some lying bastards had told the Japanese that I was an American engineer, and they had me out at dawn on that railroad to build that mother. I had never worked on a railroad in my life. I was the *hancho* [leader of a *han*, a 100-man squad]. When one of the natives decided to cause trouble, the Japanese would start beating him and yell, '*Hancho!*' That meant I had to run every step of the way down there and get beat because he wasn't doing what he was supposed to do. I learned to wave my arms a lot and shout a lot and use profanity with a little bit of Malay, a little Japanese, and a little Pidgin English. Generally, but not every time, the Japanese or Korean guard would figure I had it under control. It was all just hollering and put on, but at least I got the guards to stop beating them. The guards just generally slapped me a couple of times to save face.

"During the monsoons, when it was raining hard, we'd have to set up details at the bridges because the debris from upriver would set against the pilings and bend the bridges into a U-shape. We would send the men out on those piles of debris, and they had snakes and bugs and stuff on them that we had never seen. They had to go out there and hook a rope onto the limbs and pull them loose to go downstream.

"The hard part about carrying the timbers out, which required ten men, was that you're walking over this massive undergrowth of fern. Much of it has died over the centuries and formed pockets. If you fell into a pocket and you're carrying part of a load, you almost disappear because it may be six feet to the actual ground. That put all the strain on just a few of the men and would nearly bend them in double."

Pvt. Chambers (Burma-Thailand Railway) "We were digging dirt. You were either digging with a pick, or you were taking the dirt up top and dumping it. They would take thirty men out in one group, maybe more, and this group was referred to as a *kumi* [unit of fifty men]. I think we were the biggest *kumi* of the whole lot, with seventy-some men in it.

"If you had thirty men, they would mark off ninety square meters. They had a stick and measured around the edges to see if it was a meter deep. There was a notch cut on the stick. We got around them by moving the stakes. I liked carrying dirt the least because of my feet. I had calluses and my feet would get sore. I didn't have any shoes. I had done a lot of pick-and-shovel work on a farm before I went into the Army, and there is a little art to it. With my experience, I could loosen up more dirt with a pick than a lot of guys that had never done that kind of work.

"It didn't make any difference how hard or little it rained during the monsoon. You stayed out and worked. I believe it was in the 80 Kilo Camp when we started the Speedo and three-meter stuff.[6] When they started that, we were building a bridge. We were walking about seven miles to work on the bridge, and they'd keep us working there until late at night. We'd get back to camp late, but the Japanese would do us a big 'favor' by giving us an extra helping of rice and beans. At daylight we would go back to the bridge. This is when so many of the guys started dying. At one time I worked 133 days without a day off."

Capt. Cates (Burma-Thailand Railway) "My job was to just go out with the men and be the officer in case anything happened. The Japanese made a point that they were treating the officers nice and not making them work. I don't think there was much resentment from the enlisted men. There was none spoken."

PFC Robinson (Burma-Thailand Railway) "The best job was carrying dirt because there was a possible few seconds' lapse before you were loaded. But some of the boys liked to shovel. The least desirable job was breaking up big rocks into little rocks for ballast. Those little chips of rock could flat become an ulcer in a hurry. A working party could be any number of men from half a dozen to thirty or forty. We had several fights which were caused by your feeling that a man was goldbricking. If one man in a twenty-man work party goldbricks, that means that nineteen are filling in for him. This is usually when a fight started. As long as you worked, head down and fanny up, you were pretty safe."

Pvt. Armstrong (Burma-Thailand Railway) "We were clearing out a right-of-way for this railroad track at the 26 Kilo Camp. They would have us move a meter of dirt per day per man with a pick, shovel, and basket. The Americans worked together most of the time, as did the British and the Dutch. There were four-man crews—one would run the hoe or pick, one the shovel, and two would carry the dirt in a gunnysack on a yo-ho pole.[7] We made our mistake by finishing our

---

[6]In February 1943, aware that the war was going against them, the Japanese moved up the completion date for the railroad from November to August—the Speedo campaign. This new deadline, requiring superhuman effort from the prisoners and other forced labor, could not be met.

[7]Charley Pryor, a Marine held at 80 Kilo Camp, explains: "I guess the yo-ho pole got its name from hearing the natives when they carried

quota within a half a day. They just started adding on more to the quota. We were paid ten cents a day about once a month.

"At the 85 Kilo Camp we were making deep cuts, some forty or fifty feet deep. These cuts in the mountains were as wide as a football field and as much as a half mile long. The first thing we would do was clear the vegetation and then carry the dirt. Most of the time you had to carry the dirt two or three hundred yards. We looked like a bunch of ants working, everybody going in every direction—one picking, one shoveling, and two carrying. We also drove a lot of pilings in during bridge building. Elephants would drag the logs that were cut away from the tracks to us."

PO2 Detre (Burma-Thailand Railway) "I'd read about monsoons, but never had I ever seen rain like this. It rained all the time at the 80 Kilo Camp. Everything was wet. You couldn't get dry—you'd go to bed wet, you'd go to work wet, and you'd come home wet. This was about the time they decided they were behind schedule, and they were pushing the camp for more men. The adjutant of the camp would muster all the men, and if he wasn't satisfied with the number of workmen, he'd fill up the gaps with light-duty people who were sick. We had a fellow who continually went to work with a 104- to 106-degree temperature. He finally died with a 116-degree temperature. He died of malaria.

"When you got out to work you found a partner, and you'd work with the same guy every day if you could. You'd talk about things and just keep plugging, put yourself in neutral and let yourself go. You'd calculate your pay, or you thought about how much a new car was going to cost or how many clothes you were going to need. I built a beautiful home in my mind.

"Building bridges was different from digging dirt. The logs were brought out of the woods by elephants. They were laid in parallel rows, perhaps twenty or thirty feet long. My job was to sharpen the ends, wrap three turns of wire around the top, and drill a hole in the end. I also pulled on a rope to lift the weight. There were enough men on the ropes so that it was very easy work to lift the weight and drop it."

---

anything on those poles set up a chant as a kind of rhythm that sounded something like, 'yo-ho, yo-ho, yo-ho.' " La Forte and Marcello, *Building the Death Railway*, 152–53.

Pvt. Wisecup (Burma-Thailand Railway) "At Hintok the Americans stayed together pretty good. We didn't have to—and sometimes, you know, you'd get separated—but we stayed together pretty good. When the Speedo period started, the Japs were, well, belligerent. You know, they'd get the hell kicked out of them if they didn't produce. They had a deadline, and so they'd work you over real bad to make you produce. Plenty of guys almost got beat to death up there. Guys were falling off the damn uprights for the bridge when we first put them up, and they got hurt. Quite a few guys fell off; the bridge was pretty high.

"About three weeks before they slacked off on the bridge, they came and got me again, and I went out there because there were only about thirty guys able to work by now. When I got out there, at first, because I couldn't walk, they had me cutting wood and making tea. Everybody drank tea all day long.

"These guys didn't know how to use an ax. By this time, they were putting braces on the side of the bridge, and the Nips wanted them to be squared off. They wanted them hewed square. Now these Limeys, most of them, ain't never seen an ax except some headman in a movie cutting off somebody's head. So they're trying to square these things off, and they don't put a notch in the log. They come down on it straight, and the ax glances off and hits them in the shins and damn near cuts them off. That happened to three or four of them.

"One of the Nips came up, and I'm making the tea. He kicks me in the leg, grunts, and gives me the ax. He figures he's going to have some fun with me, I guess. So he tells me he wants this log squared away. I notched it, and he's watching. I notched it, and then I squared it on one side. I notched the other side and hewed it. I did that to two, and he said, '*Yasumi! Yasumi!*' [Rest!] He goes and gets me a cup of tea and gives me a cigarette, because I was the only one who knew how to do this. The rest of them were killing themselves. Finally, he brings the Jap sergeant to show him me doing this. That's the easiest job I had the last three weeks on that bridge."

Capt. Godbold (Woosung) "The Japanese did not require the officers to work, but they brought sufficient pressure to bear, and I think it was decided by the senior American officer that the best thing to do was for the officers to do some work, so they did gardening work, which, I think, was a good thing, personally. I ceased to be recreation officer for a while and worked in the gardens and found it not bad at all. What we grew was used in the galley. As far as I know, there was never any theft of it. The Japanese officers and enlisted men may have taken some of the vegetables for their own mess, and I would have, too, if I'd been in their position. But I don't think I recall any taking of the food and taking it out and selling it."

Pvt. Permenter (Woosung and Kiangwan) "I missed the boat when I first got to camp. My bunkie tried to get me to be a dog robber—he was what we called a dog robber. In other words, it was cleaning an officer's room and washing his uniforms, and I said, 'No deal! There ain't no way I'm going to be a dog robber.' Well, I really missed the boat there. When things got rough, they were allowed to stay in while the other people were out working ten, twelve, fourteen hours a day, and you'd stay in and do almost nothing. You could rob or steal from officers, steal their rice and food. Finally, after the latter part of 1944 or early part of 1945, my bunkie worked me in, but it was getting pretty late by that time. I was Dr. Theissen's dog robber. The other boy, he had got to doping off, and I worked in."

Pvt. Benton (Kiangwan) "We started building this mountain, hill, or whatever—Mount Fujiyama. They called it Mount Fuji. It was pick-and-shovel work. We just walked out into a field, a level plot of ground, and started digging—digging in one spot and hauling it to another. We loaded the dirt in these little cars. I guess you would say they held about a third of a yard of dirt. They were on a railroad track. We would fill the cars up and push them up an incline and dump them. First, they said about four or five loads a day, and they kept raising it and raising it. I think it finally got up to about thirty-five loads a day. Thirty-five times a third of a yard, that would be about twelve yards of dirt a day. We started out with four men to a car, and we were pushing five loads a day. We ended with two men on a car pushing about thirty-five loads a day. In my recollection, Mount Fujiyama was 25 meters high, 125 meters long, and 50 meters wide. When we finished that, we built seven small ones. That's where they fired down through at targets on the range. The big one was the backstop for bullets."

PFC Venable (Kiangwan) "Someone would always make the work quota on the rifle range. Then the quota from this point on would go up. They were always raising it. During the time, though, they would also say, 'Today is a front day.' A front day was supposedly that we were all going to show our respect because there had been a landing, in which the Japanese had landed on Guadalcanal and they had wiped us out and therefore we must work harder today. 'So we're going to raise your quota 30 percent today.' I recall one day they kept us there until midnight until the last one made their load. But we heard our Navy had sunk at least three times as many tons as previous sinkings; so we said in our minds, 'Okay, the thing that is probably happening is that when they're telling us our losses, they really are saying what their losses were, and vice versa.

"On rainy, muddy days when we couldn't go out and work on the rifle range, they marched us over to another compound and made us shine artillery shells in a very crude fashion. You'd have a pole, and it would have a straw rope wrapped around it, and you would pour some kind of abrasive liquid over that. Then you'd set the shell down and take this thing, you'd wrap the rope around the shell and move it back and forth, up and down, until that shell would be polished. It was a crude way of polishing a shell, but at least it occupied us, and I suppose that it helped them. What, I don't know!"

Cpl. McDaniel (Kiangwan) "Speaking of amusing things, about the only enjoyment we got out of Mount Fuji was riding back down the hill. We had these carts, and we'd ride back down the hill in these carts, and we'd leave some dirt in the cart. We'd throw clods at each other racing back to our own stations. This upset the Japanese."

Pvt. Permenter (Kiangwan) "I suppose, by the end of the Mount Fuji project, we were down physically about as far as you could go, because the hours were as long as ever. In fact, we went on a ten-day week basis at one time. I resented the fact that the officers did not have to work—especially the younger officers. I didn't feel like they were any better than I. Now, the older officers—older men—I could see it, you know, on light-duty details and so forth. But I did resent the fact that they'd let them stay in, and they'd take us out and work the devil out of us."

PFC Fields (Kiangwan) "They paid us ten sen [100 sen=1 yen] a day. We'd buy cigarettes or something with it, but ten sen is just about like ten cents, so you didn't have much money. They didn't have a commissary for us, so we'd just trade around. I've seen men trade food for cigarettes, but not me.

"The officers didn't move dirt like we did, but they were in charge of us on these work details. We didn't think that the officers were supposed to work. That was my feeling, and I think the majority of the men felt that the officers shouldn't have to work."

Pvt. Benton (Pusan) "We worked on little details here. I remember one I went out on. We were loading salt on a ship. Salt was one of the main things that was in very short supply during the war. It was a treat to get a little of that salt even though it was dirty. We took it and put it in water and washed it down and then let it dry out. You'd be surprised; it came out a whole lot whiter. It was a real treat. It was pretty hard work, but fortunately they didn't really drive us like they did, say, on the Mount Fujiyama project. You must remember this was well along in June 1945."

PFC Garrison (Zentsuji) "I was there for six months. They formed labor battalions, and we reclaimed mountains for farmland. They'd have us go up the side of the mountain to do it. We'd rake with a little hand rake, and we had a little, round wicker basket, open on one end and closed on the other. You got this rake, and you raked through this grass and gathered up the rocks and let the dirt stay there. Then when you got a basket full, you went down and dumped it at a wall. You would go back and pull dirt from the top end to the bottom to make a level area. When it got so wide, then you'd form another wall, you'd step up and form another wall. Then they'd put water to it. This is how they got extra farmland. This is all we did there the entire time."

PFC Evans (Nagasaki) "The largest inland dry dock in the world was at Nagasaki at the shipyard where we worked. It was about twelve hundred to fourteen hundred feet long, about three hundred feet wide, and fifty feet deep. They could build four 10,000-ton vessels at the same time in this one dry dock. We worked seven days a week with a day off maybe once a month or two. I got twenty-five sen a day, the same as a Japanese soldier. The shipyards where I worked were very dangerous because of all the toxic chemicals used there. There were also riveting fires, and danger from high-pressure hoses and high-voltage outlets of all sorts. We had scaffoldings collapse, people fall off scaffolding, and men drown. The Japanese worked ten-year-old boys in the shipyards. They had mentally retarded children working there. One prisoner got a lifesaving medal for saving a Japanese boy there.

"One time we were working in the bottom of this ship reaming holes with a seven-eighths electric drill. The drill loaded up on something, and I pulled it out. I pushed it in and pulled it out again and finally brought out Japanese cloth. A Japanese workman over on the other side had gone to sleep and the reamer had caught him in the britches' leg and just sucked them off."

Cpl. Minshew (Nagasaki) "They would blow the whistle for us to line up. We lined up according to the work party we were in. Then the Jap soldiers marched with us down to a certain point in the dock-yards where we were turned over to the Navy guards. The Navy guards would take us each to our stations where we were turned over to a Japanese *hancho*. From that time until the end of the day, that Japanese *hancho*, or boss, was responsible for you. The *hancho* was a civilian, but they also had *munji*, which actually means 'wharf rat,' which the civilians called the ship police. The *munji* were crude people. As a rule your *hancho* thought less of the *munji* than he thought of the prisoners and very seldom would he turn a prisoner over to them.

"My first work party was drilling plates on uncovered ground. There was never any friendliness between any of the workers and the *hancho* of that party. They had a system of trying to get more work out of you. If you drilled so many holes, you would be rewarded with a little piece of bread. The bread was an inch and a half wide and about two inches long. The first time someone drilled enough holes to get a piece of bread, the next day they raised the quota. We had several men almost electrocuted because we had to work out in the rain with a big, two-man, electric drill. Several times you would get one of those old, worn wire extension cords across one of those plates when the ground was wet. A guy would step on one of your plates that had been charged with electricity, and it would knock him over.

"The best job I had was in the foundry. I made a funnel that was used to pour in the molten metal. It was inside out of the weather, and you could sit down to do it. After you made so many funnels, you would have to paint them, and then they were fired. I worked in the foundry three or four months. When they took me off that job, they put me on a construction job working with cement. The prisoners had to carry sacks of cement about two hundred yards to where they would mix it and then send it up an elevator for pouring in this high-rise dock. I worked at this for six weeks. The Jap *hancho* was never friendly, and some days he would make us carry two sacks apiece, each weighing about ninety pounds. I'm sure at this time that I didn't weigh over one hundred pounds. I would bend over, and they'd put two sacks on my back, and I'd carry them two hundred yards. I was real glad to get off that party and get back to caulking. The main injuries I received while in the caulking party was steel in my eyes. One time I was sent to the bottom of the ship to stop a leak. In about two hours I got the leak stopped. They had pulled up the wooden ladder and stacked some steel plates on top of a stairway, forgetting

that I was down there. I did not want to be down there when they
started letting the water in. I took my caulking gun and stuck it in my
jacket pocket and started climbing up an air hose, rappeling in re-
verse. By the time I reached the old air pipe, I had given out. As I
rested, that whole two hundred feet of air pipe, and me, went to the
bottom of the deck. When I hit the bottom, I had half-turned around
and hit my shoulder against the bottom, and the pipe came down across
my foot. I cracked the long bone in my foot. To this day I can't tell
you how I got out of that ship."

Cpl. Brantley (Nagasaki) "I was put to work in a coal mine. Of
course, I'd never been in one before; I'd never seen one before. I
worked nine levels down. I kind of liked that because you were working with lights, and since the Japanese would bring their lunches in
and hang them on the wall, they were pretty easy to get to, and I got
my share of them. Anyway, we were drilling and picking and shoveling. They gave us each a quota. If you filled seven cars, you could
get out in a hurry. So I figured out a quick way—what I'd do, I'd load
them cars full of rocks and stuff right quick because this was the
easiest stuff to get to, then I'd put a little coal on top of it and send
them out. That went on for, oh, about two or three weeks. Then one
day I heard a Jap hollering like hell, and he came up to me and the
first thing he did was knock me down. Then he took me over and
showed me what I had done, and then they kept me down there until
I had made up all them cars of coal. I was down there for about two
or three days before I got out."

PO2 Detre (Sendryu) "For about two weeks we met in the mess
hall and went to school. The engineers came in and told us how to
mine coal and what the dangers were. We had to learn all the different words used in mining procedures. Finally, we went down and
they issued us each a pick, with our number on it. There were also
brand-new shovels with a handle about a foot and a half long with a
big scoop. They showed us how to operate the electric lights. They
gave us a mining hat, made out of paper, which the light would fit on.
It was good stuff. It took forty men to work this space. You would dig
your coal, throw it into a trough, and an endless chain would take it
out and fill the cars. We had five Japanese miners, no guards. They
were pretty good Joes. We didn't have a quota because the railroad
had been bombed out and the coal wasn't going anywhere. We'd break
the machinery down, and that would give the Japanese an excuse to
say they couldn't get the coal out. Then we'd just go to sleep. The

mine wasn't very safe. Three times we got caught in cave-ins. One time the main tunnel caved in, and Korean slaves cut steps in there so we could get out. We were in a wet mine, with water around all the time, and we had to swim to the steps. After that experience—let's put it this way—I don't like holes in the ground."

Pvt. Burns (Moji) "We were unloading ships filled with coal. What we would have to do, we'd fill these baskets with coal, and then up on deck they would have a signalman for the man who was operating the crane. When there'd be a basketful, they would take these ropes that were under the bottom and came up above the basket, and the guy on deck would motion for the winchman to let the hook drop down, and the whole thing would be pulled up. This was all shovel work on our part, and I mean these were big shovels. By the time you got through doing this, you knew you had done a day's work. We would be on the job at 8:00 or 9:00 in the morning, and it would sometimes be dark before we were through because we had to stay out there until the ship was unloaded."

Cpl. Minshew (Orio) "The first job I had was on the slag pile, two hundred yards across in either direction and thirty to forty feet high. It had caught fire and was constantly smoking. We spent days down there trying to get air down to let it burn out and quit smoking. We also tried to cover it up to smother it out, but we never succeeded. I never had to go down in the mine to work, thank goodness. They lined up about sixty of us with the Jap soldiers around and a Jap *hancho* from the mine. The *hancho* went through a pile of about forty hand tools that were used in the mine, telling us their names. He did this three times. He then held up a tool and pointed to one of the prisoners and said, 'Name!' The prisoner didn't remember the name. The *hancho* got mad and repeated, 'Name!' A soldier walked up behind the prisoner and hit him on the head with a sledgehammer handle and knocked him out cold on the ground. He picked another prisoner who couldn't remember, and he was knocked out cold on the ground. The *hancho* then went through the entire stack of tools, and there wasn't another prisoner who couldn't name every tool that was there. So don't tell me you can't have instant recall under duress, because you sure can."

Cpl. Sherman (Maibara) "We dug a canal, I guess about forty foot deep, thirty foot wide, and about eight or ten miles long to get to the bay. They gave us ten- or fifteen-minute breaks twice a day. Draining that lake was pretty hard. Those leeches, bloodsuckers, the only way we could get them off was to take a cigarette and burn them off. We could pull him, but his head would be sticking in there. When you'd pull him off and leave his head there, hell, it'd bleed everytime your heart would beat."

Capt. Weidman (Kobe) "I worked in the mines because they knew that I had been a miner. The Japs sent me to a mine in sort of a supervisory position over the eight Americans working there. I could squawk without getting beat up too badly. Anyway, I continued to complain about needing more food for the men working in the mines. They had brought a lot of English prisoners into Ikuno, English prisoners of the British Air Corps that were taken in Singapore. I'd never seen such a group. Mentally, starvation doesn't hurt you too much. You're off balance and your system is going to hell, but it doesn't seem to hurt your brain. But these fellows were just floating around in space. They were falling down the mine shafts. When I had to address one of them, I'd holler, 'You!' I'd snap my fingers and say, 'Look at me!' Then I'd tell them about the safety rules."

PFC Garrison (Osaka) "I worked on what we called the banana pile. There were sixteen of us. We worked general cargo at the docks. We'd unload raw rice one day, and Armour's corned beef the next, C & H Imperial sugar the next, and Standard Oil aviation gas that was shipped over there in 1940 the next, and then bauxite. It was just general stuff, maybe wine. As a rule, it was foodstuffs, but sometimes we'd unload coal out of cars, or they'd work slag piles at a steel mill. Just various and sundry things."

Cpl. McCall (Hitachi Motoyama) "We worked in copper mines. I was picked as a driller. There was two other Americans, and we went in to try out. That was their deal, and they put us on these drills, air drills, pneumatic drills. This was what you would say a top-notch job—in the mines this was the number one job, to be a driller. I guess those guns weighed, one of them, 160 pounds. I think out of the three hundred men, there was thirty-five drillers. Us three started, and then we started breaking in the rest for drilling. We worked by drilling tunnels and working the ore room. It was a mine that had been closed down, and they were trying to go back and pick up as much copper as they could from it.

"We'd drill, then cut our own fuses and dynamite sticks. We'd shoot a pattern so they'd all go off about the same time. Anyway, they got to putting us on a quota, and when we found out, why, we got to drilling our holes back and moving our strings back to make it look like we had done more. And, boy, they'd come around and pat you on the back—'Number one! You make your footage!' Well, probably we didn't, but that's the way we survived.

"It was a hard job. You'd go down five or six levels by stairs—wet stairs, broken stairs. And you're carrying a bunch of bits, eight or ten bits plus a box of dynamite, oil can, your lamp, and then you're swinging that gun around all day—up and down, you set it, you dismantle it. It was quite heavy."

Pvt. Blaylock (Omine) "There were only two shifts in the coal mines—all day or all night. Incidentally, a workweek was anywhere from ten to twelve days, and then they'd change shifts. It wasn't five or six days and Sunday off. Our day off could come on any day of the week. That winter I spent in Japan, we would leave camp before daylight, and we wouldn't get back until dark. Every tunnel I went into, why, I had to stoop all the time. You just dug and dug coal and loaded cars. Each work unit had tags to put on every coal car it loaded to indicate that you were making your quota. We kept working until we got so many coal cars loaded that day. We had pneumatic machinery to dig through the rock, and sometimes the Japanese would have a pneumatic tool to dig the coal. Then we'd use a scraper to pick it up and put it in little baskets. They had several shovels, but instead of doing it the American way, why, we had to use these scrapers."

Pvt. Guiles (Hitachi) "This was a huge copper-mining camp, and the mine itself was a closed-shaft mine, very deep. Of course, I had had no mining experience before, and my first trip into this thing was one of the most frightening things I've ever been in in my life. But we learned rather quickly how to mine that ore. I started off by doing what we called mucking ore. You'd take the scoop and set it down, and then you'd take a hoe and rake the ore into the scoop, and then you'd put the ore into the mine car. When the car was filled, you rolled it out and dumped it and came back and repeated the process. The workday varied. They gave us a quota of so many cars per day, and you stayed in the mine until those cars were completed. If it took you twelve hours, then you stayed twelve hours; if it took you sixteen hours, then it was a sixteen-hour day. Of course, they gradually raised the quota, and after a time they had us up to about a fourteen-hour day. We would actually fill up those cars with anything under the sun so that we could get out of there as fast as possible."

Pvt. Guiles (Ashio) "This was another copper-mining operation that I was assigned to, and we were constantly blasting in these mines.

And the one thing that stands out vividly in my mind is the terrific headaches we used to get from the dynamite fumes. Confined down in that mine, of course, you couldn't do anything but breathe them, and the headaches would be almost unbearable. Those were the most severe headaches I have ever experienced."

Pvt. Stanley (Sendai) "We worked here at one of the Triple Diamond mines. Triple Diamond Mines was the name of the company; that was the American name for it. The camp was at the foot of the mountain where we had to work. The copper mine was beneath the ground, and it was a bugger! Oh, was it a bugger! They gave you a little ol' lantern, a little ol' carbide light, like they have in mines where you don't have electricity. It was so damp, so damp, and they gave you a quota of rock to get out each day. Some days it wasn't too bad, but some days it was rough. The Japanese at night would drill holes up above you and put dynamite in and blast it. The rock would then fall out of this chute onto the ground. We would come in the next morning and load it from the ground into these little cars which would hold about half as much as a pickup truck, maybe two square yards or something like that. Then we would take it and push it to a certain spot. Boy, that was rough work! It was heavy work, and then we didn't have no food, and we was already tired. See, we had to walk a couple of miles just to get to the mine. It was a long way and up a mountain. Then when we got there, we had to work in these little cutout places underground. It was damp, and sometimes you would work with water dripping on you, and it was cold in there. Also, we would have cave-ins fairly often, but we didn't lose a man. I was scared of those cave-ins, and you could hear them coming."

Cpl. B. Allen (Osaka) "We'd go out to work at 7:00 in the morning. One military man would lead us to the job, and then he'd turn us over to a civilian. We were then broken into three- or four-man groups, each group with a civilian boss. He took you, and he knew a series of boxcars that his crew was going to unload. It might be scooping coal from flatcars or carrying bars of lead that weighed about 110 kilos each or unloading a carload of rice. You unloaded just anything, and you never knew what you were going to unload next. We worked until about 6:00, and then we were marched back to camp. It was just hard work all day long."

Cpl. Bunch (Yodogawa Steel Mill) "We were designated to go to the Yodogawa steel mill, and there were four hundred men in the group I was in. It was a pretty good-sized complex. They made all

kinds of armor for tanks and steel helmets for soldiers. It also produced nuts and bolts and sheet metal of all gauges. Then they made
steel gasoline drums and a lot of different things. The work wasn't
too bad, really, although it was physically challenging. The detail
that I worked on most of the time was in the area where strips of
steel—approximately thirty feet long, a foot wide, and a half inch
thick—were cut into, say, three feet and then put into a blast furnace
heated with coke and coal to a white-hot condition and then brought
out with long-handled tongs and then run through rollers and stretched
out to make sheet metal. Although it was physically demanding work,
it actually was a challenge because there was a real knack to handling hot steel with tongs. The Japanese in this mill, I'm sure, did it
in a primitive way compared to the way we might have done it over
here. As this metal was pulled out of the blast furnace, the Japanese
taught us to grab it with your tongs and flop it over. Then you take
your foot and hit it and mash it down. It's white-hot, and you have on
wooden shoes, see. Then you ran it through those rollers, but you had
to mash it down manually to begin with, so it was kind of a challenge
because there was a knack to doing this. I really kind of enjoyed
doing it. Since I had to work, I would just as soon have worked there
as anyplace. It was warm in the wintertime, and we worked eight-
hour shifts. We got Sunday off every week, and we used that day to
rest and wash clothes and whatever else we needed to do."

Cpl. Burlage (Hosakura) "I became a driller in the Mitsubishi
lead mine. I never drilled before in my life, but I became an expert
driller. That was the easiest job. We had three jobs—driller;
timberman, who went along and timbered up or shored up; and
mucker, a guy who did the actual shoveling. I had a pretty good deal.
I couldn't work except when somebody else cleaned up what had
been blasted. I did the blasting, the drilling, and everything like that.
It worked out pretty well. We'd go to work early in the morning and
come back at night. We usually worked singly or in pairs, two Ameri
cans, with a Jap, who was also a driller. The civilians were in charge.
We had carbide lights, and a Jap would take us in there. He would
say, 'Well, I gotta go and do something,' and he'd take off. Of course,
he'd have to walk a couple of miles back out the shaft and to the
supply room or something like that. The minute he was out of sight,
I'd blow my light out and go to sleep. We weren't allowed to have
matches, so I couldn't light it again. I'd just go to sleep, and after a
couple of hours I'd hear him. I'd get up, and I'd say the light went

out. And he'd say, 'Oh, I was scared. I thought maybe you had fallen down a shaft or something.' He was responsible for me."

Cpl. Crews (Hakodate) "All of us were apprehensive. I was born in Texas on a farm and had been outside all my life, and coal mines were something foreign to me. But the Japs didn't put us in the mines the first day for some reason. I don't know why. But after three weeks they issued us all one of those headlamps and told us we were going down into the mines to work. We had no prior training. They had two shifts—one that worked days and one that worked nights. If you worked the day shift, you didn't see daylight for a month. Or it was vice versa.

"You walked into the mine, not down on elevators like our mines. You'd go for a mile or more on an incline. There was seepage, and you had to bend over. You couldn't stand straight up even in the main shaft. You didn't have much room, and it was slick and slimy and mushy. If you have never been in one of these mines, you can't imagine how horrifying it was to have to go down there. The day the war was over, I wouldn't have walked down in that mine for five thousand dollars. But you'd do it if you had a bayonet pushing you. Anyway, when you got in the mine a mile or two, it branched off and up through little bitty holes, like rat holes. They had a ladder that you climbed up a hundred feet or so to the coal vein and another area where you dropped coal down into the main chute."

PFC Fields (Hakodate) "I worked at filling up the cars. Mucking, I believe they called it, mucking. It was spooky! You were a nervous wreck down under there because the mines weren't properly braced. We didn't have any cave-ins. I don't believe we lost anybody. But just after we came out of the mines, there was a great cave-in, and they lost lots of Koreans, who were forced labor working there after we came out. The Koreans stayed in a camp right across the fence from where we were living."

Food

Pvt. Stanley (Philippines) "When we were resting, all we ever thought about was eating. When you were as hungry as we were, that's all you think about. We sat around and dreamed up recipes. Oh, we must have had a thousand recipes for rice! That's all we ever talked about. It is a funny thing. You would know a man, work with a man, and sleep by a man for six months, and you wouldn't know whether he was married, had any children, or whatever. You would know where he was from, maybe, but all you would talk about was food. Just as soon as the war was over and you got a bellyful, every one of us started talking about our families and where we were from and all that, but when you're hungry, that's it."

Pvt. Burns (Philippines) "The biggest part of the prisoners smoked. Well, the worse-off guys were over in the hospital, and the hospital got so much canned milk issued to it for the patients. What these patients would do is take this milk and trade it for cigarettes when they should have drunk their milk. A medic would come to us and tell us these guys would trade their milk for cigarettes; and if you didn't trade with them, they'd get the cigarettes from some other source. So, okay, he'd bring over so much milk, and we'd trade cigarettes for it, and he'd take them back and give them to these patients. What the heck! The guys wanted their cigarettes. It's a shame, but these things actually happened in Cabanatuan. At certain times your cigarettes were of more value than currency or money. When the Red Cross packages came in, men would want the cigarettes, and they would sell their can of milk for maybe one pack of cigarettes. Later on, when cigarettes got scarcer, they'd cost you more. I was fortunate in that I did not smoke, so I saved my cigarettes, and I traded a lot of guys for their milk or for the various items in the Red Cross parcels."

Pvt. Blaylock (Camp O'Donnell) "A meal consisted of rice and soup. The soup had vines of some type in it. We had our own cooks, and they had these big iron cauldrons, and they just poured the rice and water in there and built a fire under it. When the rice was done, they dished it out. You didn't get much, maybe a fair-sized plate of rice or something. But, hell, how much food energy can you get out of rice?"

Cpl. Bunch (Camp O'Donnell) "The guys who went out on work details would bring back pony cakes. Now, pony cakes were a by-product of sugarcane mills, the waste sugar. They made sugar from sugarcane, and they skimmed off the top portion. It was the impurities, so to speak. They were poured into molds, and they were kind of round on the sides and flat on the bottom. It was almost like brown sugar in a cake, and the Filipinos fed the cakes to their carromata ponies. A carromata is a little one-horse, two-wheeled cart pulled by a pony. In the Philippine Islands, particularly in the small towns and villages, the carromatas were the taxicabs."

Pvt. Burns (Camp O'Donnell) "We had very poor rations. For breakfast we got what they called *lugao*. This was nothing but rice cooked with a lot of water and cooked down to where it's kind of a thick soup. Of course, most of the guys there weren't used to that kind of diet, and they just couldn't eat it. But, finally, you just had to make yourself eat it. Then they had these cones of brown sugar that would be brought into camp, and sometimes guys would get some of this and put it on the rice, and it made it taste a little bit better. Sometimes guys would get what was called a camote, a sweet potato. We would take this sweet potato to the cook shack and roast it over the hot coals, and it helped out a lot."

Lt. Burris (Camp O'Donnell) "Everybody lost weight rapidly at O'Donnell, and disease got going real good. People couldn't resist disease because they were too weak from no food. In our area we ate twice a day, and that's where I found out about the word *lugao*. It was a thin, soft, mushy rice—just real thin rice. There was no salt, no pepper, no way of flavoring it. It was just like eating flour paste with a few rice grains in it. They were even rationing our water.

"That's the first place where I learned that cigarettes were valuable, and it was that way in the hospital section, too. People who had cigarettes could trade them for other soldiers' meals. They'd trade half a cigarette for your morning meal and half a cigarette for your evening meal. In the hospital section there, I witnessed five people who committed suicide, knowing what they were doing. They traded their meals for half a cigarette and knew that they weren't going to live a week by doing that. They'd still do it. When they were giving the death rattle, they'd still be begging for a cigarette."

Pvt. Stanley (Camp O'Donnell) "There was almost no water there. I think we had one or two spigots for thousands of men, and that spigot just dripped. I don't know how long you had to stand in line, but I know I went to sleep many a time in line. You would stay in line for hours, but you were as well off there as you were anywhere else. It didn't make no difference. Hunger was bad there, but when you get short on water, that's worse than anything. Of course, your tongue is dry. Your tongue feels like it's stuffed with dry leaves. You just feel like if somebody would say, 'I'll give you a cup of water for your right arm,' you'd take your right arm off. That's all that matters. When you get thirsty, you would give just anything in the world for a drink of water because nothing else matters. You just feel like a drink of water would solve all your problems."

Pvt. Blaylock (Cabanatuan) "Even after we got our first Red Cross box, if a stray dog came into camp, somebody would kill it. You'd hear a yelp and so forth. I tasted broth, just a spoonful of broth, from soup made from a dog one time, and one spoonful of broth that some guy had made from a snake. Other than that I didn't try any other food similar to this. I'd just starve to death; I couldn't bring myself to do that."

Lt. Daman (Cabanatuan) "The Japs said, 'Look, you're our prisoners. If you want to live, you're going to work and feed yourselves, or you're not going to live. We're not going to feed you.' They provided us with one half mess kit of rice a day, one tablespoonful of unrefined sugar a week, and one tablespoon of salt a week. That was the rations that they gave us. They could have gotten out and scrounged the countryside and gotten plenty of rations for us if they had wanted to. It was a deliberate attempt on their part to starve these people down into submission. The weaker the prisoners were, the Japs knew they couldn't rebel in any way.

"When we were out in the fields, we could catch frogs. I used to catch these little bullfrogs, and I'd put them in my canteen pouch and shove my canteen down on them to hold them so they wouldn't get out until I got back into camp. As soon as I got back in, I'd clean them and dress them. Then I'd go over to the kitchen and get me a stick, and I'd roast frog meat over the coals of the fire."

Cpl. Bunch (Cabanatuan) "I saw them drink blood at Cabanatuan when they had butchered something. Every once in a while they would bring in a carabao, and they'd butcher it, and we'd get this meat. Of course, when we divided it among six or seven thousand men, you were lucky if you got a smell of the stew. But when they'd butcher the thing, the guys would get the blood, and some cooked it and some drank it. There wasn't nothing wasted.

"I never saw a guy give his food to somebody else even if he wasn't hungry. He might trade it to somebody else, but he didn't give it to them. If I couldn't eat but half my chow, I'd trade it off for half of somebody else's the next day. And this held true clear through to Japan. You just didn't give away food. You might cigarettes or something else, but not food."

Pvt. Burns (Cabanatuan) "Sometimes you were lucky if you got a third of a mess kit of rice. We had a mess officer, and he was in charge of the mess hall. He was there to watch and see that every-body got the same amount when they went through the chow line. After everybody went through, if they had any left over, they would give it out. Sometimes they would have enough to go around, and at other times maybe just a few guys would get some extra rice. That's just the way it was. The rice wasn't washed or polished, and it had the husk on it. Actually, this rice was better for you because it had more vitamins. Sometimes we got a little meat. They had a butchering detail—this was after the camp was there for a while—and they would bring in some carabao. There wasn't a whole lot of meat, though."

Pvt. Guiles (Cabanatuan) "The thought of food was constantly on our minds. You know, there's a difference between hunger and starvation, and we were starved. Now, a hungry man might think about sex and women, but a starved man, never! Sex was out of our minds because we went without food for so long."

Lt. Burris (Cabanatuan) "I never did get a piece of meat or a piece of gut or anything. One time, though, I definitely had a little bit of oil or a little bit of grease or something in my soup. I could taste that grease, probably just barely, but I could taste it, and it tasted wonderful.

"One time I got an anklebone of a carabao while I was there. I went around trying to break that thing open. I sucked out all the marrow where it was cut, then I went around trying to break it apart so that I could get some more. I cleaned the outside of that bone real good. Gristle and stuff was hanging out of it, and I ate that. Then I tried to get the marrow, but I couldn't do it. I just couldn't break that bone.

"Some people took up the habit of chewing every mouthful of rice they got in. They'd chew it a hundred chews before they'd swallow it. There were several other people who would eat the rice one grain at a time. They'd take their little ol' sticks and pick up one rice grain and chew that a hundred times before they swallowed it. I'm sure they couldn't even feel it, but after the first few chews he didn't know what he was chewing. He'd just keep it in his mouth and let the saliva work. He'd keep on counting his chews until he got to a hundred. Then he'd go after another one. They just chewed day and night. They'd make a morning meal last until they got the evening meal, and then they'd stay up half the night eating that. They were always eating."

Cpl. Read (Cabanatuan) "We had a word that we used in Cabanatuan that's supposed to have originated in China—*quan*. The most commonly used word in Cabanatuan was *quan*, and I don't even know how to spell it. Some of these old hands around there had served in China, and they introduced it, and it was a catchall word. If somebody said, 'What do you have in that package?' you'd say, '*Quan*.' That covered everything. It didn't mean anything specific, but it was just an answer if anybody asked you.[8] Now we had holidays sometimes, what the Japs called *yasumi* [rest days or holidays]. There was a big, open area there, and after our first Christmas in 1942, when we got these Red Cross packages, you'd see maybe hundreds of guys out there, each one with a little fire going, with a homemade stove of some kind. These stoves were made out of the cans that the food in the Red Cross parcels came in, and we called these *quan* stoves. Everybody had one. Everybody had their own, and there must have been a million designs. You'd look out there, and they were all squatting around—hundreds of them, a little fire going, his *quan* stove going with a little pot on it, a homemade pot made of these cans—and they were cooking something. If you wandered around among these guys and looked in these pots, you'd see all sorts of things. I remember walking by another guy, and he had a pair of duck feet in it and was boiling them. I walked by another guy, and he had a duck head cooking in his can.

"Along the way somewhere, they started paying us a small amount. It wasn't much, so you had to take a whole month's pay to buy a single thing. You could, through channels, buy a scrawny chicken or duck. If you got one—and this was few and far between—and you were carrying this chicken, which was still alive, with feathers and all still on it, you'd be besieged by a hundred people wanting the job of cleaning that chicken and preparing it for you in exchange for the guts and feet. A buddy and I pooled our resources one time and bought a chicken, and that's what happened. So many of these people were absolutely pauperized, just didn't have anything to buy anything like that, and you couldn't walk through the camp. Everybody was just like beggars, you know, grabbing you: 'How about letting me pick up that chicken for you?' They'd offer to kill it and

---

[8]In the Philippines, *quan* refers to things. In Chinese the word actually refers to people and can mean "all," "a few," or "some."

pluck it and all that in exchange for the cast-off parts. There was nothing wasted, believe me."

Lt. Taylor (Cabanatuan) "They eventually established a farm here. We didn't raise any rice because that was highland and we didn't have enough water to raise rice. But we raised sweet potatoes, corn, beans, cucumbers, onions, garlic, and various things like that."

Cpl. B. Allen (Cabanatuan) "They had one barracks that they designated as the cook shack. Then from each barracks there was somebody who was to take care of the feeding of that barracks. They simply took buckets down to the big cook shack where they were boiling rice in tremendous pots. They brought back five-gallon buckets of rice. Then they ladled it out to us individually in the barracks, and we ate in the barracks. Occasionally, they got some flour—I don't know where—and we had some biscuits. That was about the extent of it.

"As time went on, the predominant thought was food, and we dreamed up all sorts of menus. Some of these are kind of embarrassing. I can remember eating raw flour with a spoon. A friend and I sat around and ate some of that one day and decided it was as good as cake and that it was silly to cook and make cakes out of it when it was just as good this way—raw flour. I remember that discussion very well. So that was one of our things—we were going to eat raw flour when we got home.

"Sometimes they brought in some mango beans. They were tiny beans, and I've never seen any so tiny. They were about the size of okra seeds, and our cooks would cook them with the rice. To us it was very delicious, and it was like Sunday dinner to us when they had mango beans cooked in the rice. Sometimes they gave us fish heads, which they boiled and made into a soup. That was quite a treat, too."

Capt. Bartlett (Cabanatuan) "We started building a farm from scratch here. They made farmers out of us, and we finally cleared the land and planted corn and potatoes. We used to get in those rows of corn, and while nobody was looking we would eat that raw corn and the potatoes we were growing. The Japs would normally take the potatoes, and we'd get the leaves to cook for our meals."

Pvt. Bugbee (Cabanatuan) "Our main diet was rice. There were so many boys who had only ever seen rice in a cereal or in rice pudding or something. Of course, being an ol' booger from Louisiana, I'd eaten rice all my life, so they didn't throw anything different at me except for the fact that every now and then the rice had something crawling in it. Right at the first part of the time, it sort of disgusts you, but after that, when you really got hungry, you wouldn't even look to see what was in there. It was just something added to it. Of course, we were hungry all the time. For myself, I used to try to think back to the old ten-cent store, and all I could see was the candy case with that great, big block of chocolate in that candy case. And I wondered if that was really real or if it was just something that I had only imagined as being there."

PFC Bolitho (Davao Penal Colony) "Food was a constant thought. We used to sit around and dream about it. On Thanksgiving and Christmas, we'd talk about turkey and everything that went with it, all the trimmings. And you could smell it. You could actually smell the turkey cooking. I remember when a cobra got in the compound. We had these little rice knives that we harvested the rice with. They were a little, curved knife with a blade about eight inches long. It was the funniest thing in the world seeing these guys running down the company street, swinging at this cobra, and this cobra trying to stop and coil and these fellows taking a swipe at his head. They got him, skinned him, and we all had a piece of cobra. Then this monitor lizard or something like it came into the compound. This lizard was probably three feet long, four feet long, I suppose, with its tail. They're very powerful. They're prehistoric monsters. They look very poisonous with a forked tongue, enough to frighten anyone. But here's this fellow on its back, with his arm underneath, its jaw and this forked tongue going out. This guy's got nothing on but a G-string, and this lizard is carrying him right down the company street in this compound, and he's trying to cut the lizard's throat with a rice knife. Very funny. There were a lot of fellows who cracked, a lot of fellows who went completely berserk, completely out of their minds."

PFC R. Allen (Davao Penal Colony) "I've eaten every type of conceivable animal there—mouse, rat, snake, reptile, rodent, anything that would move or would crawl. You name it, and I've pretty well devoured it."

Lt. Daman (Davao Penal Colony) "We only got a piece of meat about two inches by two inches once a week. The only way we could get this, of course, is when the Japs were 'kindhearted' and would bring it in. A detail was out one time and discovered a carabao that had fallen off a bridge and down into a ravine. A guard stepped up and shot it, and they sent it into our kitchen for that night's meal.

Well, they sure lost most of their carabao that way after that. Never in the history of the Philippines did so many carabao fall off bridges as they did at that time. The POWs would deliberately drive them off there, knowing full well that if they fell down in a ravine that the Japs would shoot them.

"We grew our own rice, and for vegetables they would take a detail of us in the morning to go down and make a two-mile sweep of the ditches along the road to look for a plant that we call pigweed here in the States. We would cut this and fill bags with it, and that's the kind of vegetables we got. They would cook this with water, and occasionally the Japs would give us some oleomargarine made out of coconut oil. This stuff was nothing but a green, floating swamp weed, and we got a half canteen cup of that at night. Meanwhile, we were still on a half of a canteen cup of rice.

"Since we didn't have coffee or tea, we tried many different substitutes. For example, we found that we had some lemon trees growing in our camp. In order to have something hot to drink, we would boil water, and we would pull these lemon leaves and put them in a cup and squash them around and attempt to get tea from that sort of thing.

"The Japs had one of the finest flocks of white leghorn chickens in that part of the world, but, of course, they didn't share them with the prisoners. Well, egg production then began to fall off. The reason that egg production fell was because the Americans were stealing the eggs, breaking them, and putting them in their canteens. On top of this, the Jap officer in charge of the chickens decided to punish his birds for not producing, so he took away the oyster shells that the chickens needed so badly in forming the eggshell. As production continued to dwindle, he began to go along and pick up a chicken and throw it against the wall as another form of punishment. He almost killed the whole flock of chickens doing this.

"We were issued three Red Cross parcels while we were here, and they were really like manna from Heaven. I remember that they contained some dried fruit, but, of course, these had laid on the piers until they got wet and the fruit had started to ferment. Somebody got the brilliant idea that they could make wine out of these prunes, so they worked up a deal whereby they started a bunch of stuff going. They actually did make wine out of some of these prunes.

"They finally established what you'd call a scrip system down there. They printed money, and they paid us so much of this scrip per month. Then they would bring in things and let us take this scrip to buy sweet potatoes and things. They'd only pay us a certain amount of it. They said the balance of it was being deposited in a bank in Tokyo—you know, that old racket."

Cpl. Burlage (Palawan) "We were divided into groups of about seventy-five or so and got a bucket or two of rice for meals. What it amounted to wasn't very much. They only had to feed us 600 grams a day or something like that. Of course, we had no meat. I ate iguanas, and some of them had a rat every once in a while, a nice, fat field rat. I guess they were okay, but I couldn't quite go for rats. Sometimes after a heavy rain in the field you could get snails out of the ground or a puddle. You'd clean them pretty well. Hunger was the main thing because your stomach was always growling. That stomach never got used to being empty. You'd stretch out on the floor, and your ol' stomach would just talk back to you."

Sgt. Brodsky (Palawan) "When we first got to Palawan, we were getting three rice balls a day and some kind of a green soup, which we called whistle weed. It was a very, very thin soup. Later on, we were getting smaller rations."

PFC Venable (Wake Island) "Our Christmas Day dinner for 1941 was a drink of water out of our gasoline expeditionary cans that they used to haul gasoline in. The Japs just mixed the water in it, and I'm sure glad that no one smoked around us while we were drinking this water. The water was very strongly flavored with gasoline, and we had a little bread."

Pvt. Chambers (Tanjong Priok) "They started bringing us rice that looked like it had been swept off the floor from a warehouse. It had dirt in it, and the rats had been in it. They gave us some rotten cheese that had worms in it. We'd heat it up and try to get it hot enough to dissolve all the worms. They would bring us some vegetables, and they were giving us a little bit of meat. You would get a pint of boiled rice for breakfast, and that's all. For lunch and dinner you would get a pint of steamed rice and one of those Pet Milk cans full of soup. Sometimes there were seconds, but the cooks tried to divide it out as equally as they could and leave as little seconds as possible."

PO2 Detre (Burma-Thailand Railway) "At the 80 Kilo Camp the cook shack was an open building. The Japanese would usually give you all the rice, so it had to act as a storehouse, too. It was up to you to ration the supplies. Your food supply depended on the number of working men. The Japanese had three rations—a workingman's ration, a light-duty man's ration, and a nonworkingman's ration. You could not survive on a nonwork ration. Everybody shared equally, but the Japanese issued the rice on the basis of so many sick, so many light-duty, and so many working men. Once in a while a canteen truck would come in with sugar and some cigars. Sometimes a truckload of eggs would be an addition to our regular diet. Other than that, we got a few onions, a little horse and bullock meat, and that was it.

"Once a Japanese engineer came over and asked the guard if he could have six men to go after stores. We walked down the railroad about five miles to the supply depot. On the way back we walked fast and got way ahead of the other people. The Jap had to be last in line. The fellow on the back of my yo-ho pole ate a raw egg, so I tried it. It went down like a basketball, down and right out again. He gave me another one and said, 'Put it down and put your hand over your mouth.' That's what I did, and I kept it down. Eggs had a great deal to do with us getting through."

Pvt. Chambers (Burma-Thailand Railway) "The food supply got worse the farther back in the jungle we got. The supply truck would get stuck in the mud. The meat was quartered up and laid on a flatbed truck. It wasn't covered, and flies would get on it and lay their eggs and hatch the worms, souring the meat. It would smell like a dead cow by the time it got to the 80 Kilo Camp from Thanbyuzayat. When the trucks couldn't get through, they had dried fish for us. They wouldn't let us cook them but let them sit there and get wet from rain, and the worms would get into them. By the time they let us cook them, there wasn't anything left but the worms and the scales and the bones.

"We ate every snake we could find around 100 Kilo Camp. If you found a snake, you'd rake him in the ashes. We always had some brush burning along the railroad, and you'd stick a stake close to where you had him cooking. When they brought the food out at noon, you'd go and rake your snake out. The skin would peel off like a baked potato. Then you could take your fork and rake the meat off the bone. A Jap guard killed an eighteen-and-a-half-foot python, and we cut him up in chunks of about three feet in length and boiled him. It was gooey, but I ate some of it anyway."

Pvt. Wisecup (Hintok) "When we'd go on these working parties down to the river, we used to get some dried fish. It looked like shark. This was for the Nips. It was about three feet long and had a thick skin, just gray skin like a shark. The meat was oily, but it was beautiful! Well, en route through the jungle, we would stash some of it under logs. Then the next day we'd sneak back, or at night, and get it. By this time the maggots had gotten to it. Then we'd get back to camp, build a big fire, and beat the damned fish, and maggots would fly like salt and snow. Then we'd boil it up and eat it. It was oily, but, Jesus, that was good. I could eat anything."

PO2 Detre (Kanchanaburi) "That was the land of milk and honey as far as I was concerned. You could buy roast duck for three dollars. I got to herd the camp commandant's goats anywhere I wanted, and I'd herd them through a restricted area. It had mangoes in it, and I'd take one or two of them every day and eat them. I'd drink half of the milk the goats gave and take the other half over to the kitchen. I also helped the Aussies on the barges, boats that went down to bring supplies up from the village. You could eat all the old fruit you wanted and all the duck eggs you could eat. At that time I was getting fat."

Capt. Godbold (Woosung) "Essentially, enlisted men and officers got the same food. We were fed out of the same galley. Some of the North China people had brought some food with them. They had some American money, and occasionally they were able, through the guards and so on, to buy additional food, but the food was, as far as I recall, the same. In fact, three quarters of the time it was exactly the same, but during some short period the Japanese thought it was time to pay a little more attention to the officers, so they began to pay them in Japanese currency and allow them to buy from some merchants who would come in, and so they were able to supplement their diet some, but this was more a demonstration rather than something that had any real effect. We had pebbles in our rice, and occasionally you would find a worm in your stew. Some people knew people in Shanghai. They would send them packages, and, in fact, an individual in Shanghai whom I didn't know got my name and occasionally sent me a package of food.

"For breakfast you usually had some kind of cereal such as oatmeal or some kind of oats and maybe some rice and bread and tea. Lunch was a stew, but to call it a stew would be presumptuous because it was a thin soup with very few vegetables and, occasionally, a little piece of meat. Your dinner meal, the evening meal, was rice and a stew, and often this was a stew that had a little more substance in it than the lunch soup, and tea came along with every meal. But we got a pound of bread a day. A small loaf of bread was baked right in camp, and it was baked by Americans, and it was essentially pretty good bread! The tea was made out of tea leaves. Sometimes I think these stories of willow leaves and so on used for tea are made up by people to give their families and friends some feeling about how difficult it was or what a hard time they had. It wasn't the finest tea in the world, but it was hot tea, and it was made out of tea leaves!"

PFC Sparkman (Woosung) "You'd get up and go over to the cook house and get the rice and what they called a soup. I think there were about six pounds of meat—seems like I remember somebody saying that—for fifteen hundred men. Sometimes you'd see a chunk of it in a week. Then you'd get a cup of rice, a teacupful of rice. Of course, their rice was different from ours. Some days it was liable to be half coal, if it had fallen out and if they'd swept it up with the coal chips in it. Well, it was pretty gritty some days. I remember one morning they were serving rice, and he dipped in and he come up with a half of a rat in a cup of rice. The rat had been trying to eat at night, and it fell in and drowned. And this ol' boy said, 'I don't want it!' I said, 'Heck, give me the rat and the rest of it, too.' But the guy didn't give it to me. When you get hungry, your stomach don't care what you eat.

"One of the men had about a half a plug of tobacco, and I remember he cut it up three or four ways, gave each one of us a bite of it. And I ate it. I was hungry enough that I could eat it, and it didn't bother me. I ate it, I didn't even chew it. I don't think it made the other guys sick, either. I smoked a pipe, and it got to where it tasted like food, too, and, you know, it smelled like food did."

Pvt. Benton (Woosung) "We had rice and that old soup deal. It was sort of seaweed and green stuff. We called it Tojo water [after Japan's prime minister]. It was never good. I wouldn't eat it. I couldn't eat it. We gave most of ours away at first. But the longer you went without something to eat, well, sooner or later we began to eat a little of Tojo water, then we got to where we were eating all of it. Being hungry makes a whole lot of difference."

Pvt. Permenter (Woosung) "When the first camp commandant, Colonel Yuse, died, they lined us up there with them and so forth when they took him out. And they passed out three quarters or maybe a teacupful of peanuts. We were beginning to get pretty hungry by that time, but the peanuts were eaten up by weevils so bad that everybody just sat up and waited until they turned the lights out that night and ate the nuts where they couldn't see the weevils."

PFC Fields (Woosung and Kiangwan) "One time there was a cat that hit the fence, and we had cat stew. About the only time we could get filled up was when we would have rats in the stew, and there were some people that couldn't eat it, but we would get filled up then. Rats were fair game—in the stew."

PFC Sparkman (Kiangwan) "You'd get extra sometimes when we marched through a Chinese village. If a chicken or cat or something got out in front, well, somebody would grab it. Sometimes the Chinese would have their wheat in a little ol' basket, woven baskets out there to dry, and guys would eat that before they got to it. I got a little of it once. I kind of felt guilty. They probably didn't have any more than we did. But you'd chew that wheat, and you'd chew it a while, and it got just like gum. Anyway, it was food!"

Pvt. Permenter (Kiangwan) "The Red Cross box I got the Japs hadn't torn into, but you had to give them a cut of everything that came in, or you didn't get any of it. That was all there was to it. We got a Red Cross box just before Christmas. They'd have a pound of butter in them as a rule, a pound of powdered milk. They'd have a pound of lunch meat; they'd have a candy bar, a Baker's candy bar. I will never forget that. This candy bar was concentrated. It had twelve squares to it. There was a thousand calories in each square. I ate one of them whole one night, and I lay awake all night burning up with energy—twelve thousand calories at one time. I couldn't close an eye all night.

"They also had cigarettes in there. I'm a real heavy smoker, but not once, never, did I swap any food for cigarettes. I always kept the ones I got and smoked them; I never did trade them. There was also a pound of cheese. Incidentally, this is not a plug for Kraft, but we had, as best I can remember, three brands of cheese in pound boxes. Kraft's held up better than anybody's. Some of them would be solid mold. Kraft's sometimes would have maybe one little corner that was moldy, but the other two brands, Borden's and, I think, Sheffield's, as a rule were spoiled or moldy."

M/Sgt. Stowers (China and Japan) "Food! Food was always on your mind. You never heard about sex, hardly. You'd dream of food at night, and you'd wake up, and your whole face would be wet salivating where you had dreamed of eating some greasy beef stew or steak or pork chop or something! You'd wake up in the morning and just wipe saliva off from all over your face. You didn't dream of girls! There were hundreds of young men in the prime of their life, and you never heard, like you would normally in the barracks, about their girlfriends. They didn't talk about girls. They talked about recipes, keeping warm, and getting out alive. Sex never entered into it at all. It was hard to understand, but it's true."

Pvt. Benton (China and Japan) "Most people seem to want to hear horror tales, but I have none of these. My story is only one of starvation and hard work. That's the only horror I have. The hard work is not the horror—it's the starvation. I mean, that was my punishment. The cruelest thing that happened to me was malnutrition and starvation."

PFC Garrison (Zentsuji) "Our bodies wouldn't assimilate rice and convert it to energy. In the beginning they were probably giving us the same amount of food that they ate, but our system just wouldn't take it. We lost weight. We did get *daikons*, they're pickled radishes, and a bean-mash type thing. Once in a while a little piece of smoked salmon, some seaweed—cured seaweed. It takes a long time to get accustomed to eating that stuff. I tell you, it's pretty hard to eat."

Capt. Adair (Zentsuji) "We didn't get any Red Cross parcels in the Philippines, but, as I recall, we got eleven in Japan. Each one contained a can of instant powdered coffee, a can of powdered milk, a whole bar of Kraft cheese, a can of butter, a can of jam or jelly, and four packs of cigarettes. That was about it, I guess.

"One day the Japs brought in some large rabbits, Australian rabbits, I think. They were huge rabbits. We were to see if we could breed them. We had a Navy chief petty officer there who supposedly knew how to take care of rabbits. We'd gather grass, and they'd give them a little soybean meal, which was the residue from soybeans. Nevertheless, as hard as we tried, the rabbits would get diseases and die. Occasionally, we'd put a few rabbits in the stew pot for flavor, so at least if you never got any rabbit you got a smell."

Pvt. Burns (Moji) "In our Red Cross packages we got a can of Spam, a one- or two-pound can of milk, some concentrated stuff like chocolate bars, cheese, and cigarettes. When we got this, three or four guys would go together and pool their packages. Maybe we'd pick out a can of Spam for tonight, and then the guys would go down and get their ration of rice and concoct something.

"Sometimes we'd get a mixture of rice and barley. The barley was kind of red in color. They have a name for it, but I can't think of it right now. We'd get maybe a third or a fourth of a mess kit of that for rations. They would also make some kind of soup, and the soup would have maggots in it. Of course, what you would do is just pick them out and go ahead and eat it. Actually, our food at Cabanatuan was better than it was at Moji."

PFC Evans (Nagasaki) "We had *daikons*, which are like radishes, turnips, cabbage, and a few carrots. We also got some fish. Once a week we got beef stew, maybe twenty pounds of meat for fifty-five hundred men. Once in a while we got whale meat. Sometimes our rice came with potatoes in it and sometimes with soybeans or maize. I received a Red Cross parcel that had coffee, tea, corned beef, some bouillon cubes, and maybe some chocolate. The package was welcome, like manna from home."

PFC Visage (Nagasaki) "We always liked to see the wintertime come in Japan because of the tangerine crop. The Japanese workers would eat tangerines and throw the peelings down on the way to work, and we'd come by and clean up the peelings as we were going to work. You'd eat anything. If a dead fish washed up on the shore, you'd eat it. It was the lack of vitamins more than anything. It was gnawing at your body all the time."

Pvt. Blaylock (Omine) "I think we got less to eat in Japan than we got in the Philippines. By late 1944 the American submarines and air raids were beginning to take their toll, and the Japs probably didn't have much for themselves. When we were issued our rations, each plate was weighed. If you worked down in the coal mine, you got a bigger ration than the men who worked topside. There were hardly any vegetables to make a soup, and it was about January or February of 1945 when they didn't have any rice. Then each day we got five buns made out of soybean flour, and that was it. You got three of them when you went to work, and you could eat them any way—save one for lunch or just eat all of them. When you came back in, you got your other two buns. Nevertheless, they tasted good to me because I was so hungry."

Cpl. Bunch (Yodogawa Steel Mill) "We eventually started getting Red Cross boxes from home. When we did, we got valuable trading items. We weren't supposed to trade with civilians and they weren't supposed to trade with us, but we did trade them cigarettes for extra food. It really depended on whom you worked for, what kind of civilian he was and what his feelings were."

Cpl. Bunch (Miyazu) "The ships we unloaded were all steam-operated, and the pipes were so hot that you'd burn your hands. So in Japan everybody carried a hand towel, and they'd wrap it around their neck, or they stuck it in a waistband. When we unloaded a peanut ship, we'd steal some peanuts, put them in our towel, wrap the towel around a steam pipe, and at least get the peanuts hot. When we got a ship in that had peanuts in it, it inevitably would have oil in the bottom. In other words, the bottom would have drums of peanut oil, so we'd take our hooks that you pick up bags with, and we'd hit those drums and get the peanut oil out of them. We'd fill our canteens and drink that stuff almost like water.

"In addition to taking a box of rice with us, they gave us all the soybeans we wanted every day. Two of our men would be given permission to take the beans down to the railroad station where they had rice pots, and they'd cook those beans about 3:30 or 4:00. Those guys would bring the beans back, and we'd have a big mess of soybeans. You could cook those soybeans until they were just about like navy beans."

Cpl. B. Allen (Osaka) "Here's what you could depend on. Three times a day there was a little helping of rice, that was for sure. Sometimes you would get some soup made with fish. Occasionally, we got some seaweed soup, too. That was terrible, but we felt like it had iodine or something in it, so we ate it. Sometimes you got a little handful of dried seaweed. The Japs eat a lot of seaweed. It's candied, it's pickled, it's dried; it's every way in the world. The candied seaweed, I thought, was good. Then we got to stealing a lot of food— canned salmon, potatoes, onions, strawberry preserves in five-gallon tins, bananas occasionally. We'd bake the potatoes and onions by burying them in a foot or two of hot ashes at a nearby incinerator. We'd just eat the strawberry preserves with our hands. We got to where some of the men could read what was on the tags on the boxcars, so we knew what was inside before we had opened them."

Seaman 1/C Stewart (Ohasi) "We got breakfast every morning, got something to carry with us for lunch, and we had supper that evening when we came back. The rice was not near the quality we got in Java. The soup was some kind of seaweed soup, but once a week we would get fish soup. Once a month we might get a little bit of pork soup. There came a period when we didn't get rice at all. We got a red grain, kind of like kafir corn. It was tasteless, and the little red grains had little grains of sand in it that were awfully hard on the teeth. This grain was particularly healthy. The men stayed in good health. We had real good water piped from a mountain stream uphill. It ran all the time."

Cpl. Burlage (Hosakura) "They got short of food at the end of the war. This Jap worker, Incho, would stay home and not come to work and not eat so his wife, who was pregnant, could have his food. Mitsubishi got wise to this, and they gave the worker half his food when he came to work, and they cooked it for him. They owned him, like they owned us. We ran out of rice, by the way. We were eating what they call in this country, maize [a grain sorghum]. We were down to eating that. So we were really at the end of our rope, and they were, too. I got down to 108 pounds. I had beriberi and pellagra."

Pvt. Benton (Hakodate) "I was in the last group to arrive in camp. That was the first time the Japs brought grasshoppers for us to eat. Even though I was hungry as could be, I couldn't eat grasshoppers, I just couldn't do it. I gave mine away. I still can't eat grasshoppers. If we'd spent a winter on Hokkaido, I don't think we'd have made it. We were getting green rice. I could eat my share of it, and I'd have to go right to the bathroom. It'd go right through me."

PFC Sparkman (Hakodate) "You got rice, and you got seaweed. By then we were getting seaweed. It looked like cattails, but they eat it a lot. It wasn't bad after you got used to it. Once we passed a place in a village. They had some horse meat there with big maggots—I guess they were a sixteenth of an inch through the body—running out of it. They gave us a little. We ate it. Nothing wrong with maggots."

Clothing

Lt. Burris (Camp O'Donnell) "While I was there, my trousers rotted off at the knees. I'd sleep in them, and they'd get hot and sweaty, and pretty soon they were just rags attached. Eventually, the crotch rotted out, and I was just wearing a little skirt. And my underclothes were just rotted, gone. It didn't take a long time for them to go, so I was more or less naked. My shoes also rotted off me. When I couldn't get water, I used these pants for toilet paper—the part that rotted off. Then when I got a chance to wash them, I'd wash them. I didn't defecate very often."

Cpl. Read (Cabanatuan) "So many people died, and all their clothing and blankets and everything else was salvaged and steamed— would go into a steam thing—and then reissued. We didn't have any shoes. They were gone. We made shoes out of pieces of board. These were similar to what we call clogs now. This was an invention there in the camp, for there were people who specialized in making these. They would saw out heels and cut them to the shape of a shoe, and they took pieces of uppers of old shoes that had worn out and made a strap across. That's what everybody wore, as far as I know. As far as outer clothing went, we were reduced to wearing things like shorts. Nobody had a full set of clothes."

Cpl. Koury (Cabanatuan) "We replaced our clothing from that of dead people. As people died and were buried, they were usually buried in a G-string, and their clothing was boiled and reissued. We usually had enough clothing except for shoes. Shoes were scarce, but by then most people were going barefooted anyway."

PFC Bolitho (Davao Penal Colony) "They took our shoes away from us. We had no hats, no shirts. We did, later on, set up a weaving group of the older officers and enlisted men, and they wove hats and baskets. These hats were a protection. So far as possessions, my possessions were very few—two G-strings."

PFC R. Allen (Davao Penal Colony) "There was no way of washing clothes. The way we used to clean our clothes out, we'd get around a red ant bed and take our clothes off, throw them in that red ant bed. The ants would go in and eat the bedbugs, lice, and their eggs. Then you'd go pick your clothes up and shake them real good and hope you got all the ants out."

PFC Fields (Wake Island) "They stripped us naked after we were captured. But later, two or three days, they gave us some clothes to wear. I don't know what order came through or what changed their minds or anything else, but they did let us dress and took us up to that camp. We had shorts and a skivvy shirt, clothing that they had already gone through. It was piled up, and you just took the clothing that you could get."

Pvt. Wisecup (Bicycle Camp) "Pack Rat McCone was a Marine who could make anything. He'd pick up old tires and make shoes. Now, we call those slippers made out of tires Charlie shoes because the Vietcong use them. But we had them first. We made them in prison camp out of tires."

First Sgt. Harrelson (Sumatra Camp No. 4) "When I first got to Camp No. 4, I still had a khaki suit. I also had the street low-quarter shoes that I got in a Red Cross package. They didn't last long, maybe three or four months. I got holes in the knees of my trousers and in the seat. I cut the legs off, to start with. I had nothing to patch them with, so I made a pair of trousers out of my pup tent. After that was gone, I had a G-string. It was just a little hand towel, thin and small. You would tie a string around your waist and use the towel as a G-string."

Pvt. Armstrong (Burma-Thailand Railway) "I was barefooted all the time because my feet were so big that the shoes the Japs issued wouldn't fit them. I had one pair of patched shorts and a G-string . . . no shirt, no hat."

Cpl. Crews (Woosung) "I had an old letter sweater from my high school that was real heavy, and I hung onto that, and I wore it all through captivity. The heavy green topcoat I held onto, and some old sweatshirts. I got rid of the blouse because it was uncomfortable. It was kind of like a straitjacket. But I held onto all the heavy stuff, the old fur hat, and anything to keep me warm. I think all of us maintained a pretty good grip on all that sort of stuff.

"After a year or so our clothes began to wear out. Our shoes also wore out, and I remember tearing up one of my sweatshirts and using it for a liner. We couldn't get shoes at all. Finally, after we went through all of our clothes, you could get an old sacky-looking Japanese uniform and a pair of old loose-fitting shoes that we carried for some time."

Cpl. Burlage (in transit, Formosa to Japan) "When we left Formosa, the Japs gave each of us one Army uniform. And the Army uniform they gave me struck me right below the knees. And we had wrapped leggings. There wasn't enough leggings to wrap my whole leg, and I finally finagled somebody out of a pair—traded him a cigarette or something for his pair. So I had two pairs of leggings to wrap my legs. That's the only clothes I had when we pulled into Moji."

PFC Visage (Nagasaki) "Since it was the middle of winter, they gave us one kapok blanket for every two men. The guys paired off and slept under one blanket. Kapok is not a warm material at all. Later they gave us clothing made out of gunnysack. It was a green uniform that had a big red stripe across the back, which identified us as prisoners. These lasted no time at all. Our shoes held out for six months after we arrived in Nagasaki. When they played out, they issued us the one-toed Japanese tennis shoe. Since we had to march quite a ways to work and back every day, they just didn't last."

Pvt. Guiles (Hitachi) "The Japs issued us these wool, navy-blue suits, which I refer to as monkey suits. They had seams down the sides, and these 'seam squirrels' would get in there. I'm referring to lice. They wouldn't bother you during the daytime, as long as you were out in the cold. See, they'd get in these seams and stay there. But, as you'd lie down at night and begin to get warm, well, they'd come out and start crawling. Of course, you'd start squirming and turning, and before you knew it you were uncovered and freezing to death. Since this was a copper-mining camp with a smelter, we had a way to get rid of these critters. They had a big blast furnace for treating this ore, and we'd rotate shifts in working at this furnace. We'd take those blues and turn them inside out and put them on a rake and stick them back in this blast furnace, and that's the way we deloused our clothes. You could hear those lice popping like popcorn when you'd stick them in there. That heat was so intense that they'd just swell and pop. That was quite an experience with those cockeyed bugs, and it was a constant thing, too. By the time you rotated back to that blast furnace detail after a month, you were pretty well infested with those things, and you had to go through the process over and over."

Pvt. Blaylock (Omine) "I stayed there until the last year of the war, working in the coal mines, and I liked to have frozen to death in the winter. All we were issued was a British overcoat and a pair of long johns. The long johns were just cotton, however. We also had a kind of green coat and pants that were tight-fitting around the ankles. Of course, the pants were made for the Japanese, and they were up around my knees or calves. We couldn't wear these in the coal mines because it was for when we came back to camp and cleaned up. That was our Sunday suit, in other words."

Lt. Burris (Fukuoka) "Most of the people would combine their blankets, and all of them would lay together. Two or three of them would sleep together, and that way they'd have ten or fifteen blankets to cover up with. They'd go in there and pile up together and cover themselves with blankets, and when one guy would turn, they'd all have to turn."

Cpl. B. Allen (Osaka) "The lice were pretty bad. We'd lay our blankets down on the concrete and take a glass bottle and roll it on them and just smash them by the thousands, I guess. We had no other way to get rid of them. It'd be bloody sometimes when we'd smash them, so then we'd wash the blanket. Of course, that didn't get rid of them permanently, but it did help you to sleep for a few nights."

Cpl. Bunch (Yodogawa Steel Mill) "When we got off the ship, it was very cold, about thirty degrees. We went in a large building someplace, and they gave every man five blankets. They were cotton blankets, almost wooley things, and later all the wool or cotton came off them, and all we had left was the backing."

Personal Hygiene

Cpl. Burlage (Philippines) "We were allowed razors. If we happened to bring one with us, or if we happened to have one, we could keep a razor, but we didn't have blades for them. At this particular time I had a beard about eighteen inches long. They always clipped our hair for us, but they never did worry about shaving us. We always had crew cuts."

Cpl. Clem (Camp O'Donnell) "With these open latrines they had, there were men laying all around those things. These were the men with diarrhea, so they just stayed there at the latrines. The stench was horrible! Everything was covered with big green blowflies. People started dying off at a pretty fast rate within a couple of days after we got there."

Pvt. Stanley (Camp O'Donnell) "We just dug pits for latrines, and there were flies all over the place. You could understand why a guy never escaped dysentery. So many guys were too weak to walk to the latrines, and if they did try to walk, they didn't make it. You could walk through the barracks there, and a certain percentage of the fellows were so weak that they couldn't get up; and some of them had shorts, and some of them didn't have anything. They were like a bunch of animals."

Lt. Taylor (Cabanatuan) "Most of us who had been reared out in the country knew how to make a toothbrush. We'd get a little shrub off of a limb and split the end of it until you had a little brush on the end. That was one of the more common types. Some men were able to keep their toothbrushes when they were captured, and I suspect that never in the history of the world did toothbrushes last so long as they did over there. Those who had them did not throw them away when they got worn a little. They wore them right down to the base. For toothpaste a lot of us used soap. We did have some soap, and we reasoned like this: if soap is soap, there's likely not to be very many germs in it."

Cpl. B. Allen (Cabanatuan) "We had no bathing facilities. We dug trenches for latrines, and the faucet outside the barracks was the only running water. Now, sometimes we took baths when it rained; we'd get under the eaves and soap up quickly. The whole camp would be nude and soaping up. I never will forget one day. It just looked like it was going to rain for weeks, but it stopped suddenly and left everybody soaped up. We were all getting our canteens and rinsing each other off because the soap would chap us. Now we did get down to the river at times to bathe. There was a river—I don't know the name of it—that passed within a half mile or so of the fence, and the guards would go down with us, and we'd just all go skinny-dipping. I guess the Japs must have given us a little soap because we always had some.

"We sharpened and resharpened razor blades. We made the same blade last for months and months by resharpening them, by honing them along the concave side of a piece of a broken bottle. We'd just resharpen them over and over again, and you can keep one real sharp that way for a long time."

Lt. Daman (Cabanatuan) "I barbered here. I got hold of a pair of scissors and so on. In order to get cigarettes, I used to barber and charge the fellows a cigarette for a haircut. Cigarettes were one of the principal mediums of exchange. They were like money back here in the States or in any other country. We often bought cigarettes or traded with the guards, who would smuggle them in, for watches or whatever of value we still had."

PFC Bolitho (Camp Casisang) "In the Philippines the water level is only about two feet below the ground. Like in every other camp, the only way to take a bath was to dig wells, which we did. We'd lower five-gallon cans tied to a rope and pour water over each other. This held true in all the camps I was in."

Lt. Daman (Davao Penal Colony) "Our latrines were what we called Chick Sales fourteen-holers. Do you remember the old Chick Sales outhouse that had the star and the diamond? There were tremendous pits down below them, and they were nothing but disease breeding grounds. They would lime these things occasionally to keep the flies down to a minimum. This place was also the main source of all the rumors that came about, as you can well imagine, when you get fourteen people lined up there with nothing to talk about except their own experiences and what was to happen in the future."

Pvt. Armstrong (Tanjong Priok) "For latrine facilities you used a bucket, and you would have to carry it and dump it in the sewers. That's where John Owen got the idea of the honey bucket. The honey buckets were twenty-gallon buckets positioned under the latrines. We would pull them out from under the latrine and stick a big bamboo pole through the handle and lift it up over our shoulders. One man would be in front and one man in back. We carried the buckets to the sewer line, and everybody had to take their turn to clean the latrine and carry the buckets out."

Cpl. Minshew (Surabaja) "They built the head out over the water. They just put braces on the piers underneath and laid a platform out and built it like our outhouses here, except it was forty feet long and could accommodate twenty-some-odd people at a time. In Java they build their bathrooms out over the canals, and they use those canals for drinking water and to wash clothes. We had facilities for showers, shower heads or faucets for eight people, but no soap unless you could buy it from a native somewhere."

Seaman 1/C Stewart (Serang Theater) "The latrine facility was a hole dug in the ground. It was six or eight feet long and three feet wide, and it had boards across it. One of the fellows off the *Perth*, who wasn't too well, fell into the latrine. I thought, 'Boy, if I was him, I just wouldn't come back up.' But they got him out and took him to the river and washed him off."

Pvt. Wisecup (Bicycle Camp) "The latrine was a ditch about a foot deep with water running through. You wiped your ass with water; you didn't use paper. We used to call it 'Java, the land of the liquid toilet paper.' [Pack Rat] McCone got hold of some plumbing material and set up the first shower. The Aussies were even coming to visit us, and they didn't care that much about bathing."

PO2 Detre (Changi) "It became a way of life. You would not live any time at all if you didn't dip your mess gear. I never ceased to admire the amount of work and engineering that went into this mess gear. With the British mess gear, you could not hook all the stuff together and dip it. All through the war we just beat the hell out of it, and it lasted. The guys would sell their knives and forks, but they would never sell their spoons. I tried to get one of those Army spoons, but that was one thing they wouldn't part with."

PO2 Detre (Burma-Thailand Railway) "The latrines at 80 Kilo Camp were the worst, most scary, and horrible things I ever saw. They were just open pits; they were impossible to cover. They had to be quite large for twenty-five hundred men. They just literally boiled with maggots. You could walk out over the latrine on one of those old bamboo planks and you never knew if it was going to break or not. Most of the guys would try to wait until they were working in the jungle where it was safer. The urinals were a bit of ingenuity. They would take a five- or six-inch bamboo that was five or six feet long, dig a big pit, and cover it. They knocked the center sections out of these links, more or less like a stove pipe, and used them for urinals.

"We rigged a bamboo trough on the eaves of our hut like an eaves' drain. We cut a hole in the end. Then we cut a door through the back of the hut so we could close it and hide it. We also built a little platform outside. When we'd come in at night, we'd just open up that little door and jump on the platform, and a two-inch stream of water came down. We washed the mud off, took our clothes off, and wrung them out and dried them over a fire. I accidentally cornered all the soap in camp one time. I was the Soap King. I didn't smoke, and as I was trading around, I'd trade cigars for soap. Nobody else in camp had any soap. I had it all."

Pvt. Benton (Woosung) "The reason we shaved our heads was we found out that we could stay cleaner by keeping them shaved. We had one little siege of lice and crabs, but we got rid of them pretty fast. In some camps that became a problem, especially where they didn't have the availability of water that we did. We had plenty of water, and we could stay clean. We got a little soap all along from the Japs. It wasn't much, but you learned to use it sparingly. You'd be surprised at how long you could make a little bar of soap last. In the summertime I took a bath every day. In the wintertime I would say the majority of men bathed only once a week.

"We had quite a bit of toothpaste—I did. We had razors, and we had razor blades. It seems to me like the Japs gave the Wake Island boys some razors. Some of the boys had razor-blade sharpeners, and we'd sharpen them over and over and over. I shaved about once a week. With a double-edge razor blade and with resharpening it, you could use it for a long time. You might use a blade for six months. We just dry shaved. You'd get used to it. You get used to a lot of things you ordinarily don't do."

PFC Fields (Kiangwan) "I went from December 8 to April 3 without a bath or a shave. I had a full-length beard. My body was just fish scales. Now the doctor told us that he had never heard of anybody dying from filth, but he had heard of men dying from pneumonia. Without real shower or bath facilities you took a chance of getting pneumonia. Some took baths earlier, but I waited to my birthday, April 3. Then I gave myself a birthday present."

Capt. Bartlett (Zentsuji) "The sanitary facility was built up from the floor like our own latrines. There was a slit in the floor so long and so wide, spaced evenly. You'd go over and squat down over a concrete receiver. It was set up high enough so that on one side was a door to the outside for cleaning it out. Hell, those Japs would be dipping out that crap while we would still be shitting. That was their fertilizer.

"There was one shower head and one of these Japanese tub affairs, like a bathhouse. You could go in once a week, but there was just one for the whole works; and I would say there were close to eight hundred in this camp, so bathing was not very handy. And, oh, Jesus Christ, lice were a terrible problem, and so were bedbugs! Hell, I could have found you a greyback anytime, and it wouldn't take me all day to do it!"

Cpl. Minshew (Nagasaki) "In March 1942 they put a community bath down toward the dockyard. I got my first bath from December to March down there. We could use it once a week at the maximum. The bath felt wonderful, and they really didn't rush us very much. But the problem was that whenever they told us to get out, we had only a certain time allowed to dry off before we had to line up outside in the snow. We were hot, because the water was piping hot. Although we dried off and put our clothes on, we were still wet inside, and we would have to stand out in the snow for thirty minutes waiting for everybody before we marched that half mile back to camp."

PFC Evans (Nagasaki) "Although I didn't have a beard, my mother sent me twenty-five packages, five blades each, of Gibson razor blades. She could have sent me gold and it wouldn't have been any more money to me than that. There were no razor blades in Japan at all. They were worth a fortune to me. It was amazing that I even got them from the Japanese."

Cpl. B. Allen (Osaka) "Outside the building there was a long row of latrines. A latrine over there is nothing more than a straddle ditch in the floor, so there was a long ditch in this building. The latrines were enclosed in this building, like our outhouses here, and had a series of doors that kind of made for privacy—ten or twelve of those with that long trench underneath them. It was like the toilets in a bus terminal back here.

"We had a bath. It was a concrete tub eight feet square, two feet deep. A boiler heated the water. In most weeks they heated the water, and we took a bath. We all took a bath in the same water. If you were the first one to get in, you had clean water, but it was too hot; if you were one of the last ones to get in two or three hours later, it looked like you were taking a bath in a sump tank, and the water had cooled off and would nearly freeze you. Then sometimes the water didn't work, so some weeks we didn't take a bath."

Seaman 1/C Stewart (Ohasi) "We had hot baths in the bathhouse once or twice a week. The main bathroom was thirty feet square and at one end you had the bathtub, which was a big wooden box with an iron bottom. They would build a fire underneath it in the middle of the afternoon, and by 5:00 or 6:00, when the men got back, the water was good and warm. For the first hundred people, dipping water out of this bathtub and pouring it over yourself worked real good. For the second one hundred people, the water got kind of scarce. It was warm, however, and after being cold for a week, it helped you thaw out. The bathhouse was built for the prisoners.

"In the electrical shop there were several jars of sodium hydroxide in stick form, about four inches long and the size of a pencil. I was aware that it was a basic ingredient of lye, so I tried it a bit and found that clothes would get awful clean with just a little of it. I brought the sticks back to camp, and some of the other fellows saw what I was doing and did the same.

"The Japanese would buy toothbrushes and tooth powder, so we were able to brush our teeth very well. They charged us twenty cents for a toothbrush and ten cents for tooth powder. Shaving was a problem. Most of us managed by just growing beards. The Japanese insisted that everybody keep their hair cut off. The field artillery bunch had two or three pairs of clippers, and they would cut your hair for you. Jerry Bunch electrified one pair of clippers by building a vibrating-type motor and hooking on the blades. He'd swish through your hair two or three times and you had a haircut."

Health and Medical Treatment

Cpl. Clem (Camp O'Donnell) "I was pretty unique. I hadn't had a bowel movement during the two months I was on Bataan and then for the first two weeks I was at O'Donnell, so I was kind of worried about it, and I fell in the sick line one morning. I went up there to the doctor, and told him I couldn't get my bowels to move. He said, 'What did you say, son?' I told him again, and he said, 'Well, let me shake your hand. You're the luckiest man in this camp!' "

Cpl. Bunch (Camp O'Donnell) "I caught dysentery, and I'm convinced that I would have died if two friends had not given me some sulfathiazole. There comes a time when you can't eat, as was my case, when you have dysentery. You're too weak, and you have no desire to eat. And there's mucus that forms in the intestines that keeps coming all the time, then blood, and then you become so weak that you just die. I had dysentery for three or four days, and I was in pretty bad shape. I don't know of anybody who had dysentery over four or five days who didn't die from it, as a rule, unless they had medication of some kind. In my case it just so happened that these two fellows had the sulfathiazole and gave me some."

Cpl. Read (Camp O'Donnell) "There were a lot of doctors among the prisoners. Let me point that out. There were an enormous number of them, but they had not one aspirin pill among the whole lot—not anything. They actually conducted sick call in there, and we would line up to go see these doctors, and about all they could do was sympathize with you. They still went through the motions. Anyway, they attended the dying, and there was a place where they kept the dead ones until they could be buried. It was kind of a big building that they put them in, and I've seen that building when they were stacked up almost to the ceiling inside like cordwood. The place was lousy with green blowflies and things like that just all over the place. As a matter of fact, during this time I came to hate flies, and to this day I can't stand flies of any kind."

Pvt. Guiles (Camp O'Donnell) "With dysentery you have absolutely no control over your bowels. You have the urge, but you have no control. You start passing mucus, and that's pretty close to the end. Not only once but several times I reached that stage, but somehow I managed to survive. As far as medical treatment from the Japanese, I received none."

Cpl. Bunch (Cabanatuan) "I had malaria. Every day I had an attack, and each day as you have this attack you first start off with a little chill up your back, and the first thing you know you are just freezing to death. I've actually watched guys climb up in the bays and pile blankets and anything they could get off their buddies' beds and just lay there and just rattle the bamboo with chills. Then the chills go away, and you get a fever. Then the fever diminishes—and this whole process takes about two or three hours—and then you're just kind of weak. The next day, fifteen minutes later than the day before, you're going to get another one. It seemed to get to where you'd expect it. I don't know how long you can survive with malaria, but you obviously become weaker as time went on.

"The biggest problem was what we called tropical ulcers. Boy, those things were terrible! You could start off with a little scratch on your leg or hand, and it just kept expanding, getting larger and larger and deeper and deeper. I've seen guys covered with these things— terrible-looking things. They used sulfathiazole powder to cure these things, and we could get some of this in Cabanatuan. I don't recall whether the Red Cross or the Japanese gave it to us. I still have a scar on my knee where I had a tropical ulcer."

Lt. Burris (Cabanatuan) "I got so hot from malaria that I passed out. I got blind. I went blind because I got so hot with malaria. Somebody carried me over to the hospital area, and eventually I got back my sight. But I was weak. I didn't have any strength. I was like a little kitten.

"I know I went blind again. I was just walking up a path toward my little shack, and I went blind, and I stumbled, and my hip hit a hard, sharp rock. Shortly after that, I got paralyzed, and I couldn't move my arms or legs. Generally, it was three of them that I couldn't move, but never the same ones all the time. I guess that lasted a month or two months—something like that.

"Then I got wet beriberi. My legs swelled up like two big balloons, and I couldn't bend my knees. The swelling across my joints was so big that I couldn't hardly operate my legs. The swelling went up to my crotch, and then it didn't go any higher. After a while I started losing water, and it went down. I think I had wet beriberi at least six weeks or two months, something like that.

"I got dysentery. I started going to the latrine about thirty or forty times a day. I wasn't hardly getting any sleep. I'd lay down, and in about twenty minutes I'd have to get up and go again. I got weak from lack of sleep, and my body lost more fluid. I started defecating blood; I'd go strain and get some mucus and blood. During this period, two or three months of this stuff or longer, I got so weak that I didn't want to talk to nobody. I'd just go sit out on the little bench outside my building. I'd just sit out there. It had a kind of a board across it that you could use as a table. I'd sit out there with my elbows on the board and hold my head and just sit there until my next meal or time to go to bed.

"So I had paralysis, malaria, dysentery, beriberi, and I don't know what else. This was in late 1942, and it was a period there when I wanted to die. I wanted to go to sleep and never wake up, I'll put it that way. It was just too much effort to keep on living. I was in such bad shape that I asked the doctor to send me over to the Zero Ward. We had what we called the Zero Ward, and that's where you went to die. So I asked him to send me there, that I couldn't control my bowels and I was just making a mess around there. I wanted to die, anyway. I really wanted to go to sleep and never wake up. I had that feeling for some time—maybe three or four days. But the doctor wouldn't let me go down there.

"If beriberi went up to a guy's stomach, he died. I think it would be pushing against your stomach and lungs and everything else in the upper part of your body. Doctors would sometimes clean a mess kit knife and stick it in their legs to drain out this liquid before it went too high. Your skin is real thin, and when I had beriberi I stuck a knife in and drained that fluid out. Some people had their scrotum swell up to the size of a soccer ball. When they'd urinate, they'd spew just every which way. It would come out the pores of their skin, and it was just a terrible mess, and they couldn't clean themselves up. A guy who was in the bunk next to me, his scrotum got swelled up, and he punctured his own scrotum and drained the water out. Then he got a piece of medical tape—I don't know where he got it— and taped up that cut, and it healed. He got well, and he never got that beriberi swelling again, either. He did that all by himself. I would've been scared to death to do that."

Cpl. Read (Cabanatuan) "There was a dentist or two in our camp, and they had some equipment because we brought it in from a work detail. I had some teeth filled while I was there. There were a lot of guys from Corregidor who had coins, so they used these coins to make fillings. The dentists had these old Army field drills that looked like old-fashioned sewing machines with a treadle. They had a couple of those things and some bits and things that we'd brought in. What they'd do, they'd make a collection from people, and a lot of those Corregidor guys had silver coins. They carved them up into hunks, and then they'd drill out a hole in your tooth, make it bigger at the bottom than at the top, and then they'd take a hunk of that coin, just carve a hunk out with a sharpened instrument of some kind, and approximate the size. Then they'd take a mallet and beat it in. Some of those coins were the best fillings I ever had. I've had a lot of fillings in my time, and those were some of the best, lasted the longest, and I may even have some of them now. I'd say I had about five like that during the time I was in there.

"Now, for dysentery we'd just eat charcoal. That's based on some foundation, too, because charcoal has absorptive properties. We didn't always use charcoal because whenever they cooked rice in these iron pots—when they steamed the rice—there was always a layer of burned rice next to the iron. Of course, that's charcoal, and they then developed a system for the people who had dysentery. You had to get this prescription from the doctor. In other words, if you had a prescription for burned rice, well, you got the burned rice ration. Instead of getting the regular rice ration, you got a couple slabs of burned rice.

"The Zero Ward was the last stop inside the hospital camp. This was where you went when the doctors decided they couldn't do anything further for you—you were maybe in a coma or a near coma or something like that. So they'd haul you over there and dump you in the Zero Ward in a stack, and there you stayed until you died. That's where we picked up the bodies for burial."

Capt. Bartlett (Cabanatuan) "While we were still on Corregidor and under Jap control, I was put in charge of a detail to disinfect the grounds. As a result, I was able to go into the Army aid stations scattered about, and I took all the quinine, all the sulfathiazole, all the narcotics I could find—just a general mass of medicines. So when we left Corregidor, I had a musette bag and a Red Cross first-aid bag, and I loaded them with my medicines. Consequently, I was the medicine man for Cabanatuan while I was there.

"There's something I need to mention about our doctors. When I got there, the boys knew I had the medicine because I came in with it. A boy would come running up to me and hand me fifty dollars, and I'd say, 'What is this for?' He'd say, 'I want sulfathiazole tablets.' I said, 'Well, what does that have to do with it?' He said, 'That's the going price!' As it turned out, the doctors there were the only ones who had anything, of course, and they were selling quinine or sulfathiazole for a dollar a grain. That was a common practice among the doctors there, and there were a lot of them in Cabanatuan. I don't know of any doctor there who had medicine who gave it away! I got there a little late, and I imagine there were a lot of doctors who were not a part of this. But a big bunch of them were. They had a pretty profitable racket going on."

Lt. Daman (Cabanatuan) "My father-in-law was put in the Zero Ward because they expected him to die. Those who were put there received virtually no treatment at all—no medicine, no extra food, no nothing. Even so, you had to have one foot in the grave and the other one on a banana peel before they would say you were sick enough to go on sick call. Actually, you had to be lying on the ground before they would say you were sick enough to go on sick call. After I left Cabanatuan, I learned later from another prisoner that my father-in-law had died there."

Pvt. Stanley (Clark Field) "I had dry beriberi, but fortunately I didn't have it too long. Your bones ache; you just ache constantly. You just kind of dry up, like you have arthritis or rheumatism or something. At the same time my gums bled because I didn't get any fruit or vitamin C. But, oh, my bones ached a lot. I guess that gave me more pain than anything else in there. They had a sink or trough up in the washhouse, and I slept many a night in there and laid down and turned the water hydrant on my legs.

"I had more wet beriberi than I did dry beriberi. Take your arm, for instance, here. You could take your finger and punch a hole in your arm, and that hole would remain just like pushing a hole in the mud. Everything in you was just water. You were just soft and flabby, and you looked swollen like a guy who was an alcoholic for a long time. You looked flushed. The wet beriberi was dangerous in some ways. The way I understood it, some of the guys had wet beriberi for so long that they had swollen up around their heart and choked their heart. This is where the Red Cross packages could really help you. In other words, just a little bit of something would give you a big boost."

Cpl. Bunch (Bilibid Prison) "I had malaria very badly at Cabanatuan, but I had no medicine whatsoever until I got to Bilibid. When we got to Bilibid, knowing that we were going to Japan, the Japanese issued quinine. I don't know if it was through the Red Cross or what, but we got a ten-day course of quinine. They gave you a ten-day course, and then you would wait a week and then take another ten-day course. Of course, I'm sure that their purpose here was to get us to Japan in good enough health so we could do what they wanted us to do, and that was to work."

Cpl. McCall (Nichols Field) "This was a rough detail. At Nichols Field the White Angel would come by and wear gloves and say, 'What's wrong? Why are you out for sick call?' And if it was a fever, he'd feel your head with his gloves on, and then he'd slap you and knock you down. If it was dysentery, he'd double up his fist and hit you in the stomach. He was a naval lieutenant in charge of this camp. We called him the White Angel, I guess, because he wore a white naval uniform."

Sgt. Burk (Nielson Field) "I lost sight in my one eye here due to starvation, particularly a lack of vitamin A. Actually, the immediate cause was a perforated corneal ulcer, and I probably got something in it that infected it. It had perforated during the night, and before I knew it was there it had already perforated, and they didn't have anything to help me, anyway. That eye became runny, and then the vision just diminished. Then this other eye got to the point where a blind spot showed up in it. The doctor told me, 'You've lost your eye.' I told him, 'Well, it isn't the best news, but it isn't the worst. No need crying over spilled milk. If it's gone, then it's gone. There's nothing either you or I can do about it.' That's the way I felt. What were you going to do? That was all. Then they sent me back to Bilibid Prison because they had a hospital there. They operated on me to get rid of the perforation, and that helped some. But to this day, if you walk more than eight feet away from me, to me your head is gone even if I looked right at it."

Lt. Daman (Davao Penal Colony) "I had a really bad hernia condition, and I had an operation at Davao that would do justice to the Mayo Clinic. I was on the operating table for two hours and twenty minutes. The doctor had a little bit of anesthesia, just enough for a spinal. He blocked me out for an hour and thirty minutes. For the balance of the time, I lay there with my intestines laying on a towel while he finished operating. The doctor sewed me with 125 stitches to put the peritoneum back together inside there.

"Then while I was recuperating in the ward there, my malaria flared up, and I shook so bad that the bed they had me on collapsed. All these stitches and this underlining opened up, so I had to lie there for forty-two days with this wide-open wound trying to heal itself. We had absolutely no kind of medication to help this thing heal, but eventually I did heal up all right. But it was just a nightmare, is all I can say. Then they put me back in the regular barracks, and the next day I was assigned to a work detail."

PFC R. Allen (Davao Penal Colony) "The camp was full of beri-beri, dysentery, yellow jaundice, and dinky [dengue] fever. Dinky fever is worse than malaria. You get very, very severe headaches, very high fever, and it'll last sometimes two weeks. The only thing you could do for a man who was in that shape was just try to keep him quiet and keep compresses on him, keep him wrapped up to help combat the chills.

"We had a doctor, an American doctor, with us—Dr. Blinkey. He was Jewish. The only thing he had in the way of medical supplies was the herbs and this type of thing that he knew about that we could collect. That's what he used. He was a good doctor."

Cpl. Burlage (Palawan) "We didn't have medical facilities. We usually had a couple of corpsmen in the crowd, and they were given the recognition of being corpsmen or medics, but they had no medicine, maybe a little iodine. If a guy cut himself on something out in the field, they might be able to put iodine on it, but that was about it."

PFC Visage (Surabaja) "There were quite a few mosquitoes around, and I contracted dengue fever. I had a high fever for several days. One morning, when I woke up, I was paralyzed. I couldn't move a muscle in my body. One of my best buddies noticed my problem after he kept trying to get me to get up for roll call. The old Dutch doctor was called in, and he took me to sick bay on a stretcher. They gave me a shot with the biggest dadgummed needle I have ever seen in my life. They shot me in the bottom of my spine. I laid there for fifteen minutes, and, all of a sudden, all of the feeling came into my body. I've never run into an American doctor who knew what dengue fever was. The Dutch doctors were very good. They could make do and concoct things out of nothing to treat us."

Pvt. Wisecup (Bicycle Camp) "I got dysentery and damned near died of it. For the type of dysentery I had, bacillary and then amoebic with it, you needed a drug called emetine. They didn't have it there. When I got down to where I was crapping fifteen or twenty times a day, I couldn't go on working parties and could hardly eat. I was a walking wreck, people wouldn't come near me. I'd never been sick in my life. I believe I could have died easily, but I was a selfish son of a bitch. I wanted to get a drink, get a girl, play some more ball, get in some fights. One of the Dutch doctors told me to get on the boat to

Singapore. He said, 'Look, it's a five- or six-day trip over there, and it's going to be hell. But if I were you, I'd try to make it because they may have emetine or some other drug. If you stay here, you're going to die because we don't have anything to treat you with.' I made that trip, I got that emetine treatment, and I got over the dysentery."

Seaman 1/C Stewart (Serang Theater) "One of the ship's doctors came down and looked at my burns and told me to hang on. He figured that I wouldn't last another two days. Three weeks later, he was surprised that I was still around. The Japanese had put some bandages on my back, which was the worst. A couple of days later, when they wanted to change them, they started yanking them off where they stuck, and that hurt. On the fourth day an Australian doctor, apparently off the *Perth*, started treating me. He soaked the bandages and got them off gently. I was afraid I would lose my left arm because of infection and it being in the tropics. The Australian doctor looked at it, asked me if I could move my fingers, and said he'd have me well in a week. Well, in ten days' time this scar tissue had formed, and it was healing up. He used cod-liver oil ointment, and it did a beautiful job."

First Sgt. Harrelson (Sumatra Camp No. 4) "I got a scratch on my left ankle which started out as a little sore but kept getting bigger and bigger. My whole foot and ankle swelled up to the size of a football. An Ambonese doctor came into the camp and told me to take a cup of boiled water and pour it into the sore at least twice a day. It started closing up but not healing at the bottom. He said it wouldn't do, and he opened it up with some fingernail scissors. He then got the guards to allow him to go out into the jungle and get some leaves and herbs to boil. He wound up with a green solution that looked like antifreeze. He put a half teaspoon in the ulcer, and that started the healing from the bottom and saved my foot."

Pvt. Chambers (Burma-Thailand Railway) "I had two or three tropical ulcers. I had one on my heel and another on my toe. A guy on a work party dropped an ax on my toe and started the ulcer. It rotted out to where you could see the bone. It would never scab over. We had Dr. [Philip] Bloemsma with us, and he used a silver spoon with a sharpened edge to cut the rotten meat out of those ulcers. I finally got sick enough that I couldn't work in November of 1943. They had turned 80 Kilo Camp into what they called a hospital. It wasn't anything but a place to send you back to die. They sent me and a friend of mine back to work at that camp. We brought the guys that couldn't get up themselves around to the medics. We turned the blankets back on one who was unconscious and saw maggots in his eyes, nose, and everywhere else. These guys had ulcers all over their hands and arms."

Pvt. Armstrong (Burma-Thailand Railway) "The hospital hut at 80 Kilo Camp, which was a death camp, was just another grass shack where you'd take a person, and they cut his food down. If you were not able to work, you didn't get any food, except what we could take him. If they caught you doing that, you'd get another beating. The only thing available in the hospital hut was quinine for malaria fever, and lots of times there wasn't any of that. We always figured that they took you there to die. If the doctor said too much when the guards needed sick men to work, he'd get slapped around. Not many people made it out of 80 Kilo Camp alive."

Capt. Cates (Burma-Thailand Railway) "Our need for food was such that we would eat anything, things that we knew not to eat. All six of us in one cubicle at 100 Kilo Camp came down with cholera as a result of eating food that was open to the air. It was a thing called a rhanboetan, a hairy fruit of the jungle. I am convinced that this is the source of the disease that took Dr. [S. Hugh] Lumpkin. A native told us that if we would eat charcoal, it would absorb the contents of our stomachs that were at fault. It was effective with J. B. Nelson and me. He and I literally forced charcoal and burnt rice down each other's throats."

Pvt. Wisecup (Kanchanaburi) "When I worked in that ward, there were only two of us taking care of about seventy or eighty ulcer cases in Kanchanaburi. What you did, you had your urine bottles that we made out of sections of bamboo. Also, you had your shit pan made out of cut bamboo. We had to help them go—hold them up, like one guy who had ulcers on his buttocks, and we helped him so that the maggots wouldn't get into it. Well, they got in and all the way around it. They had to operate on him, and they cut off half of the poor bastard's butt. You could see all the ligaments and everything. Well, he had to lay on his belly, and it got gangrenous. We used to hold that bastard up to take a crap, you know. Man, he died horribly. That poor son of a bitch! I never will forget that. Boy, let me tell you, that's a hard way to go, with them ulcers. There ain't no worse. Just before you die, two or three days before, that gangrene affects your mind and everything else."

Pvt. Benton (Woosung) "Prison camp affected bigger men worse than it did the smaller men. We had one guy by the name of Birdlegs

Brown. Of course, we had a nickname for everybody. I don't guess he lost five pounds all during the war—he didn't have any to lose. He was skin and bones. If he'd lost any more, there was no way he could have made it. Before the war he lived on cigarettes, coffee, whiskey sours, and whiskey Cokes. He never suffered as far as hunger was concerned. I weighed 175, and the lowest I got down to was 125. I'm big-boned, so you can see I was mostly bone.

"Fortunately, we had the best doctors in the world there but no equipment, no medicine. Well, we did get some through the Red Cross in Shanghai; we got a limited supply. We had a doctor by the name of Foley, and as far as I'm concerned he is one of the greatest men that ever lived. He operated on me in 1943. He took a cyst off the end of my spine, but I never had a minute's trouble with it. The reason I say he was one of the greatest is not for what he did for me. I've seen the result of what he did for other people with what he had. It's amazing what the man did."

PFC Venable (Woosung) "I recall that they took one fellow in and took out his appendix without benefit of anesthetic. It's a rough way to lose your appendix, but I suppose that it saved his life, so he was grateful from that standpoint. But it was agonizing."

PFC Sparkman (Kiangwan) "I was always healthy. I didn't get sick, never did. The only thing I ever had was chilblain. Your hands stay chilled all the time. They swell up, and it itches when you sleep at night, and you just claw your hands and your feet. You just claw the skin off of them. It was caused by prolonged cold and no protection. But I stayed in camp two days, and they slipped me some hot water and I soaked them. Hot water takes it out right away, but it comes back when you get out in the cold again."

Capt. Adair (Zentsuji) "Back in the Philippines we somehow had gotten infected with body lice, and there was no way in the Philippines to get rid of this lice. They were so bad that you never could get rid of them. They were body lice, not head lice. Body lice are gray, worm-type bugs that get in your clothing right around your belt, mainly. That's where they'd stay because it was warm there. Your body warmth was good for them, and they'd bite you there. Heat would take them out, and daily you'd see guys out in the sun picking lice off them. But the next day they'd be hatched out again, so we had them constantly. This also went on during the short time we were at Osaka because they never had bathing facilities or clothing for us or anything. The moment we arrived at Zentsuji, they had us walk in the gate and pull off all our clothes, leave them, and we never saw them again. Then they burned them. It was in dead winter, January 13, and cold as hell.

"Then we had to go into a vat. It was a huge tub, almost like a swimming pool. We had a hot bath, and it was terrific. We hadn't had a bath since we'd taken one in the Philippines with a canteen cup. So now we could spend so many minutes in that bath getting all the bugs off us. Then we went outside and got new uniforms. Since it was wintertime, they gave us Japanese-type uniforms."

Capt. Bull (Zentsuji) "We were all in bad shape by the time we got here. Most of us were suffering from burning feet and were barely able to lift them. I wouldn't call it frostbite, because it wasn't due to exposure. It was just another form of malnutrition. Our extremities were dying. Our fingertips would lose their sensitivity, and so would our toes. If we hadn't gotten out of Tanagawa, we would not have lasted much longer."

PFC Evans (Nagasaki) "We had meningitis, pneumonia, bad colds, and dysentery. During the Civil War they called diarrhea the Tennessee quickstep. We called it the Nagasaki footrace. I had bronchial pneumonia, double pneumonia, and single pneumonia twice in one lung. We had a Japanese interpreter named Inouye who went all over Japan and bought sulfa drugs for us with our money. In Singapore we lost 125 men a day. During the winter in Nagasaki, four or five a day would die. I had thirty-six boils operated on at one time. I was bent over a table, and this doctor took a scalpel and cut every one of them open. Then they took a big vial, like a hypodermic needle, and drew blood out of my arm and injected it into my buttocks."

Cpl. Minshew (Nagasaki) "The medical facilities were very crude. There was just one big room that was the sick bay. We had three Dutch doctors. One of them was a baby doctor, but he worked a sick bay at the dockyard all the time. We had a couple of English doctors at different times and one or two American doctors. We had six or seven doctors there. The only thing they had to sanitize instruments with was potassium permanganate. The gauze we had for wounds was very limited and was washed and reused once a wound was healed. I had an abscess on my arm that had three or four heads on it. It had swollen twice its normal size. I went down to sick bay, and one of the orderlies first dipped an orangewood stick into the potassium permanganate and then jammed it into my abscess. It drained some, but he could see the core wasn't going to come out. He passed me on to an English doctor. He just took a scalpel, stuck it in there, and ripped it open. To kill the pain we had a towel to stick in our mouths. Yelling wouldn't be tolerated in the sick bay, so we carried a towel with us to stuff in our mouth."

PFC Visage (Nagasaki) "I had diphtheria, the only guy in camp I know of that contracted diphtheria. I had no treatment for it and ran high fevers. I was put in the 'death room' at one time. My tonsils rotted out, but after laying in there for two or three days and suffering high fever, I guess the Good Lord took care of me. It left my throat paralyzed, so I couldn't talk for three months after that. The death room was similar to our quarters. It had double bunks. They'd put you in there if they didn't think you would last, or if you had a disease that could contaminate the rest of the camp. I had a Dutchman on one side of me that died of pneumonia and was left there for two days. They'd bring his rations to him and set it at the end of his bunk. I knew he was dead, but I didn't say anything. The Japanese had two terms for a sick person. *Shisen* meant real sick, [literally, death line], and *chiryo* meant that you were up sick [literally, undergoing medical treatment or curing] and too maimed to go to the shipyard and work."

PFC Garrison (Hirohata) "About four months after we went to Hirohata, toward the last part of the war, they started bringing the boys over from the Philippines. There were sixty of us, and they brought in four hundred. Man, they had everything: dysentery, lice, crabs, scabies; everything there was, they brought. It got so big, we couldn't control things. We had this dysentery run riot. People would just die from it. There was every kind of disease you could have. If somebody got real bad, they'd go to the hospital, but there was no sterile techniques. A good percentage of the time the guy never recovered if he had to go to the hospital. We didn't have any medicine to speak of. You just toughed it out. If you got well, you got well. If you didn't, you didn't. That's all there was to it."

Capt. Weidman (Kobe) "There were 460 of us, about twenty-four Americans and the rest were mostly Scots, from the 2d Regiment, Hong Kong, and Australians. Of the 460 that first year, that first winter 115 died from beriberi. Beriberi is where your system doesn't throw water off and you swell up. I've seen a man's scrotum as big as a football. That first winter I was in good shape, although I had lost weight. It was in the second winter that I had diphtheria and pneumonia. I managed to live. Some of the boys were good to me."

Death and Burial

Cpl. Clem (Camp O'Donnell) "I believe our losses started running to between fifty to a hundred a day. The Filipinos' were about ten times what we were running. They would run anywhere from five hundred to a thousand in a day. On the burial detail you'd dig a hole probably ten feet square and about two or three feet deep. After they had one crew digging this grave, the fellows who were able to walk would bring up a file of Americans, and they'd take two men to each body. One of them would get hold of the corpse's feet, and the other would get hold of it by the hands. The Japanese wouldn't let you bury them the first day. They had to lay them out there in the sun a day or two before you could bury them. Then when you picked them up, since the bodies would bloat up in the tropics, the skin would split when you picked it up. And, generally, they were so bloated that their bellies would rupture. We had to carry them five hundred yards to where the graves were located. Then you'd just keep throwing them in there and then cover them with what dirt was left. They were just thrown in there on top of one another. Then a rain would come through there, and the ground would settle a little bit, and you'd have arms sticking out and you'd have legs sticking out. Of course, that contributed to the disease factor so much that I believe the only reason the Japanese ever moved us out of O'Donnell was that some of their own men started dying. They were losing some with this dysentery, and we'd see them holding cremation ceremonies."

Pvt. Blaylock (Camp O'Donnell) "The first burial detail that I went on, there were seventy-six Americans they had to bury. We had these bamboo litters, and there were four men to a litter. We'd pick up the corpse and put him on the litter and put the litter on our shoulder and march to the burial ground. All we could do was just dump him in a hole. At that time they weren't keeping a record of what order they were burying them in, and 90 percent of the guys didn't have dog tags anyway. When I'd go on a burial detail, I'd get me a few blades of something like Johnsongrass and wrap it around the corpse's wrist so that I wouldn't have to touch him. Then when we got to the burial ground, why, we'd just turn the litter over. Of course, the ones up front got to drop their corpse right close to the edge, and when your turn came way down the line, why, you'd have to have some strength—all four of you—to toss him into the center somewhere so they wouldn't just be in a pile. Of course, the graves weren't dug deep enough, and when the wind was from that direction, why, the stench was terrible. Naturally, the prisoners had to dig the graves. During the rainy season it was just full of water, and you just shoveled mud over the bodies. I hated the burial details!"

Pvt. Guiles (Camp O'Donnell) "They'd go through the barracks with what we called the bags, which, as I remember, was a blanket tied between two poles. You'd lay the corpse on this blanket, and you'd put the poles on your shoulders and take the body to the burial yard. It was just a constant stream to the burial yard. There they had dug a big hole, and all the corpses were piled in this one hole. After the hole was filled, it was covered, and you moved to the next one. The depth of the hole depended on the patience of the guard. Sometimes, if it had rained, the corpses would float up through the mud, and you'd see arms or legs sticking out. I personally hated to get down in that pit and stack the bodies. It was bad enough carrying them out there, but getting down in that hole and stacking them was the ultimate. The stench was overpowering, but the worst was the mere fact that you had to get down in there with all of those bodies and physically handle them again. Of course, we had very little choice in the matter."

Pvt. Stanley (Camp O'Donnell) "I was in better health than most of them, and I was put on the burial detail. My job was to dump them into the pit and fill the pit up. We throwed them in like you was throwing a log on a fire. We just piled them in, and if they fell crossways, all right, and if they fell longways, well, that was all right, too. If I'm not badly mistaken, their dog tags would be pulled off before they were throwed in. I was on that detail for several days, and I hated it. So when they came around and asked for volunteers, I volunteered to get out of O'Donnell. I wasn't there too long because, according to my notes, I got there on April 17, 1942, and I left there on May 12, 1942."

Cpl. Halbrook (Camp O'Donnell) "The guys would die in their bunks with their legs hanging off or their arms hanging down, and the burial detail would not come through for maybe two days. Rigor mortis had set in, and the guy was stiff and set. You were paid to get those guys buried underground, and if that guy's arm is sticking up, that means you're going to have to dig that much deeper. And there ain't but one way to cut down on digging all that extra dirt, and that's to cut it off. That's what they did. I've seen guys go crazy or wild in those damn burial pits, and guys really get their jollies. Guys were just as crazy above them. They were throwing people down on them and caused them to lose their bearings and go nuts. All of us were the same way. You weren't human. People don't understand it."

Cpl. Burlage (Corregidor) "About the second or third day after Corregidor surrendered, the Japs took us to do the burying of men who died in the battle on part of the island called Monkey Point. All we could do was scratch a hole in the ground and roll the person into it because they were in pretty bad shape by that time. They were bloated and started to rot. In the hot sun, bodies will do that in a day's time."

Cpl. Clem (Cabanatuan) "The Marine that I was captured with on Bataan, this fellow Rice from Louisiana, died at Cabanatuan. When we buried him, that was the only burial detail that I got on there. All the Marines who were in our group fell out for his funeral, and we were right proud of ourselves. All the [Army] dogface boys, they'd just been thrown in these pits. Since he was the only Marine who died there, we were able to hold a semblance of a military funeral for him, which we were real proud of at the time."

Cpl. Bunch (Cabanatuan) "The burial details consisted of two details, one in the morning and one in the afternoon. If you got the one in the morning, you dug the grave; if you got the afternoon detail, you carried the bodies down and put them in the grave. I've been on both of them. I helped bury some of my very close friends, my very close friends, the guys in my outfit.

"The grave-digging detail worked against time because you had guards with you who were impatient. We had an area that we went to, and the gravediggers dug one single grave, a large square hole whose size depended on how many there were to bury. Their desire, as it should have been, was to dig a hole big and deep enough to properly bury people in. But when the guard got tired, he went home, whether the grave was three feet deep or four feet deep or six feet deep. We dug as fast as we could, and then the digging detail went in, and the other detail went down later in the afternoon and buried these men all in the same grave.

"To describe how we did it, we first put the bodies on the nipa mats that normally served as the covers for the open windows. Well, these were taken off—in most cases they had fallen off or had come off in some way—and the bodies were laid on those things. Then two poles were put under the ends, and it took four men to carry the body. These dead men were nude; their clothes had been taken off them.

Many of them had been dead for twenty-four hours and were in terrible condition, swollen and with a very bad odor. It was a miserable thing. You couldn't eat for a day after you'd been on the thing, really. Then they simply walked down to the grave area, which was about three quarters to a half mile from our camp, and you walked up to the side of the grave and tipped that thing up and let the body roll in. They had two men down there picking them up and stretching them out side by side, layer by layer.

"I've actually seen them buried to where the pile came up to the top. I've actually seen it, when we came down the next day—and I've been down there two days in a row—where you'd see a hand or an arm or bloody water. There wasn't usually much dirt covering them. I also happened to be one of the unfortunate ones who one time had to get down in the grave, which was the thing everybody dreaded the worst. The guard on duty said, 'You, you, and you get down in there and straighten them out!' When you jumped in there, you had to pick them up, and your fingers would sink into the flesh. You then stretched them out side by side. That was a horrible thing, really. I didn't make the burial at O'Donnell; I made it at Cabanatuan. The death rate at Cabanatuan had dropped some, but it was still twenty, twenty-five, thirty every day."

Lt. Taylor (Cabanatuan) "The first six months, men died by the thousands. We buried a hundred or more a day, and some days, if we buried less than a hundred, we were doing pretty good. They improvised these litters, these things you carry sick people on, and four men would place the body on there without clothing or anything because clothing was so scarce. Then they'd lift this body up, and there'd be a line of them for a hundred or two hundred yards for half a day, it looked like. They would carry these bodies on these litter carriers out to the grave. At first, we buried them in common graves—no markers, no nothing—because that's the way the Japanese had us do it. The only record of those who had died was kept back in the camp, and that record eventually came back to the United States. At first, the Japanese also wouldn't allow any chaplains to go. No one knew why, but they wouldn't. Then later on they did permit chaplains to go, but before that we'd go to the morgue each morning—actually, several morgues around the prison camp—and conduct funeral services. Then the men would take them out and bury them. Man, they just died like flies during those first six months! It was gruesome—very, very gruesome."

Pvt. Bugbee (Cabanatuan) "In the beginning the burial parties were running close to a hundred a day. We were burying that many on the average. I was on one of these burial parties, and all we'd do was dig a long ditch. The bodies were nothing but skin and bones, so it was just like placing sticks in this ditch because they were so dissipated and emaciated. So we'd lay them in this ditch whose size depended on the number who died that day, and then we just put mud over them. Of course, all the dogs in the area had reverted back to their wild stage, and they'd get in there and dig up the graves and try to get at the bodies. Then the next day we'd have to go back and rebury or recover the graves. Incidentally, this was just one mass grave; there were no markers of any sort, no markings of any kind at all."

PFC Evans (Singapore) "In Singapore there were about 125 people a day dying. Early in the morning, about 6:00, the burial detail, with the Coldstream Guards playing a dirge on bagpipes, would go down. They played a quick march coming back. I remember a Limey in the hospital, an Englishman named Leggy Woods. We were both pretty sick with dysentery. Every morning I'd wake ol' Leggy up and say, 'Leggy, you hear that? You know who they're tuning up for? They're ready for you, buddy. They told me that since y'all done in ol' Mary Queen of Scots, they wasn't going to rest until they got every damn Limey up here and buried him in that damn trench.' He'd get mad and raise Cain about it. As a result, he lived through the dysentery."

Pvt. Armstrong (Burma-Thailand Railway) "We helped to bury some of them in 80 Kilo Camp. We'd carry them out, wrap them in a blanket completely, and then put that bark stuff around them. In some of those camps, if you dug over two or three feet deep, you were in water. We buried them awful shallow. We'd just put a wooden cross up. If they had a dog tag, we nailed it on the cross. If they didn't, we'd carve their name on the cross. A few prayers were said."

Pvt. Chambers (Burma-Thailand Railway) "In August 1943, when Dr. Lumpkin died at the 100 Kilo Camp, it lowered the morale of all of us. It kind of made us think a little bit that the doctor died of dysentery. Lieutenant Hampton died at the same time. I think he slept pretty close to Captain Lumpkin, and they had that kind of dysentery that you just bleed to death. Some of the graves weren't marked because they got so far behind. They didn't keep graveyards because all the rain and vegetation there just filled everything back up right away."

PO2 Detre (Burma-Thailand Railway) "Many times I volunteered to bury a lot of my friends. Funerals at 100 Kilo Camp were generally only attended by the two guys that dug the hole, maybe one or two friends, and always an officer. Mr. Hamlin usually went and said the prayers. Then the close friends would leave, and you would cover them up. The way we did it, the body was wrapped very tight in a bamboo rug or robe."

Pvt. Wisecup (Burma-Thailand Railway) "About three weeks after we got up there, to Hintok, we had the first cholera case. He was working on Hell Fire Pass. Then it hit the camp, and we started losing about sixteen, seventeen guys a day, or something like that. We'd find them laying out there outside the tents. So me and this other guy had to pick them up. At first we made individual graves, and then there were so many of them that we just couldn't keep up with it.

"There was this little Irishman from Dublin—very religious—I will never forget that. 'Hey, Paddy,' I said, 'we can't make individual graves.' He said, 'What are you going to do, lad?' I said, 'Just dig one big hole. It'll take us all morning to dig a hole about ten feet square, and we'll throw them in there.' Now, he was religious, and he says, 'Oh, mate, that's sacrilegious.' I said, 'Yeah, but we ain't going to be able to do it individually!' So he finally agreed that we'd do that, and then we'd throw them in there.

"I never will forget one rainy morning. They got these bamboo shoots that grow up overnight. And here we are. I'm barefooted, and Paddy had some shoes. The path out into the jungle was about six, seven, eight inches deep with mud, and I'm walking along, you know, out in front, Paddy in the back. We don't have this stiff headfirst; we got him with his feet toward me. I ain't got no ass left in my britches, and I'm walking along, and I'm miserable, and the lice are eating me, and the dead guy's feet keep hitting me. I never will forget. Jesus Christ, I start cussing. I never will forget this, never to the end of my days. I stopped and turned around, grabbed hold of the stretcher, and threw the whole bunch into the jungle. I said, 'Leave that son of a bitch over there!' So Paddy says, 'John!' I said, 'What?' He says, 'We can't do that, lad. No good will come of it. You can't blaspheme the dead.' I says, 'Goddamnit, he's out of it, the son of a bitch! Leave the bastard laying over there!' In a few minutes I cooled down and went and got him. I can remember that just so clear: them cold feet kicking me in the ass. I was thinking, 'Look at him! He's out of it! He ain't got to put up with this shit anymore!' Now this is how you get. We used to take what clothing they had on them worth using, if they weren't stripped by the time we got there. We never had any graveside service. We had no time for that."

Pvt. Benton (Woosung and Kiangwan) "As far as the death rate, it'd been small. Really, our camp death rate was one of the smallest of any POW camp in the Pacific."

Capt. Weidman (Kobe) "One of the details that I detested very much was when we had to burn our own comrades' dead bodies. They didn't give us enough wood to burn them up with. They only gave us about five pieces of wood, four inches in diameter and five or six feet long. Well, the dogs would eat on them at night. When the first few had begun to die, they would bring them in to these tubs. They cut their bones and muscles at the thigh and set them down in this tub of water. We had a naval officer who would give them the last rites according to military rituals. Shortly there were so many of them dying that they didn't go through that anymore."

Chapter V

General Treatment—
The Psychological

Psychological studies constitute one of the larger bodies of literature concerning American prisoners of war. In quantity they rank only behind reminiscences. In quality they include studies by outstanding psychiatrists and psychologists. However, these medical specialists do not always agree with prisoners' memoirs or with the recollections of our interviewees. A few examples of these contradictions follow.

Harvey D. Strassman, Margaret B. Thaler, and Edgar H. Schein assert that withdrawal was "the most prevalent reaction of POWs to severe and chronic physical and psychological stress." They temper their view by noting that such withdrawal, or "apathy," does not keep prisoners from maintaining their ability to respond appropriately.[1] Similarly, Willard Waller has written that prisoners of war suffer ennui more than do other soldiers. He quotes Paul Cohen-Portheim, who makes the point in a slightly different way by stating that "soldiers lead a dangerous and terrible life, prisoners a helpless and useless one."[2] Although a few of our interviewees agree, most do not remember boredom, ennui, or apathy as a particular problem. Furthermore, Peter Watson's view that men during captivity were "seclusive and taciturn" is not reflected in the statements found here.[3] There was self-pity and often misguided hope.

American officers were concerned that boredom might overtake their charges. At many camps they introduced sporting events, including softball, football, boxing, volleyball, wrestling, and races. Prisoners played cards, dominoes, and other games, if they had the

---

[1]Strassman, Thaler, and Schein, "A Prisoner of War Syndrome: Apathy as a Reaction to Severe Stress," 1001.
[2]Waller, *The Veteran Comes Back*, 76.
[3]Watson, *War on the Mind*, 256.

needed equipment. At Woosung a library of several hundred books was supplied by European civilians residing nearby in Shanghai. At Cabanatuan there was even an orchestra, and three movies.

The importance of faith and religion is another area of disagreement. N. Q. Brill, writing in 1946, stated that religious belief as a sustaining factor was never mentioned by the former prisoners. He added that none of the medical personnel examining these men, "neuropsychiatric or otherwise, included anything on religion in their reports." Brill thought that religion may have played a role early in captivity but became less important as prison routines developed.[4] However, as seen in the following pages, several prisoners found that faith and religion were important forces in their survival. At Kiangwan, also near Shanghai, they held Sunday church services. Elsewhere, this was fairly rare, although many prisoners became religious as a result of their experiences and prayed regularly. Sunday usually was a day of rest, or a day to play sports and games.

Of course, areas of agreement exist between the interviews and the psychological reports. Members of the U.S. Army team that prepared *Neuropsychiatry in World War II* confirm that the uncertainty of the duration of captivity created anxiety. In the same report it is clear that the mental condition of the prisoners varied with the type of treatment they received in captivity. When the fortunes or misfortunes of prison life rose or fell, the emotional tone of the men changed in parallel for better or for worse.[5] They all welcomed the scant amount of mail they received. Late in the war, moreover, they took great pleasure in watching American aircraft bomb and strafe nearby enemy facilities, even cheering attacks on their own compounds. A perverse satisfaction can be found in their animosity toward certain non-Americans, especially the Japanese, whom they understandably despised.

Both the interviews and the psychological reports recognize the importance of membership in small groups within the prison camps. In the Burma jungles the POWs formed cliques, and in the Philippines they got together in *quans*. Prisoners and psychiatrists also recount instances where men simply gave up the struggle to survive.

---

[4]Brill, "Neuropsychiatric Examination of Military Personnel Recovered from Japanese Prison Camps," 429.

[5]U.S. Army, Medical Department, *Neuropsychiatry in World War II,* 956–57.

This "fatal withdrawal" would last three or four days and was followed by death. Chaplain Robert Preston Taylor puts it succinctly: "A man could die if he wanted to."

According to Bernard M. Cohen and Maurice Z. Cooper, "from reported facts as to types of stress, it was apparent that excessive hard labor, physical punishment, and witnessing the punishment or killing of other prisoners were much more frequent in Japanese prison camps than in German."[6] That the prisoners suffered mentally as much as they did physically is obvious. What is not mentioned, but apparent, is that their recovery from physical maltreatment was generally quicker and more certain than from the psychological damage done them.

Boredom, Holidays, and Rest

Cpl. Clem (Cabanatuan) "There wasn't much work, and if you're in that condition, and you're confined and underfed and half sick, and there'd be no outlet through work or something like that, your mind gets dull, and one day meshes right into the next to where you lose all count of time. Consequently, your mind is a blur. I guess your mind just blocks everything out."

Pvt. Burns (Cabanatuan) "I think we got our first Red Cross packages the Christmas of 1943. Even though it was like summertime and no snow, no Christmas trees, no decorations or anything like that, with the permission of the Japanese we had a church service at night. Some of the guys got together, and they went all through the camp singing Christmas carols. For one reason or another, as far as I was concerned, I never felt, I don't think, the spirit of Christmas any more in my whole lifetime than I did that Christmas that I spent there in 1943. You could feel the spirit of Christmas. It was just everywhere, all over that camp, and in the air. The Japs let us have our service at night, and to me it was one of the most fulfilling experiences as far as Christmas goes. I don't know if the other guys felt this way, but to me, although there wasn't anything like presents or Christmas trees or decorations, you could feel the spirit of Christmas all in that camp."

---

[6]Cohen and Cooper, *A Follow-up Study of World War II Prisoners of War*, 69.

Lt. Taylor (Cabanatuan) "On days like Christmas, Easter, and even on the Fourth of July we kind of had a mixture of religion and celebration. Particularly on Christmas Eve, I think, in prison camp was a time when men enjoyed the religious performances and religious services all across the prison camp. In each of the compounds we arranged for Christmas Eve services. The Catholics held a Mass at midnight; the Protestants held their Christmas Eve service at about 11:00. Then on Christmas Day we would have some type of function, such as some of the church groups had their Communion services on Sunday.

"Then on Easter we would conduct our sunrise service. It was amazingly impressive every time we did this, how these men would come out of their bunks before daylight. You could hear them walking in their wooden shoes while coming to the sunrise or daylight service. These were great days for all of us. Amazingly, most men did not get melancholy during these times. The whole time we were in prison camp, the optimistic outlook of our people was always very good. Particularly after the first six months, when men were dying by the thousands, we didn't have a lot of this melancholy, depressed feeling among the men."

Lt. Daman (Davao Penal Colony) "On Christmas Eve of 1943 they took us over to this barn-like affair, and there they showed us pictures of Pearl Harbor. Of course, up to this time, we did not believe any of the news about Pearl Harbor, but when we saw these pictures, you can imagine how despondent we were, especially when we saw all those battleships being sunk and so on."

First Sgt. Harrelson (Sumatra Camp No. 4) "If we had a day off, like Christmas, and they allowed us to have a preacher, which wasn't the case all the time, we might have a service where everybody would turn out. Christmas generally meant a better meal for the noon meal. The Japanese would allow us to acquire stuff for that meal. We would get a couple of men with a couple of Japanese and go through the jungle and try to get a pig. Generally, we would sing Christmas carols, have a prayer, and maybe sing a religious song or two. On one occasion we were allowed the privilege of singing "The Star-spangled Banner," "God Save the King," and other national anthems. When we got to the Dutch national anthem, only the Dutch could sing it."

PFC Visage (Changi) "The only significance Thanksgiving in 1942 had was that it filled our stomachs. We ran into Major Harrigan, who had money and managed to deal with the Japs to get plenty of rice and some vegetables to make this big pot of rice. We just gorged ourselves. That was the only rice that I can recall ever having in Singapore."

Pvt. Benton (Woosung) "I think one of our main problems was they never organized a regular working detail while we were here. You had more time to sit around and think about starving to death, about how hungry you were getting. You had more time to think of yourself, which I always consider bad. That's one of the gripes in the service, that they've always got you doing something for which you do not see a reason—but the reason for it is to keep you busy."

PFC Venable (Kiangwan) "You'd come back from work, and it was to bed—dead tired. There was really not a great deal of talking at night. You were dead tired, but you might sit around and bat the breeze a little bit. But generally, it was a very humdrum existence."

PFC Sparkman (Kiangwan) "We had Sunday off. They did respect that. We had a chaplain in our camp, and I think he held church services."

Recreation and Entertainment

Lt. Daman (Philippines) "In my spare time I thought a lot about recipes because food was constantly on my mind. I'd even swap a recipe with another POW for one of his. I remember that when we went to Bilibid Prison for the last time, we parked next to a government printing office, and I got a bunch of passport papers and started to write recipes on the back of them. I still have them, and there are quite a few recipes on them."

Pvt. Blaylock (Cabanatuan) "Some fellow from Iowa got up a little orchestra, and the Japs allowed him to play once a week. I guess that in the two years I spent at Cabanatuan we had about three or four movies. I remember that one of them was Japanese, one of them was a Bing Crosby movie that I had seen in the States, and another one was a musical comedy that I had also seen. Hardly any of us stayed until the end of the Japanese movie. Now this was all out in the open. There wasn't any theater by any means, but they did allow us to build a little stage."

Sgt. Burk (Cabanatuan) "In our spare moments, we would just sit around and talk. We didn't try to tend any small personal gardens or anything because if you grew anything good, somebody would have taken it. We had cards, dominoes, so we played a lot of pinochle, hearts. Now about once a week they did put on kind of a minstrel show, you know, guys would put on different skits. That's about it."

Pvt. Stanley (Clark Field) "Now I will say one thing for the Japs— boy, they loved to play baseball! We had this one ol' boy who had been signed by the Pittsburgh Pirates before the Army got him. His name was LaRue, a Frenchman. But every once in a while the Japs would make us play baseball with them, and fortunately we could go out there and sit on the bases because they couldn't hit this ol' boy when he was pitching for us. This guy was so good that, even so weak, he could strike out the Japs, so we could go out there and sit. Fortunately, the Japs were pretty good sports and didn't beat on us if we whipped them."

Cpl. Halbrook (Clark Field) "Everybody had dysentery at Clark Field. In the evenings we would spend our time sitting out beside our old barracks, the Swali Barracks, picking a guy coming out of another barracks. And me and Bailey and Black, the three of us, would decide which one we were going to bet our rice on, to see which one would make it to the latrine. We would bet to find out which one could come the closest to getting to the head before he had to pull off the trail and do his business. You would holler at the guy and tell him you were betting on him and give him a part if he would just make it."

Cpl. McCall (Bilibid Prison) "We had plenty of tobacco in the Philippines. We could get hold of tobacco fairly often, stringy tobacco made in a big pouch like a mail pouch, chewing tobacco. It was sort of stringy, dry, hairy tobacco. Of course, we had no tobacco after we got to Japan—none to speak of, very scarce. We used to scrounge around and get paper out of an old library, where they kept case histories of prisoners at Bilibid. They had real thin paper. We'd go through these files and make our cigarette papers out of them, just a bunch of paper that had been filed and got scattered around. Toilet paper was a scarce item, too, so that was a luxury. You take so many things for granted, things that we used to think about, things that we really missed—those everyday items from the States."

PFC Bolitho (Camp Casisang) "So far as recreation is concerned, we didn't have any bats or balls to play baseball, no footballs to throw around. About all you could do would be to run races or something like that. I never did a great deal of that because the weather was too hot. But there was a lot of chess played, a lot of bridge played, and there was a lot of poker played. We had a few books but not too many. Most of the fellows that had them hoarded them and kept them pretty close—not to read primarily but to roll cigarettes with."

Lt. Daman (Davao Penal Colony) "I want to talk about one project I had to keep from going stir-crazy. I always had aspirations when I was a young man of being a farmer. I had studied accounting at this business college that I went to before I went into the Army. So in this prison camp I hypothetically bought eighty acres of good bottom-land, and I farmed this eighty acres—in my mind—for the next two and a half years. At the end of my time, I came out $17.30 in the black, so right there I said to myself, 'No, I'll never become a farmer. I don't care what I do the rest of my life.' That project took up a lot of my spare time."

Cpl. Smith (Palawan) "There wasn't no recreation at Palawan. It was all work and very little play. I started out one time that I was going to play a little ball, but after you worked in that hot sun, well, you wasn't interested in playing ball."

PFC Evans (Jaarmarkt, Surabaja) "While I was there I learned to play chess. There were some chess masters there. I played the 1941 champion of Europe to a draw. Of course, he was playing forty-nine other people at the time. He'd line them all up and play them all   an amazing man. I learned to play and enjoyed the game.

"We played baseball with the Japanese soldiers there. We did have a good rapport with them as far as playing baseball was concerned. Their officers served as umpires. They knew who Babe Ruth was, and I told them that he was my uncle. I got a little better treatment out of the Japanese because I told them he was my uncle."

PO2 Detre (Java) "We went on working parties over to a cigarette factory that had been maintained by the British. The cigarettes were called Players. It was a ten-pack cigarette in a cardboard box. Both sides of the pack were the same, and we collected as many of these as we could. We carefully dismantled them and made a deck of cards. Somebody had a stub of a pencil, and we made each suit. This is the way I learned to play bridge. These cards were handled very delicately, believe me."

T/Sgt. Stanbrough (Bicycle Camp) "A lot of volleyball went on. We'd watch the officers' side play, and we'd try to take bets on which side was going to win. The officers engaged in chess games with the Dutch, and the Dutch would always win. All the Englishmen had some talent, either reciting, singing, or putting on plays. They had a little orchestra. Some person would be dressed like a girl. It was musical slapstick comedy. During spare time in the daytime, some of the English established classes in mathematics and other subjects."

PO2 Detre (Bicycle Camp) "Shortly after we were there, we set up college-level schools. I was taking trigonometry and navigation, advanced English, and another course. Navigation was taught by a first-class petty officer named Harris off the *Houston*. The trigonometry was taught by a warrant officer from the *Perth* who was a professor of math in some university in Sydney. You could get just about any course you wanted, from music to acting. The teachers had to work from their heads because we didn't have any books. Another big thing was plays. Several plays were really outstanding. The Japanese came one night, and they had to repeat the play several nights because they invited all their friends."

Fireman 1/C Kennedy (Bicycle Camp) "They organized a volleyball team. The Australians would play the Americans, and it got to be quite a competitive situation. We always beat the Aussies, but the games were very close. We had some boxing teams. The Americans usually won most of the matches because they had more experience. We had one Golden Glover there from Illinois named Pistole. He was very good. The boxing equipment came in with the Army people."

PFC Robinson (Bicycle Camp) "I only attended a couple of the performances. One of my buddies, Freddie Quick, had a beautiful voice, and he had a knack of using his doubled-up fist, which sounded like a trumpet better than any I ever heard. The Japanese attended our shows, and there were several instances where in acting or talking out you would take a little jab at them. I remember one song especially was 'She'll Be Comin' 'round the Mountain.' That was a camp favorite. It pertained to when she got there, she would be laying thousand-pounders. It was definitely against the Nips. As far as I know, they never made any objection to it."

Pvt. Wisecup (Bicycle Camp) "Drawing cartoons was just something I enjoyed. I was always ribbing people. The Nips would give you paper and pencils to draw pictures. Sometimes I would come up with old crayons, and I got chalk from an elementary school in Batavia. I didn't draw the Japanese because I didn't want to raise any hell with them. I was warned on that. I did quite a few drawings of the ship and its sinking, the way it looked to me. A guy named McManus did terrific artwork from a model, doing portraits and stuff like that, but I was the only one there that did any cartoons. Most of the guys liked them and looked forward to them."

Cpl. Minshew (Madura Island) "There were a lot of books in the camp on the island of Madura. I remember reading *For Whom the Bell Tolls*, *Gone with the Wind*, and *The Tale of Bali*. We had a system to check them out."

Pvt. Chambers (Burma-Thailand Railway) "We had what we called wog [slur for dark-skinned Oriental] tobacco, or 'monkey hair.' Some of it was pretty powerful, and some of it could not be smoked because it had been wet and the tobacco washed out of it. If you got some out of the bottom of the pile and rolled a smoke, you could take a puff but not inhale it. If you blew that puff out of your mouth, you'd still have enough left in to strangle you when you breathed. Everybody smoked their little pocket Testaments that had one. We used them for cigarette papers."

Pvt. Wisecup (Kanchanaburi) "We had all kinds of wog tobacco, but the best was from Java. It was red. It had all kinds of names: 'wogweed' or 'Turk's beard;' 'Granny's armpit' is what the Aussies used to call it. Listen, that stuff would kill your appetite and probably kill you. You know what was a premium? Japanese paper. I think it was the *Japan Times*. It was made out of rice paper, and occasionally you could get ahold of a sheet of it. If you could get ahold of that, you had money. You'd cut that up and sell it for cigarette papers. Any kind of paper was used for cigarette papers, but you were going first class when you had the *Japan Times!* No kidding, man."

Capt. Cates (Kanchanaburi) "The camp commander was a sergeant who was, of course, socially unable to fraternize with his own people because there were no other sergeants about. He came through the camp and caught us playing mah-jongg one time, and he asked me and two of the China boys to come over to his quarters with the mah-jongg set. I had cane sugar for the first time since I'd left home. I had iced tea for the first time since I'd left home. None of us could speak to each other except in Pidgin English. We had a hilarious time."

Pvt. Benton (Tientsin) "They let some women come in at Tientsin to see some of the boys—their girlfriends. They let them come in and visit. I know because I seen it. We had one Tientsin Marine that they allowed his girl to come, and they got married. She was a White Russian. They still live together today in St. Joseph, Missouri. His name is Sydow. The Japs allowed them to get married; then after the war he went back to China and got her."

Cpl. Crews (Woosung) "We'd play blackjack, and somebody would win enough cigarettes to smoke. But there were no matches. We were forbidden to possess matches."

Capt. Godbold (Woosung and Kiangwan) "Early in the game, I was asked by the senior American officer to be the athletic officer for the camp—the recreation officer. We were given a considerable amount of athletic gear from the Shanghai foreign community, primarily through the Red Cross. We had a lot of athletic equipment. We had plenty of time. So I set up an athletic program, organized softball leagues and touch football leagues and so on. We had some top-notch softball leagues in operation. We had books. I set up a library, and eventually we had a relatively good library of several thousand volumes, and with all the sports and recreational activities we had available, there were plenty of opportunities for people to occupy themselves. We organized bridge tournaments, chess tournaments. We organized classes in various languages, such as Spanish and so on. These were the main types of recreational activities. The Japanese really allowed us great latitude in organizing these and conducting them. Obviously, they had to be performed at certain times, but within those limitations we had considerable latitude in running our own lives. There were things to be done to keep your mind and your body active. And so I spent most of my time working with athletics for many months. I was glad to have this occupation.

"We were allowed to play, for example, softball. The Japanese, as you know, loved baseball, and, insofar as baseball's concerned, we had crews of several merchant ships join the camp, and from one of the merchant ships we got one of the premier softball pitchers in the world. And he and some others of us who had some experience in athletics helped organize the softball leagues and really played top-notch softball. The whole camp came out to watch the games in the evening along with all the Japanese, and there was a great deal of enthusiasm for it and betting and a lot of animation about it, and it took the minds of prisoners off of their own plight by having these very heated and really wonderfully played games. And this went on every night during the spring, the summer, and the fall. Occasionally, a Japanese guard would come out and want to play with us, but while the Japanese were coming out and watching and enjoying it tremendously, there was little fraternization insofar as playing against the Japanese because obviously we were so much better than the Japanese. Our athletic program started at Woosung was continued at Kiangwan but not at the same pace, because we really didn't have the stamina."

PFC Venable (Woosung and Kiangwan) "In the summertime we even tried to play a little softball inside the camp. There was a little bit of recreation on Sunday, although most of the time on Sundays people just laid around. This was the time that you had to wash clothes, clean up, and take your bath. Sundays were reserved for this and just plain resting up and reminiscing."

Pvt. Permenter (Kiangwan) "You've got to remember at Shanghai there were a lot of Americans and British, and they sent books in. They sent a lot of other things in—athletic equipment and so forth—that they contributed to the camp. The Japanese let it in. We had some basketball, and people played it. I never did. I read mostly to try to save energy. It was a pretty good library—several hundred books."

Capt. Bull (Zentsuji) "In my spare time I was mostly planning to develop a new post exchange. I figured they were going to send me back to Corregidor, so I planned to build a new exchange—how much lumber I would need, how to stock it, and things like that. I even wrote it down because they did allow us to have pencils and notebooks, so that's what I was planning for. I also studied accounting a great deal. I was looking toward the future, you might say, and keeping my mind occupied.

"Fortunately, we had Ambassador [Joseph Clark] Grew's library, which was sent to this camp before we got there. They had a library, and we could check out books, so I spent most of my time reading. I must have read 150 to 200 books some novels, some other types of literature. Then after we'd been here a year, we got some books when they sent a Red Cross ship, the *Gripsholm*, over. There were a lot of textbooks, so we would form classes. We called ourselves Zentsuji University, and many of us were studying in small groups. This is why morale was so much better here, and this is why I feel fortunate in having been in this place for two years."

PFC Evans (Nagasaki) "I liked to play poker. People would lose so much rice that they would go bankrupt. We had what was called Rule Eleven; they could only take so much rice at a time. They couldn't starve you to death. It was nothing for a man to lose a hundred bowls of rice playing poker."

Morale

Cpl. Bunch (Philippines) "I don't recall any work details at O'Donnell. We simply walked around listening for rumors. Listening for rumors, that's what we thrived on—rumors. As long as we were in the Philippines, some guy would come around and say, 'I just heard. . . . This is no rumor. This is a fact. The word has got in through Captain So-and-so that there's an American convoy that will be in here the day after tomorrow at 3:30,' or some such wild thing as that. We just thrived on things like that. I honestly think it kept some guys alive, I really do. I sometimes suspect that some of our smarter officers dreamed them up to give you something to hold onto, because your buddies were sick and dying all around you. It was miserable, and there was death everywhere. I lived on rumors, and I'm sure the other fellows did, too. They just survived on them."

Cpl. B. Allen (Cabanatuan) "I witnessed men actually giving up and dying. You could tell in conversations with a man that he had lost interest. Sometimes they would make remarks such as 'I just don't care anymore.' They seemed not to fear the Japanese and wouldn't do their work. They used such remarks as 'To hell with it. I've had enough of this.' Well, it was pretty obvious in their speech, and it wouldn't be long then. They were not strong men to start with at this time—none of us were, not strong as compared to what we had once been. Some of us were much stronger than others, of course. But the men who gave up were in pretty weakened condition to start with, and it usually wasn't long from the time we noted that they were giving up until the time they died. When I say not long, I mean two or three weeks usually until they were dead."

Lt. Taylor (Cabanatuan) "People who gave up exhibited certain symptoms. You'd see him closing in. He'd quit talking. All expression of hope left him, and he was limp-like. He had no life about him. It was hard to get him to do anything, except to just lie there. You'd see him turn and face the wall if it was in the barracks or on a ship, for example. I'll give you an example that fits almost everyone to a T that I saw in this condition. A colonel—a doctor— said to me on the prison ship, 'Well, Bob, there's no use to fight this thing anymore. We've fought it now for three years, so there's no use to fight it.' Then he turned over. I said to him, 'Now, Colonel, the time is getting near. This thing is coming to an end.' You see, this was after American planes had come in, but it was after we were on our way to Japan. I said, 'Colonel, this thing's coming to an end. The Americans are on their way back. We know that. Don't forget the sight of those airplanes and everything.' But he gave up, and he was dead within five minutes. A man could die if he wanted to. This guy had fought it as long as he wanted to, and then he just gave up. It takes courage. You've got to have this hope, and you've got to have this faith that this thing will come to an end. It takes that quality in prison camp."

Cpl. Halbrook (Bilibid Prison) "The American air raids on Manila Harbor were the biggest morale booster we had. I felt better then than anything I had experienced until the time I was liberated. Guys were yelling and whooping just like they were at a basketball game, and the Japanese were cocking their machine guns and threatening to shoot if we didn't quiet down. We were hollering, 'Shoot, you son of a bitch, you ain't going to hurt nobody anymore!' "

Lt. Daman (Bilibid Prison) "During my fourth stay here, I witnessed an American air raid. It was the most fantastic thing; I'd never seen an air raid like that in my life. Here these Marine pilots were dive-bombing Manila Harbor. Boy, they were just coming down! It was beautiful! We'd see them make a dive, and then we'd see them drop their bombs, and we'd hear explosions. Then fantastic cheers would go up inside the camp. This did wonders for our morale, for we anticipated that we would be liberated shortly."

Cpl. B. Allen (Corregidor) "After being a prisoner for only a week, I still thought that the war would be very short. I just thought that America was the greatest, and I thought this country could take anybody in a short period of time, still not knowing what a complete job the Japanese had done at Pearl Harbor. This was the attitude of my buddies, too, and I think it was probably a good attitude. I would deliberately have it again, if it were to do over, because it helped to pull me through. Having hope was important. I've seen many guys say, 'This is just too much,' and it wasn't long until they were dead."

Cpl. Clem (Davao Penal Colony) "The Japanese allowed the Americans to have a stage show. I wasn't in the show, but I was one of the spectators. Some of the guys sang and told jokes, and we had a couple of skits. Just before the closing ceremonies, the master of ceremonies said he wanted everybody to stand up and sing 'God Bless America.' So everybody stood up, and they started singing. You could hear the guards; they recognized what the song was, and they didn't like it. They were hollering for us to cut it out, quit singing.

"Well, these two Americans got up, and they had a blanket they were carrying. They unfolded the blanket, and pinned to it was this American flag. They had managed to hide that thing for two and a half years through all these searches that had been going on, even though they had a pretty good idea what would happen to them if they had ever been caught with it.

"That was the first time any of the rest of us even knew that they had it, and it was the first time we had seen an American flag in two and a half years. Before these fellows stood up, everybody was singing kind of raggedly, and they just didn't give a damn, didn't feel like singing. But when they saw that flag, they all got to singing real loud and drowned out all the noises in the jungle as well as the Japanese. The guards quit muttering and saying anything about it. They could sense our feelings even though they didn't really know what was going on. Everybody was pretty hard-bitten by that time, but when we got through singing there wasn't a dry eye in the whole crowd."

Cpl. Burlage (Palawan) "Morale was surprisingly good. You didn't hear people complaining or anything because there was no reason to complain. You know, what good would it do? And people realized that, too."

PFC Garrison (in transit, Guam to Japan, 1942) "Morale was terrible. Terrible! Nobody knew what was going to happen. We didn't know what to expect, what to look forward to. We didn't . . . well, we didn't know anything."

First Sgt. Harrelson (Tanjong Priok) "We were unloading a cargo ship, and we took our noon break. This Japanese guard came over, and he was bragging in sign language and in Japanese. He put his hands together like a flying airplane and said, 'Zzzzzzzz! San Francisco—barooom! New York—zzzzzzzzz—barooom!' Dempsey Key was from Decatur, Texas, and he said, 'What about Decatur?' And the Japanese said, 'Zzzzzzzzz—barooom!' These type of incidents kept you going. The working parties or everyday existence was so desperately bleak that if it weren't for people like Dempsey Key, the comics, that would try to get you laughing at the darkest thing, you just never would have been in the frame of mind to make it."

First Sgt. Harrelson (Sumatra Camp No. 4) "You could tell somebody had lost the will to live when they just started quoting and reading the Bible pretty heavy. He'd sit down and say, 'Hey, let me read you this passage,' and he'd start reading out of the Bible. You'd say, 'Well, I'm a believer in God, and I'm a believer in the Bible, but I've seen too many of them go this route. He won't be here in two weeks.' And generally that happened. Also, once they got the blank look, you knew that tomorrow you'd be throwing dirt in their face."

Fireman 1/C Kennedy (Burma-Thailand Railway) "We saw the Japanese version of Pearl Harbor. They brought a projector and a screen in at 80 Kilo Camp, and we all got to watch the Japanese bomb Pearl Harbor. I was sorry to see it because I'd spent time in Pearl Harbor. I hated to see those bastards bragging about it. It didn't help morale."

Pvt. Chambers (Burma-Thailand Railway) "My morale never did break. I just always felt that there was going to be a way, that it was going to end. I never could picture how it was going to end, but when I left to go back to 80 Kilo Camp and I didn't have enough strength to walk up that hill, I kept telling myself, 'Well, if you can't take it, you ought to have been a milk cow where you could give it.' I just felt that if anyone else was going to make it, I was going to be one of them."

PFC Robinson (Burma-Thailand Railway) "You can look at a man and tell he's lost the will to live. When it gets to the point where you can curse him, slap him around, do everything in the world you can imagine to insult him, and there's no reaction to that, then he's given up. He's lost all hope."

Pvt. Benton (Peking) "I wouldn't say morale was too high on December 8, 1941. Then again, it wasn't too low. You'd be surprised that the morale didn't deteriorate very much. In fact, our morale never deteriorated for forty-four months. There were low points. But as far as the morale, it was kept up pretty good."

PFC Fields (Woosung) "Some of the Marines, the ones that were in North China, thought the war would last six weeks, but we found out different. The Wake Island guys were prepared to spend at least a year or two or longer. Our morale, I think, in a camp as cramped and with the mixture that we had—civilians, Guamanians, and all—it was real high. And it stayed high because we'd always have somebody who would keep it up, I mean, keep our morale high at all times."

M/Sgt. Stowers (Woosung) "You knew that if you touched the wire [fence] you were dead—you'd be electrocuted or they'd open fire. A number of young fellows actually committed suicide by going out on rainy, gloomy, dark nights, and they would grab the fence. They decided the war would last six or eight months, and they couldn't hold out that long."

PFC Venable (Woosung and Kiangwan) "I saw a number of people who became mental cases. Let me clarify that by saying that these were certainly not mentally stable people. I don't care what you say, there is a certain mental instability that creeps into prison life. I'm sure that we all did crazy-type things that, to look back on them, we would say, 'Gee whiz. Now, I wonder why a person would do that?' You are under a tremendous pressure, and the most difficult thing, the thing we used to talk about, is that if we'd been given three years in prison, we could sit there, and we could tick off the days and say, 'It will only be twelve hundred more days until release.' You could tick them off one at a time, but you couldn't tick the days off in prison camp because you didn't know quite when the war would end. You had to live one day at a time. And this is a very difficult thing to do as far as your morale is concerned."

Pvt. Benton (Kiangwan) "We were informed by the Japs when President Roosevelt died. I think they did it more to lower our morale than anything. But we knew that just because President Roosevelt died that the United States wasn't going to fold up. We knew that we would continue fighting. It didn't affect us like people might think because we knew that we had people who could step in and take his place. Outside of sorrow for the man, you hate to hear news like that; you hate to hear of any president dying."

Cpl. Halbrook (Formosa) "That camp was bad. It was terrible because of dysentery. There ain't nobody who could even sit down or move, nobody—nobody—who could break wind. It was just something to break wind. It was a feat. Well, that one day I had a new pair of poncho britches on. Ponchos was hard to come by, but we got one from somebody, and we made me a pair of britches. I was just getting ready to break them in. Well, that morning they lined us up to shake us down, and a guy in the front ranks just raised up a leg and let one go, *crraasshh*! And he just turns around and beams, just smiles up a storm, as if it was a feat, a feat that nobody else could accomplish. And there ain't nobody who could, really. Well, guys began to snicker, and the Japanese, who had opened up the ranks to shake us down, began to beat the hell out of guys. But we kept laughing at the guy with that damned fart, he thought it was such a big feat. And I commenced to laugh, and I shit in my britches, my new poncho trousers, and the more I laughed, the more I shit. I ruined them, and the guard wouldn't let me get out of ranks. I had to work all that day with them shitty pants."

Capt. Bull (Zentsuji) "At Zentsuji we had two newspapers a day, printed in English, and through them we could glean how the war was going. They were always claiming that they were shooting down ten of our planes to their loss of one, but the guards would tell us that they didn't believe their own papers. Then the Japs would put maps on our bulletin board supposedly showing the progress of the war. Despite the fact that they claimed great victories, we noticed that the battlefront seemed to be progressively coming nearer to Japan. Therefore, we knew our forces were getting closer and closer to where we were stationed. This was a great morale booster, and we gloated so much that the Japanese quit putting up the maps and took away our newspapers. But they were definitely morale boosters, and we would pass the word around as to how the war was going.

"Most people spent their time speculating as to when the war would be over and when we would be released, and most people said it would happen in ninety days. They were expecting everything to be over in ninety days. I feel I was always a little more realistic, so I couldn't see it being over that early."

Lt. Taylor (Fukuoka) "President Roosevelt's death was no blow to our morale whatsoever because we knew that our country did not depend on the president, like countries with dictators depend on their leaders. We knew we had a Congress and other leaders who could lead the country in a very efficient way even in the absence of the president."

Cpl. B. Allen (Tsuruga) "In terms of our morale, the American bombing was terrific! You should have seen us standing at the windows cheering. To heck with the guards down there! We cheered! They didn't like that too well, but they didn't do anything about it. Oh, it was a tremendous lift! Even though there was a danger that we could be hit by those bombs, it was still a tremendous feeling. We didn't go hide in a foxhole or get down on the ground. We stood in the windows and cheered and were very excited. We'd stay up all night watching."

Cpl. Brantley (Yodogawa Steel Mill) "I still had strong hopes. I didn't care how long it was going to be. I began to figure it was going to be a good while, but I had never given up hope—never did. By the time I left there, the air raids had begun. We could look up in the sky and see the B-29s, and the Japanese fighter planes would try to get up to them but never could. Our Japanese sergeant turned to me, and I said, 'One of these days they're going to be hitting here.' Up to then the American planes had not bombed where we were, so he laughed and didn't believe me. I said, 'Yes, they're going to be bombing here someday.' The guard then said, 'You never give up, do you?' I said, 'No, and I don't intend to.' Finally, in the fall the B-29s hit the steel mill, and it was a big raid. When the bombing started, we all started shouting and hollering, and they threatened to shoot us if we didn't calm down. But we kept hollering, 'Drop them here! Drop them here!' because the Japs were all out in the foxholes around us. It passed our minds that we might get killed, too, but you didn't worry about it. You got to the state that you didn't care."

Cpl. B. Allen (Osaka) "We learned to live with the possibility of death, whether by bombs or artillery shells or executions or friendly submarines or whatever. The ones who came back, I think, learned to live with it. We knew at all times that it was there, and we knew that we might get it. But so what? After a while you began to realize that the United States wasn't as all-powerful as we once thought. When you think they're going to be there in two or three months from the time you're captured, and then it's two or three years and they're still not there, then you wonder, 'Will it be ten years?' We knew that someday we would win; I never thought that the United States would not win. But sometimes you began to think, 'Is it going to be five years or ten years, or how long is it going to take?' Then you'd say, 'Well, what if you do get it? What are you leaving? Well, not too much.' But I never did want to get it. I wanted to come home and see my loved ones again. I held on, and I ate, and I took as good care of myself as I could just for that reason."

Capt. Weidman (Kobe) "I provided a slogan that kept the men's spirits up. It was an old ditty from my youth. It went: 'You know what the bluebird said to the robin?/Keep your ass a-bobbin'/For tomorrow may be a better day.' "

Friends and Friendships

Cpl. Bunch (Cabanatuan) "As you start off, you're with some of your buddies in your own outfit, and then you get divided up, and eventually you end up with one or two fellows whom you make friends with. I remember fellows I made friends with that I never met until I got to prison camp. Now I don't say that for the Philippines. However, I do remember that one night at Cabanatuan one of my best friends in prison camp went to the latrine, which was nothing more than a large hole dug in the ground with dirt piled all the way around. When it rained, these piles of dirt would get extremely slick. So he got up one night and went to the latrine, and he slipped and fell in up to his neck. Fortunately, somebody else was there and pulled him out, and he spent the rest of the night with the help of some of the rest of us washing himself off. It was a tremendously humiliating thing for him."

Pvt. Guiles (Cabanatuan) "By this time you started forming little cliques or groups and so on. In fact, a buddy and I got together because your chances of survival were much better than it was earlier when it was every man for himself. You needed somebody you could depend on or somebody who could help you, because there were times when you were out of the barracks and somebody would steal you blind if your buddy wasn't there to watch. Or, if he was gone, you were there watching. Stealing was quite a problem, especially after the Red Cross packages were distributed. I remember one guy who was caught stealing off one of the boys in his clique. There were three of them, and they took turns staying up at night and keeping him awake, just wouldn't let him sleep."

Cpl. Halbrook (Clark Field) "At Clark Field everybody formed cliques. They were like little families. I had a clique of three. There was me, a guy named Bailey, and a fellow named Robert S. Black. All three of us were Marines, and everything we received we shared. Black had a real bad case of beriberi, and the other two members of the clique, Bailey and me, brought stuff in to him to keep him alive. Black saved my life in Formosa. We were a family of three making sure we all survived."

Cpl. McCall (Clark Field) "The first time I'd ever heard about the Masons was when I'd seen one Mason sharing with a sick Mason. And they were close as thieves from then on, which I thought was pretty good because nobody shared with another man as a rule. Everybody was on their own. Most people were thinking of themselves. There wasn't too much to steal, but there was stealing."

Pvt. Armstrong (Bicycle Camp) "The survivors of the *Houston* didn't have any clothes when I came into Bicycle Camp. I know that there was a boy whose name was Blue on the *Houston*, and he and I were about the same size. I had two pairs of shorts, and I let him have one of them. What we could divide with them, we did. When that ship went down, their clothes were all oil-soaked and they had to get rid of them. We shared. I know I did, and I know several others that did."

PFC Robinson (Bicycle Camp) "I went over to meet the guys from the 131st, and one of the first things I realized was that a hell of a bunch of them were from Texas. My first real contact with one of the boys was with Rayford Harris. He was from Memphis, Texas. Rayford shared with me a portion of his possessions. He apologized, saying, 'Robby, I've only got two blankets left.' The blanket he gave me had shrapnel holes in it, but that didn't keep it from keeping me warm. He also gave me a shirt and a pair of pants."

Pvt. Armstrong (Changi) "We'd band together, just four or five boys that you knew from home. These bands would be your lifesavers. You knew that somebody out of that little group one day would get something that would help somebody. The only thing we were looking for then was something to eat. When you take that many and band together, you could pool it together and get enough food to keep you going."

Fireman 1/C Kennedy (Burma-Thailand Railway) "J. O. Burge and I used to look out for each other. We'd help each other along. We were usually on the same work party. During the short time I worked in the kitchen, I used to bring him a little extra food. He got left at 18 Kilo Camp when he got sick. One day at 100 Kilo Camp I looked up to see a guard and J. O. coming down the railroad track. J. O. had sold everything except his shorts, pith helmet, and mess gear, so I gave him some of my stuff. Later, in Saigon, he had accumulated a bunch of bananas and some money which he split with me."

PO2 Detre (Burma-Thailand Railway) "You had to have a little clique so that you could take care of each other. It couldn't be too big. Sometimes it was only two men, sometimes three or four. We had three or four in ours. What one had in this clique belonged to everybody in the true sense. They say that Americans are joiners, and this is a classic example. There was only one loner that I knew of. He survived very well, but he was a loner."

M/Sgt. Stowers (Woosung) "When we got to the Woosung Prison Camp, the Wake Island men were already there in pitiful condition. Most of them had on khaki shorts, and when we'd left Peking, it was probably zero or below. When we got down to Shanghai, it was probably about freezing or something like that, and there was still snow on the ground. But we shared our clothing with them. There were a few instances, you know, where they felt that we hadn't shared, and they tagged us as the rich Peking people. But, in general, I'd say that everybody shared his wool underwear, his shirts, his long-handled drawers, and clothes."

Capt. Godbold (Woosung) "The North China Marines came in with overcoats, fur caps, gloves, things of that nature, and it caused resentment. There was some question about whether they were going to be repatriated. They never were, but there was some thought among the Japanese officials locally that maybe they were going to be repatriated, and so they were treated, at least at the outset, with a little more courtesy than were those of us who had been fighting the Japanese. We came with tropical clothing and very little of that, so there was a difference in our creature comforts. This, of course, created some concern among our people that it was bad that we didn't have what the others had."

PFC Fields (Woosung) "The North China Marines had all these heavy clothes to come in, but we finally traded them out of most of them because they thought the war was going to be a short war, and we could see winters ahead. We made out all right, but I'd say at the beginning, yes, there was tension between the Wake boys and the North China people. But I'm not going to say whether they would share or wouldn't. I'm not going to say."

PFC Venable (Woosung) "The North China Marines had been captured the first day that hostilities commenced. Then they were transferred to the camp with us. Now we were a bunch of old ragged-ass Marines, you know, no clothing and unshaven and all of that. In contrast, the North China Marines arrived in uniforms with their overcoats and their woolen uniforms and the fur caps with flaps. Each man carried his seabag with food and all that. They even had their fat little dog running along as a mascot. You'd think the comradeship would have been deeper, but the Japs placed these Marines in a barracks by themselves, and their commanding officer decreed that we were to stay out of their barracks. We were not to go down and to associate with them.

"They were not going to have anything to do with us. I think the old selfish human nature took over. They had food; they had money. They were looking out for old number one. They weren't an elite outfit. One of them, Herbert Orr, was a good friend of mine. Because we were acquainted, he gave me some clothing, you know. They thought they were going back to the States. They thought that they had diplomatic status. A rather deep bitterness developed as a result

of this. In fact—and I ramble—they fed us rice, and in the cooking of
the rice a heavy crust formed inside the pot. They'd scrape it out and
put it aside, then they'd divide it out fairly among the people. But the
North China Marines turned down the burnt rice initially. After all, it
was beneath their dignity to eat that. But then we saw the day when
they wanted to stand in turn for their burnt rice just like everyone
else. They had found out that they weren't diplomats after all. Time
is a great leveler, and so the time came around. I'm sure that a lot of
the bitterness remains until today concerning this. This is sort of an
unhappy note."

Pvt. Permenter (Woosung) "The Wake Island guys didn't have
anything, and the Japanese let us keep this seabag full of clothes, so
it was agreed that we were going to give clothes to those people.
Most of us had two good uniforms, that is, two summer uniforms,
two winter uniforms, plus older uniforms. It was agreed that we were
going to give them one of our uniforms, but as it turned out we caught
them selling those uniforms. There was some guys that gave uniforms to them, and the Wake guys were trading them for food, cigarettes, and so forth. And so we quit. We wouldn't do it; we backed
down on it because they were selling the uniforms instead of wearing
them. So I held onto everything I had."

Pvt. Benton (Woosung) "There were two boys who were on Wake
Island that I went through boot camp with about six months before,
and we still knew each other pretty well. One of them was a guy by
the name of McWiggins, and I can't remember the other boy's name.
Anyway, when they let us get into our seabags, well, I got a bunch of
clothes. I had quite a few, I guess, about ten or twelve pair of khakis
and about five or six suits of green, and then I had my blues. So I got
a bunch out, and I got a bunch of cigarettes out, and I went down and
gave them to these two boys that I went through boot camp with.
Those were the only two because I didn't have enough to go around.
They were boys I knew, so naturally they were the boys I picked out
to help. They were very appreciative of it, too. I would like to have
had enough to give to everybody. There were other guys who divided
with some of the others, but there wasn't enough to give them all.
But we spread it around as far as we could."

Pvt. Permenter (Kiangwan) "My bunkie smoked a pipe, and he
didn't have any tobacco. I didn't smoke a pipe, but because the tobacco was so cheap—or maybe somebody gave it to me—I had a
two- or three-pound can. I told him to use that pipe tobacco, and

that's how we got to be buddies. He stayed in during the day, while I was out on work detail. I told him to keep an eye on our things, so we got to be buddies. As a result, he got to feeding me, and he'd steal rice from these officers and give me an extra ration.

"Now my bunkie was sugar crazy, and as a rule I'd give him my sweets. You got to remember, he stole from these officers and fed me. Any sweet stuff I'd give to him. I didn't crave sweets; I just craved food, period. But he craved sweets. We looked after one another. A lot of times I'd come in on a cold day, and he'd have me a bucket of warm water there, or maybe he'd do my wash for me. In turn, I'd do him the same. You slept together; you shared your blankets; you shared your food; you shared whatever you had. Whatever I had, it was his; whatever he had was mine. If he got sick, I looked after him, and if I got sick, he looked after me. In some cases there were three or four people who would buddy up, do that. In some cases a guy was an individual. T. C. Crews was like that. I could get along with him, I think, because we were from Dallas, but a lot of people couldn't get along with him. He had a pretty short temper, and he'd scrap with just about anything that could walk."

Capt. Bartlett (Zentsuji) "I don't know of any prisoners stealing from one another, but at this stage of the game it was every man for himself. You might find a friend, but you were not too close to him."

Cpl. Minshew (Nagasaki) "You had a bunk buddy, and if he was out, you looked after what few possessions he had; and if you were out, he looked after your few possessions. If you had anything he didn't have, you might share with him and he might share with you. I had four different bunk buddies that I can remember in Nagasaki. You need to have someone to talk to. You were sharing the situation with all these people, and you needed to be able to talk and let off steam."

PO2 Detre (Sendryu) "I don't even remember getting to the hospital, that's how far gone I was. Once there, I started to recover because they were giving us just a little bit more chow. Krekan and Quick raided the Red Cross storage room and brought out all the chocolate they could get. That was one of the guttiest things I ever saw two guys do, because it had a heavy guard on it. Krekan gave me some chocolate and made me eat a little bit of it every night. By God, I got right back on my feet and started working again."

PFC Garrison (Osaka) "We stole food and took it back to camp for everybody. Being only eighty of us, we were a very close-knit group. Our leader was a Navy chief, Barnum, and we generally became known as 'Barnum and his seventy-nine thieves.' "

Faith in God and Country

Cpl. Clem (Cabanatuan) "I did a lot of praying on my part. Men in these prison camps got religion very quickly. I think that was the only time in my life that I could go to bed and keep saying my prayers every night. Everybody was very religious under those circumstances."

Lt. Burris (Cabanatuan) "There was a Baptist chaplain with us, Robert Preston Taylor. He did a lot of things, and he was always baptizing people. On this ship, the *Oryoko Maru*, he started praying at night. He'd give the Lord's Prayer. I got to where I couldn't go to sleep at night without that. I figured that we were going to die on that ship anyway, and I just couldn't go to sleep until he'd give that prayer."

Lt. Taylor (Cabanatuan) "You always have time to think about home, even if it's in the evening when you lie down on the ground to sleep. You think about those things. But I'll tell you, you just can't dwell on those things too much as a prisoner of war because every moment you are challenged to survive, and in our case as chaplains we were ministering to those who were in worse shape than we were. We tried to instill hope in a frank, positive way. Opportunities came quite often to say to a man who was about to give up or wanted to give up: 'There is hope; there is faith. And the thing you need to do is to keep your chin up and keep your faith with your Lord and faith with your family and faith with your church because this thing will be over one of these days. We can't tell you when it will be, but we are in the same plight that you are, and we believe it's going to be over. So, come on, now. Let's get with it and stay with it.' This way you could encourage the men. There's nothing of greater encouragement to anyone than to believe that there's going to be an end to something like that, and we were just sure that there was going to be an end to it.

"I believe there's a difference in outlook that develops between a prisoner of war who doesn't know when he's going to be free and a person who has been sentenced to a definite prison term. A POW could always believe that something great could happen in the next six months or year, whereas a person in prison who was serving a definite term might look at five years and say, 'Gee, I just know I can't hold out that long!' But a prisoner of war who really didn't know how long he'd be incarcerated could easily in his own mind encourage himself by thinking that this thing might be over in another year or six months. Truly, this is the way it was. We didn't know.

"In prison camp you live one day at a time but with your eye to the future, with that hope and faith. I've heard numerous men say, 'If I didn't have faith in my country and, above all, faith in God and faith that we were coming through this thing out yonder in a few years, I'd have given up a long time ago.' But it takes this attitude. With this you can survive a lot that you couldn't otherwise. An experience such as this tests even a chaplain's faith."

Cpl. McCall (Cabanatuan) "One time they had church services, and I went over to the church, and the preacher said, 'Would anybody like to join?' And I had a great desire to do it, but I thought, 'Well, if I can't do it under better conditions than this, why, I'm just not going to do it.' So I decided I'd wait."

First Sgt. Harrelson (Sumatra Camp No. 4) "You're always looking for tomorrow. You live today and then hope you wake up in the morning. You really didn't know what would happen because those camps were pretty open, and roving guards would go through your barracks at night, on their payday, on drunken binges. It was kind of hair-raising. When you get into the circumstances we ran into as prisoners, you find even the so-called atheists on their knees praying. We prayed to get back home, for food, to stop hurting. I wanted MacArthur to get back through there like he was supposed to and get us back home—all of us. We held services when we were allowed to. In most of the camps, we didn't have preachers."

Capt. Cates (Burma-Thailand Railway) "I never felt that I'd be rescued. As a matter of fact, early on I didn't expect to survive. Later, I found myself able to survive for that day only and worry about nothing. I just lived for today."

PO2 Detre (Burma-Thailand Railway) "Some of the enlisted men were very religious, and they would hold services. Mostly, we had Australian or English pastors. I think the men acquired a little more religion as they went along day to day. If they weren't religious, they certainly were before they got finished because this made a believer out of you."

Fireman 1/C Kennedy (Burma-Thailand Railway) "I'm sure there were a lot of prayers said. I know I said a lot. Not too many were said outward. We didn't have organized church services until we got into Thailand. We had none in the jungle. A few prayers were said when we buried people. I prayed mostly that I'd get out of this thing alive, that people would get well, and that people at home would be all right."

PFC Robinson (Burma-Thailand Railway) "To me, religious faith is most, most vital. In spite of all my many sins, I know the Old Man's up there. Very few times did we have an opportunity to hold religious ceremonies. But you always had yourself at night, where you could think and have your own religion. My typical prayer was 'Thank you, Lord, for the good things.' I asked Him for things to be better, to be with us as a group. I asked Him to do those things that would let us continue to survive until the day of reckoning."

Pvt. Benton (Woosung and Kiangwan) "We prayed. I don't deny it. I said a lot of silent prayers during that forty-four months. I'm not ashamed of it."

PFC Venable (Woosung and Kiangwan) "We did not have a chaplain in our organization, but many of us had a deep religious conviction. More than anything else, to a man we had faith that we were going to get back."

Cpl. Halbrook (Formosa) "In the evenings this guy named Carter—he later became a preacher in Chicago—would talk to me and tell me about Christian Scientists. If you wanted to get sick, you could get sick; if you didn't want to get sick, you could get well. I began to listen to him and believe in him. I worked on it, and that, plus eating them damn fish, helped my headaches more than anything else."

PFC Visage (Arao) "I learned that the body that people think is so fragile is a very strong thing and can take lots of punishment. I learned that hard work won't kill you because we did some of the hardest work there ever was. If you're being fed right, it won't hurt you. I pretty well straightened out my life while I was there. I got more faith in God. We had many guys in prison camp with us that were never Christians, and some of them were converted in camp through guys talking to them. Some of them turned out to be preachers."

PFC Evans (Nagasaki) "I think that the Americans certainly were the most optimistic because we had faith in the ability of our people, and we knew that the United States was a bastion of freedom."

Communicating with the Outside

Lt. Taylor (Cabanatuan) "The Japanese considered radios to be contraband, so we were not permitted to have any. But I guess this was one of the most wonderfully kept secrets of all our prison life because the Japanese didn't know we had one. It was brought in piece by piece from unauthorized sources and then given to our communications specialists who put it together. Actually, Filipinos in Manila planted these pieces among the sacks of feed and rice, and eventually our men were able to piece together a shortwave radio. It functioned in Cabanatuan, I know, for more than two and a half years, and the Japanese never knew we had it. With this radio, we could receive information about the war and about the United States. The secret of our success in maintaining it unbeknown to the Japanese was the fact that only three or four men really knew where it was and anything about it. I feel real proud that we could do something like this because the Japanese would come along and they would feed us little ol' filmstrips about their great victories and their bombing of San Francisco and New York and stuff like that. They didn't know it, but we were getting direct information from our own people as to our side of the story. In other words, we felt like we were on level ground with them there. We were getting our information from the U.S. by shortwave radio even though they were feeding us propaganda about their great accomplishments."

Cpl. Koury (Cabanatuan) "We had a little smuggling system in camp, and we were able to get a radio. I had no part of this operation, but I knew when it came in. There was a Masonic group that was quite active. The Masons in Manila, as I understand it, disassembled a radio and had it smuggled in piecemeal. It was kept piecemeal by a select group and assembled periodically, and they picked up news. This group was made up of Masons who were prisoners in Cabanatuan. The news was passed by word of mouth."

Lt. Daman (Cabanatuan) "I was sure that my wife had gotten safely back to the States because it was during this time that we received three postcards through the Red Cross. I learned that she was living with her mother.

"Also, we had a Westinghouse engineer there who, somehow or other, the Japanese found out could repair radios. They had confiscated a lot of radios in the Philippines, so they put him in this little shop, and they'd take their broken radios over there to him. He would take out good parts and substitute bad parts for them. Eventually, he managed to build a little receiver about three by five and a half inches in length, and he hid it in our barracks, and we were able to get daily news from Treasure Island [Navy base at San Francisco]. Later, when we moved to Davao, he divided up all these parts among the prisoners, and then he reassembled it when everybody turned in his part. Down in Davao he built his receiver in the false bottom of a canteen. We knew in advance exactly where all of the Americans were as they came through the Philippines. We were one day behind their arrival in Manila from the news we got."

Cpl. Halbrook (Clark Field) "I got three letters, and one of them was from my sister, one was from my grandmother, and one was from my aunt who also sent me shorts. My sister started the letter off with 'We're so glad to hear that you are a prisoner.' My aunt cautioned me not to get too fat. I was glad to get the letters because I saved them and read them over and over."

PFC Bolitho (Davao Penal Colony) "We were allowed to send postcards. I don't know how many I sent, but I've still got some of them. You'd underline words on them that you wanted to indicate, like *I am well.* Then you were allowed fifteen words that you could write down at the bottom. If the wording was right and if it didn't take the censor, Running Wada, a great deal of concentration to figure it out, and if there was nothing there that might indicate something bad, and if it was in his command of English, it went through. But if it was something he wasn't too sure of, it didn't go through."

Cpl. Burlage (Palawan) "In this camp we never received any news, not down there. No, we were isolated down there. We were completely out of the mainstream of anything."

Cpl. Burlage (Las Pinas) "In this camp we were getting a daily newspaper. We were getting one sneaked in to us. It was a Filipino paper printed in English. I remember this columnist, Juan de la Cruz—John Q. Public in our language. He was writing such that you read between the lines, and you could get a pretty good idea about what was going on."

PFC R. Allen (Philippines and Japan) "I didn't receive any news from home until the day I was released, and then the only reason I did is because they had notified my family that I was released, and then I got a telegram from them."

PFC Evans (Surabaja) "It was in Surabaja that the Japanese made some propaganda broadcasts. We were taken there to make them. They were broadcast over Tokyo Rose's program or whatever, and my mother heard that 'I was doing all right,' that 'I was alive and being treated well.' What else do you say? They took us down to this studio and fed us real good. They gave us some Chinese food and sort of patted us on the back, and we went in there and made the broadcasts. I don't remember how many of us there were, but it was quite a few. I never could understand why the Japanese did this."

T/Sgt. Stanbrough (Tanjong Priok) "This sergeant named Karney said he had a radio and wanted me to fix it. I was surprised he had it, but no one really searched us. He brought it in. It was a General Electric portable in a little leatherette case. It was a nice set, similar to the ones I had worked on in a radio service shop in Wichita Falls. It used regular tubes like the one-volt series. It had a wet-cell battery that had to be charged. Karney told me that if I were to fix the radio and give him the news, I could have the set. I only messed with it at night. The first thing to do to get it to work was to get the high frequency, 455 kilohertz, back in the range. I loosened the padders all the way up and counted the turns up and counted them down, and then went back to the midrange on each one. Padders are little condensers, and they are stuck in those little intermediate-frequency transformers. Then I was able to peak up. I could hear a noise and I peaked it up. Later, I heard on the far end of the dial, at 500 kilohertz, a ship CW [continuous radio waves]. I knew that was 500, so that meant I was low frequency. I scooted that down. Before doing that I peaked up those little padders and got them in range; then I got the high frequency. I needed an oscillator coil, and somebody found a fountain-pen top. I took the little coil out and wound it several times until I got the frequency about right. I got it to oscillate. One night I turned it on, and without even touching the dial it said, 'KGEI at San Francisco.' Any good electronics person would reach over and touch it to make it a little better, but Karney said, 'Don't touch it!' I didn't, and we heard our first news.

"The Australians also had a radio in the camp. The Australian news always seemed to be not as optimistic as the American news.

Ours had a lot more propaganda than theirs. I finally learned that the BBC was the best one to listen to. In those days the commentator, who was full of overoptimism, was Mr. William Winters. It was awful nice sometimes at night to hear Dinah Shore singing. The radio was fourteen inches by ten inches by four inches. I just left it in the bedding at Tanjong Priok. The Japs didn't come in there and search. We did decide that we shouldn't let too many people know about it."

T/Sgt. Stanbrough (Bicycle Camp) "Some of the boys on the working parties brought in earphones and spare tubes. All those boys wanted was news. Sergeant Patterson knew shorthand, so we let him take it down in shorthand occasionally so we'd all get the news. He worked over in Japanese headquarters, and on several occasions, until we put a stop to it, he would type up the news and bring it back to us. Sometime during the stay at Bicycle Camp another radio showed up. It was a small Zenith. I rewired it and made a shortwave out of it. The camp guards were getting a little rougher, searching places and raising hell. We got a little tighter with the news. We traded news with the Australians, and all the people in my barracks knew about it. The headquarters unit knew all about it."

First Sgt. Harrelson (Bicycle Camp) "Jess Stanbrough was a real good ham operator from Wichita Falls prior to mobilization. He studied it a lot and was well trained in it. He was communications chief for the regiment and later for the battalion. The radio equipment he put together in the camp was kind of small, but we could pick up broadcasts from the more powerful stations. The news was passed from mouth to mouth, but it didn't take too long because any kind of news at all would go through the barracks like wildfire. It was good for our morale simply by knowing we were picking up information.

"That first Christmas, after the big masses of the battalion moved out of Java, a civilian Japanese who ran the radio station there took six or eight of us out to the station to cut a record. He had been trained in Los Angeles, I believe, and his understudy had graduated from the University of Washington. I just got to make a short announcement to my mother. I gave my name, rank, and serial number and gave my mother's name. I was allowed to say, 'I'm fine. The Japanese are feeding me well.' It was just like the card. Later, they played these records back for propaganda. A year and a half later they played these records over the radio, and a shortwave fellow in the United States picked it up and called my mother. He made a little record of what was said and sent it to her.

"This commander at Bicycle Camp liked to post information such as the Japanese forces repelling a force at Guadalcanal and killing so many thousands of troops and sinking so many ships and knocking down so many planes. Then about two months later, they would have repelled a massive force at another group of islands. Then after another three months, it would be Truk, Palau, or Iwo Jima. Every time it would get closer to Japan, so we knew the way the war was going."

Pvt. Chambers (Burma-Thailand Railway) "They gave us a little card back in the jungle. We'd been prisoners about a year. You'd just sign your name to it, and there was a little block to check that 'I am a prisoner of the Imperial Japanese Army, and I am working,' and 'I am well,' or 'I am sick.' Nobody put 'sick' on there because we knew it wouldn't go through. My mother got this card after a year. My brother was working at the Gulf refinery before the war started, and he worked there throughout the war. He didn't know that you couldn't send over a twenty-five-word letter. He wrote a three-page letter and mailed it. I don't know how in the world it got through, but it did. It was about a year old when I got it. Nobody expected any mail because you got it so seldom."

PO2 Detre (Burma-Thailand Railway) "About two years after we were made prisoners they came around with some French postcards that were from the Red Cross, printed in French and Japanese, for us to sign. There were already nice statements printed up. A lot of people wouldn't send them, and I think this was a bad mistake. My mother got hers. It was two and a half years after I was a prisoner, but she got it. I thought it was worth it, although everything on it was probably a lie. She knew I had sent it, and that was enough. She had brains to figure out the rest—that conditions couldn't be that good. I sent two cards home, and they both got home."

M/Sgt. Stowers (Woosung) "We had one fellow who was a radio expert. I can't remember his name. He was a sergeant. He made a radio out of some parts he had stolen or smuggled in with some of the other fellows. About once a week he'd get a radio broadcast, but it was a very dangerous thing. It was something you could have gotten killed for, and I wasn't in on the deal. I think he worked with Colonel Ashurst."

PFC Sparkman (Woosung) "The radioman that made a shortwave radio gave each prisoner a piece to keep. I didn't have a piece, but I knew some that did. On certain nights they would put the radio together and hook in on shortwave frequencies and bands. I think the first time they put it together the Battle of the Coral Sea was going on or had just finished, and they got that news. I think it was the battle that we first came out ahead in."

Capt. Godbold (Woosung and Kiangwan) "One guard brought in news. There were also Japanese newspapers brought in, and there were some people who could read Japanese. Also, some newspapers were in English. Then our main source were radios; parts for them were smuggled in and radios were built. The Japanese allowed radios that could only receive Shanghai broadcasts, but I guess one of these was fixed up so that you could get broadcasts from long range. For example, we heard the news of the Battle of Midway from the United States and knew that the Japanese had suffered a defeat there. We heard about [Lt. Col. James H.] Doolittle's raid [on Tokyo in April 1942] and the Battle of the Coral Sea."

PFC Venable (Woosung and Kiangwan) "We were allowed to send mail for a time. We were instructed that the only thing you could say was the state of your health and how happy you were, or else it wouldn't be sent. Our officers and NCOs urged that we not try to be cute and send anything which would try to be a coded message or something, just simply base it on fact or it wouldn't go. So there were several cards, not letters—several cards which I sent out and which did reach my parents.

"They brought in fliers from time to time who had been shot down, and, of course, they would fill us in up to the time that they had been captured. You heard things through the grapevine. It really worked, and we had pretty good news. I will always suspect there was a radio in camp. We had pretty good information as long as we were in China. Once we moved to Japan, the information ceased."

Pvt. Benton (Woosung and Kiangwan) "We could write letters— I don't remember the exact amount we were allowed—and we did receive a few letters. Some seemed to get more than others. I received very few letters. I found out after I got home that there was lots of mail that I never received. My bunkie got whole handfuls of mail. We shared everything. They'd write letters to him, about ten or fifteen, and just continue each one where the last left off. Then the censors would cut it. They were pretty scissor-happy. By the time the Americans and then the Japs would get through, you didn't have much left. You might get a letter that had two or three words. I wrote my mother a card the first day of January 1945. It was mailed. I got home

October 4, 1945, and in November my mother got that card. I beat it home. That gives you an idea of how slow the mail was."

Capt. Adair (Zentsuji) "We were allowed to write and receive letters. I think my folks got eighteen letters from me during those years, and I received probably a dozen letters altogether. We were allowed to write twenty-five-word letters. Everything was censored. The letters coming in were censored by our people and by the Japs, too.

"Of course, the Japs forbade us to receive any outside news, but the enlisted men would steal newspapers, Japanese newspapers, and bring them in. We had an American naval officer there who was fluent in Japanese—he could read it and write it—and he would interpret the news from those newspapers. Then we had a commentator who would come around to each section of the barrack as if he were lecturing on some subject. We'd put a guard at the door to make sure that no Japanese were close by, and then the commentator would give us a daily news report. In addition to that, a little later a group of Dutch officers came in from another camp, and they brought a short-wave radio with them. They put it in a wall, and they'd get the daily news reports from KGEI in San Francisco. They would bring that news around, too, so we were pretty much up to date."

Capt. Bartlett (Zentsuji) "We were writing our censored POW mail, so I had a system with my wife. I am not a religious man—never have been, still ain't. When I got to Zentsuji and started our code, I wrote just this: 'I am now reading [such and such] a paragraph in the Bible and am studying the Bible.' Then I gave the Japs the paragraph. Then I put in the next one: 'Jesus is not in Japan.' Well, the paragraph that I referred to is the portion of the Bible where Jesus is tending to the multitudes. Jesus wasn't in Japan. In other words, I was telling my wife that I was not being fed very well in Japan. That's the way I originated my code. When I would write it, I would go and look through the Bible and find something kindred. You can find anything in the Bible. I would remark that I was reading that paragraph, that part of the Bible. This would go right through the censor, and my wife would get it."

Capt. Bull (Zentsuji) "I also received a package from home while I was in Japan. It had come over aboard the *Gripsholm*, and it was a pleasure to have because it was very encouraging to feel that even the Japanese would let it come through. I felt like it wasn't pilfered, as some of the Red Cross boxes were. It contained some clothing, a wool scarf, and, I remember most of all, a pair of eyeglasses. For some reason or another my parents had had my prescription duplicated at home, not even knowing that I'd lost my glasses to the Japanese upon capture. I was thankful for the glasses because they helped me in all the reading I was able to do.

"We were allowed to send one postcard a month after we'd been there about two months. We sent our first message—thirty words—home. Then we were allowed to make a recording after we'd been there some time, in which we would send a message that they used for propaganda. Mine was picked up in the United States and sent to my parents."

PFC Evans (Nagasaki) "We could tell the war was coming closer by the type of fish we got. Certain types of fish were caught a certain distance from land. They had a type of fish they called the shit fish; it was caught close to shore and used for fertilizer. We had English people who had been fishermen for years. They knew how far you had to go out to sea to catch this type of fish. We knew that we were closing in on them when we were getting these fish that they catch closer to the shore."

T/Sgt. Stanbrough (Ohasi) "We kept the radio in the barracks. The news was distributed by word of mouth only to the Americans, the New Zealanders, and the Australians. We were particularly worried about the Black Dutch [Indonesians], because they were very sympathetic to the Japanese. The other group we were concerned about was the English, with whom we were not overly enchanted. It was very discouraging to hear on the radio every now and then that it was decided to make more of a war effort in Europe, knowing that we were secondary. When we got the news, particularly when it was getting better, you could hardly restrain yourself."

Seaman 1/C Stewart (Ohasi) "We were able to write a card home about once a month. I don't think that out of the twenty or thirty I wrote that one was ever sent out of Japan. I presume most of them were taken either to the officers at camp or to the main office of a group of camps and read and thrown out. It was a little card, like a postcard. You could write all you wanted on one side and put the address on the other side.

"In front of the electric shop there was a big signboard with a lot of Japanese writing on it. I presumed it was where the war news was posted. It was changed, but I don't know how often. They had the word 'Saipan' spelled out in Japanese letters that I could read. Having gotten word from our radio source that Saipan had been occupied, I figured out what it was. I looked at it and was reading rather laboriously that 'Saipan died.' A Japanese kid that worked in the shop was standing behind me and went to the office right quick. The next day the signboard was blank."

Pvt. Bugbee (Ashio) "One time I received seven letters, and they all came at one time. This was when I realized that my mother had passed away because there were a couple of letters from my father, a couple from my two sisters, and one from my aunt. There wasn't a word in any of them about my mother, and I had no letter from her. Knowing my mother like I did—when my brother was going to Louisiana State University, she was writing him every night—I knew that something had happened. But that was all the mail I received, and I read them and reread them. I kept them, and I still have them. I brought the letters back with me."

Attitudes toward Non-Americans

Cpl. Smith (Palawan) "I'm sure the Japs knew that we all were thinking about killing them sons of bitches. I think that would have been a unanimous feeling. I know that some others feel about like I do, and I still don't have a damned thing for Japs."

Cpl. McCall (Bilibid Prison) "I went on the outside on a couple of details into the city. That was something just to see women again, you know. And when we were downtown we went over to one of the universities and worked one day. I remember seeing a barber pick up his scissors and form a V, and the Japanese saw him, too. They went in and beat him up. But you have to hand it to the Filipinos; anytime they could get a chance to give that V, they would give it. This was the sign [for victory] at the beginning of the war when we went down the road."

PFC R. Allen (Davao Penal Colony) "The Japs brought in a thousand troops—the Black Dutch [Indonesians], Australians, English from Borneo—and put them in our camp. We got along better with the Japs, I believe, than we did with them. We Americans took care of each other, but the English didn't do this. The Jap soldier in the field is dirty. In Japan he's very clean. He's ten times cleaner than the Englishman. Even a Jap soldier is cleaner than the English. I've never been to England, but what I've seen of the English they're the dirtiest, filthiest people I've ever seen in my life. I don't think they've got as much guts as the Americans. They seem to be weak."

Sgt. Fujita (Java) "If the Dutchmen had the guts that their women did, we would still be fighting over there, I guess. Those Dutch women, I have admiration for them. They would come up there and try to get food to us and see their husbands and whatnot, and the Japs would stand out there and beat them unmercifully. But they would be by, day after day after day. If you even looked like you were going to hit one of those Dutchmen, they were long gone. The yellow-bellied devils!"

First Sgt. Harrelson (Tanjong Priok) "The British always wanted to treat us Americans as colonials, and they looked down upon us. When we got to talking to them individually, they were good people. Collectively, excuse the French, they were a bunch of bastards. They didn't have any personal cleanliness habits like we did. They didn't care whether they bathed or not, and that could have been part of the problem with the latrines and showers at Tanjong Priok when we hit there. The British liked to run things, but they liked to run them around a conference table. I never found one that would actually go out and do anything."

PO2 Detre (Bicycle Camp) "This American had a pair of wire cutters. The camp was surrounded with black barbed wire. He carefully cut some of this wire into flint size. He found a bunch of envelopes out on a working party and put ten of them into each envelope. He made a quick pass through the Australians and sold them at fifteen cents, or twenty-five cents a package. I remember seeing this one Australian put one in his lighter and trying to light it and light it. He finally looked down and said, 'Why, that bloody Yank sold me a piece of wire!' That's the only time I've ever known us to take the Aussies. Usually, they were pulling something like that on us. The Aussies were as fine a group of men as you'll ever run across."

Pvt. Armstrong (Changi) "We had trouble with our relationship with the British for a while. They were in Changi first, and they thought it was still their setup. We were supposed to take what they didn't want. Especially on working parties, they got their pick of the good tools, and we got to use the bad ones. An English major would set the tools out. We were getting the shovels with broken handles. John C. Hensley one morning got in there and told the major, 'You hand out a good one, and I'll hand out a bad one to the Americans. The next time I'll hand out a good one to the Americans.' The English major said no, and they got into a squabble. John C. had one of those big ol' square-pointed shovels and hit the major right between the eyes. Just *bam*! From then on, we got an even break on the tools.

"The incident involving the king's coconuts occurred when we were trying to gather ripe coconuts. We couldn't climb the trees because they were too high. Some of us got an ax and chopped down the trees to get the coconuts. Some Englishmen came running down and said, 'Oh, you can't do this! You've cut down the king's coconut trees!' Ray Ogle, who was with us, said, 'The king's coconut trees, hell! It looks to me like the Japs own them now!' There was a little fight over that, but those fights didn't last long."

PO2 Detre (Changi) "The British looked like rabble to me, and I think the Japanese were right when they called them rabble. The discipline in the Gordons was good. That's the only people I had contact with or wanted to have contact with, the Gordon Highlanders. The British pulled all kinds of crap on us there, and we retaliated. These guys had swagger sticks, and our men hated those swagger sticks because they were a stick to hit somebody with. I remember Pappy Starr stole something, and he got put in jail—in irons. The British threw him in there. Mr. Hamlin found out and went down and got him out. Pappy was mad as hell about getting out of jail. It was the first time he had been eating Red Cross supplies.

"On the way to work one morning we had to pass by a housing development where an old British colonel lived. He'd be up there shaving with his suspenders down over his butt. He was a big, fat one. A couple of guys took a potshot at him with their slingshots. He came down toward us, and we were yelling dirty names at him. He said he didn't mind being called names but being catapulted was the last straw. The next morning there must have been a hundred slingshots that opened up on him.

"We stayed at Changi about two months. When it came time to leave, the Gordon Highlanders stood in the best uniforms they had, with their bagpipes. We were coming up the road to the gate and they played marching music, as squealy and squally as it was. We swung right into step and gave them a salute as we went by. The old major was mad as hell. He said, 'I don't understand it! Those blokes wouldn't' play that tune for the king himself!' It turned out that it was a great honor for us. It is a regimental vote whether they play this tune for you or not, and if you are turned down it doesn't make a damn who you are."

Fireman 1/C Kennedy (Changi) "The Americans and Australians got along together famously. I think the colonial part had something to do with it. We were both used to hard work and were more individualistic. We tended to group up against the Dutch and the English."

Pvt. Wisecup (Changi) "The British officers were the worst of the lot. I did two weeks in the Changi jail for stealing rice. Everybody was stealing rice to eat, not to sell. The officers knew that two other guys put me up to stealing the rice. They said I was not responsible, but I was protecting two other people. I said I wasn't, and, without a trial, I went up and did the ten days. The officers were buying all kinds of stuff on the black market. They had their own police force, and the Nips let them run it just like peacetime."

M/Sgt. Stowers (China) "I hated the Japs; I still do. I'm not a racist, but to be honest about it I still hate them. I feel that as long as they're equal or you have the top hand, they're the most ingratiating, the most polite people you've ever seen. Once they get the upper hand on you, they're the most brutal and unfeeling people I have ever run into. Most of us never realized that human beings could be so brutal to one another, but we went through it and so we distrust them. I think you'll find throughout the prisoners that we distrust them and have no use for them as a race. Even as individuals, I don't have a single Japanese friend, and I know that's not fair, not fair at all. A whole generation has developed in the thirty years since I was captured. Youngsters like my son were born many years since then. They don't know anything about our treatment except what they read. But still, as a race I just distrust them, and I hate them."

PFC Sparkman (Tientsin) "I liked the Chinese. They're a pretty intelligent bunch of people. They're nice, polite, and they live like anybody else if they have the ways and means to do so. But life was pretty rough over there. If you'd never seen China, well, it's just hard to explain."

Cpl. Crews (Woosung) "The only Japanese that I would say anything for as far as being a human and having human feelings towards us was a medical man by the name of Shento. And he seemed to be more concerned about the health of the prisoners."

PFC Fields (Woosung and Kiangwan) "I guess I may be one of those peculiar people, but I was never bitter toward the Japanese. I'm not going to say that all of these Japanese were good fellows, but as far as hating or disliking them, I can't say that I do now, except the ones that were cruel to everybody."

Pvt. Benton (Kiangwan) "We had this fellow who was off a merchant marine ship from some country. He was Jewish. He'd come in there and didn't have nothing. So, he'd borrow an article, then he took that article and started trading, and finally he'd trade around and go get that article back plus a bunch of other stuff, and give it back to the guy that he borrowed from first. Of course, then he was on his way. He wound up, I think, with 90 percent of the money in camp before we left there. There is no way of knowing how much he got out of camp with, but he was shrewd. He didn't smoke. He was the type of guy that could get by with a minimum of food because he never had to work, which makes a lot of difference. He turned out to be, I guess you'd say, a millionaire. He was the millionaire of the camp even though he didn't have a million dollars. But speaking of articles and things that he had, he would be like a millionaire out here."

Pvt. Permenter (China and Japan) "I think really the average Japanese knew that they could never win that war in the end. You'd take an individual Japanese and get him off, 95 percent of them would be pretty nice to you if you'd be pretty nice to them. But they were just like I was; they were victims of circumstances. I got caught. I don't blame nobody for it. They didn't force me to go out there. I volunteered to go in the service. I don't blame the U.S. government. I don't blame the Japanese government."

Cpl. Halbrook (Kawasaki) "Australians were mean bastards; they didn't like nobody. We hated the Limeys worse than we did the Japanese. They'd steal from you, even if you were dying. They were worse thieves than we were. There was nothing about them that I liked. They loved to stay dirty. The only way you would have trouble with a Canadian was to call him an Englishman, and then you would have a fight on your hands."

Seaman 1/C Stewart (Ohasi) "During the last year or so, when the camp was enlarged, we had mostly French Canadians. We couldn't trust them. For civilized people, I don't see how they lived the way they did. Before they arrived, it was never a problem to keep the latrines halfway sanitary and clean. But once they got there, everything was a mess the rest of the time."

American Air Attacks

Cpl. Burlage (Las Pinas) "It was September 21, 1944. I remember the date. We were out doing our regular pick-and-shovel work. Here was Nichols Field, where the Japs had quite a few of their light bombers and fighter planes, and they were up fooling around in the air. I remember I was talking to this guy, and I was looking up at them and I said, 'They must have brought some more in last night. There's quite a few up there.' And this guy looked at me and said, 'Man, there really are a lot of them up there.' I kept watching, and this other guy said, 'I don't believe they're Japs. They don't fly in the same formation. They're flying in fours, and Japs always fly in threes.' By that time there was no question about it. Out of the sky came some planes, and two peeled off, one right behind the other, and hit this bomber that had just taken off. Boy, he didn't have a chance. He hit the ground in flames. And then it all broke loose. Out of that sky came about three or four hundred American planes, and for about two hours it was the most beautiful sight you ever wanted to see.

"Every once in a while a Zero [Japanese fighter plane] would come ripping right across going about twenty, twenty-five feet off the ground. He'd be trying to get away, and there would be one of the [American] carrier-based planes right behind him. Then he'd let go with his guns, and if he missed, the Zero would pull away because the guns would slow the pursuit plane down. He'd keep on and eventually he'd get him. And we were all shaking our fists. I got hit in the leg by a piece of shrapnel. I didn't even know I'd gotten hit. I was bleeding and yelling at the time. I was yelling and I said, 'Did you see that damn guy come by here shooting at us? He had ham and eggs for breakfast, and all I had was that damn rice!' We really enjoyed it, and then that afternoon there was some dive-bombing taking place. The most beautiful sight in the world is a dive-bomber in action. Of course, that's a thing of the past, but these planes would come out of a cloud bank and go right at them. We were right at the edge of Manila Bay, and they were after those Japanese ships. The bay was full of ships. The Americans dive-bombed all afternoon, came back the next morning, and dive-bombed again. There were about four hundred planes, chugging along at treetop level. I guess every plane that they could get off that carrier came by and flew over Manila. There wasn't a shot fired at them. The Jap planes hardly moved, and there weren't many left. Nichols Field was burning. The ships were all on fire out there in the bay, what ships weren't under water. It was a cleanup."

Cpl. Smith (Palawan) "After American bombers started coming in September or October 1944 (one or the other) treatment changed, much for the worse—food and beatings. They really started beating us on the arms, legs, what-have-you. They woke us up unannounced and just started beating on you."

Capt. Cates (Kanchanaburi) "By this time we were seeing little things on the bulletin board like, 'Prisoners will not laugh at the Japanese during the course of an air raid.' We had slit trenches all over. We were now in the position of feeling that we are again a superior race. At one camp there was a pigpen with a moat rather than a fence to retain the pigs. I spent a bombing raid down in that thing. The prisoners would walk around the parapets. The layout was rectangular. If the planes were coming from one side, we knew where to go. All the time there was one of the less strong Japanese characters on his knees and hands with his nose buried right in the bottom of that mud. We all had a feeling of superiority.

"At Kanchanaburi there was a bridge on the River Kwai [Kwae Noi River]. The B-24s would come over to bomb this bridge. The first flight they made, a bent fin brought a huge bomb over and made a crater about thirty feet deep right in the middle of our hospital shack. We could see it coming. That's when we left the parade ground and scattered. On a number of other runs, they'd fly so as to hit the piers of the bridge. It was obvious they were not deliberately attacking us, but it scared the living daylights out of us every time we'd hear a plane."

Pvt. Chambers (Kanchanaburi) "We got that bridge at Tamarkan built back, and they'd come and bomb it out. It happened two or three times. These bombers were B-24s and some B-17s, and they'd come over and drop bombs at high altitude and then circle out and come back and drop some antipersonnel bombs at the ack-ack guns the Japs had there. The first time they bombed, some fell into our camp. I think it killed twenty-six or twenty-nine Australians. A lot of them were buried that we dug out. We used the trenches around the huts, built to keep the rats out, as air-raid shelters. In addition, they let us dig zigzag trenches in a corner of the camp. We couldn't go out of the camp.

"One time, the Jap guards heard the air-raid alarm go off, and they came out of the camp and hit the road. They ran down to the end of the lane. It was just like a track race. We were laughing at them, and the camp commander saw us. He put up a sign that there wouldn't be any more laughing at the Japanese guards during air raids. The next time the guards got down to the end of the lane, the commander stepped out and headed them off. He stood there and bashed them all with his ol' saber in the scabbard. The whole gang of them turned around and had to go back. I guess he hadn't told them that he was going to stop us from laughing, but that was funnier than the other."

Fireman 1/C Kennedy (Saigon) "The day we were going out to work on the airport, we heard this buzzing sound. We were all lined up in the morning for counting. It looked like a bunch of bees over the airport circling and diving in. We immediately went to our slit trenches. It had been raining, and they were full of muddy water. They started bombing the docks, which was right by our camp. We were up to our necks in water, and when they started to strafe us, that's when we went underwater. They shot one plane down over us, and he crashed into the dock area. He turned his bomb loose right after they shot his tail off. They cleaned out every ship in the river, and they got every plane at the airport. It was [Admiral William F.] Halsey's group out in the gulf that came in, and it did a lot for our morale."

PFC Venable (Kiangwan) "On Armistice Day, 1944, B-29s bombed the Shanghai area. The Japanese didn't have any antiaircraft guns that could get up high enough to shoot them. This was a great morale booster; later, the Americans came and bombed and strafed our particular area, and they flew over our prison camp several times and created great chaos. They shot down a Japanese bomber and a trainer. They blew him out of the air, and, of course, we witnessed it. But now the Japanese soldiers went pretty wild, and, as you can imagine, they were firing around through the camp without any regard. There were twelve people bayoneted just without any provocation or any cause—just simply during the time that these people were caught up in this excitement. But for me it was a morale booster. It was pretty nice to see your side coming through again."

Cpl. Crews (Kiangwan) "We felt pretty encouraged when the P-51s started coming over. There was an airport on each side of our camp, as I remember—I say an airport, it was really a Japanese airstrip. And the Americans were coming over and bombing these airports and strafing them in the daytime. The sentries were shooting at them with their rifles from the sentry towers. They were that close!

At night the big stuff would come over and drop bombs all along the riverfront. And in the daytime, also, some B-29s would come over high up. We had one guy we called Photo Joe. He came over in a P-38 every day about the same time. He was taking pictures of everything. The Japanese wouldn't let us mark the camps. So, it was kind of nervous with all this bombing and strafing. A couple of Marines made the mistake of cheering, and they got stretched out and bayoneted for it. They didn't kill them, but they weren't in too good a shape. That's the last time anybody openly cheered during an air raid."

Pvt. Benton (Kiangwan) "When the bombers began coming over, even though the B-24 had quite a range, we knew that the Americans were getting closer. Of course, when the P-51s came in there, well, we knew they were really getting close because we knew the fighters didn't have even that much range. This was in the spring of 1945. I don't mind telling you, if you've never been through an air raid, I hope you never have to go through one, because I was scared. I was so scared I couldn't put a cigarette in my mouth. I'd finally get it in my mouth, and I couldn't light it. I was shaking that bad! I wasn't nervous, I was scared—that's all you could call it. And I wasn't the only one that was scared. When you're frightened, if you've got something to fight back with or put up a defense, it's one thing. But it's a whole lot different if you're helpless."

Lt. Taylor (Takao) "We had sailed into the harbor at Takao, and while we were getting ready to take on fuel and supplies we were bombed by American planes. Of course, the Japanese rushed us back onto the hold of the ship. This was a pretty terrifying experience to go through because you feel the impact of the explosion, and then there's the falling of debris and the flying of planks and everything from the decks. Then there's the quiet moment when seemingly everything's over—complete silence. You don't hear a scream; you don't hear a moan; you don't hear anything for a moment. Then we began to get to our feet, because when something like that happens you fall flat on your stomach and get as close as possible to whatever you're standing or lying on.

"I was kind of the leader of a group of ten men who were on the main deck receiving their rice and water. When the planes came, we just fell in a cluster right on the deck. When I was able to get up, I had been wounded in my wrist and hip by flying fragments from shells or bombs. Only about two of us got up. The rest of them were all dead in my group. Those of us who were still alive began to do our best to help those who were wounded. There wasn't much we could do except to get around among them and see how badly they were hurt. It was a pretty terrifying thing. Out of about a thousand or twelve hundred of us who were aboard, I would say that about five hundred were killed, so that left very few of us to make the trip to Japan."

M/Sgt. Stowers (in transit, Pusan to Japan, 1945) "It's hard to explain how you felt in these constant air attacks. You kind of think, 'Come on in and hit the son of a bitch so maybe I can get off of it,' but you're scared to death that they are going to hit you. It's kind of a funny feeling."

Capt. Bull (Zentsuji) "The first planes we saw over our camp occurred around January 1945. Of course, we'd never seen B-29s before. They were high in the air, and they had vapor streaks, which we had never seen before. We were not sure whether they were Japanese or American, but we soon learned that they were ours. The nicest thing of all was to hear those B-29s come over at night and drop their load. You could hear and feel the earth vibrate and see a big glow on the horizon where they had hit their target. Those planes did wonders for our morale, but we didn't know what the Japanese would do to prisoners if the Americans invaded."

Cpl. Halbrook (Kawasaki) "Kawasaki is a suburb of Tokyo. They burned it along with Tokyo, and the wind was blowing real strong and would set fires, first in one direction, then in another. Now the civilians were really up in arms. Civilians would kill you at this stage of the game. We were afraid of the civilians so, when they bombed our camp, we got brooms and mops and fought them damn fires just as heavy as the Japanese. We saved the camp. They were dropping phosphorous, and you could put water on the damn thing and it would still burn."

T/Sgt. Stanbrough (Ohasi) "Toward the latter stages of the war, when they had the big firebomb raids, they probably killed a lot more people than any atomic bomb. We were three hundred miles north of Tokyo, and the sun was obliterated by the smoke of the firebomb raids. You could smell the pine smell of the burning of Tokyo. It smelled like a fireplace burning pine wood, and the sun became dark orange."

Capt. Weidman (Kobe) "I was in prison on the morning of St. Patrick's Day, the 17th of March, 1945. I was sleeping on the third floor. The planes were coming in. They would come to this peninsula that stuck out from Kobe and pick up land, then go to the target from that point. I peeked out of the window and saw a plane drop flares. I watched it drop some more. The other planes were coming in right behind it. They took an area about a mile square. The first plane came in and laid the outline. The next ones came in and started a complete barrier of fire with those big baskets of incendiary bombs. The guards moved us out of the building. That was funny. Heretofore, they would always, for practice, go out and set up the machine guns and then evacuate us. This night they didn't set up any machine guns. They just took the oak clubs that they carried.

"Pretty soon they had the whole city, a mile square, in a mass of flames. They evacuated us, but we were also taking out sacks of rice. After we had taken out a couple of hundred sacks of rice, they left us in the middle of the soccer playing field. The Englishmen were saying, 'Come on, you bloody Yanks! Come on some more, you bloody sons of bitches!' Well, the Yanks were coming, all right. I remember one Jap came out of a building with his wife on his shoulders. She only had one leg. Three or four horses came running onto the field with their manes on fire. It began to get along toward morning. I'll always remember what one Australian prisoner did. All the shacks were made out of three-quarter boards. The fire was so heavy that the air was full of burning particles. This Australian went over and asked the Jap guard for a light for his cigarette. The Jap walloped him over the head with his club. The rest of the Australians nearby started muttering, 'You bloody bastard.' The Japs came out with their fire trucks, and they tried to fight it, but they got burned up. Two of our guards got hit as they came out of the prison. One prisoner, who had died the day before, was burned up.

"While we were out there on the field, a sergeant in the Scots Guard named MacDougall helped some women. MacDougall and I were pretty good friends. Anyway, there were four or five Japanese women up on a balcony screaming to get down. Mac went over there, and he caught the women. The guards chased the women off. A week later the Japanese moved us to another quarters that didn't burn out. And Mac, if you can imagine, was called out to receive a citation. He received it, dropped his pants, and took the citation and wiped his ass. 'God,' I thought, 'they're going to kill him.' But they didn't. I saw Mac after the war working as a guard on a ferry that ran out of Hong Kong."

Chapter VI

The Ordeal Ends

Although one might expect liberation to be greeted with unrestrained euphoria, this was not always the case. Pvt. Willie Benton, working in a coal mine near Hakodate, Japan, recalls that not a single man cheered when they all learned the war was over: "We had been waiting and praying for it so long that when it finally came we were relieved and happy, but we really didn't show the emotions like hollering and whooping. I guess we just relaxed."

Most American prisoners at the time of liberation were in Japan. They had been transferred there during late 1944 and early 1945 to work at industrial plants, in coal mines, on docks, or elsewhere, helping the Japanese war effort. They were not happy to contribute to the enemy's cause, but they appreciated the more humane circumstances in which they found themselves. Until the end of the war they generally ate better and had better housing and clothing than they had had earlier in their imprisonment. Also, the older men guarding them in Japan were less violent, in most cases.

Even the men on the Burma-Thailand Railway found themselves in better circumstances. The majority had not been shifted to the Japanese home islands; they were scattered across Southeast Asia, the bulk being kept in Thailand. Benjamin Dunn, in a camp north of Bangkok when the war ended, contradicts Benton: after a "brief moment of extreme silence . . . unimaginable bedlam broke loose."[1] The British, Australian, and Dutch soldiers among his group brought their flags out of hiding and sang their national anthems. "But strange as it may seem," Dunn notes, "we didn't sing the national anthem; we sang 'God Bless America.' It seemed to express our feelings of victory and freedom and gratitude to our country."

If gratitude is called for—and it is—the gratitude owed is that of a thankful nation. Through no fault of their own, America's prisoners

---

[1]La Forte and Marcello, *Building the Death Railway*, 234.

of war in the Orient lost three and one half years of their lives. They endured conditions that at times were unspeakable. However, by 1950, as E. Bartlett Kerr points out, the U.S. government had given them small reward for what they experienced. Their compensation consisted of their normal pay plus $2.50 per day for every day they were deprived of adequate food rations, suffered forced labor, and received inhumane treatment.[2]

Most of the American prisoners interviewed attribute their survival to a multitude of reasons. Charles J. Katz, who in 1950 was medical director of the Governor Bacon Health Center in Delaware City, Delaware, where he worked with former POWs, believed that survival depended on a man's rank and the special circumstances that it conferred, physical vigor and toughness, luck, and the ease with which he could adapt to the brutish existence in prison camp.[3] Peter Watson provides further insight, noting that "people who persistently told themselves that they were 'a soldier, a Texan, a father' survived."[4] Dr. J. E. Nardini, a prisoner in the Philippines, points out that "where the will to live was for any reason weak, death seemed to come readily even with lesser physical ailments. On the other hand, where the will was firm even in the presence of serious physical illness, life often continued."[5]

Only a few prisoners recognized the deep personality changes caused by captivity. Most thought that their return to normal life, while requiring some effort, went quickly and was complete. Henry Krystal, who worked for the Veterans Administration and was familiar with the psychological damage done to prisoners of war, wrote in 1968 that the view that prison camp survivors were cured after one or two years was familiar to those who worked for the VA, but he believed that such an opinion was "so much wishful thinking."[6]

In *Neuropsychiatry in World War II*, U.S. Army medical specialists agree. In their view, POWs found it difficult to give up their "dependent, autistic, hostile, and aggressive reactions." Many men were physically disabled and had to be rehabilitated by spending what for them were interminable days and months in veterans' hospitals, where

[2]Kerr, *Surrender and Survival*, 296–97.
[3]Katz, "Experiences in a Prison Camp as a Background for Therapy," 91–92.
[4]Watson, *War on the Mind*, 256.
[5]Nardini, "Survival Factors," 244.
[6]Krystal, *Massive Psychic Trauma*, 195.

they violated the rules. They remained angry, drank too much, and had difficulties with their families.[7] A poignant example is given by Mrs. Seldon Reese, whose husband helped build the Death Railway: "He was a very mixed-up person. He didn't trust anybody. He was antisocial and saw the black side of everything. His children grew up afraid of him. As his wife, I can say his life was miserable."[8]

Despite these problems many prison camp survivors became productive and valuable members of society, once again entering business, the professions, or even staying in the service. Several of the interviewees became general officers in the military. Still, they never forgot the experiences that made them different. Indeed, although readjusted and indistinguishable from the rest of the population, some of these men say that a day rarely passes that they are not reminded of the time when they were Prisoners of the Sun.

Liberation

Sgt. Burk (Bilibid Prison) "I know we were liberated on the 4th of February in 1945. Of course, with all of what we had seen going on around us, the noise of guns and firing and everything, we knew there were some big changes going on. I was in Ward Eleven, and all of a sudden somebody started beating on the boards that had been nailed across the windows. Of course, everybody scattered, and I got right back against the wall near the window. In the meantime the Japs had left, and I thought they were returning. They had told us that we were no longer prisoners of war, but they were keeping us locked up for our own protection. Then they just walked out. Well, I thought they were coming back to kill us, and that's why I had backed up against the wall. I thought that if they'd stick a gun in the window, they couldn't bend it around the corner to get me. Well, then somebody out there hollered, 'Who's in there?' We yelled, 'Yanks!' Off came the bolts, and that was the way we were liberated."

Lt. Daman (Bilibid Prison) "When the Americans got close, the Japs lined up their troops and marched out the front gates, but none

---

[7]U.S. Army, Medical Department, *Neuropsychiatry in World War II*, 966–67.

[8]La Forte and Marcello, *Building the Death Railway*, 283.

of us dared go near those front gates. Well, very shortly two figures came up to these gates, and they were dressed in American uniforms. Mind you now, we had never seen the new American uniforms. They looked like two people from Mars. They raised their guns like they were going to start shooting in, and somebody screamed, 'Don't shoot! We're Americans!' They said, 'We're Americans, too!' One of them said, 'How in the hell do we get into this place?' Then somebody inside said, 'Wait a minute! We'll help you!' So he rushes in under his bunk and gets this file and goes out there and files through the chain on the gate. The Americans didn't have any bolt cutters or anything to cut the chain.

"Before the Japs left, they had piled aviation gasoline all along the east wall in fifty-five-gallon drums. They had artillery zeroed in on that wall, and the morning after they left, just at dawn, they started firing at that gas. Of course, when this thing went off, it practically blew us out of Bilibid. All that aviation gasoline going up was the most fantastic fire and bombing that you ever heard of. But nobody was killed, fortunately.

"There is just no way to describe how we felt. 'We're free! We're free at last!' The first thing they did, they rushed in and started giving us food and cigarettes. The next morning I was standing out in one of the streets talking to some of our liberators when we heard this mortar go off. I didn't pay any attention to it, and I got hit in the back of the neck with a fragment of a Jap mortar shell. I was lucky. It was shaped like the propeller of a ship, and the fact that it was nearly spent is the only reason I'm here today. It put quite a gash in the back of my neck and shoulder. It wasn't an accident. The Good Lord had His hand on my shoulder. There's no question about that."

Pvt. Wisecup (Changi) "We used to get all kinds of news. The Australians would come up with the wildest news. You could never believe them. A sergeant came up and said, 'Yanks, it's going to be over pretty quick. The Yanks have a bomb that one plane can hold, and it'll blow a whole city off the map.' We said, 'Oh, man, get out of here!' We didn't believe it. I was on a working party in the garden when I heard the rumor that a plane was going to come down from Singapore and give them the word to surrender. The plane was going to be white with a green cross on it. Sure enough, one came over. Within a week's time they rigged up loudspeakers where we could hear Truman's speech from the States. We didn't have any celebrations. They let us have more rice and soybeans—we sat up eating all night long. The Japanese never made an official announcement."

Capt. Cates (Bangkok) "We were stopped at a station along the route to Bangkok and were off-boarded. We were lined up on one side of the tracks, the Japs on the other. The commanding officer of the Jap unit told his troops that the war was over. We saw them sag and start crying. Then the interpreter told us the war was over, and we started crying and sagging. A crazier situation never existed. We got back on the train and went to Bangkok, to a warehouse. We were in this warehouse on the riverfront when this mad Jap sergeant, who took delight in sending men out on work parties when they were sick at 100 Kilo Camp, walks in one door and walks diagonally across the warehouse. It's at least one hundred feet across, and every man in that warehouse knows him. Not a man got up. I don't know what that indicates, a new beginning somehow, to think that that idiot survived that walk across the floor. It just wasn't in us to pursue the conflict anymore. It was all over, and the quicker we could get out of there, the happier we would be."

Pvt. Chambers (Nakhon Nayok) "On the 16th the Japanese put out word that they were going to let everybody have a day's rest. On the 17th, when it came time to work, there was no bugle call. About 10:00 they blew the bugle, and everybody grabbed their canteens and headed for the parade ground. The Japanese told this British sergeant what they wanted. He got up on a stand and said, 'Men, this is the happiest moment of my life, to tell you that the war . . .' He didn't get to complete what he started to say because we got to hollering, and some of the guys were crying and throwing their hats up in the air and hugging each other. It was a heck of a sight. This guy, Ben Dunn, a close friend, was standing beside me. I said, 'Well, I'll be damned!' He said, 'What's the matter with you, Slim?' I said, 'Well, I'm going to get back to East Texas just in time to start picking cotton!'"

Pvt. Armstrong (Saigon) "This captain who was the commander of the camp where we were made a little talk. He just said that the war was over. I don't think he ever said that they had surrendered. He just calmly started talking to us about it—that it was over with and there wouldn't be any more fighting. He told us to stay in the camp until the authorities had taken it over. We just carried on wherever we wanted to go. We went downtown to Saigon. There wasn't much celebration at camp because we didn't have much to celebrate with.

The next morning there was a homemade American flag flying over the top of our prison."

Fireman 1/C Kennedy (Saigon) "One day a B-29 flew over dropping leaflets. He was two thousand or three thousand feet high, and that damned antiaircraft gun cut off on him. He got away, but I remember hearing staff cars racing out to the antiaircraft operation to cut him off because they had already received the emperor's message to cease and desist. Anyway, the leaflets told us the war was over. I was real happy and just wanted to go home. The leaflets said, 'You're still in Japanese hands. Behave yourself because you'll be out soon. Don't do anything rash.' The Japanese moved us to a new camp, issued us the first issue of clothing that we'd had in years, and the food improved. All the Korean guards were moved out, and new Japanese guards moved in.

"After we had been in the new camp a few days, the Americans flew in at Tan Son Nhut Airport. They set up at a downtown hotel. I volunteered to go downtown to help them. I was given a submachine gun and put on guard duty at the radio station. The next day we were being shown around Saigon when the revolution started. We nearly didn't make it back. The fact that we could speak a little Japanese to let them know we were Americans finally enabled us to get through the lines and into the hotel. We were about ten blocks from the hotel when all the shooting started. It scared the hell out of us. We had guns stuck in our stomachs two or three times until we got through to the hotel. The OSS [predecessor of the CIA] colonel in charge got hold of a Japanese general in Saigon and told him in no uncertain terms to protect the hotel. He threw a ring of soldiers around it to protect us. The natives were firing at the hotel, and everybody stayed below window level for a while. I was thinking, 'My God! I got through this whole thing, and now I'm going to get killed!' But things settled down."

Lt. Taylor (Hoten) "General [George] Parker called us together bright and early in the morning and told us the war was over. Oh, man, it went high! The emotions went very high. You could hear the boys parading and rejoicing all about the place. We chaplains got with our camp commander, and he said, 'By all means, now let's have a big thanksgiving service.' So we had a campwide songfest and a big thanksgiving service over the victory.

"The Japanese guards protected us for four or five days until the Russians came in and formally liberated us. At that point the Japanese guards came into camp all in formation, and they went through a ceremony with the Russians and the Americans. They turned their guns over to General Parker and his American guards. Then the Japanese were marched off as prisoners, and that was the end of it. I might add that when the Russians came in they brought their interpreter, and he gave a speech to us about how glad they were to liberate us from these Japanese warmongers and pigs. The American POWs then grabbed him up on their shoulders in the American style and paraded around the grounds with him. From a formality viewpoint the Russians liberated us, but they got there after we had already learned that the war was over, but that was all right. The Russians offered to do anything in the world they could do for us."

Sgt. Brodsky (Taihoku) "While we were up in the mountains, they decided to move us because something was happening. We could tell because everybody was jumping around. The Japs were running all around. Well, they moved us down to what I think was Taihoku. It's what is now Taipei. They put us in a place of confinement, a big building that had a bamboo fence around it. This was in August. We were there just a short time. Apparently, this was after the A-bomb was dropped, because they told us that peace negotiations were being discussed and that American planes would fly over and drop food, medicine, and clothing by parachute. Well, the next day everybody was happy. We figured we were going to get food and clothing, and they did drop these parachutes and stuff in fifty-five-gallon drums. But some parachutes didn't open, and they came right through the building and killed a few people and injured a lot of people. So I was moved out with the injured people to a hospital. It wasn't a real hospital, but they took the doctor and me and a couple of other corpsmen. They were mostly British. I think there were only eight or nine Americans in the bunch.

"As a sidelight, we retrieved the stuff they dropped, and there was medicine. Among the medicines was something called penicillin, which we had never heard of. I remember it was in ampoules of dried powder, and then an ampoule of sterile distilled water. Penicillin was a tan color and was very impure compared to what we see now, a pure white material. You took the powder, and you shot the distilled water in, and you shook it, and you injected the patients with it intermuscularly. A lot of guys had ulcers from the coral, and we couldn't cure them in the prison camp. We had one guy operated on for appendicitis, and he had infection. I started shooting these guys with penicillin, and in two or three days all these damn infections started to clear up, and these guys thought I was God! It was just miraculous! I've received letters from guys in Great Britain who had been prisoners thanking me for saving their lives when it was simply penicillin. These were really just happy days. We got canned fruit, and the guys gobbled it up. I mean, we had so much food and clothing—more than we could use. And these guys started to get well.

"Then I remember this pilot walking down the corridor. He heard me talking to a British corpsman, and he stopped me and said, 'Are you an American?' I said, 'Yeah.' He said, 'Are there any other Americans?' I said, 'Yeah, we have six or seven that are sick.' He said, 'Well, can you round them up and put them in an ambulance and take them up to the airfield?' I said, 'Yeah!' He said, 'Can you get ready in a half an hour?' I said, 'I sure can!' So I got these guys dressed and loaded them on litters, those who couldn't walk, and put them in an ambulance. Well, we flew to Nielson Field in the Philippines, which was close to the place where I was stationed before the war—Nichols Field. They had a general hospital set up out near the airport there. They took me in there, and they put me in a hospital bed and examined me. I was in bed for a while. I weighed somewhere between ninety and a hundred pounds. But around the end of September 1945 they decided to ship me back to the United States."

Pvt. Burns (Moji) "There were no celebrations that took place after the announcement of the surrender. Of course, we were glad it was over, but as far as making a hullabaloo of it, no."

Cpl. Brantley (Nagasaki) "On the day they dropped the atomic bomb on Nagasaki, I counted two hundred and some bombers, and you couldn't even begin to count the fighter planes because there were so many. And right after that, one lone plane came over and dropped the atomic bomb. I saw the mushroom, and I thought they had hit a gasoline dump. I saw all this white smoke and stuff boil up, and we all laughed and said, 'Well, we really lowered the boom on them this time!' With the regular bombing and then the atomic bomb, the ground was really rattling.

"Then daylight came, and they marched us back into our barracks. They then brought in a big ration of rice and told us that it was a big Japanese holiday. The next day we didn't have to go to work. They said it was another holiday. We didn't go out the next day, either, and, boy, they really shot the rice to us. Then the next day they called us out and told us that they had reached a peace agreement with the United States and that the war was over. They also told us to stay in the compound until American troops came and got us. Well, another boy who'd been bunking with me turned and said, 'Well, Loren, we made it.' And then he immediately dropped dead—took one deep breath and died right there. Before this he hadn't been sick or anything. He just had a heart attack and died right there."

PO2 Detre (Sendryu) "The first thing that happened was the bomb dropped on Nagasaki, which was forty miles away. We knew something terrible had happened because, when we came out of the mine, the mine shaft was lined with refugees. This mine was dangerous, yet people were down in there as deep as they could get. When we came up on the surface, the hillsides were covered with people. That afternoon the major, who was the commandant, gave a big, long talk. He said that hereafter, when he blew the whistle for air raids, we must run because the latest bombs were very powerful. That was an understatement if there ever was one, but that was the way he intended it.

"The day the war ended we knew it before they told us because of the reaction of the people. They took us down to the mine where we worked for two or three hours. Then we came back up and just goofed around. When we came up, they had a big blackboard that served as a newspaper. Old Pop said, 'The war is over!' We went back and got cleaned up, and the Japanese called us together. They said they were ready to surrender to the Americans. They were not surrendering to the British, the Australians, the Dutch, or anybody: 'We either surrender to the Americans or nobody at all.' Weeks, a first-class petty officer, accepted the surrender from the major. We had a feeling of relief and gladness that the war was over, but there wasn't any hurrahing. We went back to the barracks and got some sleep.

"The first thing we did the next day was to have a meeting with the town officials, chief of police—*Kempei*—and the mine officials. We told them we wanted some meat, and they brought a cow into camp that we killed and ate. Supplies came in by B-29. They dropped thousands of those little cans of shoe polish. What they sent that for, I'll never know.

"When the Japanese quit, they quit completely, and they followed everything to the letter. We went into Sasebo about four days after the war was over, and the *Kempei* got me a man who had been an English professor during the war. He told me it was the death sentence to speak English during the war. However, three days after the war, they put English back into the public schools. That night on the way home, a formation of kids got on the train. This one ol' guy eased up to me, opened a book, and said, 'Cow?' I nodded my head. Before we got too far, all the kids were over with us reciting, 'This is a cow.' The *Kempei* was glowering over in the corner. We were the last prisoners of war out of Japan. We didn't leave until the last of September."

PFC Visage (Arao) "The camp commander called all the prisoners together in the street and announced it. It was a sad announcement, as far as he personally was concerned. Unbeknown to us, he had cleared out the Japanese guards before he made this announcement. The whole camp was ours, and we had our freedom. That was part of our shock. 'Who's to tell us what to do?' First thing you know, we started doing things soldiers normally do—they go out hunting for beer somewhere and hunting for guns. We brought barrels of beer back to camp from a brewery that was about two miles away. The airplanes immediately started dropping food to us. There was Spam and cheese in little packages. We ate and ate until we got ourselves sick.

"About the second day after the war was over, eight of us went to the railroad station because we got to wondering about a few guys we left behind in Nagasaki. When the bomb was dropped there, we heard it from up at our camp. It was about 125 to 150 miles from Nagasaki. It was a big, thundering blast. We were working that day down in an air-raid shelter when we heard it. We said, 'Good gosh, that must be something!' Anyway, we took this train away from the engineer and railroaded that thing all the way to Nagasaki. The whole city was wiped out. We were kind of in a state of shock. The whole city was just flattened. The machine shops on the outskirts were melted down like candles. The thing that caught our attention more than anything was that there was no noise, no birds, no nothing. It was a ghost city, and we were leery about it. One of the guys, Paul Stein, just happened to kick the curb for some reason, and it just powdered. There was a terrific smell. When we got to the camp, the prisoners wouldn't let us in. We wanted to see about these two or three Americans, but the Dutch wouldn't let us in because of the contamination.

"We returned to the train and ran into a bunch of Japanese civilian officials going back to Arao. We started to drink some water on the train, but the Japanese warned us against it: 'Don't. It's contaminated.' They gave us hot tea. When we got back to the camp, five days after the end of the war, there was a contingent of American forces there. They found out that eight of us guys had been through Nagasaki, and they immediately quarantined us. They put us in one of the rooms and kept us for twelve hours. Boy, that was the longest twelve hours I ever spent! I've read many articles about people claiming they were the first Americans through Nagasaki after the bomb. We were the first ones in there, and we were there because we didn't know what it was."

PFC Evans (Orio) "We found out about peace about 2:00 in the afternoon. We kept waiting for the evening crew to come on and relieve us at the mine. A Japanese soldier at the coal mine office had this letter. He would read this letter, look at us, and read the letter again. When it came time to go back to camp, we were all marched back just like nothing had happened. When we got back to camp, we were told that the war was over. The only words the Japanese said to us were that the war was finished. They were downcast and didn't know what to anticipate.

"The next morning, the only Japanese anywhere around was the camp commandant, a captain, I believe. He was a pretty decent kind of man. He wasn't harsh and ran a pretty good camp. I wanted to do all the natural human things that anybody else wanted to do—get drunk, get a woman, whatever. The main thing I wanted was to get home. I felt remorse that the war was over and I hadn't contributed any more to it than I had. I guess I had some satisfaction in knowing that in order to keep us there, they had to keep a certain number of people occupied.

"The B-29s started dropping food to us. The first run that they made on the camp was actually a bombing of our camp with these fifty-five-gallon drums. The drums were so heavy that they would strip loose from the parachutes. On the first run our camp commandant's samurai sword got broken. There was a Japanese house that got hit by a fifty-five-gallon drum of Melba peaches. We went down there and found a woman, all her insides and brains and guts mixed in with those Melba peaches. I couldn't eat a Melba peach for years after that. Sometimes they'd drop two or three times a day. In the drums they had leaflets that said, 'Do not overeat or overmedicate.' The parachutes were different colors—red, white, and blue. We had a tailor, Marvin Snulling, make us a flag, an American flag. It wasn't over three feet by two and a half, with forty-eight stars and thirteen stripes. The next morning we hoisted it above camp.

"The Japanese were raiding our drop zone, so we formed an MP [military police] detachment of ten Australians, ten Dutchmen, ten Englishmen, and ten Americans. We told the guy at the mine that we wanted all those *hanchos* out at camp. We were going to have a kangaroo court and gather information from them. The next morning, they were all there. We got all their names and listed all the damn mean things they had done. We gave them a honey bucket and made them dip it in the latrine and then go fix our garden. We turned them loose after that. The next day we went downtown. I disarmed a whole trainload of soldiers—made them pile their rifles, bayonets, swords, and pistols separately. I then put them back on the train and sent them whichever way they were going. I got a horse, and I rode it around carrying a saber. I was pretty well the cock of the walk there.

"We went down to Nagasaki and saw all the devastation down there. That's probably the most frightening thing that I can recall. We knew some of the general landmarks of Nagasaki at the time we left there. To go back and see nothing—literally nothing—left except one big old building. They had a big coal-gas plant that had big twenty-four-inch I-beams to hold up some of the superstructure. They were melted down just like a candle and just draped over. Streetcar and railroad tracks were twisted out of the ground. I remember seeing a streetcar that was turned over on its side, and it was literally burned and melted down like it was made out of wax. Another guy showed me the shadow of a person on the side of a building. A person had been walking along there—now just the shadow. We were not molested in any way. We were not spoken to. They had had crews working on the streets since the 9th, and this was about the 20th. It seems to me that it was a terrible, tragic thing for a man ever to have to see something like that happen."

Cpl. Halbrook (Kawasaki) "Our Japanese commanding officer didn't show up for roll call. We went to the guardhouse and started asking the Japs about it, but they wouldn't say anything. We went over to the galley, and guys reached over to get some rice, and the Japs didn't do anything about it. Then all hell broke loose. The whole goddamn camp started breaking into warehouses. We didn't know that they surrendered, but we knew something was wrong, so we took advantage of it. That evening the Japanese commanding officer called our senior officer, an American Navy commander, and told him that we'd be going home. They didn't say they had surrendered; they said they were going to end the war. He came back and told us, 'Shit, men, the war is over!' "

T/Sgt. Stanbrough (Ohasi) "When I heard the war was over, I wasn't shocked. I was listening, really hanging in there on our radio in the middle of the night. I crawled down my ladder and went over by the foot of [Captain] Zeigler and Captain Epley, I believe. I told them in a hushed tone, 'It's all over.' They elected that we keep quiet until the Japanese heard about it, because you couldn't afford to turn the whole camp loose. That was a hard secret to keep.

"The townspeople were told that the emperor would address the people on the radio. They were not going to let any prisoners hear the emperor because it would be sacrilege for us to hear the 'god's' voice. That day we marched to work and were moved into the tunnel where the ore cars went. After that we came out, and there were girls sitting around crying. The men were sitting and just looking strange and staring. Our guard hadn't heard the news, and when they told him, his face fell, too. That was the last day we worked. The guards disappeared, all but the good ones. Later, a group came down to the village and made Zeigler the mayor. They also gave him a Buick that belonged to the previous mayor."

Cpl. Burlage (Hosakura) "One day the camp commandant and interpreter disappeared, but for a reason. They were called to Yokohama for a conference with the Americans. A couple of days later the commandant came back and told the British Army captain, the senior man, that he wanted us to fall out. So we lined up, and he said, 'I have been to Yokohama. I have instructions from your friends. The war is over. We are going to feed you, make you fat, make you healthy. You can go home to your wife, your friends, sisters, and mothers'—all that old jazz. But that was it. He turned around and handed his sword to the captain and took off. All the guards had disappeared."

Pvt. Blaylock (Omine) "This coal mine was in the same province as Hiroshima. Well, the same day, the very time, that they dropped the atomic bomb, we were in formation on the parade ground fixing to go to work. As we were standing there, we heard this rumble and rumble and rumble. Oh, it just kept rumbling and rumbling, and we thought that it would never end! It was like thunder, and we were looking around and looking at each other and trying to figure out what was happening because we hadn't heard any planes.

"A short while later, before we broke formation or before we left camp, this one B-29 flew over our camp. I don't know if this was the one that dropped the bomb or the one that was following up to take pictures. Then a few days later, a Jap told us that the Americans had dropped one bomb and that people were still dying. Incidentally, that day we heard all the rumbles, we didn't see the sun the rest of the day because the wind was coming our way, and there was smoke and haze for, oh, maybe several days.

"Several days later, early in the morning before daylight, I heard the guards holler 'attention!' Well, they only did that when the camp commander was coming through, and I wondered why he was coming into camp this early. Then everybody began getting up, and we were wondering why they hadn't awakened us to go to work. Pretty soon, word got around that the war was over, and then later that morning the Jap camp commander called the American and British officers together and told them the war was over. Then they made the official announcement to us.

"We couldn't leave. The Japs still had the guns, and we got a radio by this time, and the fleet was telling us to stay where we were. Then the Americans dropped us clothes and food and medicine by parachute. They even dropped us notes and things.

"Finally, we got orders to move, and the Japs had this special train for us. We boarded this train, and we went to a port where we met the American Navy. They disinfected us and saw if there were any emergency cases or anything. We stayed here a full month after the war was over waiting for orders. They kept us supplied with food and cigarettes and medicine and things. We were told that the reason we had to wait so long was because the POW camps were scattered all over the islands, so that was the best they could do."

Cpl. Bunch (Miyazu) "We were told by our Japanese commandant that if the Americans landed on Honshu, we would be executed. I don't know if he knew what he was talking about or not, but we were told that. Fortunately, the war ended before the American forces landed on Honshu, and when they dropped the atomic bomb, attitudes among our guards changed tremendously.

"I think that within a week the emperor made a speech one day at noon over the radio, and I know we knocked off early because the Japanese there wanted to hear the speech. We had fellows who could understand Japanese, and they overheard the emperor's speech at a distance. It was obvious that he was telling the Japanese people that the war was coming to an end. I don't know what he told them exactly—whether they were whipped or whether they were going to try to make peace or what—but when we got the word, it was that they were going to make peace with the United States, that they had not surrendered but that they would make peace. After the emperor made his speech, we never went back to work again. The next day they didn't take us to work. We stayed in the barracks, and they didn't say anything. Finally, they called us out about 10:00 and said that we would not be working any longer. Of course, they were real nice, and we went back to our barracks and loafed around. The next day it was the same thing. Our guys would sit around and play cards, and the guards would stand around and watch."

Cpl. Koury (Honshu) "It was kind of an anticlimax, really. I think everybody believed it was a foregone conclusion that it was just a matter of days. The Jap commander called on our commander and told him that the war was over, but he said that for our own protection we should stay in our compound, and we did. We stayed there for about two weeks after the war was over because we were so far north. We were waiting for our orders on what to do.

"In the meantime, we put 'POW' signs on top of everything, and then B-29s came over and dropped more food than we could ever eat. I think this is something that is indicative of the American character because when we left there, the extra food was left for the Japanese. Rather than destroying it, we left it for the guys who had been guarding us because they had been kind of short on rations, too. I think this is indicative of how forgiving the American is. I think that all those guys who were so bent on revenge were so damn glad the war was over and so damn glad to be alive and to be going home that they immediately forgot those thoughts. I know I did. I couldn't have done any of them any harm. Then, too, we were treated better in Japan than we were anywhere else."

Pvt. Stanley (Hanawa) "We knew that the atomic bomb had been dropped, because we had heard the Japanese talk and we could understand their language a little bit by this time. As we lined up one morning to go to work, they told us to go back and rest. Well, buddy, this was very unusual because the only days they didn't work us was on Jap holidays. So they didn't fool with us all that day, and the next day the same thing happened. Man, we was beginning to really feel big. On the third day they lined us up out there and then told us to sit down for a while. Then I guess it was about 10:00 in the morning when the Japanese officer in charge and another guy, a high-ranking American, called us together. The Jap got on a little stand and told us that the war was over, that we were now friends and that we were going back to our homes. He never said that Japan had been defeated. He said they had made peace terms and that we would be going back to our homes. So, boy, we felt like a million dollars! Then we all cried and raised the American flag. There wasn't a man there that didn't cry. Some guy had made the flag and had kept it hidden until this time."

Cpl. B. Allen (Honshu Camp No. 7) "When the Americans dropped the atomic bomb on Hiroshima, the next day the Japanese told us about an awful bomb that had killed things for five miles around. Then they began to act differently, really differently. They were friendly to us for the first time—very friendly, overly so—and tried to help us. Finally, in a few days, after the second atomic bomb had been dropped, they told us we didn't have to go to work. They were going to let us have the day off; we needed some rest. This seemed very funny to us, but we enjoyed it, and we sat around and speculated: 'Why are they being so good to us? I wonder if the war is over.' But they didn't say anything. Another day went by. 'We're going to let you have another day off.' We really began to think it was over then.

"The third day we got up, and there were no guards outside. We were the only ones there. Well, we figured it was over, which it was, but we didn't dare leave camp right yet. Where were they? Where were the guards? We couldn't find them, so we gradually began to walk out of camp and walk to little stores. We walked in, and the proprietors would just back away from us and bow and tell us to help ourselves to whatever we wanted. Then we knew the war was over. In our minds we were sure. Well, that same day a B-29 came over at a very low altitude and dropped out leaflets that Japan had surrendered unconditionally: 'Mark your camps and we'll drop supplies to you.'

"I guess to me it was one of the most touching things that ever happened to me in my life. We got rags, red ones and white ones and blue ones, and sewed a flag together. One guy still had his old bugle with him, and after we made our flag and took down the Japanese flag, he was blowing the bugle when we put up our flag. We were all standing there crying. That's the way it ended. It was the greatest feeling that one could ever have. I would imagine that the winners of the Super Bowl felt nothing compared to what we felt on that day when we put up the flag and the bugler was standing there blowing his bugle. We were all standing there and crying like babies. It still chokes me up to think of that one thing."

Pvt. Guiles (Ashio) "Liberation is the period I like to talk about best! We were on our way to work early in the morning, about 8:00, when this plane flew over and dropped literally millions of these leaflets that told us to go back to camp and stay there. Up until this time, we had no news or hint whatsoever from the Japs that the war was over. Of course, we knew the Americans were coming closer by the day, but we still didn't really know how far things had progressed. Well, we went back to camp, and shortly thereafter a Navy pilot flew in in a fighter—there wasn't a landing strip there— and landed on a sandy piece of the beach. He advised us that the war had ended and for us just to hold tight.

"Well, that night I'll never forget. It was a full moon that night. I sat on the ground with my back propped against the barracks, and I cried like a baby. I could no more stop than get up and fly. I just couldn't control it!"

Pvt. Bugbee (Ashio) "One day the Jap camp commandant called all the guards into his office. When they came out, they were all standing around with their heads bowed and were crying. Then shortly thereafter our interpreter came over and said that we had done such a good job that the emperor was going to give us all a holiday. Well, we knew this was a bunch of malarkey because they didn't know what a holiday was. Then all kinds of speculation took place at that time as to what was really going on. The Japs never did actually come out and tell us that the war was over.

"Then, a few days after that, our commanding officer came over and told us that the war was over. He reminded us that we were still POWs and that if we got out of line in any way the Japs had a perfect right to punish us in any way they saw fit. He said it would be rather dumb, after all that we had been through, to think about starting foolishness, that we were to be patient and that we would soon be liberated by our own troops.

"A couple of days later some Navy carrier planes flew over, and the pilots dropped seabags containing their own personal gear along with various little goodies that we hadn't seen in a long time. Then in a short while the B-29s made some passes, and when their bomb bays opened, out came these multicolored parachutes attached to rafts containing drums filled with food and clothing.

"At first we had made up our minds that we weren't going to give the Japs anything. We really didn't have any scores to settle with the guards, though, at least not any more than I had with that damn Marine drill instructor I had in boot camp. I thought I'd like to tear that drill instructor apart, but after I had gotten out of boot camp, it was all forgotten."

Capt. Bull (Roku Rushi) "Our Japanese commandant left the camp about August 18, a couple of days after the surrender. Then I remember him coming back into camp with his head hung very low. He came up to our officers and said that a peace treaty was about to be signed. He didn't say there had been a surrender, but rather a termination of hostilities. Our immediate reaction was to hold a thanksgiving service, thanking God that the war was over. That night we kind of had a pep rally like we have at football games in the United States. We had a serpentine and built a big bonfire. I think it frightened the civilians who lived about a half mile away. I believe they thought we were going to come out and burn down their town, but we had no intention of doing that.

"The Japanese guards disappeared. They just left camp and opened their warehouse to us, and in the warehouse we found a lot of warm clothing that we immediately appropriated. We really needed it because it got cold at night at that altitude—we were very high in the mountains—even though it was in August. Then we were instructed to remain there until a rescue party came to us. So during those ten or fifteen days, we would go on hikes to nearby towns only to find them abandoned. We surmised that the civilians were afraid that we would rape all the women and destroy the towns, so they just evacuated to somewhere, and we didn't see a soul. But we were pretty harmless at that point and came back without incident.

"About two days later, this rescue party of about two doctors, two nurses, a couple of signal corpsmen, and photographers came to us and examined us and weighed us. Then the next day we went by truck to Fukui and then got on a train to Yokohama. From there we went back to the Philippines, where they fattened us up and gave us uniforms, and then they took us by ship back to San Francisco."

Capt. Adair (Roku Rushi) "On August 22 they told us the war was over, and shortly thereafter we went down to the village to look around. We didn't bother anybody, and the Japanese were as nice as they could be down there. They'd lost the war, and, naturally, they were bowing and scraping and smiling. We had an interpreter with us, and we asked him if he could get us some *sake* [Japanese liquor of fermented rice]. Well, this clown brought back enough *sake* to fill a washtub. We got the whole camp drunk. You've never seen such a wild bunch of people in your life. That night we built a bonfire, and we used these log poles that made up the fence around the camp; it went up about fifty feet in the air. We continued to drink, and then we decided to do an Indian war dance. Some Englishman had an accordion, and another one had a trumpet, and I got a five-gallon can and made a drum out of it; and we had a band, and everybody was dancing. You never saw such a wild bunch, just like a bunch of kids. One guy started doing a striptease, and you never saw anything funnier in your life. He was funny-looking, anyhow, with his potbelly and skinny body. All night long this went on, just snake dancing through the barracks and just drunk out of our minds. It's a wonder we all didn't get killed.

"In our camp, at least, nobody thought of taking revenge on anybody. The Jap military had left our camp except for this one sergeant who had been pretty mean. He'd slapped some people around, and I'm surprised that somebody didn't slug him, to tell you the truth. But everybody was so happy to get out of there that they felt they could turn in a report and get him later, which they probably did."

PFC Venable (Hakodate) "The Japanese colonel—I can't recall his name—said that America had dropped a cruel and inhumane bomb and had threatened to annihilate the Japanese race if they did not surrender. The emperor said that they should surrender and so forth, so Major Devereux took over the camp. The Americans flew in food, and we gathered it up. Then the next morning, Major Devereux fell us out and announced to us for all concerned that we were back in the Marine Corps again, and so we fell out for close-order drill to get back in shape: 'You've been away from it too long, but you're a Marine, and don't you forget it,' that sort of thing. Of course, we were anxiously waiting to get to the States, and I can assure you that we didn't take kindly to Devereux's maneuver at that point. We talked about how quickly we were going to get out of the Marine Corps, you know. You were going to get back in civilian life and do all of these things. It was a great emotional feeling that came over us."

Cpl. Crews (Hakodate) "They told us one morning: 'Today, you do not work in the mines.' They didn't say why. They made a big speech. We had a pretty good idea something was afoot, because they just didn't tell you that you don't work because they had us work regardless. Some of the boys had learned to read Japanese, I don't remember who, but they got hold of a Japanese paper somehow, and they read that we had dropped a bomb that wasn't ordinary. They came out in the paper and told you that it wasn't an ordinary bomb. Anyway, after our boys read that, they decided to give it a try. This guy ran and climbed up the stockade fence—the Jap guards were still on duty, still there—and he climbed over, jumped out, and ran into the hills, and all the Jap guards said was, 'Come back, come back!' They didn't shoot him. So we knew then that this wasn't some sort of publicity gag; we knew it was true that the war was over. So the Japs called us together and told us they were having to surrender, that America had been cruel and inhuman and they had been forced to surrender. They said they were going to turn the camp over to us, which they did. The guards had disappeared, so we just took over and formed our own guard, and we kept the Japanese camp commander there."

M/Sgt. Stowers (Hakodate) "A sergeant major senior to me, named Dietz, said the signs showed that the war was over. So he says, 'Each one of you go back and tell everybody to get any weapon he has.' The Japs told us, you know, if they lost the war they would kill us all and commit hara-kiri. They were so fanatic we weren't sure it wasn't true. We halfway believed them. At any rate, this arsenal of knives and clubs and everything suddenly appeared. I didn't know they had these things. I didn't want to know. Of course, I had a couple of items myself. Well, we went down to the fence and told the guard to come to the fence. He came and Sergeant Major Dietz said, 'Lieutenant, the Americans won the war, and we want the surrender of this garrison. I'll take your sword, and we'll treat you as honorable prisoners of war.' The lieutenant stood there a long time and looked at Dietz, and finally he just unbuckled his belt and handed his sword to Dietz and then wheeled and saluted and walked off. An hour later the lieutenant marched all the guards off."

Pvt. Permenter (Hakodate) "After the surrender they dropped clothes, cigarettes, food, candy bars—you name it— to us. The Army Air Force did, I guess. Oh, did we get sick! Food was going in one end and coming out the other. You'd poke it in one end, and it'd come out the other. It was the grease. We hadn't had grease, and the way they fixed the food was to make goulash out of it. The kitchen stayed open twenty-four hours. We just had a big ol' three-gallon bucket to bring it in. If it'd get cold, somebody would go back, pour it in the pot, and get some hot and bring it over. We ate around the clock."

Survival

Cpl. B. Allen "Of course, there was some luck involved. Then, too, there was my background, what my parents had instilled in me. I think my parents did a good job mentally preparing me. Finally, there was just a strong desire, a very strong desire, to get home and see those same parents."

Capt. Bartlett "Damn stubbornness! The will to live! Also, what helped me is that I'm a fatalist."

Pvt. Benton "I think faith more than anything else is why I survived—faith in the Good Lord, faith in our country, and faith in myself. I never lost confidence in my country. I never lost confidence in myself. I never lost confidence in my buddies who were with me. I guess that's about the extent of it."

Cpl. Brantley "My opinion is that many of those who died had given up, and the ones who gave up were the ones who had lived a pretty easy life before they went in the service. I was raised in East Texas on a farm, and I knew how to hunt and fish and knew a little bit about the land. Of course, my constant thought there was to figure out a way to survive, and I knew that you had to eat to keep up your strength. Everything I could turn into food in one way or another, that's what I did. And those people who didn't know nothing about such things and who didn't know how to take care of themselves, actually their will to live was less than mine."

Pvt. Bugbee "I'm not what you would call a religious man, but I do believe that the Man Upstairs has our numbers, and regardless of what we do, when our time is up it's going to be that way. We can do things to make our existence a little bit more comfortable on earth, but my feelings are that you can't extend your life any. So with the help of the Lord, I made up my mind that I was going to do anything I could to get back. I thought that I had capitulated once, and I was going to do everything in my power not to capitulate again. I was going to come back come hell or high water, any way I could. I was criticized one time by our lieutenant for digging in garbage cans. I told him, 'I'm sorry. I may be a Marine, and I may be disgracing the

Marines as far as you are concerned, but I made up my mind, with the will of the Lord, that I'm coming back any way I can. I'm hungry and I'm going to find something to eat.' And that's why I survived."

Cpl. Bunch "To begin with, I'd say it was the good fortune to have a couple of good friends who had medicine for me when I had dysentery. Secondly, when I got malaria, I had the good fortune of being sent to Japan and getting two good ten-day doses of quinine, which took care of my malaria problem. And thirdly, I would say that eating my rations and not trading them off helped a lot. We had some fellows over there who just couldn't control themselves. For instance, I've seen guys who would trade the weaker-willed fellows a half bowl of rice today for the guy's full bowl tomorrow. Well, that could go on indefinitely, and tomorrow he's going to trade for another half, and the first thing you know he's on permanent half rations. So we had some guys who literally almost starved doing this."

Cpl. Burlage "I pulled through the ordeal because I was healthy as far as physical fitness; I had a good body, as did a lot of us. A lot of us came from where I did. I came from the farm, and a lot of prisoners were sharecroppers' sons. They didn't have the best; they didn't have the best food in the world. They had, like this colored friend of mine says, soul food—pork and black-eyed peas or something. But the body was strong, and the mind was healthy. I had a good outlook, and a lot of luck. That was it, I think."

Capt. Cates "A sense of humor, I think, is perhaps essential to survival. I think the feeling that there's something that you ought to be a part of again is necessary. Faith is vital. Something carries you that is not literally life itself."

Pvt. Chambers "I didn't get so scared of getting sick like a lot of guys that had never been sick in their lives. When I came back, my granddaddy asked me, 'How was it?' I told him, 'Poppa, other than not seeing your folks, it was just about like East Texas. They worked the hell out of you and starved you to death.' He thought that was a pretty good explanation. I think the kind of raising up I had really helped me. I had done twenty-one years of training before I got caught."

Cpl. Clem "I think a lot of it was luck. I was fortunate enough to be in a particular place when something happened. It might have been that if I had come back to the States instead of staying in the Philippines, I could have gone to Guadalcanal. If I hadn't gone from one prison camp to another, something could have happened back at this one. I was fortunate because during the two years I had spent in China I had been eating Chinese food, and my system was accustomed to raw vegetables. Also I had been drinking the water for a long time. But these boys who had come out of the States with the New Mexico National Guard didn't have a chance."

Cpl. Crews "Here's something that will surprise you, I think, and anyone else. The civilian people from Wake Island, most of them were older people, and believe it or not the older people survived and remained in better condition than the young two-hundred-pounders, the young Marines. And I think the reason for that is that everyone got a certain ration, and it didn't take as much for these older men to survive as it did for the younger ones. I mean, it was real surprising to me that the older ones made out a lot better than the young, stronger types.

"Time wasn't of any importance to us. We lived from day to day, but if you didn't have a glimmer of hope that someday with the help of the Lord you'd get out of there, you never would have made it. I think we made it through our prayers and our hopes. You had hopes, or you wouldn't have made it."

PFC Fields "What brought me back home? I really can't pinpoint it to one thing. I know one thing was willpower. I wanted to come home. And another thing, I think, was love. I was in love with a girl who was real nice, and I wanted to see her, and if I was going to pinpoint anything, I'd put it on her because I just wanted to get back."

PFC Garrison "I made it, but I don't see how it could be any rougher. I'd been beaten until I bled, until I had no control over my bowels, till I was unconscious. They'd stand you up and get a flat board, and they'd start slapping you on the cheeks with this flat board. And I promise you, when they got through, your head was three times as big as normal. You can't imagine what the pain was like. *Fire!* They'd do it to you until you're unconscious, but I'm here. When the planes started coming, I'll be damned if those people were going to kill me. I wasn't going to die. They would have had to kill me, and they weren't going to do it! That's the way I felt about it. I made up my mind I was coming back. I like this country. It is the greatest country there's ever been—the United States. There's nothing like it in the world."

Pvt. Guiles "My faith in the Good Lord is primarily responsible. I think I probably had a few more things to live for than some of them did. I had a real fine mother and father to come back to."

Cpl. Halbrook "It was the will to live and nothing more. People didn't die because they were that sick. They gave up—they just gave up and quit. I was as sick as most other people, but I didn't want to die, and I lived."

Fireman 1/C Kennedy "The fact that I was used to hard work and was fairly healthy, the fact that I was small, the fact that I did what I was told and kept a low profile were keys to my survival. That, and a lot of luck. I didn't get sent to Japan and get sunk on a ship. The scalding I got didn't turn into ulcers. Even getting off the *Houston* was luck. When you're exposed to a lot of danger, luck becomes more and more a factor."

Cpl. Koury "I survived because I knew, without any doubt, how the war was going to end. There never was any doubt. I think that if you ever doubted for one minute that America was going to win, you would have died. I don't think anybody who survived ever doubted America would win; I don't think the Japanese ever doubted it. Then, second, was the constant hope that it was going to be over next week, that liberation was just around the corner. I think all the survivors felt this way."

Pvt. Permenter "Hope is why I survived. Knowing that there was a better life than what I had there because I knew once I got out of there, there was a better place back here in America. Now if I'd had no hope, if I had had what the Japanese had to look forward to, I don't think I'd have survived. That's the one thing—hope. I knew we were going to win the war in the end. There wasn't ever any doubt in my mind. You had to have hope to keep alive—that's what kept a majority of us alive. Two or three of the guys gave up in camp and died. That's a pitiful sight to see. All you had to do was to beat the game there and live through it, and you had it made. And the majority of us beat it."

Cpl. Read "If I had to single out one thing, I would say it would have to be adaptability—ability to change with the environment. In my term as a prisoner, I've seen hundreds of guys—many of whom were personal friends of mine—sit down and die for no good reason because they could not adapt to circumstances. There were a lot of people who died from simply feeling sorry for themselves and from homesickness. It was awfully easy to feel sorry for yourself, and I've seen people die from it. And you can do it! Maybe I ought to clarify a little bit what I said. I was an orphan, along with my two brothers, so I had a pretty rough time growing up as a kid. It was pretty tough out around the creeks and woods and so on, and I had always shifted for myself as a kid, while those who gave up almost invariably were people who were raised in sheltered ways and had never really faced any kind of tough situation before in their life."

PFC Robinson "I think that you have got to have the will to live. There's no ifs, ands, or buts. You have got to have that will or you won't make it. I saw Englishmen lay down and die with sores on their backs just because they were too lazy to get up and take the opportunities—the few opportunities we had—to have a bath and to keep the camp clean. The key to my survival, however, is the fact that I have an Old Man right up yonder. The Good Lord was looking after me."

PFC Sparkman "I have a hard head, and I was just determined not to let it get me down. If you got through one day, okay, but don't worry about the next. Keep going. Don't feel sorry for yourself. A lot of guys got to feeling sorry for themselves in the prison camp, and they were dead."

T/Sgt. Stanbrough "We had our shots when we got into the service, we had our shots when we were to go to the Philippines, we had our shots by our doctor when the Japs landed, and damned if we didn't have shots again! That is why the Americans survived more than the others. The food was part of it, but the other was that we had cholera shots up until the time we got into camp."

Pvt. Stanley "In my survival one of the key points, I think, is the way I was born and raised. I was born and raised in the country, and my dad died the year I was born, and I worked from the time I was a little boy right on up until I was grown. Obviously, being a prisoner was a big change for me, but it wasn't as big a change as it was for some guy who was raised in a home with a gold spoon in his mouth all his life. In fact, a good portion of the fellows who got back were small-town boys, country boys. The big-city boys, a lot of them who was drafted, came from well-to-do families, and their percentage of survival wasn't as good as ours."

M/Sgt. Stowers "The death rate for young people was extremely high. You'd tell a young eighteen-year-old boy that, when you see a Chinaman drinking cold water and splashing it on his face in the canals, 'Don't you do it! He's immune to it. You'll get cholera, dysentery.' You'd tell him that, and suddenly he'd break ranks and go out there and start drinking it. Three or four days later you'd bury him. That was the cruelest part. We old-timers were disciplined, and I think the old-timers went through it better than the lesser-trained younger men did."

Lt. Taylor "I think it boils down to maturity and experience. We had youngsters of seventeen and even younger in some cases. Seventeen to twenty are actually pretty formative age brackets in a person's life, and I think the sheer shock of becoming a prisoner of war and suddenly not having the necessities of life that they have been accustomed to at home or in the barracks takes a severe toll on these kids. Then, too, of course, there was the separation of them from their families completely, their parents. And most of these young men were single. I think, as I analyze it, it was our maturity over their youth. Timewise, agewise, they were just not old enough. They just hadn't gone through any hard knocks, so to speak. That's the only way I can answer it. They were just too young—just too young.

"Take my own case. I grew up on a farm. From the time I was seven years of age, I was plowing furrows. I was kind of seasoned to an outdoor type of rugged life. This meant a lot to me over there. I never had malaria over there, even though the same mosquitoes that bit the other men also bit me. I asked the doctor about it, and he asked if I had ever had malaria. I answered that I did—every summer, with chills and fever. My father and mother broke it up on me with quinine and chill tonic or something. The doctor said that I had obviously built up an immunity against malaria. You see what I mean? This is where experience comes in."

PFC Venable "First, I think that my Marine Corps training had disciplined me to accept life. I think the fact that I had good physical stamina when I went into prison camp. I think the fact that I never lost confidence that I would make it through—I was always confident about the future. I think that I had a good religious background, which stood me in good stead in a lot of dark moments. I just knew that I was going to make it back. This really brought me through."

PFC Visage "I believe the key to my survival was mainly staying busy and doing something all the time in these camps—just continually having your mind occupied with something. Determination is a big thing. I was determined that I was going to come home. Also, a key to my survival was getting food at the right time and withstanding the beatings. Maybe a little trickery was involved. Chance was as important as anything."

Capt. Weidman "I survived because I didn't give up. Twenty-five percent died because they didn't want to live. They didn't have the guts."

Readjustment

PFC R. Allen "To be honest with you, I never thought about getting even. About all I could think of was getting back home to my loved ones and going out and eating all I could eat. I had made up my mind that when I came back to the United States, there wasn't going to be a soul on earth tell me what I had to do again for the rest of my life and I would never go hungry."

Pvt. Armstrong "After a few stops, we landed in Washington and went to Walter Reed Hospital. They gave us a lot of treatments there, put us to bed, and checked us out real good. We had to talk to a psychiatrist. I'm sure everybody did. I guess he decided that most of us were all right. He didn't lock us up.

"I know it sounds funny to us after we got out, but I missed the boys. I missed being with them. I was glad to be with my family in Jacksboro, Texas, but I would meet some of the boys from the Second Battalion downtown on the courthouse lawn. It had benches, and we would have a bull session right there on the lawn. I finally got a job on a drilling rig, but I still missed being around that bunch of boys."

Pvt. Benton "When I first got home, I was restless. I drank a lot, which I don't do anymore. Of course, I wasn't married. I drank quite a bit for a couple of years after I got home, but I saw that was no good. That wasn't going to solve anything, so I got off that stuff. I didn't want to get hooked. I guess you could say I had problems. My wife has been quite a help to me. I've known my wife all my life. We married after I came home. When we were first married, we'd argue. I was high-tempered. I had a chip on my shoulder; I didn't want anybody telling me what to do. I'd been taking orders so long unwillingly that I just didn't want nobody giving me orders. Well, I've overcome that. We go for months and months and never have a cross word. I'm still awfully nervous. You notice tonight that I'm pretty nervous. I'm not this way all the time. What makes me nervous is that you are a stranger. It doesn't make me nervous talking about being a prisoner of war, it's the stranger. I can't help it. Strangers make me nervous. It's hard for me to talk to strangers."

PFC Bolitho "I came back to Letterman General Hospital and then to Walter Reed in Washington in September of 1944, and I didn't get out of the service until September of 1945. I was in and out of the hospital, all that time. I was discharged on Friday and started back to college at Montana School of Mines on Monday. I think if I had not gone back to school, I may have had an awful time of adjusting. I think having to get my nose back to the grindstone took away a lot of worries and depressive attitudes that I might have had."

Sgt. Brodsky "I've been married for forty-two years now to the same wife. I honestly believe that most of these prisoners who are pretty well adjusted are those who have found wives that have stayed with them. I mean, they've had a lot to contend with—nightmares and other problems. We have a lot of men who need a lot of help, and I just hope that they get it. Those wives are gems! They really are. Tears come to my eyes when I think of it.

"I started to work for the Food and Drug Administration on January 2, 1951. Then around 1964 they started sending some of the doctors from Washington abroad to inspect some antibiotic plants because the United States Government was making inspections of plants that were sending drugs through the Agency for International Development. AID wouldn't approve drugs unless they were passed for safety and effectiveness by the FDA. They started using some of the more experienced drug inspectors. I was teamed up with a Dr. DeLorenzo, who was one of the heads of the antibiotic division in Washington. We made trips around the world, including the Philippines. While I was in the Philippines, I was inspecting a Parke-Davis plant, and they took me out to the cemetery where they buried a lot of these guys who were killed in the Philippines. And there I saw this big, beautiful memorial with the names of all the military that were killed in the Philippines. There I saw Bancroft's name—my buddy—and then I went through the cemetery. They had a very well-kept cemetery with crosses and Stars of David lined up. It was well taken care of. Gee, it just made me feel so good to see my friend's name there! It just so happened that later, in 1975, they disinterred these bodies and brought them back to the United States and buried them during memorial services at Jefferson Barracks in St. Louis. I attended that ceremony. Well, I have a son, Richard B.—Richard Bancroft Brodsky. He was named after my friend that died at Palawan. I have a son who was named after my friend Bancroft."

Cpl. Burlage "I don't think I had good sense for a long time after I got home. You're kind of in a daze, I might say; you're kind of in a fog. You just can't see things clearly. It takes time to get perspective again."

Cpl. Crews "I guess that if I had any adjustments to make, and I'm sure I did, I wasn't really too aware of them. I know I had a little trouble in movies—I was real anxious to get out and not stay inside a place for any length of time. I know when I went to work for the Police Department, one time I heard that I might have to do a little time up in the jail. I went to the captain and told him that I didn't have anything against jails, but I couldn't work in one, and I told him why I didn't want any part of it. If I was going to have to be even a guard in the jail, well, I'd just quit. So he didn't make me go to work in the jail."

PFC Evans "When I got back, I got my discharge, but this general, General [Jonathan] Wainwright, was in San Antonio where we got our discharge. He wanted us to reenlist, stay in the Army. I told him that I done had all of this damn Army that I wanted."

Cpl. Halbrook "After I got back, I had a heart murmur that was causing some trouble. I had amoebic dysentery, and I had malaria. They put me in the hospital in Corpus Christi, Texas. I was down there for seven months. At the end of the seven months, I wanted a decision made to either get out or stay in the service. They eventually kicked me out on a medical discharge. I was discharged in 1946 on 100 percent disability. I couldn't get a job because I needed a physical every time. I made a deal with the government: If they wouldn't bother me, I wouldn't bother them, and when I died they could put a flag over my casket. I appreciate everything they have done for me, but I no longer need medical treatment, and they don't have to bother me anymore."

First Sgt. Harrelson "The train took me out to El Paso, Texas, William Beaumont Army Hospital near Fort Bliss. It's kind of funny. I went into William Beaumont, and they started running me through one place and out the other. Then they transferred me to Moore General Hospital in North Carolina for three or four months. A year to the day, exactly, from when I entered Beaumont the first time, I wound up there again in the same ward down at the same annex in the same stinkin' bed I'd first had when I got there. They hadn't given me as much as an aspirin, but they had kicked me from pillar to post. All I wanted was medical treatment, and they just wouldn't give it to me."

Fireman 1/C Kennedy "In Calcutta they issued us khakis and good clothes for a change and gave us some tests in the hospital. We ate a lot of food and went on liberty. They paid me five hundred dollars. I saw my first American movie since being captured. The short subject before the featured movie was Spike Jones. I thought, 'What the hell has happened to American music?' They were beating on dishpans and all that crap, and I thought, 'Good God!'

"I have had nerve problems as well as back problems. I had some trouble adjusting to civilian life. I had few social graces. I remember one time blowing my nose without a handkerchief, with my fingers. When you were out in the jungle, you just blew your nose. It takes a little time to get back on the civilization track. That was my biggest problem."

Cpl. Minshew "After I returned, I was in school in Fort Worth when I got a letter from a U.S. agency offering to pay my way back to Japan to testify at the war crimes trials. I dropped it in the wastebasket because I had just been to Japan. I didn't want to interrupt things to go through all that again. You'd say I've been a loner ever since the war. I haven't formed any close relationships other than my wife and children. I just never have felt safe in forming close relations for some reason. It just doesn't seem like the right thing to do or an important thing to me."

Pvt. Permenter "I'd been gone for five years, and everything was different. I drank a little bit when I got back. I got mixed up and drank. Then I met Nadine, and she didn't drink, so I quit. We got married and have lived happily ever afterwards."

Cpl. Read "My biggest trouble was that I had been out of circulation so long that I had trouble with monetary values and things like that because I was pretty naive. I got stung everywhere I turned when I bought something. I got stung on it because I didn't appreciate the differences, the changes, that had taken place in the value of things—you know, like used cars and all that."

PFC Robinson "When we arrived in Washington, it was strictly an interrogation situation. They wanted every Japanese name, every camp, every detail. I had no idea what the real names of Brown Bomber and Liver Lips were. I hated them, and that was unusual for me because I do not bear that deep-rooted hatred toward the Japanese. The Marine Corps asked me where I wanted duty, and I told them I was from Fort Worth, Texas. They sent me to Eagle Mountain Lake near Fort Worth. At Eagle Mountain Lake I told them I wanted sea duty. They said, 'Forget it.' Because I had been a prisoner of war, they wouldn't allow a person with biased feelings against Japan to be seagoing, so I terminated my duty."

Cpl. Smith "I was discharged on September 29, 1945, and I didn't do anything for quite a long while due to illness. I was still eaten up with malaria fever. That malaria fever like to have killed me, I guess, the first three years back. I got married the first day of December 1945. I had no job. I was sick, so I couldn't even hold a job. They gave me a pension for disability when I got discharged, so we survived on that for a couple of years, mostly. It was only $157 a month then. Other than that, I'd pick up an odd job now and then, and that would help out."

T/Sgt. Stanbrough "I told my wife I was going back to college in Texas. I had always wanted to go to Texas A & M. Well, I drove from Wichita Falls to Texas A & M, drove into the front of the campus, drove around, and took a look at that bleak place for a second. I saw a sign that said, 'Don't park, by order of the commandant.' I saw GIs policing around the grounds. I didn't even stop the motor. I drove over to Austin to the University of Texas."

Seaman 1/C Stewart "Most of my problems were with my left arm on the inside of the elbow, where there was a heavy keloid formation. It made moving my elbow a problem. They sent me to the National Naval Medical Center in Bethesda, Maryland, and two surgeons who specialized in skin grafting were able to excise the keloid formation and put a skin graft on it. Nowadays, my arm is close to normal."

M/Sgt. Slowers "In my case, food was such an obsession with me that I built a restaurant—and I still have it—in North Carolina. Otherwise, I don't think ever in my life I'd have had the idea of being a restaurant man."

PFC Venable "I would say that I had some problems adjusting, but it was a matter of nerves being a little more taut than they should be. But as far as adjusting at that time, why, I, of course, did a foolish thing. I commenced to drink some, and I did more of that than I should have. And I'm sure that there were other things that I did that I'm not particularly proud of, you know. Nothing bad. What I'm talking about is carousing around, you know, just kind of living it up, generally. I think that I would have been better off not to have done that."

PFC Visage "The only medical care that we got was on the hospital ship at Nagasaki. Along the other stops there was no doctor to talk to us, no officers. We were just on our own when we'd hit a place. During the time they were taking us prisoners back, they were also getting a lot of the soldiers out of Asia as fast as they could.

"When we got to San Francisco, I was sent to Letterman Hospital. From there I was with a group that they sent to McCloskey Hospital in Temple, Texas. About eight of us ended up in McCloskey Hospital. About half of the men were put in the nuthouse. There was no reason for that whatsoever because the guys weren't crazy—they were just about four years behind the rest of the Americans. That was the hardest part about coming back home. We were thinking about America as it was in 1941 and 1942, rather than in 1946."

Pvt. Wisecup "We were sent to Washington, DC, and Charles and I went over to 8th and I Streets, which was Marine headquarters. They treated us like real psycho cases. They had a corporal stay with us at all times. They kept this Marine chaser on us for three days. On the first day I said, 'Hey, why are you following us around?' He said, 'I was told to stay with you. You guys ain't responsible. You guys are Asiatic.' But after the second day, they saw we were okay."

Bibliography

American Ex-Prisoners of War Inc., National Medical Research Committee. *Alphabetical Index to Microfilm Copies of Recovered Records, Philippine Islands, November 4, 1945*. Tampa, FL: American Ex-Prisoners of War Inc., 1976.

———. *The Japanese Story*. Packet #10. Marshfield, WI: Stan Sommers, 1980.

Bailey, Ronald H. *Prisoners of War: World War II*. Chicago: Time-Life Books, 1981.

Barker, A. J. *Prisoners of War*. New York: Universe Books, 1975.

Biderman, Albert D. *March to Calumny: The Story of American POWs in the Korean War*. New York: Macmillan, 1963.

Bird, Tom. *American POWs of World War II: Forgotten Men Tell Their Stories*. Westport, CT: Praeger, 1992.

Blair, Joan, and Blair, Clay, Jr. *Return from the River Kwai*. New York: Simon and Schuster, 1979.

Brill, N. Q. "Neuropsychiatric Examination of Military Personnel Recovered from Japanese Prison Camps." *Bulletin of the U.S. Army Medical Department* 5 (April 1946): 429–38.

Calvocoressi, Peter; Wint, Guy; and Pritchard, John. *Total War: The Causes and Courses of the Second World War*. Vol. 2, *The Greater East Asian and Pacific Conflict*. Rev. 2d ed. New York: Pantheon Books, 1989.

Carano, Paul, and Sanchez, Pedro. *A Complete History of Guam*. Rutland, VT: C. E. Tuttle, 1964.

Cohen, Bernard M., and Cooper, Maurice Z. *A Follow-up Study of World War II Prisoners of War*. Veterans Administration, Medical Monograph, Department of Medicine and Surgery. Washington, DC: Government Printing Office, 1954.

Devereux, James P. S. *The Story of Wake Island*. New York: J. B. Lippincott, 1947.

DeWhitt, Ben, and Heaps, Jennifer Davis, comps. *Records Relating to Personal Participation in World War II: American Prisoners of War and Civilian Internees*. Reference Information Paper 80.

Washington, DC: National Archives and Records Administration, 1992.

Dower, John W. *War without Mercy: Race and Power in the Pacific War.* New York: Pantheon Books, 1986.

Falk, Stanley L. *Bataan: The March of Death.* New York: W. W. Norton, 1962.

Fooks, Herbert C. *Prisoners of War.* Federalsburg, MD: J. W. Stowell, 1924.

Frank, Benis M., and Shaw, Henry I., Jr. *Victory and Occupation: History of the U.S. Marine Corps Operations in World War II.* Vol. 5. Washington, DC: Historical Branch, G-3 Division, U.S. Marine Corps, 1968.

Garrett, Richard. *P.O.W., The Uncivil Face of War.* Devon, UK: David and Charles Publishers, 1981.

Harries, Meirion, and Harries, Susie. *Soldiers of the Sun: The Rise and Fall of the Imperial Japanese Army.* New York: Random House, 1991.

Holmes, Richard. *Acts of War: The Behavior of Men in Battle.* New York: Free Press, 1985.

James, D. Clayton, ed. *South to Bataan, North to Mukden: The Prison Diary of Brigadier General W. E. Brougher.* Athens: University of Georgia Press, 1971.

Jane's Fighting Ships. New York: McGraw-Hill, 1942.

Johnson, Clarence R. *Prisoners of War.* Social Science Series, No. 22. Los Angeles: University of Southern California Press, 1941.

Jones, Waller F. "Japanese Attitudes toward Prisoners of War: Feudal Resurgence in *Kokutai No Hongi.*" Master's thesis, University of North Texas, 1990.

Junghans, E. A. *History of Wake Island, 1568–1946.* Washington, DC: Navy Department, 1947.

Katz, Charles J. "Experiences in a Prison Camp as a Background for Therapy." *Mental Hygiene* 34 (January 1950): 90–96.

Kerr, E. Bartlett. *Surrender and Survival: The Experience of American POWs in the Pacific, 1941–1945.* New York: William Morrow, 1985.

Knox, Donald. *Death March: The Survivors of Bataan.* New York: Harcourt Brace Jovanovich, 1981.

Krystal, Henry, ed. *Massive Psychic Trauma.* New York: International Universities Press, 1968.

La Forte, Robert S., and Marcello, Ronald E., eds. *Building the Death Railway: The Ordeal of American POWs in Burma, 1942–1945.* Wilmington, DE: Scholarly Resources, 1993.

Maga, Timothy P. *Defending Paradise: The United States and Guam, 1898–1950.* New York: Garland Press, 1988.

Miller, Andrew. "The Historian's Corner." *The Quan* (September 1992 and April 1993): n.p.

Morison, Samuel Eliot. *History of United States Naval Operations in World War II.* Vol. 3, *Rising Sun in the Pacific.* Boston: Little, Brown, 1948.

Morton, Louis. *The Fall of the Philippines: The War in the Pacific: United States Army in World War II.* Washington, DC: Office of the Chief of Military History, Department of the Army, 1953.

Myers, Hugh H. *Prisoner of War: World War II.* Portland, OR: Metropolitan Press, 1965.

Nardini, J. E. "Survival Factors in American Prisoners of War of the Japanese." *American Journal of Psychiatry* 109 (October 1952): 241–48.

New York Times, 1945–1951 passim.

Office of Naval Intelligence Weekly. Vols. 12, 13, 16 (April 15, 22, May 13, 1942). Washington, DC: Navy Department, 1942.

Onorato, Michael P., ed. *Forgotten Heroes: Japan's Imprisonment of American Civilians in the Philippines, 1942–1945: An Oral History.* Westport, CT: Meckler, 1990.

Perret, Geoffrey. *There's a War to Be Won: The United States Army in World War II.* New York: Random House, 1991.

Piccigallo, Philip R. *The Japanese on Trial: Allied War Crimes Operations in the East, 1945–1951.* Austin: University of Texas Press, 1979.

Pomeroy, Earl S. *Pacific Outpost: American Strategy in Guam and Micronesia.* Stanford, CA: Stanford University Press, 1951.

POW: The Fight Continues after the Battle. Report of the Secretary of Defense's Advisory Committee on Prisoners of War. Washington, DC: Government Printing Office, August 1955.

Provost Marshal General, American POW Information Bureau, Liaison and Research Branch. "POW Camps in Japan and Japanese Controlled Areas as Taken from Reports of Interned Prisoners" in "U.S. Army Center of Military Historical Manuscript Collection: The War against Japan." Microfilm, Reel 48 (Scholarly Re sources print), University of North Texas Library, Denton.

Reid, Pat, and Michael, Maurice. *Prisoner of War.* New York: Beaufort Books, 1984.

Roland, Charles G., and Shannon, Harry S. "Patterns of Disease among World War II Prisoners of the Japanese: Hunger, Weight Loss, and Deficiency Diseases in Two Camps." *Journal of the History of Medicine and Allied Sciences* 46 (1991): 65–85.

Simon and Schuster Encyclopedia of World War II. Edited by Thomas Parrish. New York: Simon and Schuster, 1978.

Strassman, Harvey D.; Thaler, Margaret B.; and Schein, Edgar H. "A Prisoner of War Syndrome: Apathy as a Reaction to Severe Stress." *American Journal of Psychiatry* 112 (June 1956): 998–1003.

U.S. Army, Medical Department. *Neuropsychiatry in World War II: Overseas Theaters.* Office of the Surgeon General, Department of the Army. Washington, DC: Government Printing Office, 1973.

U.S. Naval Chronology, World War II. Naval Historical Division, Office of the Chief of Naval Operations, Navy Department. Washington, DC: Government Printing Office, 1955.

Veterans Administration, Studies and Analysis Service. *POW: Study of Former Prisoners of War.* Washington, DC: Office of Planning and Program Evaluation, 1980.

Waller, Willard. *The Veteran Comes Back.* New York: Dryden Press, 1944.

Watson, Peter. *War on the Mind: The Military Uses and Abuses of Psychology.* New York: Basic Books, 1978.

Wolf, Stewart, and Ripley, Herbert S. "Reactions among Allied Prisoners of War Subjected to Three Years of Imprisonment and Torture by the Japanese." *American Journal of Psychiatry* 104 (September 1947): 180–93.

Index